EUROPEAN HISTORICAL DICTIONARIES
Edited by Jon Woronoff

Historical Dictionary
of
Ireland

Colin Thomas
Avril Thomas

European Historical Dictionaries, No. 20

The Scarecrow Press, Inc.
Lanham, Md., & London
1997

SCARECROW PRESS, INC.

Published in the United States of America
by Scarecrow Press, Inc.
4720 Boston Way
Lanham, Maryland 20706

4 Pleydell Gardens, Folkestone
Kent CT20 2DN, England

British Library Cataloguing in Publication Information Available

Library of Congress Cataloging-in-Publication Data

Thomas, Colin, 1939–
    Historical dictionary of Ireland / Colin Thomas, Avril Thomas.
       p.   cm. — (European historical dictionaries ; no. 20)
    Includes bibliographical references and index.
    ISBN 0-8108-3300-X (cloth : alk. paper)
    1. Ireland—History—Dictionaries.   2. Ireland—Chronology.
I. Thomas, Avril. II. Title. III. Series.
DA910.T39   1997
941.5'003—dc21   97-2136
                                     CIP

ISBN 0-8108-3300-0 (cloth: alk. paper)

CONTENTS

Tables

Editor's Foreword

Ireland, for those who do not know it well, often appears indistinctly through a haze of clichés. Tourists and readers of photographic essays like to imagine it as the Emerald Island with tiny farms, quaint villages, and rolling hills. For many, it is the "old country," clinging to charming customs and traditions. For others, it is just an old country, hopelessly stuck in assorted ruts that impede its progress to more modern, enlightened ways. They do not associate it with a dynamic economy, highly educated youth, and lively political system. They do not realize that attitudes toward politics, the church, and society in general are changing dramatically. Nor are they aware that the Irish are among the more active supporters of the European Union.

To help put the clichés (with their kernel of truth) in perspective and balance them against fresher realities, it is worthwhile taking a new look from time to time. This *Historical Dictionary of Ireland* facilitates such a look. It does have entries on previous leaders, earlier events, ancient souvenirs—the past, in short. But it also features contemporary leaders, current events, economic and social progress, namely, the present. The passage from there to here is traced in an informative chronology. Obviously, a historical dictionary does not cover all aspects, but its broad bibliography is an excellent place to seek the many books and articles that can fill gaps.

A country can be approached from various directions. Less common, but certainly providing a remarkable vantage point, is geography. The authors of this book, Avril and Colin Thomas, are both geographers. Avril Thomas, who grew up and studied in Dublin, has focused on Ireland's towns and cities and has written extensively on the subject. Colin Thomas, presently Reader in Geography at the University of Ulster, Coleraine, has for over a decade been a member of the Royal Irish Academy's National Committee for Geography. Both know not only the land but also its people and history, and they have done an admirable job of conveying this.

Jon Woronoff
Series Editor

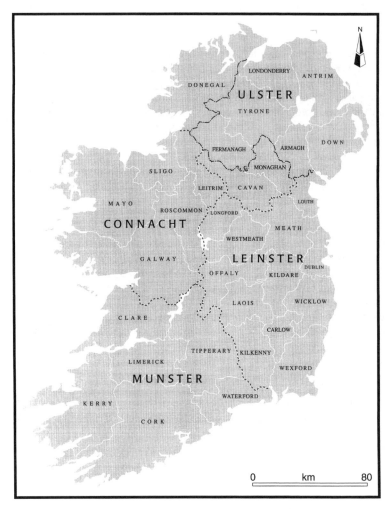

Map 1. Ireland: Provinces and Counties

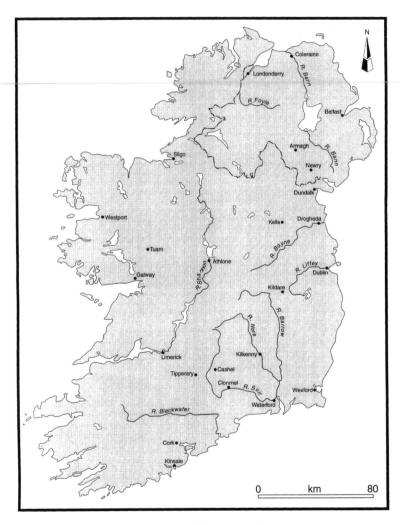

Map 2. Ireland: Rivers and Towns

Acronyms

AOH	Ancient Order of Hibernians
BBC	British Broadcasting Corporation
CBS	Christian Brothers School
CG	Cumann na nGaedheal political party
CIE	Coras Iompair Eireann
Co.	County
CUI	Catholic University of Ireland
CVO	Commander of the Royal Victorian Order
DL	Democratic Left, political party in the Republic of Ireland
DMP	Dublin Metropolitan Police
DUP	Democratic Unionist Party in Northern Ireland
E(E)C	European (Economic) Community, now European Union
EMS	European Monetary System
ESB	Electricity Supply Board in Republic of Ireland
EU	European Union
FF	Fianna Fail political party in Republic of Ireland
FG	Fine Gail political party in Republic of Ireland
FRS	Fellow of the Royal Society
GAA	Gaelic Athletic Association
GB	Great Britain, i.e., England, Wales, and Scotland
GDP	Gross Domestic Product
GOC	General Officer in Command
ICTU	Irish Congress of Trades Unions
IFS	Irish Free State (1922–37)
ILP	Irish Labour Party
INLA	Irish National Liberation Army
IPLO	Irish People's Liberation Organisation
IPP	Irish Parliamentary Party
IRA	Irish Republican Army
IRB	Irish (Revolutionary) Republican Brotherhood
ITGWU	Irish Transport and General Workers Union
ITUC	Irish Trades Union Congress
KCB	Knight Commander of the Order of the Bath
MP	Member of Parliament, Great Britain/United Kingdom
MRIA	Member of the Royal Irish Academy

NI	Northern Ireland, since 1922
NICRA	Northern Ireland Civil Rights Association
NILP	Northern Ireland Labour Party
NUI	National University of Ireland
OS	Ordnance Survey
PD	Progressive Democrats political party in Republic of Ireland
PIRA	Provisional Irish Republican Army
PRONI	Public Record Office of Northern Ireland
PROI	Public Record Office of Ireland
QUB	The Queen's University of Belfast
QUI	The Queen's University of Ireland
RBAI	Royal Belfast Academical Institution
RCS	Royal College of Surgeons
RDS	Royal Dublin Society
RHA	Royal Hibernian Academy
RHC	Red Hand Commandos
RIA	Royal Irish Academy
RIC	Royal Irish Constabulary
RSAI	Royal Society of Antiquaries of Ireland
RTE	Radio Telefis Eireann
RUC	Royal Ulster Constabulary
RUI	Royal University of Ireland
SDLP	Social Democratic and Labour Party
SF	Sinn Fein political party
TCD	Trinity College Dublin
TD	Teachta Dala, member of the Dáil (parliament), Republic of Ireland
UCC	University College Cork
UCD	University College Dublin
UCG	University College Galway
UDA	Ulster Defence Association
UDR	Ulster Defence Regiment
UFF	Ulster Freedom Fighters
UK	United Kingdom (of Great Britain and Northern Ireland)
UN(O)	United Nations (Organization)
UPNI	Unionist Party of Northern Ireland
UUUC	United Ulster Unionist Council
UVF	Ulster Volunteer Force
WP	Workers Party
WWI/II	World War (1914–18/1939–45)

Historical Chronology

6500 B.C.	Ireland separated from Britain by rising sealevel.
6000 B.C.	Evidence of earliest known inhabitants, Ulster.
3800 B.C.	First farming communities.
3000 B.C.	Earliest megalithic tombs.
1500 B.C.	Irish bronze and gold work exported.
300 B.C.	Arrival of Celtic-speaking peoples.
100 B.C.–500 A.D.	Ogham inscriptions; proto-Irish language.
52–51 B.C.	*Hibernia* used in Caesar's *De Bello Gallico*.
130–180 A.D.	Map of Ireland in Ptolemy's *Geographia* that names physical features and peoples.
297–450	Irish raids on Roman Britain.
431	Palladius sent as first bishop to Ireland by Pope Celestine; *Annals of Ulster* begin.
432	St. Patrick begins mission in Ireland (traditional date).
457/461	Death of St. Patrick (492/493 annals/tradition).
535–546	Derry monastery founded by St. Columba.
550–600	Earliest Irish law texts.
563	St. Columba founds monastery at Iona, Scotland.
580–680	Latin literature developed at monastic centers e.g., Cathach psalter C. 597.
590	St. Columbanus begins Irish mission on the Continent.
635–651	St. Aidan's mission to Northumbria, Lindisfarne founded from Iona.
650	*Book of Durrow,* earliest Irish illuminated manuscript.
670–690	Primacy of Armagh asserted; St. Patrick's *Life* written.
700–750	Climax of achievement in Irish metalworking and stone sculpture.
750–800	*Book of Kells* illuminated; flowering of Old Irish lyric poetry and sagas.
770–840	Ascetic *culdee* reform movement in Irish church.
795	First Viking raids on Ireland.
836–876	Viking fleets raid interior along rivers; coastal bases established; frequent clashes with Irish kings.
841 (c.)	Foundation of Dublin by the Norse.
845	John Scotus "Eriugena," scholar, joins the imperial school at Laon.
875	Union of Norse kingdoms of Dublin and York attempted.

902	Norse forced out of Dublin.
913	Renewed Viking activity challenged by Irish kings.
920–952	Joint Dublin-York kingdom partly formed.
924–937	Intra-Norse conflicts, Dublin-Waterford vs. Limerick.
938	High king besieges Dublin unsuccessfully.
981/989/995	Dublin captured briefly by high king, Mael Sechnaill II.
995 (c.)	Norse mint established at Dublin (ceases to operate by 1135).
1002	Brian Boru displaces Mael Sechnaill II as high king.
1014	Battle of Clontarf between Leinster Hiberno-Norse and Munster Irish; death of Brian Boru.
1063 (c.)	Augustinian canons arrive.
1111	Synod of Raith Bressail: territorial dioceses planned.
1127–34	Cormac's chapel at Cashel built in Irish romanesque style.
1132	St. Malachy becomes Archbishop of Armagh.
1142	First Cistercian house founded at Mellifont.
1152	Synod of Kells: diocesan organization completed.
1155–56	Invasion of Ireland by Henry II of England proposed and approved by Pope Adrian IV.
1162	Mac Murchada, king of Leinster, gains control of Dublin.
1166	Mac Murchada banished by Ruaidri Ua Conchobair, whose rule as high king is generally opposed.
1167	Mac Murchada receives permission from Henry II to recruit help in Wales; recovers kingdom with help of Flemings.
1169	Anglo-Norman invasion begins in south Wexford.
1170	Richard de Clare (Strongbow) takes Waterford; Dublin falls to Mac Murchada and Norman allies.
1171	Mac Murchada dies, succeeded by his son-in-law, de Clare.
1171–72	Henry II in Ireland; grants charter to Dublin and receives submission of some Irish kings; grants Meath to Hugh de Lacy.
1175	Treaty of Windsor between Ruaidri Ua Conchobair, as high king, and Henry II.
1177	John de Courcy invades Ulster, builds castle at Downpatrick; other Normans less successful in southwest.
1185	Visit of Prince John, son of Henry II and "lord of Ireland," grants lands and builds castles.
1187–88	Giraldus Cambrensis's *Topographia Hibernia* and *Expugnatio Hibernia*.
1199	Normans settle beyond Limerick city and take Derry.
1204	Dublin castle built to house king's treasury.

1210	John's second visit, Waterford to Carrickfergus.
1224	Cathal Crobderg Ó Conchobair, last independent king of Connacht, dies; arrival of Dominicans, first mendicant friars in Ireland (followed by Franciscans c. 1224–30; Carmelites c. 1270; Augustinians by 1280).
1235	Anglo-Norman invasion of Connacht by Richard de Burgo.
1244	Irish kings and lords join Henry III in Scottish campaign.
1251–54	Dublin mint operating.
1260	Battle of Downpatrick: justiciar defeats Ó Conchobair and O'Neill kings.
1261	Battle of Callan, Kerry; Mac Carthaig king defeats justiciar and Norman lords; result reversed in 1262.
1264	Parliament held at Castledermot (earlier assemblies of representatives not called parliaments).
1274	Hostilities in Leinster lead to defeat of justiciar.
1275	Merchants of Lucca and Florence collect Irish customs for Edward I.
1302–6	Ecclesiastical taxation of Ireland (rich documentary source for medieval church).
1315–18	Bruce invasion; Edward Bruce killed at Faughart.
1333	Murder of the "Brown Earl" of Ulster; extensive lands come under crown control.
1348	"Black death" appears in east coast ports.
1353	Statute of the Staple applied in Ireland.
1361–94	Irish exchequer moved from Dublin to Carlow.
1366	Anglo-Irish forbidden to adopt Irish customs by the "Statutes of Kilkenny."
1384 (c.)	*Book of Ballymote* compiled as part of revival within Gaelic-dominated areas.
1394–95	Richard II visits for the first time, defeats Leinster Irish led by Art Mor Mac Murchadha, and receives submission of Irish kings.
1399	Richard II campaigns again in Leinster.
1423	Observantine movement opens its first priory, in Connacht.
1426	The Pale raided by Gaelic forces.
1430	Parliament in Dublin grants aid for building castles to defend the Pale.
1436 (c.)	"Libelle of Englyshe polycye" outlines strategic importance of Ireland.
1449	Richard of York, heir to Meath, Ulster, and Connacht lands, arrives as "lieutenant," operates through

	Anglo-Irish "deputies" until his death in 1460 during the Wars of the Roses in England.
1460	Parliament at Drogheda reaffirms supremacy of Irish parliaments in Ireland; Irish currency devised.
1462	Battle of Pilltown: Desmond defeats Butlers in Anglo-Irish conflict.
1468	Execution of Desmond.
1479–1513	Gearóid Mór, or Gerald, Great Earl of Kildare, as Anglo-Irish deputy; frequent campaigns to regain control of Dublin, lost during previous century.
1487	Lambert Simnel crowned "king of England" in Dublin; first known use of firearms in Ireland, by Ó Domnhaill troops.
1491–97	Second English pretender, Perkin Warbeck, seeks support periodically, but unsuccessfully, in Ireland.
1494–95	Parliament, held by English deputy, Sir Edward Poynings, passes laws restricting independence of the Irish parliament, following Anglo-Irish support for the pretenders.
1500 (c.)	*Book of Lismore* written.
1504	Battle of Knockdoe: Kildare with Ó Domhnaill and the English of the Pale defeat the renegade Burke of Clanricard and Ó Briain associates.
1513	Gearóid Óg Kildare succeeds his father as deputy following battle with O'Mores of Leinster, in which the Great Earl was mortally wounded.
1534	Kildare goes to London (Feb.), leaving his heir, Thomas, as deputy; dies in the Tower (Sept.); "Silken Thomas" besieges Dublin briefly and seeks help in Europe.
1536–37	First Reformation parliament meets in Dublin; acts for suspending Poynings' Law; supremacy of Henry VIII and suppression of monasteries proposed.
1537	Execution of Silken Thomas and his five uncles in London.
1539	Dissolution of monasteries within the Pale begins.
1539	Geraldine league formed by Anglo-Irish lords as a union of north and south to protect Kildare child heir.
1540–48	Sir Anthony St. Leger's policy of surrender and regrant toward Irish chiefs.
1541	Parliament in Dublin declares Henry VIII "king of Ireland"—Irish and English used in text.
1542	First Jesuit mission to Ireland.
1547–53	Edwardian reformation in Ireland, revoked under Queen Mary (1553–58).

1550	Preparations for plantation of Leix and Offaly.
1551	*Boke of the common praier after the use of the Churche of England,* the first book printed in Ireland.
1557	Leix and Offaly renamed Queen's and King's Counties.
1560	Elizabethan settlement restores Anglican Church in Ireland.
1562–67	Shane O'Neill, Lord of Tyrone, at war in Ulster until killed by MacDonnells at Cushendun.
1566	Sir Henry Sidney appointed lord deputy, campaigns in Ulster.
1567	Robert Lythe, cartographer, at work in Ireland.
1568–73	First Desmond rebellion; Irish Catholics offer allegiance to Philip II of Spain.
1569–70	Presidencies of Connacht and Munster created as bases for administration by Dublin government.
1571	First book in Irish printed in Dublin: J. Kearney's *Aibidil Gaoidheilge & Caiticiosma* (Gaelic alphabet and catechism).
1572	Colonization schemes for Ulster begin in Ards.
1573–76	Earl of Essex campaigns in Ulster with a view to colonization, but dies in Dublin.
1579–83	Second Desmond rebellion aided by the pope and by Spain.
1581	Edmund Spenser, author of *The Faerie Queene,* appointed secretary to lord deputy.
1584	Papal appointee Dermot O'Hurley, archbishop of Cashel, hanged in Dublin.
1585	Composition of Connacht and plans for plantation of Munster developed.
1588	Ships of the Spanish Armada wrecked off Irish coasts.
1592	First Irish university, Trinity College, founded on site of former priory in Dublin.
1595–1603	Rebellion of Hugh O'Neill, Earl of Tyrone, and the Northern Confederacy, receives Spanish and Munster aid later.
1598	Tyrone victorious at the Yellow Ford; Sir Henry Bagenal killed.
1600	Tyrone campaigns in Munster; Lord Mountjoy made lord deputy; Sir Henry Docwra reestablishes fort and settlement at Derry.
1601	Spanish fleet arrives at Kinsale (Sept.); Tyrone and allies defeated there by Mountjoy (Dec.).
1603	Tyrone surrenders; death of Queen Elizabeth I and accession of King James I.

1607	"Flight of the earls"—Tyrone and Tyrconnell—from Ulster (Sept.) results in forfeiture of lands.
1608–10	Preparations for Ulster plantation: survey of six escheated counties; agreement with City of London for plantation of Derry city and Coleraine County.
1613	Charter incorporating Derry as Londonderry.
1621	Smaller plantations arranged for parts of Leinster.
1622	Survey of Co. Londonderry, with maps and illustrations.
1626–28	The "Graces" (concessions) offered by Charles I in return for Irish subsidy.
1632–36	Compilation of the *Annals of the Four Masters* begins in Donegal.
1633–40	Wentworth (Earl of Strafford) lord deputy.
1637	Discovery and mining of coal at Castlecomer, Leinster.
1641	Strafford executed (May); beginning of Ulster rising (Oct.), in which insurgents kill Protestant settlers.
1642	Monro's Scottish army arrives in Ulster (Apr.); Owen Roe O'Neill lands in Donegal (July); beginning of the Civil War in England (Aug.); Catholic confederacy formed at Kilkenny (Oct.).
1643	Ormond made lord lieutenant; negotiates truce with confederates (Sept.).
1645	Archbishop Rinuccini at Kilkenny as papal envoy.
1646	Rinuccini's forces reject Ormond peace (Sept.).
1647	Parliamentary force under Col. Michael Jones lands near Dublin; Ormond surrenders Dublin (July); confederates defeated by Jones in Co. Meath (Aug.).
1648	Last meeting of Kilkenny assembly; Owen Roe O'Neill proclaimed traitor.
1649	Charles I executed (30 Jan.); Rinuccini leaves Ireland; Jones defeats Ormond near Dublin (Aug.); Cromwell lands and captures Drogheda (Sept.) and Wexford (Oct.); Owen Roe O'Neill dies (Nov.).
1650	Cromwell's campaign resumes and main towns surrender; Cromwell departs, leaving his son-in-law Henry Ireton in charge.
1651	Ireton's forces successfully besiege Limerick (June-Oct.); Ireton dies there.
1652	Cromwellian war ends (June).
1653	Cromwellian land confiscation based on Civil Survey.
1654	Sir William Petty maps lands reserved for soldiers (Down Survey); transplanted Irish to be in Connacht and Clare by March 1655.

1660	Poll tax produces first Irish census (Apr.); Restoration of Charles II (May).
1662	Duke of Ormond returns as lord lieutenant; Act of Settlement to resolve conflicting claims of Cromwellian settlers and former royalists.
1663	English act prohibits importation of Irish cattle into England as well as Irish trade with colonies; renewed 1685.
1665	Act of Explanation: Cromwellian settlers to give up one-third of their holdings to provide land for restored Catholics.
1666	Act of Uniformity requires schoolmasters to be licensed by bishops of the Established Church.
1667	Second Cattle Act; charter incorporating the College of Physicians in Dublin.
1673	Test Act requires officeholders to take Anglican sacrament; order for Catholic clergy to be banished; religious houses and schools closed.
1678–81	"Popish plot"; Archbishop Talbot arrested.
1680	Kilmainham Royal Hospital for retired soldiers established.
1681	Execution of Archbishop Oliver Plunkett.
1684	Dublin Philosophical Society established.
1685	Accession of James II; *Dublin News-letter,* first newspaper; Petty's *Hiberniae Delineatio.*
1687–91	Richard Talbot, Earl of Tyrconnell, acts as Jacobite lord deputy.
1688	Derry gates shut against Jacobite forces (7 Dec.).
1689	Arrival of James II (Mar.); Derry besieged (18 Apr.–31 July); James II's Irish parliament (May–July) revokes Restoration laws.
1690	French force enters Cork (Mar.); William III joins Danish force near Belfast (June) and defeats King James's army at the Boyne (1 July); James II sails to France (July); sieges of Athlone and Limerick (July–Aug.); Sarsfield destroys Williamite baggage train.
1691	William's general, von Ginkel, takes Athlone (June); defeats Jacobite force at Aughrim (July); successfully besieges Limerick (25 Aug.–24 Sept.); treaty of Limerick (Oct.); Sarsfield sails for France with remnants of Irish army.
1691–92	Catholics excluded from Irish parliament and office.
1692–1700	Williamite land settlement.
1695	Beginning of penal legislation against Catholics.

1696	Linen manufacture encouraged by duty-free access to England.
1697	First English act restricting export of Irish woollens.
1699	Act (10 Will. III c.12) obliges landholders to plant and preserve trees.
1700	Subsidy paid to Louis Crommelin to manufacture linen.
1701	First public library in Ireland built by Archbishop Marsh in Dublin.
1704	Test Act against Catholics and Protestant Dissenters; Dublin Workhouse Act for care of the poor.
1713	Jonathan Swift installed as Dean of St. Patrick's Cathedral, Dublin.
1718	First large emigration from Ulster to the American colonies (again in 1729); first charitable infirmary in the British Isles opened in Dublin.
1719	Toleration Act exempts Protestant Dissenters from Test Act.
1720	Declaratory Act: British parliament asserts right to legislate for Ireland.
1722–25	Patent to William Wood to coin halfpence and farthings for Ireland.
1724	Swift's *Drapier's letters,* opposing Wood's coinage.
1726	Swift's *Gulliver's Travels*; C. Threlkeld's *Irish Flora.*
1729	New parliament building started in Dublin, outside medieval city.
1730	First Turnpike Acts; commissioners appointed for inland navigation.
1731	Dublin Society for Improving Husbandry, Manufacturing . . . , founded.
1737	First issue of *Belfast News-letter.*
1740	W. Harris publishes first Irish county history (Down).
1740–41	Famine mortality estimated at 200,000–400,000.
1742	Newry canal in use, first in Ireland; Handel's *Messiah* premiered in Dublin.
1747	Edmund Burke founds philosophical club; John Wesley's first visit.
1751	Rotunda (maternity) Hospital begun in Dublin.
1756	Grand Canal from Dublin to Shannon begun.
1758	"Wide street commissioners" appointed for development of Dublin.
1759	Removal of restrictions on importation of Irish cattle into Britain; Arthur Guinness leases brewery in Dublin.
1760	Catholic committee formed by Curry, O'Connor, and Wise in Dublin.

	rejected; Tone leaves Belfast for America; Royal College of St. Patrick Catholic seminary opened at Maynooth.
1796	Insurrection Act; French invasion fleet with Tone in Bantry Bay (Dec.).
1797	General Lake's disarming of Ulster; election of last Irish parliament; E. Bunting's *A general collection of the ancient Irish music.*
1798	Arrest of Leinster directory of United Irishmen; arrest and death of Lord Edward Fitzgerald; United Irish rising (May–June) in Leinster and Ulster; French force under Humbert in Connacht; defeat of French squadron off Lough Swilly (Oct.); capture, court-martial, and death of Tone (Nov.).
1800	Daniel O'Connell's first public speech against proposed union; Orange lodges oppose union; Act for legislative union of Ireland with Great Britain passed by British and Irish parliaments (July/Aug.); Maria Edgeworth's *Castle Rackrent;* Dublin Society sponsors statistical surveys of Irish counties.
1801	Union of Great Britain and Ireland (1 Jan.); Copyright Act applied to Trinity College and King's Inns, Dublin.
1803	Rising of Robert Emmet in Dublin (July); Emmet tried and executed (Sept.).
1808	Controversy over proposed royal veto on appointments of Irish Catholic bishops; Christian Brothers Order of lay teachers founded at Waterford.
1809	Drainage of Bogs (Ireland) Act; establishment of Sunday School Society for Ireland, and of Belfast Harp Society to teach blind children and promote Irish culture.
1811	Kildare Place Society founded to run nondenominational schools.
1813	Grattan's first Catholic Relief bill defeated; first unrest in Belfast between Protestants and Catholics (July).
1814	Belfast Academical Institution opened.
1815	Bianconi runs first car for passengers from Clonmel to Cahir; Mary Aikenhead's Irish Sisters of Charity convent opened in Dublin.
1816	Potato crop failure, first famine since 1742, followed by typhus outbreak.
1817	Acts establish public works for employment of poor and asylums; first European total abstinence society started in Skibbereen.
1818	Fever Hospitals Act, with extension of dispensary system (established 1805).

1821	First population census (6,801,827); Belfast Natural History (and Philosophical) Society formed; potato crop fails.
1823	Catholic Association founded in Dublin.
1824	O'Connell initiates Catholic rent as a campaigning fund; parliamentary inquiry into education; Thomas Colby directed to make cartographic survey.
1826	Waterford election: O'Connell successfully mobilizes Catholic voters; act provides for uniform valuation of lands and tenements for local tax.
1828	O'Connell elected MP in Clare by-election.
1829	Catholic emancipation achieved.
1831	Tithe war begins; "national" (primary) education system instituted; Zoological Gardens in Dublin and Belfast museum opened.
1833	First six-inch Ordnance Survey map (Co. Londonderry) published; parliamentary commission of inquiry into municipal corporations (report 1835–36).
1834	First railway opened, between Dublin and Kingstown.
1835	British Association for the Advancement of Science meets in Dublin.
1836	Constabulary (Ireland) Act.
1838	Tithe Rentcharge Act; English Poor Law Act extended to Ireland.
1840	Municipal Reform Act; Irish Archaeological Society founded.
1841	O'Connell elected lord mayor of reformed Dublin corporation; Hall's *Ireland: its scenery, character,* based on five tours 1825–40.
1842	Fr. Matthew's total abstinence crusade; first issue of *The Nation* (Oct.).
1843	O'Connell proclaims 1843 as the "Repeal (of union) year" (Jan.); "monster meetings" agitate for repeal; O'Connell charged with conspiracy; Devon Commission into law relating to land occupancy (Nov.).
1844	O'Connell sentenced to one year's imprisonment (May), judgment reversed by House of Lords (Sept.); Society of St. Vincent de Paul introduced to Ireland.
1845	Report of Devon Commission; Earl of Rosse's new telescope is largest in world; dispute between O'Connell and Young Ireland over Queen's Colleges (May); Colleges (Ireland) Act (July); potato blight in eleven counties; Thomas Davis dies.
1846	Public Works Act to relieve distress; Fisheries and

	Drainage Acts; repeal of Corn Laws; disastrous potato crop failure; Central Relief Committee of Society of Friends set up.
1847	Irish Confederation established (Jan.); soup-kitchens system established; famine at its height; death of O'Connell; Poor Law amended to extend its remit.
1848	Mitchel founds *United Irishman,* but is convicted under treason-felony act and transported (May); letters on land question by J. F. Lalor; Young Ireland rising in Munster (July), leaders sentenced to be hanged, but later transported to Van Dieman's Land (later called Tasmania); general failure of potato crop; first Encumbered Estates Act; cholera outbreak (Nov.).
1849	Kilkenny Archaeological Society formed (predecessor of Royal Society of Antiquaries of Ireland, 1890); potato blight reappears (May); Queen Victoria's first visit; revival of *The Nation;* Queen's Colleges at Belfast, Cork, and Galway opened (Oct.); second Encumbered Estates Act, commission meets for first time; evictions from agricultural holdings begin.
1850	Tenant Right League formed (Aug.); university charter to Queen's University of Ireland (Sept.).
1851	Census includes Irish language inquiry.
1852	Telegraph cable link completed between Holyhead and Howth; National Exhibition in Cork (June); General election (July), 40 MPs promise support for tenant-right question; Keogh and Sadleir accept office in Aberdeen's ministry; Conference of Tenant League in Dublin, adopting policy of independent opposition in parliament (Sept.).
1853	Irish Industrial Exhibition in Dublin.
1854	Catholic University opens in Dublin.
1855	C. G. Duffy emigrates to Australia.
1856	Irish Academy of Music founded.
1857	Sectarian rioting in Belfast (June/Sept.).
1858	Foundation of Fenian movement, Irish Revolutionary/ Republican Brotherhood; first trans-Atlantic cable between Valentia and Newfoundland; Harland and Wolff partnership begins at Belfast shipyard.
1859	Building of National Gallery in Dublin begun; *Irish Times* first issued (Mar.); religious revival in Ulster.
1860	Deasy's Landlord and Tenant Law Amendment Act.
1862	Dublin United Trades Association formed (Oct.–Nov.).
1863	Registration of Births and Deaths (Ireland) Act (Apr.); Registration of Marriages (Ireland) Act (July).

1864	Stephens declares Fenian insurrection in 1865.
1865	Dublin International Exhibition (May); Magee College, Londonderry, opened (Oct.); Stephens arrested, but escapes to France.
1866	Suspension of *Habeas corpus* continued until 1869; Fenian council of war rejects plan for an immediate rising; Devoy arrested (Feb.); Fenian raids on Canada (Apr.–June); Archbishop Cullen made first Irish cardinal; Alexandra College, Dublin, opened for higher education for women.
1867	Abortive Fenian attempt to seize Chester Castle (Feb.); Fenian rising starts in Kerry, spreading to Dublin (Mar.), Cork, Limerick, Tipperary, and Clare; Irish Republican Brotherhood convention at Manchester appoints Col. Thomas Kelly to succeed Stephens; Kelly and Deasy rescued from police in Manchester; Allen, Larkin, and O'Brien executed at Manchester; explosion at Clerkenwell jail, London, in abortive attempt to rescue Fenians.
1868	Michael Barrett publicly executed for his part in Clerkenwell explosion, the last such in UK; J. O'Hagan made first Catholic lord chancellor since reign of James II.
1869	Amnesty for 49 Fenian prisoners, Church of Ireland disestablished and disendowed.
1870	Home Government Association founded; Michael Davitt sentenced to 15 years penal servitude; Gladstone's Landlord and Tenant Act.
1871	Release of 33 amnestied Fenian prisoners.
1872	Ballot Act introduces secret voting; first horse-drawn tramcars in Dublin and Belfast.
1873	Home Rule Confederation of Great Britain founded in Manchester; Fawcett's Act abolishes religious test in Trinity College Dublin; Gladstone's university bill defeated; Home Rule League formed in Dublin.
1874	General election: 60 "home rulers" returned, form distinct party; Butt's home rule motion defeated.
1875	John Mitchel elected MP for Tipperary (Feb.), barred from taking his seat, reelected but dies (Mar.); Parnell elected for Meath (Apr.).
1876	Supreme council of Irish Republican Brotherhood withdraws support from home rule movement (Mar.); Society for the Preservation of the Irish Language formed.
1877	Parnell elected president of Home Rule Confederation in place of Butt; Davitt released from Dartmoor.
1878	Intermediate Education Act; Cardinal Cullen dies; "new

	departure" policy developed by Davitt, Devoy, and other Fenians in the United States.
1879	Land agitation opened with Davitt's meeting in Co. Mayo (Apr.); Parnell at Westport meeting; National Land League of Mayo founded at Castlebar; Irish National Land League formed in Dublin; Irish Convention Act of 1793 repealed.
1879–82	The "land war."
1880	Parnell addresses U.S. Congress; charter founding Royal University of Ireland (Apr.); Parnell elected chairman of Irish Parliamentary Party (May); ostracism of land agent, Capt. Boycott in Co. Mayo (Sept.–Nov.); trial of Parnell and others for conspiracy (Dec.).
1881	Arrest of Davitt (Feb.); Peace Preservation Act (Mar.); disorders in west Cork; first number of *United Ireland* Parnellite weekly (13 Aug.); second Land Act; arrest of Parnell and others, "No rent manifesto" issued from prison (18 Oct.); Land League proclaimed an unlawful and criminal association (Oct.).
1882	"Kilmainham treaty" (Apr.–May); Parnell and others released from jail; murder of Cavendish and Burke in Phoenix Park (May); Prevention of Crime Act (July); Arrears of Rent Act (Aug.); Irish National League founded (Oct.).
1883	Arrest of "Invincibles" for Phoenix Park murders (Jan.); dynamite campaign in England, conspirators arrested (Apr.); Portrush-Bushmills electric railway opened (second in the world).
1884	First women graduate in Ireland at Royal University; Gaelic Athletic Association formed.
1885	Ashbourne Land Purchase Act; Parnell holds balance between British parties in House of Commons after general election (Nov.–Dec.); Gladstone's conversion to home rule announced prematurely.
1886	Ulster Loyalist Anti-Repeal Committee organizes demonstrations against home rule (Jan.–Feb.); Gladstone introduces Home Rule Bill (8 Apr.), defeated (7–8 June); "Plan of Campaign" announced in *United Ireland* (23 Oct.), journal proscribed (18 Dec.).
1887	"Parnellism-and-crime" articles in *The Times* (Mar.–Apr.); Criminal Law and Procedure Act (July).
1888	Papal circular condemns "Plan of Campaign" and boycotting (Apr.); W. B. Yeats and others publish *Poems &*

	Ballads of Young Ireland; commission appointed to investigate charges against Parnell and others; Belfast granted city charter (Nov.).
1889	Pigott forgeries exposed before special commission; O'Shea files for divorce, citing Parnell (Dec.).
1890	Special commission exonerates Parnell; verdict of divorce court goes against Mrs. O'Shea and Parnell (17 Nov.); Parnell's re-election as chairman of Irish Parliamentary Party (25 Nov.) followed by publication of Gladstone's letter to Morley disavowing Parnell; Parnell's manifesto to the Irish people (29 Nov.); debates on Parnell's leadership result in majority decision against him and split of Irish party (Dec.); Parnell's candidate defeated at Kilkenny by-election.
1891	Congested Districts Board formed by Balfour Land Act; death of Parnell (6 Oct.); John Redmond holds Waterford seat for Parnellites.
1892	Ulster Convention opposes home rule (June); Irish Education Act abolishes fees and makes schooling compulsory for ages 6–14; Belfast Labour Party formed, the first in Ireland (Sept.).
1893	Gladstone's second Home Rule bill (Feb.); electric tramway opens in Dublin suburbs; foundation of Gaelic League; Home Rule bill passes House of Commons but is defeated in House of Lords (Sept.).
1894	Irish Agricultural Organisation Society formed by Sir Horace Plunkett.
1896	Irish Socialist Republican Party formed in Dublin.
1897	First Oireachtas and Feis Ceoil—Irish literary and music festivals—held.
1898	Irish Local Government Act established county councils; women granted limited franchise; first issue of Connolly's *Workers' Republic* (12 Aug.).
1899	Irish Literary Theatre founded; first issue of Griffith's *United Irishman* (4 Mar.); Catholic Truth Society of Ireland founded; first issue of *An Claidheamh Soluis,* official organ of Gaelic League (17 Mar.).
1900	Redmond elected leader of reunited Irish Parliamentary Party; foundation of Cumann na nGaedheal party.
1901	Lady Gregory's *Ideals in Ireland* published in London.
1902	First performance of Yeats's *Cathleen ni Houlihan.*
1903	Wyndham Land Act (Aug.); St. Patrick's Day to be a bank holiday.

1904	Griffith's *Resurrection of Hungary* begins in *United Irishman;* Abbey Theatre opened in Dublin by National Theatre Society; Ulster Unionist Council formed.
1905	Dungannon clubs formed in Belfast by Bulmer Hobson; first Carnegie free library opened in Cork; Redmond secures promise of home rule from Campbell-Bannerman, leader of Liberals (Nov.); Griffith proposes policy of "Sinn Fein" at National Council.
1906	First issue of *Sinn Féin* (5 May); Belfast City Hall opened; first issue of *The Republic* in Belfast.
1907	*Ne Temere* decree, affecting interfaith marriages, issued by the pope; industrial unrest in Belfast; Evicted Tenants Act; National Council and Sinn Fein unite.
1908	Irish Universities Act substitutes National University of Ireland and Queen's University of Belfast for Royal University; James Larkin forms Irish Transport Workers' Union; Housing of the Working-Class Act sets up house construction fund (Dec.).
1909	Health Resorts and Watering-Places Act (the first related to tourism); Birrell's Land Act; first cinema opened in Dublin.
1910	General elections: Irish Party holds balance; Sir Edward Carson elected leader of Irish Unionist Party.
1911	Parliament Act restricts House of Lords' power of veto.
1912	Third Home Rule bill passes House of Commons; Solemn League and Convenant subscribed in Ulster (28 Sept.).
1913	Ulster Volunteer Force formed; Home Rule bill twice defeated in House of Lords (Jan./July); mechanism for provisional government of Ulster set up by Ulster Unionist Council (Sept.); labor unrest in Dublin: Larkin arrested and imprisoned; Irish Volunteers formed (Nov.); Irish Citizen Army launched in Dublin; import of arms into Ireland forbidden by royal proclamation.
1914	Curragh incident (Mar.); Ulster Volunteers' gun running into Larne and Down ports (Apr.); Home Rule bill passes House of Commons for third time (May); Buckingham Palace conference (21 June–4 July) fails to resolve Ulster problem; Howth gun running (July) for Irish Volunteers; further gun running into Kilcoole (Aug.); UK declares war on Germany (4 Aug.) and Irish divisions begin forming; Nationalists, mostly Supreme Council of Irish Republican Brotherhood, meet to consider insurrection before end of war; Redmond calls on Irish Volunteers to serve the allied cause, thereby splitting movement; Gov-

ernment of Ireland Act receives royal assent, but its operation is suspended (Sept.); Sir Roger Casement arranges for Irish brigade to serve German cause.

1915   *Lusitania* sunk off Kinsale with 1,198 lives lost; coalition formed under Asquith includes Carson as attorney general; Patrick Pearse joins reorganized supreme and military councils of Irish Republican Brotherhood.

1916   The *Aud* arrives in Tralee Bay (20 Apr.) with arms but is apprehended; Casement lands from German submarine in Co. Kerry (21 Apr.); Easter rising begins in Dublin (24 Apr.) with proclamation of Provisional Government and capture of key buildings; martial law proclaimed in Dublin (25 Apr.); Pearse orders surrender (29 Apr.); leaders of rising executed (3–12 May); Lloyd George's proposals for immediate implementation of home rule, with a temporary exclusion of six Ulster counties (July); Anti-Partition League formed in Derry; Casement hanged (3 Aug.).

1917   Count Plunkett elected as Sinn Fein candidate for North Roscommon (Feb.), but does not take his seat in parliament; Ford Motor Co. sets up tractor factory in Cork; remaining Irish insurgents released from prison (June), including de Valera, who is elected as Sinn Fein candidate for East Clare (July); Irish Convention meets in Dublin (July), boycotted by Sinn Fein; de Valera elected leader of Sinn Fein and Irish Volunteers (Oct.).

1918   Redmond dies (Mar.); Military Service Act, extending conscription to Ireland, opposed outside Ulster; Sinn Fein leaders arrested in German plot; mail boat *Leinster* sunk by German submarine with 500 lives lost (Oct.).

1919   Proportional representation implemented for first time in Sligo municipal election (Jan.); "war of independence" begins as Sinn Fein representatives in Dublin adopt constitution for Dáil Eireann (21 Jan.) and issue declaration of independence; de Valera escapes from prison and is elected president of Dáil Eireann (1 Apr.); general strike in Limerick, soviet formed; Dáil Eireann declared illegal (Sept.).

1920   Royal Irish Constabulary recruits former British soldiers ("Black and Tans"); unrest in Derry and Belfast; assassinations by Republicans provoke Bloody Sunday in Dublin (21 Nov.); Michael Collins commands Irish Republican Army (formerly Irish Volunteers); imposition of martial law (Dec.); Government of Ireland Act.

1921   Sir James Craig succeeds Carson as leader of Ulster Unionists; Craig and de Valera meet in Dublin before general election for new parliaments; Northern Ireland parliament opened by King George V (June); Anglo-Irish truce signed (July); Sinn Fein's 124 representatives meet as second Dáil Eireann (Aug.); Anglo-Irish Treaty signed in London (6 Dec.).

1922   Treaty ratified by Dáil Eireann (7 Jan.); de Valera seeks re-election but is defeated by pro-treaty Arthur Griffith; Michael Collins becomes chairman of provisional government; James Joyce's *Ulysses* published in Paris; Irish language to be taught daily in national schools; Irish Free State (Agreement) Act (Mar.); Civil Authorities (Special Powers) Act (NI) for one year (made permanent in 1933); Royal Ulster Constabulary formed (May); Irish Free State (IFS) general election (June), majority pro-treaty; civil war begins (28 June), buildings in Dublin held by anti-treaty forces destroyed by Provisional Government forces, including the Four Courts; Griffith dies, Collins killed in ambush (Aug.); W. T. Cosgrave elected president of Provisional Government (Sept.); rebels (Irregular IRA) tried by military court and 77 executed (Nov.); Irish Free State Constitution Act approved (Dec.), T. M. Healy becomes first governor-general; Northern Ireland parliament decides to opt out of IFS and Duke of Abercorn becomes first governor; first IFS postage stamps issued.

1923   Customs barriers between Irish Free State (IFS) and UK set up (1 Apr.); end of civil war follows suspension of operations announced by de Valera (17 Apr.); de Valera imprisoned without trial (Aug.–July 1924); IFS joins League of Nations; Yeats awarded Nobel Prize for Literature.

1924   Reorganization of IFS army leads to mutiny; Leinster House given to Irish government by Royal Dublin Society; British Broadcasting Company (now Corporation) opens Belfast station; first performance of Hamilton Harty's *Irish Symphony* given in Manchester.

1925   Shannon Electricity Act authorizes Irish-German hydroelectric project; report of boundary commission submitted but not published (Dec.) due to furor following *Morning Post* forecast (7 Nov.).

1926   Broadcasting station opens in Dublin; de Valera leaves Sinn Fein and sets up Fianna Fail party; first Royal Dublin

	Society international horse show; George Bernard Shaw awarded Nobel Prize for Literature.
1927	General elections in Irish Free State (IFS) (June/Sept.), Fianna Fail enters Dáil as largest opposition party; Currency Act creates separate IFS currency.
1928	Galway Gaelic Theatre opens; Irish Manuscripts Commission set up; Library Association of Ireland founded.
1929	Northern Ireland general election follows abolition of proportional representation; Irish Free State Censorship of Publications Act.
1930	Irish Hospital Sweepstakes established in Dublin; National Exhibition of Irish Manufactures at Royal Dublin Society.
1931	Statute of Westminster (Dec.) provides separation of British and Dominion laws; An Oige (Irish Youth Hostel Association) set up.
1932	Irish Free State general election results in Fianna Fail victory, de Valera becomes president of executive council; British and Irish governments fail to resolve differences on constitutional details, economic restrictions follow; Northern Ireland parliament buildings at Stormont formally opened; de Valera chairs League of Nations assembly at Geneva.
1933	Constitutional Amendment Acts passed by Dáil.
1934	Town and Regional Planning Act passed in Dáil; Anglo-Irish cattle and coal agreement; R. L. Praeger's *The Botanist in Ireland*.
1935	Sale or importation of contraceptives forbidden in Irish Free State; Irish speakers from Connemara move to Meath Gaeltacht.
1936	First flight by Aer Lingus; IRA declared illegal in Irish Free State (IFS) following period of atrocities; IFS Constitutional Amendment and External Relations Acts passed.
1937	New IFS constitution; Eire replaces IFS (29 Dec.).
1938	Anglo-Irish Agreement settles trade and annuity dispute, treaty ports restored to Ireland; Douglas Hyde becomes first president of Ireland; Short and Harland's aircraft factory opens in Belfast.
1939–45	Ireland remains neutral in World War II; Northern Ireland excluded from conscription; IRA bombing activity in England until March 1940; German bombs dropped intensively on Belfast industrial sites (April–May 1941),

	with 700 fatalities; Dublin and other fire brigades sent to help.
1942	American troops arrive in Northern Ireland, protest by de Valera; naval base set up in Derry.
1944	Transport Act establishes Coras Iompair Eireann (CIE).
1945	Northern Ireland Housing Trust set up; de Valera asserts Eire is a republic (July); opera singer John McCormack dies.
1946	Ireland applies for membership of UNO; Northern Ireland Elections and Franchise Act increases business votes in local elections; Industrial Relations Act sets up labor court for Eire; Shannon airport declared customs-free area.
1947	Northern Ireland Education Act provides secondary schooling for all (Mar.); Eire Health Act (Aug.) disapproved by Catholic hierarchy.
1948	General election in Eire: Fianna Fail defeated and first coalition government formed under J. A. Costello (Fine Gael); National Health Service established in Northern Ireland; External Relations Act (1936) repealed.
1949	Republic of Ireland declared (18 Apr.), Eire leaves Commonwealth; Ireland Act (UK) confirms that citizens of Irish Republic should not be treated as aliens in UK or colonies; last tramcar runs in Dublin.
1950	Agreement between Eire and Northern Ireland on Foyle fisheries and Erne Drainage and Development Act; first peat-fired power station in operation.
1951	Catholic bishops' opposition to "Mother-and-child" scheme forces resignation of minister, Dr. Noel Browne, and of Costello's government; de Valera returns to office (May); first Wexford opera festival; Prof. E. T. S. Walton shares Nobel Prize for Physics.
1952	Bord Failte (Irish Tourist Board) formed.
1953	Comhairle Radio Éireann set up by Erskine Childers, minister for posts and telegraphs (Jan.); car ferry *Princess Victoria* lost in storm off Larne; Chester Beatty library opened in Dublin; Health Act provides free mother-and-child care in Republic of Ireland.
1954	Second interparty government under Costello; IRA raids on military bases in Northern Ireland; first Cork international choral and folk dance festival.
1955	Ireland admitted to UNO (Dec.).
1956	IRA attacks in Northern Ireland (campaign lasting until 1962).

1957	De Valera again taoiseach following general election (Mar.); first Dublin International Theatre Festival; Roman Catholics boycott Protestants in Fethard, Co. Wexford, during interfaith marriage dispute; Gaeltarra Eireann formed to run small industries in Irish-speaking areas; Jack B. Yeats dies.
1958	Irish officers serve with the UN in Lebanon; Industrial Development Act removes restrictions on foreign ownership of manufacturing industries; first Programme for Economic Expansion in Republic of Ireland published.
1959	De Valera succeeds S. T. O'Kelly as president of Republic of Ireland; S. F. Lemass becomes taoiseach; new Irish Congress of Trade Unions formed with special Northern Ireland committee; Ulster Television initiated (Oct.).
1960	Appointment of commission on higher education (Sept.); Broadcasting Authority Act forms Radio (Telefis) Eireann; Irish troops serve with UN forces in Congo; F. H. Boland elected president of UN General Assembly.
1961	Republic of Ireland applies for membership of EEC (Aug.) and joins UNESCO (Oct.); television service inaugurated (31 Dec.).
1962	Republic of Ireland government compulsorily acquires mineral rights in Tynagh, Co. Galway; M1 motorway opened from Belfast to Lisburn.
1963	Regional plan produced for Northern Ireland by Sir R. Matthew; Terence O'Neill succeeds Brookborough as prime minister of Northern Ireland; second Programme for Economic Expansion in Republic of Ireland.
1964	Irish troops serve with UN forces in Cyprus; E. McAteer elected leader of Nationalist Party in Northern Ireland; Ulster Folk Museum opened.
1965	Northern Ireland's prime minister O'Neill and Republic's taoiseach Lemass exchange visits (Jan./Feb.); Nationalist Party accepts role of official opposition in Stormont parliament (Feb.); Lockwood committee recommends a new university at Coleraine and an end to university status for Magee College, Londonderry; New Towns Act in Northern Ireland leads to creation of Craigavon; Anglo-Irish free trade agreement.
1966	Opening of new Abbey Theatre (July); Lemass resigns, succeeded by Jack Lynch (Nov.); meeting between Taoiseach Lynch and Northern Ireland Prime Minister O'Neill; Armagh planetarium opened.

1967	Northern Ireland Civil Rights Association (NICRA) states objectives; Republic of Ireland Commission on higher education reports (Mar.), proposing separate university status for National University of Ireland's constituent colleges, but rejected by minister who announces countermeasure involving merger of Dublin's two universities; second round of cross-border visits by O'Neill and Lynch.
1968	New University of Ulster opens; civil rights marchers clash with police in Derry; Nationalists cease to be official opposition party in Stormont parliament; O'Neill announces five-point reform proposals, opposed by part of cabinet.
1969	People's Democracy march from Belfast to Derry attacked by militant Protestants near Claudy; Republic's third Economic Programme published; Bernadette Devlin wins Mid-Ulster by-election for Westminster as Unity candidate (Apr.); riots in Derry over banned civil rights march; O'Neill resigns, succeeded by James Chichester-Clark (Apr.); rioting in Co. Londonderry (July); Republic's Finance Act exempts artists and writers from income tax on proceeds of their work; severe rioting in Derry and Belfast (Aug.), British troops brought in to support the police; Downing Street Declaration announces security is now the responsibility of General Officer in Command for Northern Ireland and outlines general policy principles; tribunal of inquiry into disturbances in Northern Ireland set up under Sir Leslie Scarman; Samuel Beckett awarded Nobel Prize for Literature.
1970	IRA split into "Official" and "Provisional" wings at Dublin Ard-fheis (Jan); Rev. Ian Paisley and Rev. William Beattie returned to Stormont parliament in by-elections (Apr.); Alliance Party of Northern Ireland formed; Ulster Defence Regiment replaces B Specials; Irish Council of Churches and Roman Catholic Church set up joint group on social problems; two recently dismissed Republic of Ireland ministers arrested on arms-importing charges, later acquitted; Roman Catholic bishops remove ban on Catholics attending Trinity College Dublin; Social Democratic and Labour Party formed as opposition in Stormont parliament.
1971	Decimal currency introduced in Republic of Ireland and UK; Housing Executive Act in Northern Ireland (NI) concentrates all public housing in single authority (Feb.);

Chichester-Clark succeeded by Brian Faulkner as prime minister of NI; bill to liberalize Republic of Ireland law on contraceptives introduced into senate by Mrs. Mary Robinson, but rejected; reintroduction of internment without trial in NI (Aug.); NI, Irish, and British prime ministers meet to discuss NI problems (Sept.); Paisley and three others form Democratic Unionist Party in Stormont parliament; Social Democratic and Labour Party meets at Dungiven as alternative assembly; natural gas discovered off Kinsale.

1972   Bloody Sunday; civil rights march in Derry banned, 13 civilians shot dead (Jan 30.); Stormont parliament suspended and direct rule from Westminister introduced under Home Secretary, William Whitelaw (24 Mar.); Scarman tribunal reports on September 1969 events, and Lord Widgery's inquiry attributes blame for Bloody Sunday deaths to NICRA (Apr.); Republic of Ireland referendum on EEC entry; special criminal court set up in Republic to deal with terrorist cases (May); Official IRA suspends operations and Provisionals cease fire while discussions take place with government (June/July); "no-go" areas of Belfast and Derry reoccupied by army; SDLP's new policy proposing joint sovereignty over Northern Ireland, a provincial assembly, and all-Ireland senate outlined in *Towards a new Ireland* (Sept.); Whitelaw's Green Paper accepts an Irish dimension to the Northern Ireland problem (Oct.); Offences against the State (Amendment) Act passed in the Republic; referendum in the Republic amends articles 16 (voting age) and 44 (status of the Roman Catholic church) of constitution; Diplock Commission recommends changes in administration of justice in Northern Ireland for terrorist cases.

1973   Republic of Ireland and UK join EEC (1 Jan.); Republic general election (Feb.): Fine Gael-Labour coalition government; Northern Ireland (NI) referendum produces majority for remaining in the UK (boycotted by Social Democratic and Labour Party); NI Assembly Act sets up 78-member assembly to be based on proportional representation system (May); NI Constitution and Emergency Powers Acts (July): parliament and office of governor abolished and replaced by an executive appointed by the secretary of state; conference at Sunningdale between UK and Republic of Ireland governments and new NI power-sharing Executive affirms

	rights and creates framework for cross-border cooperation (Dec.).
1974	Northern Ireland (NI) Executive takes office to protests from members of United Ulster Unionist Council (UUUC) (Jan.); general election in UK (Feb.), UUUC majority in NI and Labour Party returned in Great Britain; Merlyn Rees, Secretary of State for NI, announces phased release of detainees; Ulster Workers Council enforces general strike (14–29 May), state of emergency declared, NI Executive resigns and NI assembly prorogued as direct rule is reimposed; Sean MacBride shares Nobel Peace Prize; Prevention of Terrorism Act in UK.
1975	Secret talks between Northern Ireland (NI) officials and Provisional Sinn Fein (Jan.); elections in NI for new Convention (May); detention without trial ended in NI (Dec.).
1976	Northern Ireland Convention fails to agree on power sharing; murder of UK ambassador to Republic of Ireland; Republic's president requires Criminal Law (Jurisdiction) bill to be tested in Supreme Court, found to be constitutional (Mar./May); Northern Ireland Fair Employment Agency created (July); death of three small children in Belfast during a terrorist incident leads to formation of the Peace People (Aug.); European Commission of Human Rights report finds UK guilty of torture of republican prisoners (Sept.); Anne Dickson elected leader of Unionist Party of Northern Ireland (first woman to lead political party in the island); Republic's Supreme Court alters capital sentences to life imprisonment for death of a policeman.
1977	Loyalist strikes fail in Northern Ireland (May) and UUUC parliamentary coalition dissolved; general election in Republic (June): Fianna Fail returned with record majority; American naval communication base in Derry closed; founders of Peace People awarded Nobel Peace Prize.
1978	European Court of Human Rights declared 1971 internees did not suffer from torture, but did receive inhuman and degrading treatment; rioting in Derry following tenth anniversary celebration of civil rights march (Oct.), most injuries inflicted by loyalists on police; Northern Ireland representation at Westminster increased by five MPs; Provisional IRA warn of "preparing for a long war" after widespread series of bombings in Northern Ireland.

1979	Unionist MPs decisive in Labour government's defeat (Mar.) leading to general election in UK (May); Conservative government formed under Margaret Thatcher; first European parliamentary election: three Northern Ireland seats contested under proportional representation; terrorist violence at a ten-year peak with 18 soldiers killed near Warrenpoint, and Lord Mountbatten of Burma and some of his party killed off Sligo (Aug.); papal visit to Ireland confined to Republic for security reasons; the pope appeals for end to violence at Drogheda mass; John Hume becomes leader of Social Democratic and Labour Party (SDLP).
1980	Constitutional conference opens at Stormont (Jan.), but adjourned indefinitely (Mar); "special category" status withdrawn from terrorist prisoners; European Commission of Human Rights rejects case of H-block prisoners; Northern Ireland devolution of government document rejected by Unionists and SDLP (July); H-block protesters undertake hunger strike (Sept.–Dec.); Thatcher-Haughey talks in Dublin set up joint studies.
1981	Paisley protests at Anglo-Irish talks at series of large rallies; hunger striker Bobby Sands wins Fermanagh-South Tyrone by-election (Mar.), rioting follows this and his death (May); sporadic rioting following ten other deaths during the summer, strike called off (Oct.); IRA bombing campaign extended to British army targets in Europe; British-Irish Inter-governmental Council set up.
1982	General election in Republic of Ireland, Fianna Fail returned with support of minor parties (Feb.); first person charged in Dublin with a crime committed in UK; Secretary of State James Prior fails to gain support for Rolling Devolution idea; SDLP decides to contest Assembly elections (Oct.) and refuses to take seats; general election in Republic (Nov.); Fine Gael-Labour coalition forms government.
1983	Republic's government sets up New Ireland Forum, but Alliance and Unionist parties decline to take part; general election in UK: Unionists take 15 out of 17 Northern Ireland seats (June), John Hume elected, but Provisional Sinn Fein oust former SDLP leader Gerry Fitt from the West Belfast seat; referendum on abortion in Republic; 38 terrorist prisoners escape from Maze prison; pre-Christmas bombing in London.
1984	Northern Ireland (NI) Assembly votes against extending

1967 Abortion Act to NI; Irish National Liberation Army leader Dominic McGlinchey extradited to NI to face murder charge, first such case; New Ireland Forum report suggests federal and joint-authority solutions within a united Ireland (May), rejected later by UK government; de Lorean sports car project partly developed in West Belfast from 1977 but closed after owner's arrest in United States, castigated as a "grave misuse" of public money by British parliamentary committee; Democratic Unionist Party devolution scheme proposed; Provisional IRA bombs Conservative Party conference in Brighton (Oct.); European Commission on Human Rights agrees that use of plastic bullets by security forces in NI was justified in riot conditions.

1985   Hume holds abortive meeting with Provisional IRA; Anglo-Irish Agreement signed by Thatcher and FitzGerald (Nov.), massive loyalist rallies object; both Republic of Ireland and UK parliaments endorse Anglo-Irish Agreement.

1986   Unionists resign seats in protest, by-elections result in loss of two seats to SDLP, but increased majorities in other 15; compromise reached by Unionist leaders, Paisley and Molyneaux, with prime minister in London but later reneged on after consultation with grassroots supporters in Belfast; British government refuses to suspend Anglo-Irish Agreement and dissolves Northern Ireland Assembly; John Stalker replaced in inquiry of alleged Royal Ulster Constabulary shoot-to-kill policy of 1982; Republic's referendum rejects divorce proposal; Provisional IRA extends list of "legitimate" targets to those servicing security installations; Anglo-Irish Conference's first meeting held in Dublin (Oct.).

1987   General election in Republic results in minority government (Feb.); Unionist leaders end 19-month boycott of government ministers (Sept); seizure of arms and explosives on *Eksund* off the French coast indicates scale of IRA stockpile of arms; 11 civilian bystanders killed by IRA bomb at Remembrance Day ceremony in Enniskillen; Republic's Extradition Act becomes effective (Nov.).

1988   Hume meets Adams for talks in Belfast; 17.6 percent unemployed in Republic (Jan.); first extradition under new act; talks between SDLP and Sinn Fein break down; direct statements by paramilitary spokespersons banned on radio and TV (Oct.); De Rossa replaces Tomas MacGiolla as leader of Workers' Party; IRA activity in mainland Europe endorsed by Martin McGuinness; European Court of Human Rights rules against detention without charge beyond four days, affecting Prevention of Terrorism Act's seven-day detention provision, British government seeks derogation from European Convention; difficulties experienced with extradition arrangements from Republic.

1989   Adams seeks unarmed political movement for national self-determination in Ireland; new Prevention of Terrorism Act allows seven-day detention (Mar.); restrictions on Sinn Fein in council elections lifted (Apr.); Haughey wins Republic general election (June), but is rejected as taoiseach by the Dáil with Progressive Democrat (PD) support; coalition of Fianna Fail, PD, and one Independent formed, with Lenihan as tanaiste (July); Adams supports IRA right to armed struggle (Oct.); widespread calls to suspend Anglo-Irish Agreement.

1990   Fair Employment law takes effect; Irish Supreme Court rejects appeal over 1988 assertion that Republic's territorial claim on Northern Ireland was a legal right (1 Mar.); Dublin Supreme Court rejects extraditions to UK, overruling High Court's decision on political motivation grounds (Mar.–Apr.); abolition of capital punishment proposed, but retaining mandatory 40-year jail sentences for treason and murders of police and diplomats (Apr.); Cardinal Ó Fiaich dies (May); Lenihan dismissed by Haughey (Oct.) under Progressive Democrat duress in the coalition; having resigned from Labour in 1985 over Anglo-Irish Agreement, Mary Robinson, with Labour/Workers' Party support, is elected president with 52 percent final vote against Fianna Fail nominee Lenihan's 46 percent, a final margin of 86,000 votes; Haughey survives attempted party coup by 55–22 (Nov.), and Dáil no-confidence vote by 84–81; leadership challenger Reynolds dismissed as minister of finance; John Bruton takes over as Fine Gael leader from Alan Dukes (November); Thatcher resigns as Conservative leader and prime minister (Nov.) and is replaced by John Major; Archbishop Daly installed (Dec.); IRA three-day Christmas cease-fire, the first in 15 years.

1991   At Fianna Fail (FF) conference (Mar.) Haughey promises reforms on contraception, divorce, telephone taps, and official secrets; FF and Fine Gael losses in local elections

(June); Sinn Fein states it will in future no longer comment on Provisional IRA activities; Archbishop Daly becomes a cardinal (June); Northern Ireland Emergency Provisions Act (Aug.).

1992   Haughey resigns (6 Feb.) over his knowledge of the phone tapping of a journalist in 1982; Reynolds succeeds him in Fianna Fail and by 84–78 votes as taoiseach in Dáil; High Court refuses permission to travel for nine months to a pregnant 14-year-old girl seeking an abortion despite her suicide threats (17 Feb.); Republic's attorney general Whelehan grants injunction while the girl is already in England, imposing fine or imprisonment on parents; Supreme Court lifts ban on travel (Feb.), citing the Constitution's safeguards for equal rights of the mother and European right to freedom of movement; Democratic Left formed from Workers' Party by De Rossa (Feb.–Mar.); Conservatives win British general election with a majority of 21 (Apr.); Adams loses West Belfast seat to SDLP; Dr. Eamon Casey resigns as Roman Catholic bishop of Galway over revelations that he had fathered a child 20 years earlier; 21 May issue of *The Guardian* banned for abortion advertisement, Irish government denies involvement in ban, De Rossa reads sections in the Dáil, thereby allowing publication; Ulster Defence Association banned in Northern Ireland (Aug.); Republic of Ireland referendum endorses Maastricht treaty (June); 3,000th victim of terrorism dies in Northern Ireland; Dublin High Court prevents students from offering information on abortion in UK, though the decision conflicts with Maastricht provisions on freedom of information (Aug.); Northern Ireland Roman Catholic schools allowed full state funding; Irish People's Liberation Organization disbanded (Nov); Anglo-Irish intergovernmental secretariat begins; Reynolds loses confidence vote by 88–77 (Nov.).

1993   Fianna Fail-Labour coalition under Reynolds, with largest-ever government majority of 36 (Jan.); Sinn Fein receives only 1.6 percent first-preference votes; three referenda in Republic: right to information passed by 64 percent, right to travel by 67 percent, but right to life rejected by 66 percent; Tanaiste Spring spoke of possible flexibility on articles 2 and 3 of Constitution (Feb); unemployment in Republic at 16.8 percent (Feb.); Hume-Adams talks (Apr.) reject devolution, seek "national self-determination," in contrast to Mayhew's stance of self-determination "within Northern Ireland"; Anglo-Irish Intergovernmental conferences; SDLP membership expresses some concern at Hume's actions; Dáil decriminalizes homosexual behavior between consenting adults over the age of 17 (June), since the British Offences Against the Person Act (1861), still in force in Ireland, breaches the European Convention on human rights; to stop AIDS, condoms are declassified as contraceptive devices; Adams argues for "demilitarization"; IRA bombings continue throughout the year, culminating in Shankill Road bomb in Belfast, which kills ten (Oct.); Reynolds publishes six-year National Development Plan (Oct.) to create 20,000 jobs, 40 percent of the required IR£20,000 million being sought from European Community structural-cohesion funds; O'Malley (leader of Progressive Democrats since 1985) resigns, succeeded by his deputy Mary Harney, the first woman party leader in the Republic; Ulster Freedom Fighters murder seven at Greysteel; UK government-Sinn Fein contacts revealed; Downing Street Declaration issued (15 Dec.) by Major and Reynolds, Forum for Peace and Reconciliation set up in Republic; IRA Christmas ceasefire for three days only.

1994   Crisis for Bruton in Fine Gael opposition, the party having received only 13 percent support in opinion poll (Feb.); June election reverses for Fianna Fail (two seats lost to Fine Gael and Democratic Left parties in Dáil), European elections and for 80 local councils; Sinn Fein announces Provisional IRA had "instructed its units to implement a complete cessation of military action" from midnight 31 August, "struggle not over, but a new phase," by now 3,170 dead due to terrorism in Northern Ireland; broadcasting ban on Sinn Fein lifted (Sept.); loyalist paramilitary groups spokesmen express "abject remorse" for the suffering inflicted on innocent civilians and announce an end to hostilities, "as permanent as that of the IRA" (13 Oct.); UK government removes the broadcasting ban on spokespersons for paramilitary organizations, including Ulster Defence Association, Ulster Volunteer Force, Ulster Freedom Fighters and Red Hand Commandos; in the Republic Labour withdraws from coalition government, Reynolds forced to resign (17 Nov.) over attempted appointment of attorney general Harry Whelehan as president of the High Court; Bruton becomes taoiseach with a cabinet comprising eight Fine Gael, six Labour, and one Democratic Left members (15 Dec.).

1995   Dáil lifts 1976 Emergency Powers Act (Feb.) (though some provisions of the 1939 Offences Against the State Act remain in force) and calls on London not to renew Prevention of Terrorism Act as a gesture of faith in the so-called peace process; *The Times* publishes what is claimed to be a draft of the "Framework document" to be discussed by British and Irish governments in which intergovernmental bodies with executive authority are to be created; angry Unionist reaction unallayed by Mayhew/Major assurances, since the content of the leaked document is not denied, although British and Irish spokesmen emphasize that, even if it was agreed to discuss such content, the ultimate acceptance or rejection of such institutions would be subject to a Northern Ireland referendum; several Unionist politicians threaten to withdraw support from the Major government, by now in effect a minority in view of the removal of the whip from nine Conservative rebels; Dáil passes by 85–67 votes a bill giving citizens legal right to freedom of information on abortion services available outside the state (8 Mar.), the Senate approves (14 Mar.), following support at the November 1992 referendum; when referred to it by President Robinson, the Supreme Court rules (12 May) that the bill is constitutional; David Trimble succeeds Molyneaux as leader of Ulster Unionists (Oct.); a bitterly contested referendum on the clause in the Republic's constitution banning divorce results in a wafer-thin majority in favor of permitting legal separation (Nov.); British and Irish governments agree on establishment of a three-man commission, chaired by former U.S. Senator George Mitchell, to examine the issues of decommissioning weapons held illegally by paramilitary organizations (Dec.); Seamus Heaney awarded Nobel Prize for Literature.

1996   The IRA announces the end of its cease-fire and simultaneously explodes a bomb in London, killing two civilians and causing extensive damage to property (9 Feb.); an IRA terrorist accidentally triggers an explosive device on a London bus, killing himself and injuring other passengers (19 Feb.); British and Irish governments jointly announce (27 Feb.) a sequence of procedural measures intending to culminate in all-party talks on Northern Ireland issues on 10 June; Hume and Adams meet leaders of the IRA.

Introduction

Ireland's geographical setting is of fundamental importance to its historical development. With an area of 84,400 square kilometers, it is situated between 51½ and 55½° north latitude and 5½ and 10½° west longitude. As the smaller and more westerly of two islands toward the edge of the continental shelf on the Atlantic seaboard of northwestern Europe, it is the more remote of the two from the rest of Europe, while being closer to North America than any part of the continent except Iceland. Contact with mainland Europe is at its shortest via the Irish Sea and across Britain. From the northeast corner of Ireland, Scotland is within sight, only 20 kilometers away, and Wales is about 100 kilometers from much of the southeast coast. Nevertheless, relative isolation has meant that some widespread European experiences (the Roman Empire, certain developments of early Catholicism) did not reach Ireland or were filtered through Britain (e.g., Celtic and Norman settlements). Conversely, more peripheral movements have been especially important (prehistoric megaliths, Viking-Norse raids and settlements). The Atlantic Ocean is the source of prevailing westerly wind systems and cyclonic depressions, and it serves to moderate the temperate climate even further through the influence of the relatively warm waters of the North Atlantic drift. However, increased frequency of high winds, particularly near the north and west coasts, not only limits tree growth and periodically disrupts contact with offshore islands but in the past has been reflected in vernacular house styles. Weather patterns are characterized by short-term variability; extreme conditions are rarely experienced. Generally mild, moist conditions endow the whole island with a long growing season for grass, reducing the need to house farm livestock during the winter. The mean January temperature is 4–8° C, and July, 15–17° C; the mean annual rainfall is between 700 and 3600 millimeters, decreasing from west to east and from high to low ground.

Irish ports were formerly important as the first landfall for trans-Atlantic shipping. North America became a popular destination for Irish emigration in the 18th century, being particularly important from the mid-19th century. Ireland's proximity to Britain has been of crucial significance historically in that its location meant that it could act as a back door to the larger island. Both islands share similar geological variety, but Ireland is less well endowed with the minerals essential for early industrialization—iron ore and coal. Consequently, it lacked the capacity to mirror Britain's late 18th- and 19th-century development. On the other hand, its population was able to benefit from seasonal or periodic labor emigration, while in earlier periods the proximity factor worked in reverse, with peoples moving from Britain to Ireland, sometimes as part of a general westward movement through Europe. The political and economic domination of Britain in the modern period has inevitably complicated the cohesion implicit in the notion of "the British Isles," a term that encompasses the Irish Sea, which simultaneously links and separates the two main islands.

Physical Features

Ireland is shaped like a saucer, having a central plain that covers more than half the island and a discontinuous mountain rim. Neither terrain is seriously impenetrable because the plain is drained by many rivers, including the Shannon, which at over 320 kilometers is the longest in Ireland and Britain. The uplands are segmented by valleys, many of which provide good access to the coastline. Except in the northeast, the mountains are remnants of the oldest geological formations, which have been structurally complicated and/or intruded by igneous masses, often granite. Those of the northwest are part of a tectonic system that extends through the highlands of Scotland to Scandinavia, while those of the southwest are related similarly to southwest England and Brittany. The plain is underlain by Carboniferous limestone with a variable cover of glacial drift, and thus it is not uniformly flat or featureless. The limestone is best exposed in the Burren area of northern Co. Clare where it descends to sea level in a series of terraces. The post-Carboniferous periods are represented by only small deposits in the northeast, where they are overlain by extrusive volcanics, mostly basalt, forming a structural plateau. Glaciation during the Pleistocene period came from the northeast, although some localized movements occurred in the uplands too. It affected most of Ireland, altering the shape of many valleys and producing small depositional hills to which Irish names have been given— drumlin and esker. These are particularly common in the northern half of the island and, where associated with poor drainage, can produce a landscape as difficult to traverse as higher mountain areas. The latter are not particularly elevated by European standards, generally rising above 300 meters, with numerous peaks over 900 meters, the highest being Carrauntoohil in Co. Kerry (1,041 m.), but locally they appear quite impressive. Their more level sections are masked with thick blanket bog that has accumulated since about 2000 B.C. Similar but more extensive and deeper peat deposits are a feature of the central plain and other low-lying areas. Soils based on this geomorphic and geological complex are similarly varied, but tend toward acidity and have a marked tendency to be shallower in the west. There are many lakes, small ones of glacial origin in the mountains or the drumlin-dominated lowland, and a number of larger ones associated with the river systems. The Corrib, Erne, and Shannon groups are the most extensive, but the largest single lake in Ireland or Britain is Lough Neagh (400 sq. km.). The coastline is very long (3,200 km.) with a considerable variety of deep embayments, representing submerged former river valleys, which often extend far inland, high rock cliffs, and extensive sandy beaches. Only a few offshore islands are still inhabited, principally Rathlin, Tory, and the Aran group.

History

As temperatures rose and woodland developed in the early postglacial era, settlers with early Mesolithic cultures seem to have come from Scotland, where their predecessors were already established in Paleolithic times. They were probably attracted initially by land that could be seen and explored from their home bases, and where they found along the coast useful supplies of flint for tools. Evidence of simple dwellings and a fishing-hunting lifestyle have been found at Mountsandel in the lower Bann valley, dating from 7000–6500 B.C., along the north and east coasts on raised beaches (worked flints found abundantly at Larne, Co. Antrim, led to the name Larnian being given to the latter culture groups) and at a few inland sites beside lakes farther south, particularly in the Shannon basin. Hitherto, evidence for Mesolithic settlement in Ireland has come from a small number of lowland sites in the northern half of the island, but it is possible that others may be concealed by the subsequent development of peat.

Neolithic Period, c. 4000–2000 B.C.

In contrast, the Neolithic period is characterized by primitive agriculture, as peoples utilized interior upland areas where the soils were lighter and the forest cover less dense. Possibly three millennia separated the Mountsandel fishers from the megalith builders of the Neolithic heyday. There was much transitional development. Again, few settlement sites have been found, but the use of pottery and the clearance of woodland by fire is known from mid-Ulster sites c. 4000 B.C. Some Neolithic peoples may have come to Ireland over longer distances, from both the south and the north, to judge by their most characteristic remains—megalithic tombs. These are sufficiently numerous and diverse to make Ireland an important area of study for Neolithic Europe. There are three main types—court, wedge and passage graves—all of which were originally covered by tumuli, or mounds, some of which also survive. Each type has parallels in Britain or mainland Europe, but the precise connections are still the subject of debate: diffusion into and/or through Ireland (e.g., long or court cairns common in the area north of the drumlin belt between Clifden and Dundalk). Among the most interesting features of the distributions, which being of stone are probably relatively unchanged, is the correlation with later regional differences within the island.

The most formidable example is provided by the famous passage graves of the Boyne valley and other concentrations (such as 30 on the Loughcrew Hills). They are in the richest part of the east-central plain and are distinctive in their use of hilltops and decoration on some of the stones; wedge tombs are the most numerous (about 400 recorded), particularly west of the river Shannon; portal tombs, characterized by imposing entrances, are most common in the southeast, while court tombs, to which they may be related, are found most often north of the "drumlin belt," usually on lower hill slopes. There are almost 300 of these in Ulster alone, which gives some idea of the scale of just one facet of Neolithic life. Their use, differing sizes and styles, and broadly discrete locations indicate a complex society with organizational and technological skills beyond those required for agriculture.

Bronze Age, c. 2000–500 B.C.

Some tombs and other Neolithic sites were used in subsequent periods, the distinguishing new feature being the use of metals, initially bronze and later iron. Beaker folk, associated with the first use of copper and characterized by their pottery and single, cist-type cremation burials, probably arrived from Britain c. 2000 B.C., but many of the new developments may have been acquired more accidentally and spread among existing settlers. Finds suggest settlements on lower ground, particularly on morainic deposits providing routeways, probably indicative of a greater degree of internal trading. Many consist of hoards of tools and ornaments, which although essentially haphazard, imply widespread use of metals throughout the island and local styles of pottery. Mixed agriculture, in which pastoralism became more important, seems to have been practiced, with the further reduction of forest cover and the possible introduction of horses.

Evidence from settlement sites is still rare, but it points to continuity and some degree of permanence, probably alongside transhumance. Some sites are on crannogs (artificial islands in small lakes), a form of settlement that persisted in some cases to the 17th century A.D. At the hillside Lough Gur site, Co. Limerick, are remains of wooden "house" structures. Few great stone circles from this period are known in Ireland, unlike Britain, though there are some small ones. With a plentiful supply of copper and associated metals, the Bronze Age in Ireland is characterized particularly by a vigorous trade in its products, including bronze axes, copper halberds, and gold ornaments, examples of which have been found all over Europe. Those from c. 1000 B.C. show evidence of technical changes and a high degree of social organization. Consequently, existence of an "industry" can be inferred, with substantial contact with developments at such major European centers such as Hallstatt, Austria. A further contrast with the previous period is the appearance of specialized tools for warfare, which suggests different trends in social relations.

Iron Age, c. 500 B.C.–A.D. 500

This period illustrates further development of existing Bronze Age culture, particularly defensive structures, with a new element—the gradual introduction of the use of iron—bronze being reserved increasingly for decorative objects. There is little evidence of more than minimal immigration, even of the notionally Celtic peoples associated with the Halstatt and the La Tène cultures, and it now seems likely that the origin of the Celtic language that became dominant in Ireland is to be found in the last major prehistoric influx of people, the Beaker folk. Settlement forms that are specifically Irish and date to the late prehistoric period—raths, cashels and crannogs—may also have their origins in the earlier Bronze Age. Also pointing to stability within the island, certain characteristics of Iron Age Britain, or La Tène culture, multivallate hill forts or burial customs and pottery forms, are rarely found in Ireland. The surviving forts are less complex and are associated with locally dominant tribes. Most are earthen structures, like Tara and Emhain Macha, and some are at least partly of stone, like Grianan of Aileach and the coastal promontory forts such as those on the Aran Islands. In many ways they are larger and more elaborate versions of the most common settlement forms, the earthen rath, or ring-fort, and stone cashel, and, while they may have had ceremonial and/or defensive functions, they may also represent the dwelling places of the most prominent family in any area.

The ubiquitous and uniquely Irish rath, also known as dun, lios, and cathair, was a small level area enclosed by a circular bank and ditch, varying in diameter from 15 to 50 meters. Over 30,000 known sites have survived all over the island, mostly in previously forested lowlands, but generally on the slopes between 30 and 120 meters above sea level. They were typically dispersed, single-family units with space for dwellings, usually wooden framed and often circular; storage places, including underground systems (souterrains); and coralling of animals. Their names are still dominant elements in Irish place-names, and, like crannogs, many were used for long periods, possibly from the Bronze to the Middle Ages. The names of some leading tribes and individuals are also known. Their heroic exploits form the basis of early Irish mythology, first commemorated by the bards of this period. Many features—such as roadways, settlement forms, building styles, and economic activity—preserved their prehistoric features well into the medieval period. Politically and culturally, the Celtic system developed for the most part independently in Ireland as Roman expansion ground to a halt close by in Britain. Until 1995 it was believed that no Roman settlement had occurred in Ireland, but this view may have to be revised in the light of the discovery of a coastal fort north of Dublin, apparently occupied about A.D. 79–138.

Medieval Period, c. 500–1500 A.D.

Early medieval Ireland was unique in Western Europe, trading with the Roman world, including partially Romanized Britain, and receiving Christianity via such contacts, yet retaining a distinct, separate identity. The basic political unit was the *tuath,* a small pastoral-agricultural territory ruled by a chief or king (*ri*), that was about one-sixth of a modern county in size. It may be related to later baronies. *Tuatha* tended to cluster into larger groups under a dominant king, and some of these "overkingdoms" may be reflected in early dioceses from the 12th century. The overkingdoms in turn often formed federations, which by the end of the Iron Age consisted of the "Five Fifths"—Ulaid (Ulster, north), Connachta (Connaught, west), Munha (Munster, south), Laigin (Leinster, southeast), and Mide (Meath, east). These later became the four provinces of Ireland, with the last two combining. Fluidity typified the system. Alliances formed and reformed following battles that often became the subject of epic poetry. One example was the breakup of Ulster and the linking of the western parts with Meath under the Uí Néill. Meanwhile, east Ulster kings established closer links with southwest Scotland in the kingdom of Dál Riada, which straddled the narrow sea and produced a different traditional emphasis there.

Tuatha-based society was hierarchical, with the warrior king and related nobles at the top. They were followed by free farmers who paid food rent, joined in armed hostings, and contributed to local assemblies. Last came the numerous servile classes. There were also highly valued jurists, bards, harpers, specialist craftsmen, and later clerics and Latin scholars. Land and rights, including kingship, were originally structured in terms of the extended family, as defined over a number of generations, and were inalienable. Succession was by division of land among all male heirs and by election to the kingship, both processes tending toward intermittent strife, but also to the consolidation of extensive familial loyalties. There were legal safeguards for women, clerics, and children. Even in pre-Christian times an aura of sanctity surrounded the king. Eventually an equally dispersed church system developed in which the ruling families often played a key role, enhancing their political centers with monasteries or moving to be near those that were especially prestigious. Similar realignments took place with regard to the Norse towns that rose to prominence toward the end of the millennium.

Viking and Norse Period, A.D. 795–1169

At the end of the eighth century Ireland received a new wave of immigrants. Arriving as raiders, as some of their prehistoric predecessors may have done, they were drawn to wealth concentrated at the monastic centers, where the losses they inflicted were severe. Unlike previous immigrants, they came from northern, rather than western or central, Europe via Britain. Since they were equally interested in the rest of the British Isles, they reinforced contacts between Ireland and the islands to its north and east. A plundering phase soon gave way to trading, at first from small fortified coastal bases and later from well-established towns. These nuclei filled two voids in the Irish settlement pattern—few ports and few truly urban centers, although some of the more prominent monastic locations may have been at least prototowns, with substantial populations, markets or fairs, and discrete internal functional areas based on a complex division of labor. Small Norse colonies around towns such as Dublin and Limerick joined the Irish political scene with their fleets as a new element, sometimes in alliance with, sometimes in opposition to, the Gaelic kings. The O'Brien kings of Munster virtually took over Norse Limerick and gained a famous victory under Brian Boru, then high king, against Norse Dublin and its Leinster allies at the battle of Clontarf in 1014.

As they grew and were fortified, the towns acted as magnets for the people and produce of the rest of Ireland and became essentially Hiberno-Norse in culture. The Norse became Christian, and the Irish experienced a renewal of long-distance trade, through which they had more frequent and direct experience of the unfamiliar social, religious, and political traditions of feudal Europe. The first coins known to have been minted in Ireland were made in Dublin, which was also closely connected politically to the Norse settlement in northern England, via the city of York. There, unlike the Irish experience, rural settlement was also a feature of the Scandinavian immigration. Place-names of coastal features (especially inlets and islands) and towns (e.g., Waterford and Wexford) derived from these settlers were, however, joined by their versions of Irish political units so that most of the provincial names are now used in their Norse form (e.g., Ulster).

The Anglo-Norman Period, 1169–1485

This period is typified by renewed in-migration that directly affected over two-thirds of the island, with indirect effects on the western and northern margins. It was comparable in many ways to the Norman invasion of England a century earlier, in that a relatively small number of immigrants produced an administrative and land-owning stratum. There was also a local dynastic context. Diarmuid Mac Murchada (Dermot McMurrough), king of Leinster, had lost his kingship to his rivalry with the

Ua Conchobair (O'Conors) of Connacht, then in the ascendant among the Irish kings. In 1166 Mac Murchada sought help from Henry II of England. Henry already had ambitions toward Ireland and gave Diarmuid permission to recruit knights and their followers, which he did mostly in south Wales. Not appreciating the danger, the high king allowed Diarmuid to reestablish himself in south Leinster, with a Norman force taking the nearby Hiberno-Norse town of Wexford in 1169. The next year a larger army under Richard de Clare, earl of Pembroke (Strongbow), arrived and captured Waterford, where he married Mac Murchada's daughter and only heir. The Leinster and Norman force met the Irish under the high king at Dublin and lifted their blockade of the city. Mac Murchada died suddenly, leaving his Leinster lands to Strongbow. Henry II arrived to assert control over his knights and the whole island as part of his large west European hegemony. His ultimate authority was a papal bull, issued some years earlier, allowing him to aid the reformation of the Irish church. The Irish kings readily swore their fealty, but there was a wide divergence between the concept of overlordship, as developed in traditional Gaelic Ireland, and a more modern feudal Europe, the former being rather fluid and the latter much more exact.

Ireland presented a fine opportunity for the land-hungry Normans to develop a rich agricultural area in western Europe, parallel to the contemporary colonization of eastern Europe by Germans. To a large extent the Normans' more cereal-based economy complemented the more pastoral Gaelic one, while their settlement forms of lord's manor, nucleated village, and market town, though new, could be fitted into the existing pattern. It was in a very real sense a meeting of two different worlds. Because the Irish were less modern, they were the ultimate losers. As individual Normans spread through the fertile valleys, the Irish were squeezed westward and into the less productive areas. The two cultures often coexisted closely, but Anglo-Norman society was unified around trading via the ports. Initially the ports belonged to the king because he had acquired the existing Hiberno-Norse towns. Anglo-Norman society was also unified by loyalty, including tax-paying, to a common, although generally absent king. Politically, the Gaelic system was more loosely structured and was much more fragmented physically. This both aided and limited the Anglo-Norman success, so that the conquest, being incomplete, also contained the seeds of its own destruction. Another widespread introduction to the landscape was the castle. Initially it was a wooden structure on a mound (the motte-and-bailey type). Later large stone castles were constructed at ports and river crossings on important routeways. Dublin Castle became in effect the center of the administration, although the king's representative, a local or an English lord sent over for a time as justiciar, often went on tours and held parliaments in different towns in southeast Ireland. Economically and politically, this lordship probably reached its peak in the late 13th century. Early in the next century it was increasingly beset by problems, some emanating from the adjacent Gaelic areas and some from within.

Intermittent warfare followed, which increasingly involved Scots mercenaries and included a major incursion in 1315–18 by the brother of Robert Bruce, the Scottish king who had successfully resolved an English problem on his border in 1314. Difficulties with a wider provenence—deteriorating European trade and climatic conditions, and plagues, especially the Black Death—bore most heavily on the settlers, now increasingly Anglo-Irish in composition through intermarriage and long separation from Britain. The English crown had preoccupations in Wales and France as well as Scotland that overshadowed the decline in Ireland, and both men and funds were raised that could be ill spared. Repressive legislation against Gaelic practices, together with seasonal military campaigns against areas of Gaelic strength, became increasingly the norm, but failed even to contain the situation. The "land of war" gained over the "land of peace," and by the late 15th century Dublin rule could only be assured in a very small area of the eastern coastal plain, the Pale, which was demarcated by a double ditch and defended by a series of castles and walled towns. Even there, raids from Ulster in the north and the Wicklow mountains in the south were not infrequent and had to be endured without aid, as the political upheavals of the Wars of the Roses dominated England. Simultaneously, large areas of Norman settlement had fallen under the sway of a few dominant families, such as the Butlers of Ormond or the Kildare and Desmond Fitzgeralds, who, when acting as justiciars, sometimes had priorities at odds with those of the king and who, within their own areas, assumed powers and practices akin to Gaelic kings of an earlier period.

Tudor and Stuart Period, 1485–1691

It was this diversity of residual Gaelic lordships, Anglo-Irish magnates with palatine powers, and a shrunken crown administration that faced the Tudor rulers who emerged supreme from dynastic warfare and united England and Wales at a time of great technological, artistic, and philosophical change in Europe.

The first step at retrieval was "Poynings's Law" (1494), which limited the power of the Irish parliament to meet or legislate without the prior approval of the English crown. The second was a policy of "surrender and regrant" toward Gaelic or over-independent Anglo-Irish lords that redefined the renewal of crown control of land and loyalty through grants of new titles. To these limited measures, whose success was also partial, in time was added a more active policy of resettlement by new plantations of settlers from Britain, following local wars such as those in the center against the Gaelic O'Mores and in the southwest against the Anglo-Irish Fitzgeralds. These local wars had only limited success. The last major campaign in Ulster, following the most concerted Gaelic rebellion by the combined forces of the O'Neills and the O'Donnells, was the most effective. But as part of a policy of limited military campaigns and subsequent garrisoning, they eventually achieved the desired effect of bringing the whole island under crown control by the end of the 16th century. By then, Ireland had become the old colony and was seen once more as ripe for development, just like the new colonies being founded farther away in America during this age of discovery.

The other great contemporary development, the Reformation, proved to be a further complication. It was too closely connected with the English administration to be even slightly attractive on an island where traditionalism was inherent. As elsewhere in northern Europe, monasteries were suppressed, the associated lands being redistributed and the basis of a reformed church was established. Another related complication which appeared increasingly during this period was the internationalization of England's relations with Ireland. Foreign powers, such as Spain and France, could wage a proxy war on England by helping their coreligionists in Ireland. By the end of the 17th century a full-blown European conflict was fought partly in the island as James II tried to regain his English crown through Ireland, England's "back door." This was only the last of a series of military struggles that blighted Ireland with barbaric war during this century, with towns besieged (Londonderry, Limerick, Athlone) and, from time to time, populations massacred (Drogheda and Wexford) as either "settler" or "native" was in the ascendant.

The Eighteenth Century, 1691–1801

The reality of Ireland in 1700 was of an even richer diversity than before, but it had grown out of strife and was built on so much displacement of those, whether Gaelic or Anglo-Irish Catholics in origin, who regarded themselves as natives. The rising class of Protestant British settlers (now comprising the majority of landlords) and government administrators were still fearful, both locally and in the wider European sense, should Catholic Ireland again become a major issue.

The country was exhausted, and quiescence was desired by all; yet, in this context, it was perhaps too much to expect that it might be achieved with magnanimity. Initial prohibitions against Catholic clergy and ecclesiastical practices were gradually relaxed as the church instituted reforms, and the hierarchy was restored by the middle of the century. But it was the Penal Laws that generally came to characterize the period. Uniquely in Ireland, they were directed against the majority (unlike measures against Dissenters in Britain or Huguenots in France) as a means of ensuring their conformity (if they wished to play a public role) or else their subjection. The oath required of administrative and military office holders was unacceptable to Roman Catholics, although a few—already practicing lawyers and most of the surviving great landowners—did join the Established Church. What most Catholics found more oppressive was being forced to pay tithes to a church they did not attend, especially when their standard of living could only fall due to the meager amount of land (7%) and other resources left in their hands. Those penal laws, which required attendance at the Established Church, were seldom firmly enforced, although at first Catholic mass houses and schools could only operate unofficially. Protestant Dissenters also suffered some of these restrictions and shared Catholic objections, particularly to paying tithes and being excluded from official positions. Where this was felt most strongly, in parts of Ulster, some Presbyterians left for North America, but their creed was granted legal toleration from 1719 and their right to hold land and to vote were never restricted. For the Catholic majority the net effects also meant impoverishment of wealth and of culture in that there was no longer the capacity to sustain the Gaelic system of bards, and many of the natural leaders had left at the end of the wars.

The Irish parliament was dominated by the Protestant ascendancy, and it was also powerless to operate independently of London. Thus it was unable to defend Ireland's economic interests when they conflicted with those of Great Britain (the Irish woollen industry fell into decline as a result). Later under the guidance of Henry Grattan it found a subtle approach whereby funds were "required" for major Irish projects, such as the development of Dublin and especially its university. What little unrest that did occur was usually based on localized land issues aggravated by oppressive landlords. In the context of previous history, such occurrences usually produced panic measures that fueled a sense of grievance rather than a rational investigation of the causes.

During this period parts of the countryside were transformed by "improving" landlords who created imposing mansions surrounded by large parks and redeveloped associated villages or small towns (e.g., Carton House and Maynooth village by the dukes of Leinster). Many have survived, usually without their houses, and show the Irish contribution to the Age of Enlightenment, particularly in terms of architecture, glassware, and silver. Some of the expertise came from abroad, as did the development of the linen industry in which Huguenot emigrés were important.

Toward the end of the century the atmosphere in Ireland changed under the influence of the American War of Independence and the French Revolution and the new thinking underpinning them. Catholics and Dissenters made common cause, and the renewed threat of war in Europe changed the British government's approach to Ireland. However, these changes did not harmonize, and armed struggle was once more seen as necessary. The Volunteer movement found considerable support, as did the later United Irishmen under Wolfe Tone, especially in Belfast, then beginning its rise to prominence as Ireland's second city.

Some of the penal laws were repealed, but calls for Ireland's greater independence and acceptance as a distinct nation led ultimately to the opposite—the end of the Dublin parliament and closer integration through the creation of the United Kingdom of Great Britain and Ireland in 1801. This came in the aftermath of the 1798 rising that broke out in Wexford and extended to Dublin. Although it failed to elicit the expected level of French support, it did highlight the old fear of Ireland as England's Trojan horse.

From Union to Partition, 1801–1922

This period saw almost continuous internal conflict. The quest for complete Catholic emancipation was led by Daniel O'Connell, the first major Catholic/Gaelic figure in a century. O'Connell was enormously popular and successfully mobilized public opinion, which was expressed in huge public meetings. The need for equity in land distribution was made all the more urgent as the almost landless Catholic majority grew ever larger. The Home Rule movement, whose aim was ultimately taken up by the British Liberal party under Gladstone, pressed for restoration of a local parliament but failed to produce the necessary legislation. In time in Ireland it came to mean independence under the leadership of more radical groups such as the Fenians and was a major source of political and religious division within the island, ultimately leading to its partition.

The land issue produced intermittent violence and spawned extreme political groups too, but its aims were taken up with some success by Charles Stewart Parnell and the Irish Parliamentary Party. A series of land acts solved the problem over some decades, reducing the large estates and effecting a major redistribution, made easier with the contemporary reduction in population pressure.

The Act of Union was devastating for Dublin as a city and its housing stock suffered severe decline, as did its craft industries. At the same time Belfast and Londonderry were becoming manufacturing cities closely linked to the industrialization of central Scotland. The Union therefore came to have positive advantages in Ulster, and the new developments there added to its urban population at a time when famine was stalking the rural areas of the island. The Great Famine of 1845–47 occurred when the potato crop, on which the peasantry had become almost totally reliant, failed due to blight. Emigration had long been endemic, but it increased enormously immediately after the famine struck on a wider scale than ever before. Consequently, the island's population decreased by a fourth (two million) in 1845–50, due almost equally to mortality and emigration: this was a scale unknown anywhere in 19th-century Europe, where neither problem was uncommon. Not surprisingly, the "year of revolutions" (1848) was also marked in Ireland by a rising, this time by the Young Ireland movement, which, although it failed, served as an inspiration for later political leaders.

The last years of the century witnessed a cultural revival based particularly on literature, often written in English but strongly nationalistic, inspired especially by Gaelic poetry and legend. The poet and dramatist W. B. Yeats was the leading figure. This movement was complemented by the specifically Irish-based Gaelic League, which sought to revive the native language and foster other Gaelic traditions in games and music.

With home rule suffering from stalemate in parliament up to 1914, such efforts at raising national consciousness had an impact in the political sphere with the development of republicanism (especially through Sinn Fein and the Irish Republican Brotherhood). Socialism, gaining ground in Europe, was also seen as a route for Irish salvation. While republicanism, as expounded by people like Patrick Pearse, grew in Dublin, home rule lost its popular attraction. In Belfast Unionism was developed as a cause by Edward Carson, with the grassroots backing of the populist Orange movement in Ulster generally and the Conservative party in Great Britain.

By 1914 it was clear that both these extremes were prepared to resort to arms and that although Parliament could no longer prevent home rule, the actual issue had changed. War froze matters for many of those involved. Numerous Irishmen served as volunteers in the British army, while republicans saw the war as their great opportunity. The 1916 Easter Rising in Dublin was limited in scope but raised Unionists' fears to new levels. Coming as it did in the middle of a world war, it is hardly surprising that the rising was put down with some brutality, which itself served to fuel the cause. The 1918 general election gave Sinn Fein 73 seats and the Unionists 26. The former turned itself into Dáil Eireann under Eamon de Valera. The ensuing guerilla war (1919–21) caused much bitterness due to atrocities committed on both sides. The war ended with a compromise treaty granting dominion status to 26 counties; thereby Irish nationhood was accepted and independence gained. It was hoped that the six Ulster counties, to which home rule had come in 1920, would be persuaded to join in time. This was not to be; in the south civil war continued over the treaty provisions until 1923 and republican unrest became endemic in the north due to the existence of a large non-Unionist minority in parts of Belfast and the border areas, especially around Derry and Newry.

Northern Ireland remains part of the United Kingdom, although its administration changed to direct rule from London in 1974, following sustained republican terrorism and failure to produce a universally acceptable local administration. The Irish Free State effectively became a republic in 1936, and a new constitution institutionalized the position of the Roman Catholic Church, to which the overwhelming majority of its inhabitants belonged. Neutrality was established in its foreign policy (even during World War II), but it left the British Commonwealth only in 1948. These developments served to widen further the gulf with Northern Ireland. With both the UK and the Republic of Ireland joining the European Economic Community on 1 January 1973, there has been an external forum for closer cooperation untainted by the emotions of the past. This "return" to Europe has also widened horizons, modernized industries, and raised rural prosperity in the south, so that disparities in living standards between Northern Ireland and the Republic have diminished. Routine relations are improving as political attitudes seem to soften under more general changes in both personal issues and world politics.

The Dictionary

-A-

ABBEY THEATRE. Created in Dublin on 27 December 1904, when the National Dramatic Company merged with the Irish Literary Society. It occupied the Mechanics Institute building, which had been purchased with funds from Miss A. F. Horniman. At first it specialized in works written for it by J. M. Synge, W. B. Yeats, Lady Gregory, and Sean O'Casey (qq.v.). Since 1924 it has been state subsidized.

ADAMS, GERARD (Gerry) (1949–). Born in Belfast, formerly employed as a barman, involved with republican groups, and interned as suspected leader of Provisional IRA (PIRA)(q.v.) in Ballymurphy in 1971. He was imprisoned again in 1973 with other leading republicans in Belfast but was released in 1976. Since then he has denied ever having been a member of the IRA. Increasingly he has been influential in republican political policy making, seeing it as a parallel tactic to "armed struggle." In 1982 he was elected to the Northern Ireland Assembly and in 1983 to the Westminster parliament for West Belfast, but in the Sinn Fein (SF)(q.v.) abstentionist tradition did not take his seat. He lost the 1991 election when the Social Democratic and Labour Party (SDLP)(q.v.) candidate regained it. He became president of Provisional Sinn Fein in 1983, wresting power from a Dublin-based leadership and promoting a more active political stance. In 1988 and again in 1994 he had talks with the SDLP. While appearing to accept the proposition that "civilian killings" had retarded the republican cause, he failed then to persuade the IRA to cease its terrorist activities. A "cessation of military operations" was announced by SF on 31 August 1994 but ended with a bomb in London in February 1996, resulting in the deaths of two civilians. While the British and Irish prime ministers were announcing measures intended to lead to acceptance of a main SF demand, "all-party talks" in Northern Ireland, Adams and John Hume (q.v.) of the SDLP secretly met leaders of PIRA in an unsuccessful attempt to reinstate the cease-fire.

ADMINISTRATIVE DIVISIONS. The four provinces of Ireland (Connacht, Leinster, Munster, and Ulster) seem to reflect very ancient

15

regional cultural variations that had crystallized into political entities by the early Christian period. They formed the basis for fluctuating native kingdoms until the Anglo-Norman invasion (q.v.). They were originally five in number, but Meath, "the middle kingdom," had been absorbed into Leinster by the time Elizabethan administrators considered adapting them to contemporary needs in 1568. The system whereby each was to have been ruled by a lord president lasted only until 1672. Subsequently, the provinces have retained only archaic historical significance. In popular usage some confusion still exists between the ancient nine-county province of Ulster and the post-Partition Northern Ireland, which has only six counties but is often referred to by the same name.

Connacht (4,230,700 acres) includes the counties of Galway, Leitrim, Mayo, Roscommon, and Sligo. The royal seat of the legendary Queen Maeve was located at Rathcroghan, Roscommon.

Leinster (4,851,300 acres) includes the counties of Carlow, Dublin, Kildare, Laois (formerly Queen's), Longford, Louth, Meath, Offaly (formerly King's), Westmeath, Wexford, and Wicklow. The royal seat was at Tara (q.v.), Meath.

Munster (5,961,800 acres) includes the counties of Clare, Cork, Kerry, Limerick, Tipperary, and Waterford. The royal seat was at Cashel, Tipperary, to the 12th century.

Ulster (5,456,381 acres, including 3,476,651 acres in Northern Ireland) includes the counties of Antrim, Armagh, Cavan, Donegal, Down, Fermanagh, Londonderry, Monaghan, and Tyrone. The royal seat was at Emhain Macha, Armagh. *See also* Navan Fort

Counties, or shires, under the responsibility of sheriffs, were introduced into Ireland by the Anglo-Normans in the late 12th century in the same way that they were created from local lordships in Wales when that country was united with England in 1536–42. The pattern was completed by 1606 when a blend of medieval and new urban centers constituted nodes in an administrative network that survived in outline until the Local Government Act of 1898. That provided for minor boundary alterations and designated the towns of Belfast, Dublin, Cork, Londonderry, Limerick, and Waterford (qq.v.) as county boroughs.

Broadly in line with proposals for local government reform in Great Britain, in the 1960s the Stormont (q.v.) administration undertook a review for Northern Ireland, a report in 1969 advocating the creation of 16 area councils, plus one for Belfast, that would essentially reflect main functional urban spheres. Reaction to this desirable restructuring was heavily molded by party political considerations in relation to a redrawing of councils' electoral boundaries, a response deplored by the Cameron Commission (1969), which attributed civil disorder partly to failures in the existing local government system. The 1970 Macrory review endorsed the 1969 report's principles, but opted for a greater number of locally elected bodies in the interests of democratic accountability. Under the Local Government Act (Northern Ireland) 1972, 26 district councils were set up to replace the former county councils and rural/urban districts. They now form the framework for most official published statistics.

Baronies were often pre-Norman territorial units that became extended after the conquest and continued to exist, subject to various modifications, until the local government (q.v.) reforms of 1898. Civil parishes ceased to carry any practical importance after that legislation.

Townlands represent the fundamental territorial units throughout Ireland, varying in size and configuration. Like most very old divisions, they are clearly derived from practical considerations of land utilization and settlement in antiquity. As such, they are usually bounded by natural features such as streams or hillcrests. Historically they may be traced to single farmsteads or clusters of holdings that exploited a variety of agricultural potential from meadow through arable land to hill pasture. Great continuity of ownership or occupancy has endowed townland names with remarkable durability in many rural localities, for example in Co. Fermanagh where the introduction of systematic postal codes related to road names failed to replace everyday use of townland names in modern house addresses in the countryside. *See also* Ecclesiastical Organization

Rural and Urban Districts no longer have the administrative importance they possessed in the 19th and earlier 20th centuries, particularly since advances in public and private transport have enabled people to participate in town-based employment while residing in the surrounding countryside. Concurrently, the former social and economic distinctions between the two have been further diminished by cultural transformations and the physical expansion of suburbs.

District Electoral Divisions originated as territorial bases for electing Poor Law guardians and were thus intended to be relatively uniform in size, but differential population growth between urban and rural communities gradually rendered them obsolete. *See also* Poor Law Commission

ADVENTURERS. A term applied to those willing to purchase, at a rate of £200 per 1,000 acres, land totaling about 2.5 million acres to be confiscated in Ulster under an Act (16 Chas I, c. 33) of 19 March 1642 intended to achieve the "speedy and effectual reducing of the rebels in his majesty's kingdom of Ireland." Land grants were also used to pay off soldiers by dispossession and displacement of "Old English" (q.v.) and Irish settlers.

AER LINGUS. The Irish state airline, created under the Air Navigation and Transport Act of 14 August 1936, having been inaugurated on 27 May by a flight from Baldonnel military airfield to Bristol. Operations were transferred to the new Dublin airport at Collinstown in 1940, expanding routes after 1945. Aer Rianta (Airports Authority) was created in 1937 to include services from Shannon (which became a major trans-Atlantic airport) in 1945 and from Cork in 1961.

AGRICULTURAL CREDIT CORPORATION. Formed in May 1927 as the first state-sponsored body in Ireland to provide capital on loans, it proved too small to achieve much. It became a public company in 1965 when the Agricultural Credit Act allowed it to acquire deposits from any source.

AIKEN, FRANK (1898–1983). Born in Camlough, Co. Armagh. Joined the Irish Volunteers in 1913, the Gaelic League in 1914, and organized Sinn Fein (qq.v) in south Armagh in 1917. As an IRA company commander, he opposed the Anglo-Irish Treaty (q.v.) and the Provisional Government. He became chief of the Irregulars/IRA in 1923 and was elected TD for Louth (1923–73). A founder member of Fianna Fail (FF) (q.v.) in 1926, he was minister of defense in 1932–39 and held other ministerial posts in 1945–68, becoming tanaiste (deputy prime minister) in 1965–69.

AIKENHEAD, MOTHER MARY (1787–1858). Born in Cork, a convert to Roman Catholicism like her parents, she founded the Sisters of Charity in Dublin in 1816 and the first St. Vincent hospital. *See also* Hospitals

ALL-FOR-IRELAND LEAGUE. Formed in 1910 by William O'Brien (q.v.) in a split with the United Irish League, demanding "conference, conciliation, and consent" to resolve the Irish question. Rejected by the Irish Parliamentary party (q.v.), it opposed partition, but faded out in 1918.

ALLIANCE PARTY. Founded in April 1970 in Belfast as a nonsectarian political party, attracting support from the old Northern Ireland Labour Party (NILP) (q.v.) and some pro-O'Neill Unionists. In 1973 it won 13.6 percent of the vote in district elections and 9.6 percent in the Assembly election. Two members, Oliver Napier and Bob Cooper, served in the short-lived Executive set up by the Sunningdale Conference. In the 1975 Convention it produced a scheme of government by committees, composed in proportion to the strength of parties in the Assembly. In the early 1980s it was the party most supportive of the

British government's idea of "rolling devolution." It has never secured a Westminster seat, despite an initial total vote of over 10 percent. In 1985 it gave conditional support to the Anglo-Irish Agreement (q.v.). Since 1988 the new leader, John (now, Lord) Alderdice, has sought links with the Liberals/Social Democrats in Great Britain and the Progressive Democrats (q.v.) in the Republic of Ireland. Its main policy objective is a devolved power-sharing government in Northern Ireland. *See also* Sunningdale Agreement

ALLINGHAM, WILLIAM (1824–89). Born in Ballyshannon, Co. Donegal. Left school at 14 to work in a bank where his Anglican merchant father was also manager, while collecting folk ballads and airs at rural fairs around his home. In 1846 he became a customs officer in Donegal town, transferred to Coleraine in 1853–54, then worked in London and Hampshire until 1870.

Feeling profoundly isolated from intellectual, as opposed to artistic, stimulus in northwestern Ireland, he lived in England from 1863 and married the watercolorist Helen Paterson in 1874. In the same year he became editor of *Fraser's Magazine,* to which he contributed several Irish items. His poetry, occasionally lapsing into moralizing or dreamy sentimentality, was admired by W. B. Yeats (q.v.) and by his Pre-Raphaelite acquaintances Browning, Leigh Hunt, Rossetti, and Tennyson. He maintained long friendships with George Petrie, Samuel Ferguson, and the historians Lecky (qq.v.) and Carlyle. In addition to verse collections *Poems* (1850), *Day and Night Songs* (1854), and *Blackberries* (1884), he wrote a long, vivid narrative poem on the theme of agrarian poverty and unrest, *Laurence Bloomfield in Ireland* (1864), which had first been serialized in *Fraser's* in 1862–63. He compiled *Irish Songs and Poems* (1887) and published travel impressions in *Rambles* (1873). His *Diary* (1907) was edited by his widow and appeared posthumously. He contemplated, but never wrote, a history of Ireland.

ALL-PARTY ANTI-PARTITION (Mansion House) COMMITTEE. Created in January 1949 by Costello, Norton, MacBride, de Valera, Aiken, and O'Dalaigh (qq.v.) to achieve peaceful reunification of Ireland. Essentially, it performed a propagandist role and financed antipartition Nationalist Party (q.v.) candidates in the north via the Anti-Partition League.

ANCIENT ORDER OF HIBERNIANS (AOH). Founded in 1641 with the motto "Fidelity to Faith and Fatherland." It was especially strong in south Ulster. It became active in the United States in the 1880s under Clan na Gael (q.v.), but split over a definition of membership in

1878–84, supported Redmond's Irish Parliamentary Party campaign for home rule (qq.v.), and saw itself as protector of Roman Catholic rights in Northern Ireland in the 1920s. Its title dates from 1838, as successor to the American Knights of St. Patrick, but its origins go back to the rebellion of 1641 (q.v.) and 18th-century Catholic organizations. Its purpose is to defend the Catholic faith and to promote Irish nationalism. Its activities are social rather than political, based on community halls, particularly in rural areas, from which parades rather like those of the Orange Order (q.v.) are organized. Its links with the more political American AOH have not always been harmonious.

ANDREWS, JOHN MILLER (1871–1956). Born in Comber, Co. Down, into a linen-manufacturing family, he was elected MP for Co. Down (1921–29) and for Mid-Down (1929–53). He served as prime minister of Northern Ireland (1940–43) and as grand master of the Orange Institution of Ireland in 1948.

ANGLESEY, FIRST MARQUIS OF (Henry William Paget) (1768–1854). Educated at Oxford, elected MP for Caernarvon Boroughs in 1790. As a cavalry officer, he was seriously wounded at the battle of Waterloo. Wellington (with whose sister-in-law he had eloped) sent him to Ireland at the height of agitation for Catholic emancipation (q.v.). He was lord lieutenant in 1828–29 and 1830–33, supported emancipation, took a progressive stance in relation to tithes (q.v.) (in which he was opposed by Wellington), favored nondenominational education (q.v.) and provision of finance for Catholic bishops for educational purposes. He opposed Daniel O'Connell's (q.v.) repeal activities in the 1830s. He introduced the "national" education system in 1831.

ANGLO-IRISH AGREEMENT (25 April 1938). Concluded between Neville Chamberlain and Eamon de Valera (q.v.) as a resolution of the economic war that had been waged since 1932. Its main provisions were return of the Treaty ports to Ireland, payment of £10 million by Eire as one-tenth of a claim of unpaid land annuities, and reestablishment of free trade between Britain and Ireland.

ANGLO-IRISH AGREEMENT (1985). In committing the governments of the Republic of Ireland and the United Kingdom (UK) to working much more closely on Northern Ireland (NI) through a structure of intergovernmental meetings and a secretariat in Belfast, it is possibly the most far-reaching political development since 1920. While leaving ultimate authority for NI with the UK, it effectively institutionalized consultation with the Republic and for that reason has been vigorously opposed by most Unionist politicians. Its provisions for monitoring matters of particular concern for the minority have found favor with the Social Democratic and Labour Party (SDLP) (q.v.), and its official recognition of the two traditions in NI has found broad support.

The first article of the agreement reaffirms that the status of NI can only be changed with the consent of a majority in NI. Devolution of power to NI is a stated aim, on a basis of "widespread acceptance throughout the community." But lacking the full cooperation of Unionists, this has not been achieved. Closer cross-border cooperation on security matters is an ongoing activity, as are joint projects of an economic or social nature.

ANGLO-IRISH TREATY (6 December 1921). Following the 1919–21 war and de Valera's rejection of Lloyd George's (qq.v.) July compromise, Griffith, Collins (qq.v.), Barton, Duffy, and Duggan were sent "as Envoys Plenipotentiary of the Republic of Ireland" [*sic*] to negotiate a treaty "between Ireland and the . . . British Commonwealth," though their hands were in fact bound by the cabinet in Dublin. The only other cabinet members not attending were de Valera, Brugha (Defence), W. T. Cosgrave (q.v.)(Local Government), and Stack (Home Affairs).

The terms were rejected as unacceptable by the Irish cabinet on 3 December on the grounds of dominion status, exclusion of the six northern counties, and obligation to swear the Oath of Allegiance. Lloyd George issued an ultimatum to the Irish to sign or face resumed war within three days. The Treaty signed on 6 December 1921 created the Irish Free State (IFS) as a Commonwealth Dominion. It was accepted by the Irish cabinet by four votes (Griffith, Collins, Barton, Cosgrave) to three (de Valera, Brugha, Stack). On 8 December de Valera repudiated it, but it was accepted by the Dáil (q.v.) on 7 January 1922 by 64 votes to 57. De Valera refused to recognize Collins's Provisional Government, but accepted Griffith as president of the parallel Dáil. In the June 1922 election pro-Treaty candidates won 239,193 votes (58 seats), and anti-Treaty candidates 133,864 votes (35 seats), to which were added 17 Labour, four Unionists, seven Independents, and seven Farmers' Party members.

The IFS became a dominion, creating its own laws with a governor-general (like Canada) and an oath sworn to the IFS constitution and King George V (as common citizens of Great Britain and Ireland). Ireland undertook to repay debts; the IFS became responsible for its own coastal defenses as well as for maintaining a proportionate defense force; both countries allowed free access to each other's ports; the IFS was to provide compensation for retiring officials, except members of the Royal Irish Constabulary or the Auxiliaries (qq.v.); the Government of Ireland Act (q.v.) was to remain for Northern Ireland, whose elected representatives were not members of the IFS parliament, unless both Northern Ireland houses of parliament agreed within one month. If not, they were to have no legal powers in Northern Ireland, an issue that might be discussed at a later date. Neither parliament was to pass any law that would give any religious preference or disability of status concerning educational provision. It was signed in Irish by the five IFS delegates (Barton, Collins, Duffy, Dug, and Griffith) and for Britain by Lloyd George, Austen Chamberlain, and Winston Churchill. An annex referred to the so-called Treaty ports, Berehaven, Queenstown, Belfast Lough, and Lough Swilly, defenses retained in British care.

ANGLO-IRISH WAR ("War of Independence," 1919–21). Supposedly began when a Royal Irish Constabulary (RIC) (q.v.) patrol was ambushed in Co. Tipperary on 21 January 1919, on the day of the declaration of the Dáil by Sinn Fein (qq.v.) MPs, and the declaration of independence. Guerilla raids were repeated later in the year under Frank Aiken (q.v.), Liam Lynch, and Sean MacEoin. In August 1919 the IRA was formed from the 1916 Volunteers, with Michael Collins (qq.v.) as minister of finance and Cathal Brugha as minister of defense, attacking tax offices to deprive the UK government of revenue. Reprisals were exacted by members of the RIC, the Black and Tans, and the Auxiliaries (qq.v.).

The focus of activity was in counties Tipperary, Cork, Kerry, and Limerick, in which martial law was declared on 10 December 1920, and was extended to Clare. The violence was condemned by the Roman Catholic hierarchy, though some openly sympathized with republicanism. Some 165 members of the RIC had been killed by the end of 1920, when overtures for peace were rejected by the IRA. Eamon de Valera (q.v.) formally declared war on 11 March 1921 via the Dáil after his return from the United States. A truce was agreed on 9 July 1921, and the Anglo-Irish Treaty (q.v.) was eventually signed on 6 December. Some versions of operations conducted by small groups with a military structure of divisions, brigades, and companies, and inflicting devastating casualties while incurring few themselves, are difficult to credit, especially when most sites of reprisals were only tiny villages.

ANGLO-NORMAN INVASION (1169). An event of fundamental importance for the history of Ireland, it was not a formal invasion like the Norman conquest of England led by William the Conqueror a century earlier. William's descendant, Henry II, ruled the extensive Angevin empire from Scotland to Aquitaine. On his western borders were Wales, over which he had a sovereign claim, and beyond, the island of Ireland, in which he had expressed an interest at the very beginning of his reign. The bull *Laudabiliter* (1155) from the English pope, Adrian IV, was claimed to commission him to reform the Catholic Church in Ireland.

Meanwhile, Irish politics remained independent of wider European affairs and were volatile. This volatility was due to the often shifting alliances that resulted from the pursuit of supremacy by regional kings. One of these, Diarmuid MacMurrough (q.v.) of Leinster (the province closest to Wales and the rest of Europe), allowed his personal life to complicate matters. He abducted, briefly and not unwillingly, the wife of Tiernan O'Rourke of Breifne. Many years later, in 1166, the score was settled when O'Rourke and his allies drove MacMurrough from his kingdom. He went to Bristol, the chief English port for trade with Ireland, and on to France to seek aid from Henry II, offering fealty, a feudal concept as yet unknown in Ireland. He received only an open letter authorizing an expedition to Ireland because Henry felt too busy to get involved directly. MacMurrough even had difficulty finding recruits in Britain until he turned to south Wales, where the Norman settlers were often opposed by the native Welsh and were thus both experienced campaigners and still eager for land. He recruited one of the foremost, the earl of Pembroke (popularly known as Strongbow), who in return sought MacMurrough's eldest daughter in marriage and thus the right of succession to the kingdom of Leinster, another concept alien to Irish politics.

Lesser Norman-Welsh knights and the Flemish colony in Pembroke promised their support, and a few went with MacMurrough to Leinster in 1167, helping him recover his power base at Ferns. The invasion proper started at Bannow Bay in May 1169, with 600 mounted knights and men armed with crossbows, both still unknown in Irish warfare. Joined by MacMurrough's army, they marched on Wexford (q.v.), which soon capitulated. Further forces, including one led by Strongbow, landed in August and captured Waterford (q.v.), one of the largest Hiberno-Norse towns. There Strongbow married Aoife MacMurrough. Despite having already made his peace with the Irish high king, Rory O'Connor of Connacht, MacMurrough marched with Strongbow on Dublin, the center of an independent Hiberno-Norse kingdom allied to the high king. Dublin was taken in September 1170, but MacMurrough died within months. The invaders faced increased opposition, including a prolonged siege of Dublin.

The Normans withstood these onslaughts, and their success encouraged their king to arrive with reinforcements in October 1171. Henry II received the homage of all—Normans, Irish and Norse—and a treaty was signed at Windsor in 1175, formalizing his overlordship of Ireland and recognizing the role of the Irish high king in unconquered parts of Ireland. The power of both of these was limited—the one by distance and numerous other concerns and the other by close rivals. A further complication was the very different political systems of Gaelic Ireland and feudal England. The treaty became ineffective as Irish kings and Norman barons pursued their own agendas, the latter of necessity being more territorially based. Both could be accommodated to some extent and for some time in one of the relatively undeveloped areas of medieval Europe.

The Normans concentrated on lower terrains that were best suited to their more cereal-based agriculture, particularly in the southeast where they developed port and riverside towns to facilitate an export trade. Their military success, however piecemeal, was followed by the introduction of feudal land tenure and legal administration. Settlers were drawn in from England and Wales. Inevitably, this meant a similarly piecemeal contraction of Irish core areas, particularly into uplands and toward the northwest. Meath soon ceased to be an Irish kingdom, being "granted" (in contravention of the treaty) by Henry II to Hugh de Lacy. Northeastern Ulster was conquered and colonized from 1177 by John de Courcy, also not one of the original invasion leaders. By such individualistic, if often authorized, schemes almost two-thirds of Ireland came under varying degrees of Anglo-Norman settlement and control, which altered those parts of the country fundamentally while also influencing the adjacent one-third in which the Gaelic-Irish tradition dominated the way of life, if not the broader political development.

The ultimate impact of the Anglo-Norman invasion was therefore strongly influenced by its partial nature insofar as this provided a potential for opposition. This in turn was also partial, and was never fully successful, largely because it had become geographically very fragmented. A stalemate emerged within a century of the initial invasion, the details of which varied from time to time, but the consequences of which have influenced relations between the two islands ever since.

APPRENTICE BOYS OF DERRY. Founded as Apprentice Clubs in 1814, a Protestant unionist organization based on the "no surrender" action of 13 apprentices in shutting the gates of Londonderry in the face of a Jacobite force on 7 December 1688. Its main parade is held on the 12 August to celebrate the end of the subsequent siege of 1689. The traditional route along the walls came to be seen as provocative to the Roman Catholic stronghold in the adjacent Bogside and was restricted to streets of the walled town in 1975.

ARDAGH CHALICE. Found in Co. Limerick in 1868, it was presented to the Royal Irish Academy in 1878 and is now in the National Museum (qq.v.). In fact, two chalices and three silver-gilt annular brooches were discovered under a flagstone in a ring fort. On the basis of their bird and animal decoration, they have been dated to the eighth century A.D. *See also* Derrynaflan Hoard

ARMAGH. Saint Patrick's (q.v.) church was established around A.D. 445–457 on the pagan site of a hill fort and developed into a circular monastic enclosure. The great antiquity of the site was attested by the discovery of Neolithic pottery and remains of Iron Age industries on Cathedral Hill. The eighth-century bishops' claim to primacy, an ecclesiastical parallel to the high king's secular claim over all other provincial kings, was recognized by Brian Boru (q.v.) in 1004. In 1129 the ascetic reformer St. Malachy (q.v.) was nominated archbishop but did not assume office unchallenged until 1132, later welcoming Augustinian canons and securing for Armagh its reputation as the chief 12th-century school in Ireland, despite repeated attacks by the Anglo-Normans in 1184–89. The first Primate, Gilla-meic-Liag, was acknowledged by the papal legate at the Synod of Kells (1152).

A Franciscan priory was founded in 1263–64, but the 14th-century English archbishops resided at Termonfeckin, near Drogheda, Co. Louth, in order to be near the safe area of Dublin. In 1557 the Augustinian abbey was closed and in 1566 the Franciscan friary was burned, although a high cross has survived. The cathedral itself was heavily restored in 1834–37. An astronomical observatory was founded in 1793 by Archbishop Robinson, during whose primacy the city's appearance was considerably improved under the architects Thomas Cooley and Francis Johnston (q.v.), the former being responsible for the Georgian public library (1771) and the archbishop's palace (1770), and the latter for the classical style of the chapel, market house, courthouse, and observatory. Saint Patrick's Roman Catholic cathedral, originally designed by Thomas Duff, was begun in 1840, but was mainly constructed under the supervision of J. J. McCarthy between 1854 and 1873.

ARMY, BRITISH. Prior to 1969 a British garrison of 2,000 was maintained in Northern Ireland. It was first used in support of the Royal Ulster Constabulary (RUC) (q.v.) on 14 August 1969 when police became exhausted in an attempt to contain prolonged rioting. This new role involved a change in Westminster-Stormont relations because control of the army lay with the former. The army was initially welcomed in Roman Catholic residential areas because it was seen as a safeguard against loyalist attacks, but this soon changed as republicans, led by the Irish Republican Army (IRA) (q.v.), protested. In due course army operations had political repercussions, e.g. the events of

Bloody Sunday (q.v.) in Londonderry. About 7,000 British troops were stationed in 1970. This number rose to 21,000 by 1979 and fell to about 10,000 by 1982–88. Temporary reinforcements were brought in to meet special situations, and the Special Air Service performed specific covert operations along the border with the Republic. The army handed control of security policy back to the RUC in 1977, but army operations remained under the General Officer in Command. The whole period has seen adaptations by the army as its function changed from crowd control to antiterrorism, especially as the illegal paramilitaries became more sophisticated in arms and training.

ARREARS ACT (May 1882). This legislation aimed to allow a further 130,000 tenants in arrears with their rents to benefit from the 1881 Land Act. It paid off £800,000 of debts and reduced violent protests on that issue. *See also* Land Acts

ASCENDANCY. A term coined by Orangeman John Giffard, editor of *Faulkner's Dublin Journal.* It was in use by 1792 and connoted members of the Church of Ireland (q.v.) after the 1691 settlement. This group was not necessarily non-Irish in an ethnic sense but upheld the penal laws (q.v.) against Roman Catholics in general. Rooted in Henry Grattan's (q.v.) Irish Parliament and Trinity College Dublin, they became distinctly Irish vis-à-vis English in outlook and even quasi-nationalist. Being equally anti-Dissent, they resisted reform from whatever quarter or form (religious emancipation, parliament, or land), and were attracted to home rule (q.v.) to preserve their power. Their main material achievement may be seen in urban and rural rebuilding, and landownership.

ASHE, THOMAS (1885–1917). Born near Dingle, Co. Kerry. A teacher, he joined the Irish Volunteers and the Gaelic League (qq.v.) and took part in fund raising in the United States. He was arrested and court-martialed after a battle with the Royal Irish Constabulary (q.v.) at Ashbourne, but was released in 1917. He died while on hunger strike in Mountjoy jail in pursuit of political status for Sinn Fein (q.v.) prisoners.

AUGHRIM, BATTLE OF (12 July 1691). Following the fall of Athlone, this was a decisive conflict near Ballinasloe, Co. Galway, in which William III's forces led by General von Ginkel defeated a Jacobite army and the French marshal St. Ruth was killed. Galway (q.v.) fell nine days later, and Patrick Sarsfield (q.v.) retreated with his troops to Limerick, where they were besieged.

AUXILIARIES (27 July 1920). Recruited from ex-World War I British officers and commanded by their founder, Brigadier-General F. P. Crozier, to boost the Royal Irish Constabulary after the IRA (qq.v.) had started to target the police, leading to proclamation of martial law on 10 December.

-B-

BALFOUR, ARTHUR JAMES (1848–1930). Scottish-born nephew of the Earl of Salisbury, educated at Cambridge. He was elected Conservative MP for Manchester in 1885. He served as chief secretary for Ireland (1887–91), favoring land reform. He mixed conciliation with coercion and became known as "Bloody Balfour" when three people died in the "Mitchelstown massacre" (9 September 1887). That incident arose when, during Land League agitation, a protest meeting was fired upon outside a police barracks in a Co. Cork village. Balfour introduced the Light Railways Act (1889) and Land Purchase Act (1891), which was extended in 1896 by his brother, Gerald (1853–1945), during his period as chief secretary (1895–1900). He set up the Congested Districts Board (q.v.) and opposed home rule (q.v.). He succeeded his uncle as British prime minister.

BALL, SIR ROBERT (1840–1913). Astronomer and tutor to the sons of the earl of Rosse at Birr Castle, Co. Offaly. He held the Chair of Astronomy at Dublin University (1874–92), while concurrently Royal Astronomer of Ireland, and the Chair of Astronomy at Cambridge University (1893–1913). *See also* Parsons, Charles

BALLOT ACT (1872). Secret voting encouraged tenants who possessed the franchise to elect their own candidates, instead of being subject to landlord coercion, and led to Irish Parliamentary Party (q.v.) success in 1880.

BEATTY, SIR ALFRED CHESTER (1875–1968). A mining engineer born in New York, he collected oriental manuscripts and moved to Dublin in 1953. He left his library and his art collection to the Irish people, in recognition of which he was made the first honorary citizen of Ireland. The Chester Beatty Library, at Shrewsbury Road, Dublin, is government supported.

BEAUFORT, DANIEL AUGUSTUS (1739–1821). Son of a Huguenot refugee pastor who had joined the Church of England and went to Ireland with Lord Lieutenant Harrington, becoming rector of Navan in 1747. Educated at Trinity College Dublin, from which he received an honorary LL.D. in 1789, he was ordained in 1762, succeeded his father at Navan (1765–1818), and was vicar of Collon, where he built the parish church. He was very active in promoting education, including Sunday schools, and in the formation of the Royal Irish Academy (q.v.). He published an original map of Ireland in 1792 with an accompanying detailed *Memoir* of the country and an index of place-names. He married Mary Waller, co-heiress of Allenstown, Co. Meath; their daughter Frances married R. L. Edgeworth (q.v.), and their younger son, Francis (q.v.), became the husband of Honora, Edgeworth's daughter by a previous marriage to Elizabeth Sneyd.

BEAUFORT, SIR FRANCIS (1774–1857). Invalided from the navy in 1803–4, he helped R. L. Edgeworth (q.v.) construct the Dublin-Galway telegraph line and pioneered systematic weather observation. In 1805 he devised a scale, named after him, for measuring wind velocity. It was adopted internationally in 1874. He served as British admiralty hydrographer in 1829–55 and became a rear-admiral in 1846. He was made a Knight Commander of the Order of the Bath in 1848, and he was elected Fellow of the Royal Society, Fellow of the Royal Astronomical Society, and Member of the Royal Irish Academy.

BECKETT, SAMUEL BARCLAY (1906–89). Born in Foxrock, Dublin, and educated at Portora Royal School, Enniskillen, and Trinity College Dublin (TCD). He lectured in Paris (1928–30), and at TCD (1930–32) before emigrating to France, where he met James Joyce (q.v.). He lived mainly in Paris from 1937 and was active in the French resistance during World War II. Apart from a dozen novels, many of his short stories and plays for stage, radio, and television are contained in *Collected Poems 1930–1978* (1984), *Collected Shorter Prose 1945–80* (1984), and *The Complete Dramatic Works* (1986). He was awarded the Nobel Prize for Literature in 1969.

BELFAST. Largest city in Northern Ireland (population 279,237 in 1991). Situated at the head of a long sheltered sea lough, it received its charter of incorporation as a borough in 1613. It grew around Sir Arthur Chichester's (q.v.) castle and was fortified in 1642. The port built up a flourishing trade in agricultural produce with England, Scotland, France, and America by the 1660s. A bridge across the river Lagan was constructed in 1682. The city's development was especially promoted by the earls of Donegall, who funded and encouraged the construction of public buildings, including the Exchange and Assembly Rooms (1768), Millgate Theatre (1768), Chichester Dock (1769), a poorhouse (Clifton House, 1771–74), Chamber of Commerce (1783), St. Anne's parish church (1774–76), the White Linen Hall (1784), a Methodist preaching house (1784), Belfast Academy (1785), Linen Hall Library (1788), the Academical Institution (1807–14), St. Patrick's Roman Catholic parish church, and Frederick Street General Hospital (1815).

From 1778 the Smithfield area became the focus of cotton and (in the 1840s and 1850s) flax spinning, iron foundries, and gasworks (1823). The Lagan Navigation Company canal (1756) gave access to linen from the basin of Lough Neagh, "Ulster's inland sea," and by 1835 Belfast was the premier port in Ireland, handling half its linen exports. Communications were improved by the Queen's Bridge (1843), while maritime activity was fostered by the creation of the Harbour Commission in 1847 in succession to its 1785 Harbour Board. Modern shipbuilding dates from the arrival of William Ritchie from Saltcoats, Ayrshire, in 1791, the first wooden steamboat being completed in 1820, and the first iron ship in 1838. From 1849 the Victoria Channel gave the shipyards access to the deep-water lough, and in 1853 Robert Hickson opened premises on Queen's Island opposite the docks, appointing Edward Harland (q.v.) from Tyneside as manager in 1854, and selling out to him in 1858, after which there was founded a partnership with G. W. Wolff. Employment in the shipyards increased from 100 men to 9,000 men between 1858 and 1900, and the tonnage constructed increased to over 90,000, including the whole White Star fleet, making it the largest yard in the world. Shipbuilding was also undertaken on five sites by Workman, Clark & Co. from 1879 to 1935.

Power-loom weaving replaced hand looms in the cotton industry in the 1850s and linen overtook it in the 1870s, both trends stimulating mechanical engineering. Local flax cultivation received a brief but dramatic stimulus during the American Civil War in the 1860s, when that source of cotton fiber became unavailable, though it declined equally markedly by the end of the 19th century, when imports from the Baltic states sustained the Irish linen-manufacturing industry. Queen's College was opened in 1849, and the Custom House in 1857, followed by the City Hall (1902–6). City status was awarded in 1888. Already by 1881 a network of horse-drawn trams carried 1 million passengers, the number rising to 10 million in 1891 and 28 million in 1904.

Between 1757 and 1841 Belfast's population increased ninefold, from 8,500 to 75,000 (Dublin's was then 233,000). The greatest absolute growth occurred between 1871 (175,000) and 1901 (349,000). An outburst of residential construction occurred in 1880–1900, especially to the south beyond the river Blackstaff, while socioeconomic and cultural changes were equally profound. From 1857 sectarian riots erupted periodically with the rapid growth of the Roman Catholic component of the city's population. In the 20th century, particularly since 1950, foreign competition resulted in a sharp decline of employment in the linen industry. Shipbuilding, too, experienced a collapse during the economic depression. Suburban sprawl, civil unrest, and central redevelopment in recent decades have contributed to a reduction in the resident population of the city, though it remains Northern Ireland's dominant industrial, commercial, and employment focus.

BERESFORD, JOHN CLAUDIUS (1738–1805). Born in Dublin, educated at Kilkenny College and Trinity College Dublin, elected MP for Waterford from 1760 to his death. Appointed First Revenue Commissioner in 1780, he was influential in attracting James Gandon (q.v.) to Dublin in 1781 and in constructing Sackville (O'Connell) Street and new quays. He was largely in control of Ireland under Pitt's ministry and supported the Union against the opposition of Grattan (q.v.).

BERKELEY, GEORGE (1685–1753). Born in Kilkenny and educated at Trinity College Dublin. In 1709 he published an *Essay towards a New Theory of Vision,* as a thesis on the psychology of perception, and *A Treatise Concerning the Principles of Human Knowledge* in 1710. He was appointed dean of Derry in 1724, and he spent several years in Rhode Island, having tried to promote a college in Bermuda, partly with a bequest from the companion of Dean Swift, Esther Vanhomrigh. He was bishop of Cloyne from 1734 until his death and wrote a critique of Newtonian mathematics, *The Analyst.* Throughout his life he sought social and economic reform and religious toleration, greatly influencing the philosophical ideas of Hume and Kant.

BESSBOROUGH COMMISSION (1880). Headed by the sixth earl, Frederick George Brabazon Ponsonby, a Trinity College-educated lawyer with estates in Kilkenny. Its purpose was to investigate the working of the 1870 Land Act, to improve landlord-tenant relations, and to facilitate tenant purchases. The Commission, opposed by the Land League (q.v.) over its membership, took evidence from about 1,300 witnesses and produced its report on 4 January 1881, recommending that the "three Fs" (fair rents, fixity of tenure, and freedom of sale) be granted, although a minority report wanted outright peasant ownership. Its key points were endorsed by the Richmond Commission (q.v.) in February.

BIANCONI, CHARLES (Joachim Carlo Giuseppe)(1785–1875). Born in northern Italy, he opened a shop selling prints in Thurles and then in Waterford in 1807. In 1809 he moved to Clonmel, where he set up workshops. He became mayor in 1844. His horse-drawn jaunting car was used for transport between Clonmel and Cahir in 1815, the service extending throughout Munster and more widely over 3,000 miles of road by 1845, facilitating contact between rural areas and small towns for passengers and mail at speeds of up to eight miles per hour. The capacity of the cars (known as "bians") increased to 20 passengers. Later he bought shares in early railway companies while retaining some road routes in Ulster and Connacht, and became a director of O'Connell's National Bank in 1835. *See also* Railways

BIRRELL, AUGUSTINE (1850–1933). Chief secretary for Ireland in 1907, prepared the Irish Council Bill in an attempt to promote devolved power in the face of intense and increasingly violent home rule agitation by the Irish Volunteers (q.v.). He achieved passage of the Irish Universities Act (1908) and the Land Purchase Act (1909). He resigned in 1916.

BLACK AND TANS. Formed from ex-soldiers on 2 January 1920 and arrived in Ireland in March. Their nickname derived from their black-green/khaki uniforms, and they acquired a reputation for forceful reaction to IRA attacks, expressed as violence against the civilian population, especially in Munster. *See also* Auxiliaries

BLOODY SUNDAY. The term *Bloody Sunday* is used to refer to three separate incidents.
1. Dublin, 21 November 1920, Michael Collins's (q.v.) "Special Intelligence Unit" murdered 14 suspected British agents; in response, the Black and Tans fired on a crowd at a Gaelic Athletic Association (qq.v.) football match in Croke Park, killing 12 onlookers.
2. Belfast, 10 July 1921, Orange/Special Constabulary attacks killed 15.
3. Londonderry, 30 January 1972, in the aftermath of a banned civil rights march, British troops shot dead 13 people in what was claimed to be a return of fire; in protest, the British embassy in Dublin was burned on 2 February.

BLOUNT, CHARLES (1563–1605). Lord Mountjoy and earl of Devonshire, appointed lord deputy in 1600 to quell the Tyrone rebellion in Ulster. Munster was pacified by Sir George Carew. Sir Henry Docwra was sent to Derry to set up an alliance against Tyrone, adopting a scorched-earth policy. Tyrone's Spanish allies collapsed at Kinsale in 1601 and submitted at Mellifont (q.v.) in March 1603. As lord lieutenant in 1603, he banned Roman Catholic public worship. He was succeeded by Arthur Chichester (q.v.) who implemented a full plantation policy. *See also* Plantations

BLUESHIRTS. Formed in July 1933 as the Army Comrades Association under General Eoin O'Duffy (1892–1944). He renamed them the

National Guard and mounted a volunteer fascist brigade on Franco's side in the civil war in Spain in 1936–37. O'Duffy was a founder and president of Fine Gael (q.v.) from September 1933 to September 1934, having been dismissed by Eamon de Valera (q.v.) after only two weeks as commissioner of the Civic Guard in 1922 on grounds of likely bias.

BOARD OF WORKS (Barrack Board). Re-created in October 1831 (1 & 2 Will. IV, c. 33). Its commissioners held extensive powers to conduct inquiries and to initiate schemes to improve the whole country's infrastructure and ease unemployment, under an inspectorate of engineers, e.g., building roads and harbors, constructing railways (1838), inland navigation (1839), drainage systems (1842), fisheries (1842), and housing. It also undertook famine relief works in 1845–49. *See also* Famines

BORD NA MONA. Created under the Turf Development Act 1946, it replaced the 1934 state-supported private Turf Development Board, initially producing sod or milled peat for the Electricity Supply Board (q.v.) and providing rural employment while reducing import dependency. It acquired bog for mechanized production and later manufactured briquettes for domestic fuel and moss peat for horticulture. An output of over five million metric tons of fuel was achieved in the mid-1980s, representing about 1.3 million metric tons oil equivalent, or one-eighth of national fuel consumption.

BORU, BRIAN (c. 941–1014). Succeeded his brother as king of Dal Cais and became king of Munster in A.D. 978; embarked on war with Mael Sechnaill of Tara (q.v.) in 980, winning supremacy over the southern half of the country after campaigns in Connacht, Meath, and Breifne. In 997 he accepted partition of Ireland with Mael Sechnaill at Clonfert, and two years later his forces plundered Viking Dublin after a Leinster revolt. He married the mother of the Dane Sitric, king of all Ireland. In 1005 he confirmed the primacy of the See of Armagh. He was killed at the battle of Clontarf, although the opposing Norse and Leinster men were defeated.

BOULTER, HUGH (1672–1742). London-born, Oxford-educated chaplain to George I (1719) and tutor in English to Prince Frederick. He was translated from the bishopric of Bristol to the primacy of Armagh in 1724 and became a member of the Irish Privy Council dealing with government business. He joined William King and Jonathan Swift (qq.v.) in opposing Wood's copper coinage, but, unlike them, favored a reduction of gold for silver currency. He opposed moves toward independence and upheld the penal laws (q.v.), excluding Catholics from the legal profession and depriving them of the vote. He promoted charter schools as a means of converting Irish Protestants to Anglicanism, supported numerous charities, and was an influential lord justice in the absence of successive viceroys. Having been patronized by Walpole as the English administration's mouthpiece in Ireland, he was decried as a well-intentioned interloper in Ireland by George Faulkner, who published his collected letters in Dublin in 1770.

BOUNDARY COMMISSION. Set up in 1924 under article XII of the Anglo-Irish Treaty (q.v.) to define the border between Northern Ireland and the Irish Free State, which had been created as separate entities by the Government of Ireland Act (1920) (q.v.). Its three members—Dr. Eoin MacNeill (q.v.), James Fisher, and Justice Feetham—received representations from local inhabitants, public and private bodies and toured the border to collect evidence that might justify a realignment of the boundary in either direction. It was not empowered to conduct a plebiscite, but assumed that people's political wishes would follow their confessional adherence and, consequently, that the most useful guide would be the most detailed religious data from the 1911 census. The commission's supposed recommendations were leaked by *The Morning Post* newspaper on 7 November 1925 amid protests, and the commission was dissolved without official publication of its report. By another agreement of 3 December 1925 the boundary of 1920 was reaffirmed.

BOYCOTT, CAPTAIN CHARLES CUNNINGHAM (1832–97). Land agent and owner of Lough Mask House, Co. Mayo, who defied the Land League (q.v.) in 1880 by refusing to implement agrarian reforms. He was isolated so completely (thus adding a new word to the dictionary) that farm laborers from Monaghan and Cavan had to be brought in under military guard to complete his harvest.

BOYLE, RICHARD (1566–1643), first earl of Cork. Descended from a Herefordshire family but born in Canterbury, where he was privately tutored before entering Corpus Christi, Cambridge, in 1583. Prevented by lack of private means from rapid advancement in the legal profession, he sought his fortune in Dublin in June 1588, married a Limerick heiress in 1595, and inherited a large estate on her death in childbed in 1599. He was imprisoned on a charge of embezzlement, but defended himself against several accusations of financial impropriety at the onset of the Munster rebellion in 1598. He resumed his legal studies in England until Essex gave him a position in Ireland. He again came into conflict with the treasurer, Sir Henry Wallop, was summoned before the Court of Star

Chamber, but was rescued by the patronage of Sir George Carew, who made him his clerk of council in Munster.

An introduction to court circles gave him the opportunity to acquire by purchase Raleigh's estates in Cork, Waterford, and Tipperary, where he energetically introduced manufactures and ironworks. He built bridges and harbors, garrisoned castles, and strictly controlled papists. He was knighted on his marriage to a daughter of Sir George Fenton in 1603 and was made Privy Councillor for Munster (1606) and for Ireland (1612). He was created baron of Youghal (1616), then viscount Dungarvan and earl of Cork (1620). Renowned as "the Great Earl," in 1629 he became a lord justice of Ireland and lord high treasurer in 1631.

From 1633 he was in conflict with Thomas Wentworth (q.v.), who deprived him of almost all his Youghal revenues. Yet he concealed his resentment publicly, though he acted as a witness at Strafford's trial in 1641 and expressed no regret at the latter's execution. He left seven sons and eight daughters, many of whom married well or achieved distinction through their own abilities.

BOYLE, ROBERT (1627–91). Seventh son and fourteenth child of the "Great Earl" of Cork. Born at Lismore castle, but spent most of his life in England. One of the first notable Irish scientists, he discovered Boyle's law: the volume of a gas varies inversely with its pressure. With others he formed the Invisible Society, which led to the foundation of the Royal Society. He was an alchemist and theologian, and he had the first Irish Bible published.

BOYNE, RIVER. Overlooking a bend in the river, which flows to the Irish Sea at Drogheda, east of Slane are several Neolithic tombs, including Dowth, Knowth and Newgrange (qq.v.), and the remains of a stone circle. Proposals to create a Boyne Valley Archaeological Park were approved by the government in 1987. The area is also famous as the location of the battle (1 July 1690) in the last British religious dynastic war, when the international Williamite army routed the Jacobites, who fled from Kinsale to France three days later. A memorial obelisk to the event was erected at Oldbridge in 1736, but was surreptitiously demolished in 1923.

BREHON LAWS. *Brithemin,* or brehons, were medieval Gaelic law interpreters of traditional practices by which clans were collectively accountable for the actions of their members. Such concepts of customary law were supplanted by English notions of individual responsibility by the 17th century. A version of the laws was published by Charles Graves (q.v.) in 1851.

BROIGHTER HOARD. A collection, possibly of Mediterranean origin, discovered near Limavady, Co. Londonderry, in 1896. It consists of La Tène-style gold ornaments, bracelets, necklaces, a collar, a bowl, and a boat. The find was eventually passed to the Royal Irish Academy (q.v.) by the British Museum and is now in the National Museum (q.v.), Dublin.

BROOKE, BASIL (1888–1974), Viscount Brookeborough (1952). He served on the western front in World War I and formed the Ulster Special Constabulary (q.v.). He was a member of the Northern Ireland Senate in 1921, Ulster Unionist MP for Lisnaskea (1929–68), and a minister from 1933. He was critical of J. M. Andrews (q.v.), whom he succeeded as prime minister of Northern Ireland (1943–63), and stimulated economic development in the province with a new group of young ministers. He introduced internment in 1956 during the IRA (q.v.) campaign.

BROWNE, DR. NOEL (1915–). A Trinity College graduate in medicine and a socialist, he was a member of several small parties during his period in the Dáil, or Senate, having become a TD in 1948. As minister of health, he achieved eradication of tuberculosis in Ireland, but his "Mother-and-Child" care scheme proved controversial and was opposed by the Roman Catholic hierarchy. As a result, Sean MacBride (q.v.) pressured him to resign from government and from Clann na Poblachta in April 1951. As a consequence the coalition government of J. A. Costello (q.v.) fell in the subsequent general election (30 May).

BRUCE, EDWARD (?–1318). Younger brother of King Robert of Scotland, for whom he overcame Galloway against the English in 1308 and was a commander at the battle of Bannockburn (1314). He led a Scottish campaign in Ulster in May 1315 as part of a Gaelic revival, the aim of which was the ending of the English lordship based on Dublin. Though condemned by Pope John XXII as a rebel against Edward II, he captured Carrickfergus and was crowned king of Ireland near Dundalk. His progress south as far as Limerick caused much misery, and his brief siege of Dublin shocked the administration. In 1318 he again recklessly attacked the reinforced Leinster colony, and was defeated and killed in the battle of Faughart (14 October) near Dundalk.

BRUTON, JOHN (1947–). Born in Dublin, educated at Clongowes Wood College, University College Dublin, and King's Inns. Elected for Meath in 1969 as the youngest-ever TD, he held ministerial office in Industry and Energy (1982–83), Industry, Trade, Commerce and Tourism (1983–86), and was minister for finance (1986–87) in the Fine Gael-Labour coalition government. He became Fine Gael (FG)(q.v.) party leader in November 1990, and was elected taoiseach in December 1994 at the head of a coalition between FG, the Labour Party, and the Democratic Left (qq.v.). He opposed dialogue with Provisional Sinn Fein (SF) in 1993 and upheld the broadcasting ban on paramilitary spokespersons. But he did take part in talks with members of SF following the 1994 Provisional IRA (q.v.) cease-fire. He reimposed the embargo on ministerial meetings with SF after the IRA bombings in London in February 1996. On Northern Ireland policy, while supporting the Downing Street Declaration (q.v.), he has expressed tentative agreement with a need for flexibility regarding the Republic's constitution (q.v.) and has always emphasized adherence to the principle of consent in any proposed political settlement. A convinced European, he was a member of the parliamentary assembly of the Council of Europe (1989–91) and has been president of the Irish Council of the European Movement since 1990.

BURKE, EDMUND (1729–97). Born in Dublin of a Protestant father and a Roman Catholic mother, he was educated at the Quaker school in Ballitore, Co. Kildare, and at Trinity College Dublin and the Middle Temple, London, but was not called to the Bar. He published *A Philosophical Inquiry into the Origin of our Ideas of the Sublime and the Beautiful* (1756), edited the *Annual Register* from 1759, and established a literary circle in London. He was secretary to the Chief Secretary for Ireland, Hamilton, in 1761–63, was elected MP successively for Wendover (1765), Bristol (1774–80), and Malton (to 1795). He was appointed Privy Councillor and paymaster general in Rockingham's government (1782–86). He advocated a conciliatory approach in the American colonial crisis of 1774–77, as well as in Ireland. His *Thoughts on the Present Discontents* appeared in 1770. Having failed to have Warren Hastings impeached, he wrote *Reflections on the Revolution in France* (1790).

BUTLER, JAMES (1610–88), twelfth earl of Ormond. Born in London, he married his cousin, heiress of the earl of Desmond in 1629. As a Protestant landowner and a loyal crown administrator during a difficult period in English and Irish history, he supported Thomas Wentworth (q.v.) after his fall and commanded government forces during the rebellion of 1641 (q.v.), though he was hampered by officials loyal to parliament. From 1643 his efforts to make peace in Ireland in order to release forces for the king were thwarted by the Catholic Confederation led by Rinuccini. Following the 1646 treaty granting toleration, he supported Charles II after the execution of Charles I, but handed Dublin over to parliamentary forces in 1647. In 1649 he tried unsuccessfully to make peace with Owen Roe O'Neill before Oliver Cromwell (qq.v.) arrived and was forced to flee to France for ten years in the face of Cromwellian successes in 1650. He received an Irish dukedom at the Restoration in 1661, was appointed lord lieutenant (1662–69), and was again restored to favor in 1677–82 when he reluctantly supported James II, restored the Established Church, enforced the Settlement and Explanation Acts in 1665, confirming Cromwell's land settlement, and was granted an English dukedom in 1682. He retired to England in 1685 and died in Dorset. He was succeeded by his nephew, James, who supported William III. *See also* Settlment, Act of

BUTT, ISAAC (1813–79). Born in Glenfin, Co. Donegal, the son of the local rector, educated at Raphoe school and Trinity College Dublin, where he was professor of political economy (1836–41). A leading barrister, he set up the weekly *Protestant Guardian.* Initially a conservative, he was converted to a nationalist viewpoint during the famine, was elected MP for Youghal (1852–65), defended Fenians (q.v.) in the later 1860s, was president of the Amnesty Association seeking release of Irish (Revolutionary) Republican Brotherhood (q.v.) prisoners, and founded the Home Government (Rule) Association (q.v.) in 1870. He was elected MP for Limerick in 1871, but despite victories in the 1874 election, lost out to the more radical Parnellites. *See also* Famines

-C-

CAMPBELL, JAMES HENRY MUSSEN (1851–1931), first baron Glenavy (1921). Born in Dublin, studied law at Trinity College Dublin, became a barrister, and was elected MP for Dublin constituencies (1898–1916). He was appointed solicitor general (1901–5), attorney general (1905/1916), and lord chief justice (1916–18), became a member of Sir Edward Carson's (q.v.) provisional government, lord chancellor of Ireland (1918–21), and chairman of the Irish Free State senate (1922–28).

CANALS. In 1715 a statute was passed "to encourage the draining and improving of the Boggs and unprofitable low grounds, and for easing and despatching the inland carriage of goods from one part to another within this kingdom," identifying "undertakers" to make the river Shannon navigable from Limerick to Carrick. They were empowered to levy tolls and were regulated by MP and justices of the peace commissioners. A similar project was mounted for the rivers Liffey, Boyne, Barrow, Foyle, and Bann, but these proved largely ineffective.

The statute led to the 1730 Act (3 Geo. II, c. 3) appointing commissioners to accomplish what had been required of previous undertakers, resulting in the Newry canal to the upper Bann and Lough Neagh, and from Coalisland to Lough Neagh in Tyrone. Under 25 Geo. II, c. 10 (1752) the administration was constituted as a "Corporation for promoting and carrying on an Inland Navigation in Ireland," with public funds. Consequently, there began the Grand Canal (1753–1830) from Dublin to the Shannon, the Lagan navigation to Lough Neagh (1753–94), the Barrow (Athy to St. Mullin's) canal lock system (1759–1812), the Boyne (Navan to Drogheda), and Shannon navigation to the Lough Allen collieries (1755–1850).

When divested to private companies or local corporations in 1787, these projects were augmented by the Royal Canal (Dublin to the Shannon, 1789–1822), and the Foyle navigation to Strabane by Lord Abercorn. In 1800 (40 Geo. III c. 51) a statute authorized the lord lieutenant to appoint a Board of Directors of Inland Navigation, absorbing all works accomplished thus far. Continued concern existed over the use of public money, with the result that in October 1831 (1 & 2 Will. IV, c. 33) the Board of Works (q.v.) took over all property and powers previously held by directors general. Subsequent completion of the Suir navigation from Carrick to Waterford by 1840, the Erne-Shannon waterway from Ballinamore to Ballyconnell by 1859 (complicated by lakes, and only viable by steam barges), Bann (Blackwater to Coleraine), Corrib (1842–59), and Ulster systems (Upper Erne-Lough Neagh, 1826–41) at a total cost of £4.7 million, provided foci on the ports of Dublin, Belfast, Limerick, and Waterford (qq.v.).

Passenger boats provided the main means of transport in central Ireland until a stagecoach network about 1810. Nevertheless, at an eight-mile-per-hour maximum horse-drawn speed, these were slow. The network was accompanied by a hotel chain, but soon discontinued when railways (q.v.) were constructed along similar routes. Primarily, river and canal transport handled bulky commodities such as peat, coal, bricks, timber, sand, grain, flour, porter, and fertilizers. *See also* Bianconi, Charles

CARLETON, WILLIAM (1794–1869). Born near Clogher, Co. Tyrone, the youngest of 14 children of a farmer with a treasured memory of folk tradition, and a bilingual, musical mother. Educated at a hedge school (q.v.) and at Glasslough, he studied classics with the intention of joining the church, an idea rejected after a visit to the pilgrimage site of Lough Derg. He became tutor to a farmer's family in Louth and later in Dublin, writing an account of his pilgrimage. His numerous, widely translated works include *Traits and Stories of the Irish Peasantry* (1830 and 1833), *Tales of Ireland* (1834), *Fardorougha the Miser* (1839), *Valentine M'Clutchy, the Irish Agent, or Chronicles of Castle Cumber* (1845), *The Pious Aspirations of Solomon M'Slime* (1846), *Rody the Rover, or the Ribbonman* (1845), *The Black Prophet* (1847), *Tithe Proctor* (1849), *The Black Baronet* (1852), *The Emigrants* (1857), and *The Squanders of Castle Squander* (1853). Several novels deal with contemporary Irish themes, such as various aspects of the land question, and were acclaimed by W. B. Yeats (q.v.) as faithful portrayals of Irish character and dialect. Others, however, considered his style to be exaggerated and melodramatic. He was awarded a government pension under Lord John Russell.

CARLISLE, seventh EARL OF (1802–64) (George William Frederick Howard, later viscount Morpeth). Born in London, educated at Eton and Oxford. He became MP for Morpeth (1826), chief secretary for Ireland (1835–41), and lord lieutenant (1855–58). He supported Burdett in introducing Catholic emancipation (q.v.), and he helped Mulgrave and Drummond pass the Irish Tithes Act (1838) to end the tithe war, which had dragged on since 1830. He also promoted the Municipal Corporations Act (1840) to reform town councils and the Irish Poor Law Act (1838), which created Poor Law Unions.

CARSON, SIR EDWARD, Baron of Duncairn (1854–1935). Born in Dublin, educated at Portarlington and Trinity College Dublin, he became a barrister and was appointed solicitor general for Ireland in 1892 and achieved prominence in cross-examining Oscar Wilde (q.v.). He became leader of the Ulster Unionists in 1910, and in September 1912 he led the campaign for the Solemn League and Covenant to resist home rule (qq.v.), formed the Ulster Volunteers after passage of the Home Rule bill in January 1913, but received assurance from Lloyd George (q.v.) that the six northern counties would not be coerced into union with the south. Elected MP for Duncairn, Belfast, in 1918, he accepted the Home Rule Act (1914) and supported the Government of Ireland Act (1920) (q.v.) as an alternative.

CASEMENT, SIR ROGER (1864–1916). Born at Sandycove, Dublin; educated at Ballymena Academy. He served in the colonial administration in Africa before becoming British consul general in Rio de Janeiro. He was active in denouncing the inhuman treatment of native workers in the Belgian Congo and Peru, was knighted in 1912, joined the Irish Volunteers (q.v.) in 1913, and sought German help for Irish independence via arms shipped on the *Aud* to Kerry. He was tried for treason and executed on 3 August 1916.

CASTLEREAGH, VISCOUNT (1769–1822); Robert Stewart, second marquess of Londonderry. As Conservative MP for Co. Down from 1790, he supported the Catholic Relief Act in 1793 and the United Irishmen (q.v.). He was horrified by the excesses of the French Revolution and became less liberal. As chief secretary of Ireland in 1798, he became convinced by that year's uprising of the need for legislative union and facilitated that process by dispensing largesse in 1799–1800. He resigned his Irish post after a duel with his political rival George Canning (also Ulster-born). He attended the Congress of Vienna in 1812 as British foreign minister; overwork led to mental breakdown and suicide.

CATHOLIC EMANCIPATION (April 1829). The Roman Catholic Relief Act (10 Geo. IV, c. 7) gave Catholics the right to sit in parliament without swearing the old oath of supremacy and repealed their exclusion from other public office. The campaign was led by Daniel O'Connell (q.v.) and Sheil's populist Catholic Association (1823–29, suppressed by Goulburn's Act in 1825–27). It was financed by church collections after the unsuccessful Catholic Committee of 1805 and Catholic Board (1812–14), which achieved electoral success in Waterford and Clare by-elections. Peel's bill was supported by Wellington, but the Irish Parliamentary Elections Act (10 Geo. IV, c. 8) changed the franchise property qualification from 40 shillings to £10. *See also* Forty-Shilling Freeholders

CATTLE ACTS (July 1663/January 1667). A series of measures also applied to prohibition of imports of sheep, pigs, and meat from Ireland, while another act of 1681 added dairy produce, as an act of May 1662 had done for wool. In 1759 restrictions on imports of livestock to Britain were removed, but a 1776 act confined exports to Britain and the colonies. Such complex legislation should be viewed, together with the Navigation Acts (q.v.), in the context of prevailing economic and political philosophy. Contentious assertions have been made concerning consequential shifts between pastoralism and tillage in Irish agriculture, with hypothetical repercussions on unemployment and unrest, as trade was periodically curbed, confined to Britain and its colonies, or diverted to the continent. In the absence of comprehensive analyses of meagre documentary evidence on such themes, no objective conclusions are yet available.

CAULFIELD, JAMES (1728–99), Dublin-born first earl of Charlemont. He defended Belfast against the French in 1763, was rewarded with an earldom, moved to Dublin and built Charlemont House, later the Municipal Gallery of Modern Art (q.v.). He helped found the Royal

Irish Academy (q.v.) in 1785–86, was commander in chief of the Volunteers in 1780, and was active in the Dungannon Convention. He allied himself to Henry Grattan (q.v.) in the move for securing the independence of the Irish parliament, supported Catholic emancipation, (q.v.) and opposed the union before it was enacted. *See also* Union, Act of

CELTIC CHURCH. Christianity was established in Ireland in the early fifth century, the first area beyond Roman Europe to receive missionaries. Of these the most famous was Patrick (c. A.D. 390–461) who probably came from west Britain to Ulster, initially as a slave. After studying in Gaul, he returned as a bishop, eventually to become the country's patron saint. He established several churches, particularly in the northeast, making his center at Armagh (q.v.) close to Emhain Macha. Armagh has remained the focus of Irish Christianity ever since.

Despite its episcopal background, Patrick's church developed a looser, more monastic structure that reflected the different political systems in Ireland and Romanized Europe. This "Celtic" form had parallels in Scotland, Wales, and Brittany. While its emphasis on local saints was distinctive, it used the common language of Latin. Despite later medieval rededication of churches to the Virgin Mary and the apostles, many still retain the names of local or regional Celtic saints such as Brendan, Brigid, Ciaran, Colman, Finnian, and Patrick.

This new development in Ireland brought it into contact with the mainstream of European thought and in turn allowed its monks to mount missions to other areas, initially to Scotland and northern England, and later to south-central Europe. The most influential missionary was St. Columbanus, who founded monasteries from A.D. 590 onward in Burgundy, Switzerland, and at Bobbio in northern Italy where Irish influence persisted for centuries.

The growth of Irish monasticism led to a general flowering of culture that produced for Ireland the title of "island of saints and scholars" by the eighth century. It found expression in carved stone crosses, fine metalwork such as the Ardagh chalice (q.v.), and illuminated gospels like the *Book of Kells* and the *Book of Durrow*. When the Latin alphabet was applied to the Gaelic language, scholars from Europe, especially Anglo-Saxons, came to the monasteries, while natives went abroad as Latin scholars, the most notable being John Scotus "Eriugena" who from about A.D. 845 was the foremost philosopher at the court of Emperor Charles the Bald at Laon.

The Irish monasteries provided the strongest and most enduring foci within the island. The road network was influenced by them and commercial life in the form of markets or fairs was often related to their locations, most of which were in the interior. Some became large centers of population, for example Kildare (q.v.), Clonmacnoise, and Cashel, particularly if they also later became seats of powerful Irish kings. The monastic nuclei were usually small, simple, and informal, surrounded by earthen ramparts or stone walls. Toward the end of their heyday they often acquired a tall "round tower," which acted as both a store and a defense. *See also* Monasticism (Medieval)

CENSORSHIP OF PUBLICATIONS. In the Republic of Ireland censorship is exercised, according to provisions of the 1929 and 1946 acts, by a Censorship of Publications Board that uses criteria of indecency, obscenity, and advocacy of artificial methods of contraception or abortion. Since 1946 its decisions have been subject to appeal, but may only be overturned by the minister for justice. Banned books were listed in the *Register of Prohibited Publications*. Much of the conservatism and xenophobia engendered by the 1929 act was attributed by its victims to the postindependence atmosphere of insecure national identity, to a historical context of poor general cultural awareness, and to Irish Catholicism's misplaced desire to shelter its adherents, together with other citizens of the state, from reality by discouraging rational discussion and having its own *Index* of proscribed publications imposed by law. In July 1967 an amendment provided for a review of all banned books, those which had been banned for more than 12 years being allowed to lapse from the list. Films are controlled by the Censorship of Films Act (1923) and Amendment Acts (1925, 1930) to issue certificates, and to prohibit, restrict, or cut material if it is considered indecent, obscene, or blasphemous. There is no official stage censorship, although in the past particular works, including some by W. B. Yeats and J. M. Synge (qq.v.), faced opposition campaigns when first performed.

Intellectual rejection of the principle of arbitrary literary and artistic censorship, arising from complaints brought by individuals or the Catholic Truth Society, ostensibly on grounds of the subversion of public morality, led to the formation of the Irish Academy of Letters in 1932 by Oliver St. John Gogarty, Frank O'Connor, Sean O'Faolain, Liam O'Flaherty, George Russell, George Bernard Shaw, Edith Somerville, William Butler Yeats (qq.v.), and others.

Since the 1980s fierce debate has surrounded another issue—suppression of open access to published information and advice on artificial methods of birth control [allowed under the Health (Family Planning) Act, 1979], combined with freedom of women to travel outside the country in order to obtain a pregnancy termination, which remains illegal in the Republic of Ireland. *See also* Referenda

CENSUS OF POPULATION. After an abortive and partial attempt at conducting a population count in 1813–15, the first census on the English model was taken in 1821 under the Commissioner W. S. Mason (q.v.). Its operation suffered from the absence of well-defined townland boundaries, lack of synchronization, and a mistaken belief among enumerators (often in the persons of mistrusted local tax collectors) that they were being paid by results. Its totals were therefore rendered suspect because of omissions, double counting, and confusion over mobile population elements, and were considered to be an underestimate of actual numbers. In 1831 Commissioner George Hatchell adopted the procedures followed in England and Wales by the experienced John Rickman, though some sources of error remained. The first census acknowledged as being reasonably reliable was that organized by Thomas Larcom (q.v.) on Sunday, 6 June 1841. Censuses were held at ten-year intervals under British administration until 1911. The few manuscript household returns that survived the fire at the Four Courts in 1922 may now be consulted at the National Archive, Dublin. *See also* Population; Public Record Office

CHICHESTER, ARTHUR (1563–1625). The Devon-born and Oxford-educated Chichester captained a ship against the Spanish Armada (q.v.) in 1588 and was with Francis Drake on the expedition to Cadiz, after which he fought on the continent. He was sent to Ireland by Cecil about 1599 with a regiment of 1,200 against Tyrone's rebel forces, was made governor of Carrickfergus by Essex, and appointed sergeant-major-general of the army in Ireland. He benefited from the patronage of Mountjoy (earl of Devonshire), who recommended to Cecil that he be made sole governor of Ulster, became a member of the Irish Privy Council in 1603, and served as lord deputy from 1604 until 1614.

He favored a strategy of control by settlement rather than by military conquest, but was relentless in suppressing rebels and native customs through the imposition of strict civil law and disarmament. He sought to abolish traditional clan dues in favor of free tenancies under the crown, tried to enforce church attendance fines on Roman Catholics, yet promoted translating the prayer book into Irish (1608) and tried to arbitrate in the Tyrone-O'Cahan dispute before the "flight of the earls" (q.v.) in 1607. He wished to place native tenants first on the escheated lands in Ulster, and only then introduce Scottish-English settlers on the remainder, but his advice was not heeded. When he was made Lord Chichester of Belfast (1613), he was obliged to revert to a policy of forced conversion and displacement. He was recalled to retirement in England for his moderation, though received the position of lord treasurer of Ireland. He married a daughter of Sir John Perrot, the widow of

Walter Vaughan of Golden Grove, but had no heirs, and was buried at Carrickfergus. The viscount's title passed to his brother Edward, whose eldest son Arthur (1606–75) became MP for Antrim in 1639, governor of Carrickfergus (1643), and earl of Donegal (1647).

CHICHESTER-CLARK, JAMES DAWSON, Lord Moyola (1923–). Born in Castledawson, succeeded Terence O'Neill (q.v.) as Northern Ireland prime minister in May 1969 with a one-vote majority over Brian Faulkner (q.v.). He offered amnesty for political detainees, but intensified rioting in the Bogside, Londonderry, in August 1969 forced him to request British Home Secretary James Callaghan for troops to be sent in. His inability to have order restored, especially in July 1970, together with concessions made in the face of British anti-discrimination demands, led to increased loyalist paramilitary activity and finally his resignation in March 1971 after he had failed to achieve massive army intervention in republican areas.

CHILDERS, ERSKINE HAMILTON (1905–74). Born in London, son of R. E. Childers (q.v.), educated in Norfolk and at Trinity College, Cambridge. Following several years' business experience in Paris, he became advertising manager of the *Irish Press* in 1932. As TD for Athlone-Longford from 1938, he held various ministerial offices in Fianna Fail (q.v.) governments (Posts and Telegraphs, Lands, Transport, Power, Health), and set up Radio Telefis Eireann (q.v.) in June 1960. He was elected president of the Republic on 30 May 1973, a position held until his sudden death on 17 November 1974.

CHILDERS, ROBERT ERSKINE (1870–1922). Born in London and educated at Haileybury School and Trinity College, Cambridge. He was a clerk in the House of Commons from 1895 until 1910, when he decided to enter politics. In 1903 Childers published an espionage novel, *The Riddle of the Sands*, interpreted as a warning against the German military threat to Britain. He imported German arms for the Irish Volunteers (q.v.) to Howth in July 1914 on his yacht *Asgard*, but served in the British navy during World War I and was decorated. As TD for Wicklow in 1921, he acted as secretary to the Irish delegation during the Treaty negotiations, but opposed it. Having fought on the side of republican forces in the civil war (q.v.), he was captured at his mother's home in Co. Wicklow by Irish Free State troops, court-martialed, and executed on 24 November 1922.

CHURCH OF IRELAND. After the Reformation, the Established Church held a privileged position throughout Britain and deeply influenced many facets of economic, social, and political life. Feelings of injustice held by growing numbers of Protestant dissenters, for example at having to pay tithes (q.v.) for the upkeep of a church to which they did not belong, were even more intense in Ireland, where the vast majority of the population had remained loyal to the Roman Catholic Church. There, too, social cleavages were deepened by the rift between indigenous Catholic tenants and landowners, who were often Anglican.

The Church Temporalities Act (3 & 4 Will. IV, c. 37) of August 1833 reduced the number of bishoprics from 22 to 12, created a board of ecclesiastical commissioners to administer surplus funds for the parish clergy and churches, and abolished the church cess, a tax levied on all inhabitants of a parish for the upkeep of the church, as distinct from the county cess, raised by grand juries on occupiers. On 26 July 1869, after the 1868 election, the Church was disestablished; from 1871 it operated under a synod and commissioners, providing rights of tenants to purchase, and offering a grant to St. Patrick's College, Maynooth. *See also* Education; Religion

CIE (Irish Transport System). *See* Córas Iompair Éireann

CIVIL WAR (1922–23). On 7 January 1922 the Dáil voted to accept the Anglo-Irish Treaty (q.v.) of 6 December 1921. Following a split in the army over the question of allegiance, republican opposition insurgents seized the Four Courts on 13 April. In an attempt to restore its authority, on 28 June the Provisional Government ordered an artillery attack to dislodge them, causing a fire that largely destroyed the building and its historical documents before its surrender on 30 June. The remaining dissidents were forced into a southern guerilla campaign. After the death of Arthur Griffith and the assassination of Michael Collins in August, W. T. Cosgrave (qq.v.) was elected president of the Executive Council. From September 1922 the minister of defense, Richard Mulcahy, and the minister of home affairs, Kevin O'Higgins, introduced military courts, imposing the death penalty for unauthorized possession of arms. Some 77 Republicans, most notably Erskine Childers (q.v.), were executed. The IRA (q.v.) under Liam Lynch, having threatened reprisals, met on 24 March 1923 to discuss a truce, peace being favored by Eamon de Valera and Frank Aiken (qq.v.). Their views were rejected by six votes to five, and one opponent, Lynch, was murdered the same day. De Valera and Aiken announced a cease-fire for 30 April that did not include surrender of arms, a move rejected by the government, though on 14 May it was agreed neither to continue the war nor to give up arms, despite being ordered to do so by Aiken on 24 May. Mass arrests followed. Part of the political fallout was the formation of the pro-Treaty Cumann na nGaedheal (CG) party, later to become Fine Gael (qq.v.). Sinn Fein then split, leading to de Valera's creation of Fianna Fail (FF)(q.v.) in 1926, while the Sinn Fein-IRA campaign against both CG and FF governments continued. Military conflict occurred in Dublin in June–August 1922, Limerick in July, Waterford and Wexford in June–July, and Cork, Tipperary, Dundalk, and Kilmallock in July–August.

CLANCY, GEORGE (1879–1921). Member of a Limerick Fenian family, educated at the Catholic University of Ireland. A Gaelic Athletic Association (q.v.) enthusiast, he joined the Gaelic League (q.v.) under Patrick Pearse (q.v.) and taught Irish at Clongowes Wood College. Mayor of Limerick in 1921 and the model of "Davin" in James Joyce's *Portrait of the Artist,* he was shot by the Black and Tans (qq.v.).

CLAN NA GAEL. Formed on 20 June 1867 among Irish immigrants in New York, allied to the Irish (Revolutionary) Republican Brotherhood (q.v.), whose Supreme Council was viewed as the provisional government of Ireland. It was rivaled by O'Donovan Rossa's United Irishmen (1880) and shipped German guns to the Irish Volunteers (q.v.) in 1916.

COLLINS, MICHAEL (1890–1922). Youngest of eight children of a tenant farmer near Rosscarbery, west Cork. He worked as a postal clerk in London (1906–15), joined Sinn Fein (SF), the Irish (Revolutionary) Republican Brotherhood (IRB) in 1909, and the Irish Volunteers (qq.v.) in London in 1914. He played a minor part in the 1916 rising and was interned at Frongoch camp in Wales. He opposed the socialist program put before the first Dáil by SF in 1919 and became secretary/treasurer of the IRB and president of its Supreme Council, while also minister of finance in the Dáil. He held an ambivalent view of relationships between the IRB and the newly created constitutional government, objecting to Brugha's motion that Volunteers should swear allegiance to the Dáil, wishing to retain his hold on the IRA (q.v.) as its director of intelligence and through a hand-picked assassination squad.

With Arthur Griffith (q.v.) and Barton he was sent by Eamon de Valera to negotiate the Anglo-Irish Treaty (qq.v.) in October 1921, becoming chairman of the Irish Free State's Provisional Government established by the Treaty in January 1922. Caught in a conflict of personal loyalties and between absolute principles and pragmatism, he manipulated IRB members in irregular raids on Northern Ireland in May 1922, ostensibly in defense of nationalists under attack. However, he was forced to back down and was castigated by former colleagues over suppression of de Valera's republicans for the sake of upholding the Treaty. He became commander of government forces in the civil war (q.v.), and was shot dead in an ambush in Co. Cork.

COMMUNIST PARTY. Until November 1921 it was called the Socialist Party of Ireland, founded on an all-Ireland basis in June 1933, but split during World War II into the Communist Party of Northern Ireland and the Irish Workers' Party in the Irish Free State. Reunited in March 1970, it has sought a united Ireland and an end to political violence. It was critical of the Anglo-Irish Agreement (q.v.), but has never succeeded in winning a seat at an election in Northern Ireland.

CONGESTED DISTRICTS BOARD. Set up by A. J. Balfour (q.v.) in 1891 as a group of commissioners to give assistance in counties Clare, Cork, Donegal, Galway, Kerry, Leitrim, Limerick, Roscommon, and Sligo to promote harbor construction, the autumn mackerel fishing and curing industry, spinning and weaving, land drainage, modernization of farming practices, and facilitating short-distance migration. It collected data on family budgets to assess domestic economic conditions. The Purchase of Land Act (1891) identified counties in which more than 20 percent of the population lived in electoral divisions where the rateable value averaged below 30 shillings, i.e., about 3.5 million acres and a 1901 population of 0.5 million, placing an emphasis on land quality rather than overcrowding in terms of crude density.

Under the 1903 land act tenants were allowed to buy land from estates to enlarge small holdings by amalgamation or consolidation by exchange, reversing generations of subdivision and morcellation. The scale of purchases of estates increased greatly in 1899, and compulsory purchase powers were granted from 1909, redistributing about 2 million acres. The board was abolished in 1923 by the Irish Free State government and its powers passed to the Land Commission, leading to Sir Horace Plunkett's (q.v.) Co-operative Movement. The Land Commission had been established under the 1881 act to establish fair rents and land-purchase schemes. From 1923 it arranged transfers to tenants on payment of land annuities by them to the UK treasury, a procedure agreed by W. T. Cosgrave (q.v.). After independence the Blueshirt campaign for nonpayment, led by Duffy, agitated for such payments to be retained in the Free State. They were withheld by de Valera and Fianna Fail (qq.v.) from June 1932, provoking economic retaliation from the UK. *See also* Land Acts; Blueshirts

CONNOLLY, JAMES (1868–1916). Born in Edinburgh, served in the British army at the Curragh. A socialist trade unionist, he founded *The Workers' Republic* and the Irish Socialist Republican Party (q.v.), organized the Ulster branch of the Irish Transport Workers' Union, and founded the Irish Citizen Army (q.v.) after the imprisonment of James Larkin (q.v.) and the Dublin lockout of 1913. He acted as Irish

(Revolutionary) Republican Brotherhood military commander in the 1916 Easter Rising (q.v.) with Pearse (q.v.) and MacDonagh, and was executed following the General Post Office battle and the proclamation of the Irish Republic. *See also* Trade Unions

CONSTITUTION. The first constitution (16 June 1922) was drawn up by a committee chaired by Michael Collins (q.v.). It consisted of 79 articles plus the Anglo-Irish Treaty incorporated into the Irish Free State (Constitution) Act. Under Cosgrave's bill to implement the Treaty, the Free State (Saorstat) was to remain a member of the British Commonwealth as a dominion, with a governor general representing the monarch as head of state. Its law-making body, the National Parliament (Oireachtas), comprised the House of Representatives (Dáil) and the Senate (Seanad). The Saorstat became effective on 6 December 1922. The governor general occupied the vice-regal Lodge in Phoenix Park (later Aras an Uachtaráin), but the office, whose only holders were T. H. Healy (q.v.) (1922–28), James MacNeill (1928–32), and Domhnall O'Buachalla (1932–37), was abolished under the 1937 constitution.

From 1935 Eamon de Valera (q.v.) had requested the preparation of a new republican constitution. *Bunreacht na hÉireann* was published on 1 May 1937 and was approved by the Dáil on 14 June. On 1 July it was subjected to a referendum and received approval by 685,105 votes to 526,945, becoming effective on 29 December 1937. Article 2 stated that "the national territory consists of the whole island of Ireland, its islands and the territorial [*sic*] seas." Article 3 affirmed that laws passed by the Dáil are applicable to 26 counties only. Article 4 declared the title of the state to be Éire. Article 5 defined it as a "sovereign, independent, democratic state." Article 8 proclaimed Irish as the first official language, with English second. The Oireachtas was to include the president, the Dáil and the Seanad, the cabinet being composed of 7–15 members. Article 41 prohibited divorce. Article 44 recognized the special position of the Roman Catholic Church (which lasted until the 1972 referendum) but provided equal rights for other named and existing denominations. The 1937 *Bunreacht* ended the provisions of the 1922 Anglo-Irish Treaty (q.v.) and was narrowly adopted with de Valera as president of the Executive Council. Subsequently, it has been considered faulty in law and in the efficacy of its institutions. It was amended by W. T. Cosgrave (q.v.) in 1931 to set up military tribunals to counter republican violence. The Republic came into being on Easter Monday, 18 April 1949, under the Republic of Ireland Act 1948, which repealed the Executive Authority (External Relations) Act of 1936 and declared "the description of the State shall be the Republic of Ireland." Thereupon the UK government passed the Ireland Act, which stated that Eire ceased to be part of the dominions, while Northern Ireland remained, affirming "in no event will Northern Ireland or any part thereof cease to be part of His Majesty's Dominions and of the United Kingdom without the consent of the Parliament of Northern Ireland."

The president, elected by direct vote for a term of seven years, once renewable, must not be a member of either the House of Representatives (166 members) or the Senate (60 members) as legislative bodies. The president appoints the *taoiseach* (prime minister), who has been nominated by the Dáil. The Senate has 11 members nominated by the *taoiseach,* 43 elected by professional and vocational groups, three each by the National University of Ireland and the University of Dublin. The Council of State is composed of former presidents, former *taoiseachs,* chief justices, chairs of the Dáil and the Senate, the attorney general, and the president of the High Court.

Teachtai dála (TDs, Dáil deputies) are elected by single transferable vote from 41 constituencies that send three to five members in proportion to their population, each member representing between 20,000 and 30,000 inhabitants. Eligible electors must be registered citizens who are aged at least 18 on the qualifying date. The maximum term of a Dáil is five years. Elections to the Senate must take place within 90 days of the dissolution of a Dáil. Meetings of both chambers are held in public, and their proceedings are published. Although the number of ministers was limited to between seven and 15 by the constitution, de Valera appointed two more during the Emergency (q.v.). The finance secretary is head of the civil service, while other current ministries are Enterprise and Employment; Agriculture, Food, and Forestry; Tourism and Trade; Foreign Affairs; Environment; Education; Social Welfare; Health; Justice; Equality and Law Reform; Arts, Culture, and the Gaeltacht (q.v.); Transport, Energy, and Communications; the Marine; and Defence. The titles and responsibilities of these departments of state have varied in the past.

At district level the country is administered by five-year elected county councils plus four county borough corporations, boroughs, and urban districts for health, roads, social services, sanitation, housing, vocational education, fire service, libraries, levying property rates, plus state grants for national policies formerly via the ministry of local government and finance, their managers now being appointed by the minister of the environment.

CONWAY, ARTHUR WILLIAM (1875–1950). Born in Wexford, educated at University College Dublin (UCD) and Oxford. He was professor of mathematical physics at UCD from 1901 and was elected Fellow of the Royal Society in 1915. He was influential in the establishment of the Dublin Institute of Advanced Studies in 1940 and served as president of UCD (1940–47).

COOTE, SIR CHARLES (?–1661). Descended from a Devon family, son of a ruthless but successful army commander with extensive lands who had been in Ireland since 1600 during the O'Neill wars. As MP for Leitrim (1639) and provost marshal of Connacht, he withstood a siege by rebels in 1641 at Castle Coote, Co. Roscommon. He relieved Athlone and captured Galway in 1642, becoming governor of Dublin (1642–45) and lord president of Connacht (1645). He was besieged in Derry, but agreed a truce with Owen Roe O'Neill (q.v.) and cleared the city's hinterland, later defeating Munro's Scottish army at Carrickfergus in 1649 before moving on to subdue Sligo and Galway (1651–52) and then defeat the earl of Clanricarde in Kerry. He was Commonwealth commissioner in Connacht in 1659, but accepted and worked to establish the restoration of Charles II, for which he was appointed president of Connacht in 1660 and was given lands in Westmeath. In 1661 he was made earl of Mountrath, the name taken from the place of one of his father's successful exploits. He was a lord justice of Ireland and received large sums of money for his services under the Act of Settlement. *See also* Settlement, Act of

CÓRAS IOMPAIR ÉIREANN (CIE, Irish Transport System). This statutory body came into being on 1 January 1945 after the Transport Act (1944) merged the Great Southern Railways Company and the Dublin United Transport Company. It became publicly owned in 1950 and was subdivided in 1961 into five regional enterprises centered on Dublin, Cork, Limerick, Waterford, and Galway (qq.v.), operating buses and train services, now via three subsidiary companies, throughout the Republic and maintaining links with Northern Ireland. At that time it was the largest employer in the Republic.

CORK. County borough (population of 127,253 in 1991), major port, commercial, industrial (woollen textiles and rubber) and regional center for southwestern Ireland. Its history begins with the monastery founded by St. Finnbarr (ob. c. A.D. 630) near the present Church of Ireland cathedral, which subsequently became an important nucleus for the south Munster church. Following Viking raids, a small trading settlement was established closer to the islands that were a distinct feature of the river Lee. Its development does not seem to have been as spectacular as that of Norse Limerick or Waterford (qq.v.), but by the early 12th century Cork had become a political focus for the Irish kings of Desmond (South Munster). Despite the submission of the MacCarthy king, Cork was taken by the Anglo-Normans and formed the hub of their colonization of its rich agricultural hinterland, the town itself being reserved to the Crown. Development took place on two of the larger islands that were further fortified by a town wall enclosing the harbor between them. During the late 16th century Desmond plantation Cork was the main refuge in times of difficulty and became a garrison town with a large fort built to increase its defenses. Remains of these fortifications, but little else of the premodern town, survive. In the 17th century it experienced a number of sieges, the last by John Churchill, later duke of Marlborough.

Industries began to flourish in the 18th century, especially silver and glass, and, in the 19th century, cottage crafts such as lace making (examples may be seen in the museum). During the same period Cork began to assume its present position as the second most important town in southern Ireland with a thriving commercial life and agriculturally based industries, especially brewing and butter. A new town developed as land was reclaimed from the river, lined by terraces of red brick houses, interspersed by public buildings of local white limestone, for example, the Mansion and Custom Houses (art gallery attached). Most of the churches are modern or 18th- and 19th-century rebuildings of older structures. The University College was founded in 1845, and there are many other educational establishments. There is a modern opera house, a ballet company, and an annual international film festival.

The new quays were supplemented by the development of deepwater shipping facilities downstream, allowing Cork to maintain its preeminence as the port of the region, while Cobh developed as an outport, originally for the navy and later for trans-Atlantic liners. Heavy industry (steel, shipbuilding, oil refining, chemical works, and for some time car assembly) has concentrated on the extensive shores of Cork Harbour, and an airport was opened in 1961. *See also* Plantations; Viking Settlements

CORRIGAN, SIR DOMINIC JOHN (1802–80). Son of a tradesman in the Dublin Liberties, he was taught at a Maynooth school and by the village doctor before going to Edinburgh University, from which he graduated in medicine in 1825. A specialist in cardiac disorders, from 1833 he lectured in Dublin, was physician to the House of Industry hospitals (1840–66), was appointed physician to Queen Victoria and was made a baronet in 1866. In 1847 he was bitterly criticized by Robert Graves (q.v.) for allowing the Central Board of Health, of which he was a member, to pay only five shillings a day to doctors overwhelmed by cases of famine fever. He was five times president of the Irish College of Physicians. He was MP for Dublin city (1870–4), though he allegedly had no interest in politics. A collection of his lectures was published in 1853, showing that he was aware of the distinction between typhus and typhoid fever. He also wrote on cholera, though only in 1866 when all the most serious epidemics had passed.

CORRYMEELA COMMUNITY. Founded in 1965 at Ballycastle, Co. Antrim, by Rev. R. Davey, Presbyterian chaplain to the Queen's University of Belfast. His mission is to promote reconciliation by bringing together people from both sides of the Northern Ireland community.

COSGRAVE, WILLIAM THOMAS (1880–1965). Born in Dublin, and joined the Irish Volunteers in 1913. After the Easter Rising (q.v.) a death sentence imposed on him was commuted to life imprisonment, but he was released from Frongoch camp in Wales under the amnesty in 1917. Having been elected Sinn Fein MP for Kilkenny, he became a Dáil member, supported the Anglo-Irish Treaty (qq.v.), and, after the deaths of Griffith and Collins (qq.v.), was elected president of the Executive Council of the Irish Free State to 1932. He led the Cumann na nGaedheal (q.v.) opposition party from 1932 to 1945.

COSTELLO, JOHN ALOYSIUS (1891–1976). Born in Dublin, studied languages and law at University College and King's Inns. He was attorney general (1926–32) and a member of the Dáil (q.v.). He did not become prominent until the interparty government of 1948, which issued the declaration of a republic in 1949. In 1950 he introduced Noel Browne's (q.v.) "Mother-and-child" health scheme, which was fiercely opposed by the Roman Catholic hierarchy. He set up the Industrial Development Authority and in 1954 led a coalition government, which was overthrown by an IRA (q.v.) campaign and a motion of no confidence proposed by Sean MacBride (q.v.) in 1957.

COUNCIL OF 300. First proposed by *The Nation* and taken up by Daniel O'Connell (qq.v.) in 1843 as a mirror of the old Irish parliament, which had 300 members. Sixty Irish MPs were to join 240 others to be elected from districts to draft a repeal bill as an independent Irish parliament under the crown. It led only to the trial of William Smith O'Brien, John Mitchel, and T. F. Meagher (qq.v.). The idea was floated again unsuccessfully by Arthur Griffith (q.v.).

CRAIG, SIR JAMES (1871–1940), Viscount Craigavon (1927). Son of a Belfast distiller, he saw army service in the Boer War and was elected MP for East Down in 1906 as a fervent opponent of home rule. He organized the Ulster Volunteers, took part in World War I, and was knighted in 1918. He succeeded Sir Edward Carson (q.v.) as leader of the Ulster Unionists in 1921, becoming first prime minister of Northern Ireland in June of that year and agreeing to safeguard minority rights, but abolishing the proportional representation voting system in 1929. *See also* Ulster Unionist Party

CROMMELIN, SAMUEL-LOUIS (1652–1727). A craftsman invited from Holland along with 25 Huguenot families by King William III. He was granted a ten-year patent to spin and weave linen and hemp. At Lisburn and Hilden, Co. Antrim, he set up businesses that were further promoted by the Linen Board, which operated in Dublin from 1711 to 1828. Exports increased from 0.3 to 2.4 million yards between 1690 and 1720, doubled again by 1730, and rose by almost tenfold a century later, virtually replacing cotton manufacture during the 19th century.

CROMWELL, OLIVER (1599–1658). Elected to parliament for Huntingdon in 1628 and for Cambridge in 1640, he acquired a firm reputation as a devout Puritan and an implacable defender of commoners' rights. He spent his own money defending Ireland in 1642, and he served in Essex's army. In Ireland itself his historical significance derives from his military campaign from mid-August 1649 to May 1650, during which massacres of garrisons followed the storming of Drogheda and Wexford. Subsequently, his forces moved inland through Cashel, Kilkenny, and Clonmel to punish previous massacres inflicted against them. He believed the clergy to have been responsible for the rebellion and therefore imposed strict repression of Roman Catholicism. Yet he sought to create an impartial system of justice for poorer tenantry, reacting mercilessly to prohibit plunder and atrocities committed by his soldiers against innocent civilians. When faced with organized opposition, he implemented parliament's program of forced resettlement to Connacht of Roman Catholics who had resisted. He created a brief effective union by proroguing the Irish parliament and sending 30 members to the Commons in London. Seldom has so short a period of activity led to such complete demonization of an individual, and only now is the mythology of his campaign in Ireland being disentangled from its objective reality.

CULLEN, CARDINAL PAUL (1803–78). Born in Co. Kildare, son of a farmer whose wife was a priest's sister; educated at the local Ballitore Quaker school, Carlow College, and in Rome (from 1820), where he eaerned an impeccable reputation as a scholar. Ordained into the priesthood in 1829, he later became rector of the Irish College in Rome, and in 1848–49 rector of the Propaganda College where he had been a pupil, protecting its students from expulsion by Mazzini in the 1848 revolution by enlisting American diplomatic help. He negotiated the Irish bishops' interests with the Holy See and was made monsignor as a papal adviser. He watered down the official condemnation of Daniel O'Connell's (q.v.) repeal campaign and expressed Pope Gregory XVI's opposition to mixed education. He returned to Ireland on being appointed Roman Catholic archbishop of Armagh in 1850 in preference to three candidates nominated by the archdiocese. He was translated to Dublin in 1852. In 1850 he summoned the first Irish synod since 1642 at Thurles, attacking the Queen's Colleges proposals and advocating a Catholic university, while denouncing Anglican Archbishop Whately's (q.v.) texts for the "National" schools system as subversive of Catholic education. In 1853 he forbade involvement of priests in political activity during the tenant rights agitation. He also reacted strongly against the Young Ireland (q.v.) movement and Fenianism (q.v.), supporting the Crown, the law, and the constitution. In June 1866 he became the first Irish cardinal and was reputedly the author of the doctine of papal infallibility (1870), maintaining cordial relations with Pope Pius IX. A proponent of ultramontanism in the church, he was a firm disciplinarian and promoted many new churches and schools in Dublin. *See also* Universities

CUMANN NA mBAN. Founded in April 1914 as the women's section of the Irish Volunteers, it rejected the Anglo-Irish Treaty (qq.v.) in 1922. It has since played a significant role, not only in support but also in active service with the IRA (q.v.); it was declared an illegal organization in both Northern Ireland (1922) and the Irish Free State (1931).

CUMANN NA nGAEDHEAL. Formed originally in September 1900 by Arthur Griffith (q.v.) to oppose the Boer War, it had links to the Fenians (q.v.) and the Irish language movement, but sought an independent parliament and led to formation of Sinn Fein (SF) (q.v.). When SF split, it became the pro-Treaty wing, willing to form a government and to introduce conservative legislation such as the censorship (q.v.) of films (1923) and publications (1929). Almost by default, in view of the abstentionism of its opponents, from 1923 it found itself branded as a party liable to make concessions to Britain, rather than upholding stridently independent nationalist aspirations. Indeed it curbed them during the civil war (q.v.) and imposed economic retrenchment while espousing free trade. By 1932 it had attracted more right-wing followers, including the quasi-fascist Blueshirts (q.v.) under O'Duffy, until he was replaced as leader of Fine Gael by W. T. Cosgrave (qq.v.) in 1935.

CURRAGH INCIDENT. On 20 March 1914 British cavalry troops were ordered to move to Ulster, allegedly to enforce impending home rule against the Ulster Volunteers. Most officers threatened to resign rather than refuse to accept orders to confront opponents of home rule. A potential mutiny was diplomatically avoided.

-D-

DÁIL ÉIREANN. After the general election in December 1918, 73 elected Sinn Fein (SF) (q.v.) abstentionists met in the Mansion House, Dublin, and on 21 January 1921 formed an independent Irish parliament, first under Cathal Brugha and then Eamon de Valera (q.v.). It was declared illegal on 12 September after its members and the Irish Volunteers (q.v.) swore an oath of allegiance in August. Under the Government of Ireland Act (1920) (q.v.) the southern parliament would have been made up of 124 SF members and four independents (from Dublin University), nominated for the uncontested election in 1921, but they abstained and met as the second Dáil Éireann. For the third Dáil in September 1922, 17 Labour, ten Independent, and one Farmers' Union candidate were elected, along with 58 pro-Treaty and 36 anti-Treaty (republican) SF members. Subsequent main party performance and representation (percentage of first preference votes and seats in the Dáil) is shown in Table 1 on the following page.

Elections to the Dáil are conducted by a single transferable vote system of proportional representation in multiseat constituencies, where the number of seats varies according to the size of the electorate. The present Dáil chamber is the former Royal Dublin Society theater at Leinster House.

DARGAN, WILLIAM (1799–1867). Prominent contracting engineer who was responsible for building almost all mainline railways (q.v.) in Ireland. Born in Co. Carlow, he worked with Thomas Telford on the Holyhead road. In 1834 the first train ran from Dublin to Kingstown, and five years later the Ulster railway was linked to his Lough Neagh-Upper Erne Canal (1834–42). Dargan built lines to Carrickfergus, Bangor, Ballymena, Newry-Warrenpoint, Dublin-Cork, and Drogheda. He promoted and largely financed the Dublin Industrial Exhibition (1853). His house at Mount Anville, Dundrum, Dublin, contained a collection of paintings that he bequeathed to the National Gallery of Arts, constructed as a testament to him on the grounds of the exhibition, Leinster Lawn, in 1864. *See also* National Gallery of Ireland

DAVIES, SIR JOHN (1569–1626). Born in Wiltshire, educated at Winchester, Oxford, and the Middle Temple. Davies was a poet and a writer of epigrams who produced verse translations of the Psalms

Table 1
Party Performance and Representation

	FF		FG [CG]		Labour		SF	
	%	seats	%	seats	%	seats	%	seats
1923	27.4	44	[39.0	**63**]	10.6	14		
1927 June	26.2	44	[27.4	**47**]	12.6	22	3.6	5
1927 Sept.	35.2	57	[38.6	**62**]	9.1	13		
1932	44.5	**72**	[35.2	57]	7.7	7		
1933	49.7	**77**	30.4	48	5.7	8		
1937	45.2	**69**	34.8	48	10.3	13		
1938	51.9	**77**	33.3	45	10.0	9		
1943	41.8	**67**	23.1	32	15.7	17		
1944	48.9	**76**	20.5	30	8.7	8		
1948	41.9	68	19.8	31	8.7	14	(interparty)	
1951	46.3	**69**	25.8	40	11.4	16		
1954	43.4	65	32.0	50	12.1	19	(interparty)	
1957	48.3	**78**	26.6	40	9.1	12	5.4	4
1961	43.8	**70**	32.0	47	11.7	16	3.1	—
1965	47.7	**72**	34.1	47	15.4	22		
1969	44.6	**75**	33.3	50	16.6	18	(interparty)	
1973	46.2	69	35.1	54	13.7	19	1.1	—
1977	50.6	**84**	30.6	43	11.6	17	WP	
1981	45.3	78	36.5	**65**	9.9	**15**	1.7	1
1982 Feb.	47.3	**81**	37.3	63	9.1	15	2.2	3
1982 Nov.	45.2	75	39.2	**70**	9.4	**16**	3.3	2
1987	44.2	**81**	27.1	51	6.5	12	3.8	4 PD	11.9	14
1989	43.7	**77**	29.6	55	8.5	15	5.6	7 **PD**	5.0	6
1992	39.1	**68**	24.5	45	19.3	**33**	DL2.8	4 PD	4.7	10
1994	FG-Labour-DL (former WP) coalition							

Figures in bold print indicate parties in government.
CG: Cuman na nGaedheal; DL: Democratic Left; FF: Fianna Fail; FG: Fine Gael;
PD: Progressive Democrats; SF: Sinn Fein; WP: Workers' Party.
Source: Sinnott, 1995, pp. 299–305.

(1624). He was called to the Bar in 1595, was disbarred in 1598 for assault, but was readmitted after an apology in 1601 and was elected MP for Corfe Castle. Since Davies was a friend of Francis Bacon, James I obtained for him the position of solicitor general for Ireland in 1603 under Lord Mountjoy. Davies's correspondence to Sir Robert Cecil includes vivid accounts of prevailing famine and disease there, as well as expressions of optimism for the country's future. He was critical of the Protestant clergy, restored regular courts, and was praised by Arthur Chichester (q.v.) for his energy in traveling everywhere banishing Catholic priests. He was attorney general (1606–19) and left an account of the flight of the earls (q.v.) of Tyrone and Tyrconnel, whom he indicted, subsequently touring the escheated lands in Ulster in 1608 and setting up plantation commissions in 1608–10, for which he himself received a grant of land. The first plantation of Cavan (1610) was contested by the dispossessed, but Davies encouraged further Stuart plantations (q.v.) in Ulster. He represented Fermanagh and in 1613 he was elected speaker of the Irish parliament. He helped Sir Robert Cotton revive the Society of Antiquaries, to which he contributed several papers. From 1619 he undertook legal practice and was a judge in England, being appointed chief justice of England in November 1626, but dying a month later. His complete literary works were edited and published by A. B. Grosart in 1869–76, many of the original Irish letters being preserved in the Carte Mss in the Bodleian Library, Oxford.

DAVIS, THOMAS OSBORNE (1814–1845). Born in Mallow, Co. Cork, son of an army surgeon and an Irish mother. Educated in mathematics and history at Trinity College Dublin to 1836, he became a barrister in 1838 and was active in the College Historical Society, also writing for the *Citizen* magazine. He became one of the relatively few Protestant members of the Repeal Association in 1839, but allied himself with Young Ireland's more assertive outlook, as opposed to Daniel O'Connell's (qq.v.) constitutional approach. In 1840 he contributed to the Dublin *Morning Register,* which he briefly edited with J. B. Dillon. In 1842 with C. G. Duffy and John Dillon he founded *The Nation* (qq.v.) as the mouthpiece for radical nationalists. A member of the Royal Irish Academy (q.v.), he was also interested in art. Having begun to write a life of Wolfe Tone (q.v.), he died of fever in September 1845. His influence as a poet was acknowledged by Arthur Griffith (q.v.). *See also* Newspapers

DAVITT, MICHAEL (1846–1906). Son of a Mayo tenant farmer evicted in 1850, he joined the Fenians in 1865 and helped to organize the Irish (Revolutionary) Republican Brotherhood (q.v.). He was imprisoned from 1870 to 1877, and then went to America and collaborated with John Devoy (q.v.). He founded the Land League (q.v.) in 1879, advocating direct action by tenants to obtain the "three Fs" (fair rents, fixity of tenure, and freedom of sale) from the 1881 land act, personally favoring nationalization of land rather than peasant ownership. He was elected MP for North Meath (1892) and then for South Mayo (1895–99), after which he took to journalism. *See also* Land Acts

DECLARATORY ACT (6 Geo. I, c. 5). In April 1720 British supremacy over the Irish parliament was affirmed, and the Irish House of Lords was denied appeal status. The act revived Poynings's insistence that Irish legislation had to receive approval of the British parliament. Henry Grattan (q.v.) tried unsuccessfully to have it repealed in February 1782, but it was repealed on 21 June. Flood secured a concession that no such measures be introduced at a later date, a move which led to "Grattan's parliament," which lasted until the Act of Union in 1801. *See also* Poynings' Law; Union, Act of

DELARGY, JAMES HAMILTON (1899–1980). Born in Cushendall, Co. Antrim, but moved to Dublin where he graduated in Celtic Studies at University College (UCD), having assimilated much of the Irish oral tradition from holidays in Co. Antrim. As a lecturer at UCD, he founded and edited *Béaloideas* in 1927, became head of the Irish Folklore Commission (q.v.) in 1935, and Professor of Folklore (1946). The culmination of his work may be considered the creation of the Department of Irish Folklore at UCD (1977).

DEMOCRATIC LEFT. *See* WORKERS' PARTY

DEMOCRATIC UNIONIST PARTY (DUP). Founded in Northern Ireland in September 1971 by Rev. Ian Paisley (q.v.) from the Protestant Unionist Party, which he had started c. 1964, and by former Unionist MP Desmond Boal, both of whom opposed Northern Ireland Prime Minister Terence O'Neill's (q.v.) policy of reconciliation. In the 1970s, in partnership with other Unionists, the DUP opposed power sharing. Its support rose from 10 percent to over 25 percent at elections in the early 1980s, during which it rejected membership of the European Community, but supported the Assembly. At Westminster it has had three MPs since 1979 and in the European parliament one member. Fiercely protective of the constitutional link with Britain, it has consistently opposed the Anglo-Irish Agreement and the Downing Street Declaration (qq.v.).

DERRY/LONDONDERRY. The fortified town was built in 1610–18 on an elevated island site on the west shore of the river Foyle where a Columban monastic settlement had existed in the sixth century. Its original purpose was as a strong point and refuge for the settlers who came from England and Scotland during James I's plantation of west Ulster, and consequently it depended on maritime trade. The prefix *London* was added in recognition of the crucial role played by London livery companies in financing and organizing plantation settlement. Its Protestant cathedral dates from 1633. During the Williamite wars (1688–89), it withstood a Jacobite siege, earning itself the name of "the Maiden City."

The city's most famous industry was based on the linen market. At the beginning of the 19th century, most hand-loom weavers lived in the rural hinterland. With the introduction of mechanized factory weaving a severe crisis in employment was alleviated after 1850 by the expansion of shirt-making, to such an extent that a shortage of workers was experienced by the 1890s. Most were women and much of the sewing was done at home in places up to 50 kilometers distant from the finishing factories in the city itself. The dearth of employment opportunities for men hindered migration of complete families from the countryside of counties Donegal and Londonderry.

In 1830 a slipway was built for the repair and construction of wooden vessels made from local oak. Port and Harbor Commissioners, established by parliament in 1855, promoted developments, especially after 1865, but Biggar's shipyard closed in 1892. Reopening under new management in 1899, it suffered from the fact that hulls had to be fitted out on the rivers Clyde or Tyne and could not compete with Belfast (q.v.) shipyards. Trans-Atlantic commerce flourished, Derry also becoming a key emigrant port for North America in the later 19th century. With the subsequent collapse of both shipping and textile industries, and the demarcation of the post-1922 border between the Irish Free State and Northern Ireland, the whole locality suffered economic decline, high male unemployment, and acute social deprivation, which resulted in sectarian conflict. New industries began to emerge slowly in the 1960s after its designation as a growth center. From 1967 Magee College became part of the New University of Ulster. The city's population in 1991 was 72,300. *See also* Martha Maria Magee; Plantations; The Honourable the Irish Society

DERRYNAFLAN HOARD. Found in 1980 in a pit at a sixth-century monastic island site 13 kilometers southeast of Thurles, Co. Tipperary, the collection consists of very fine metalwork, including a chalice and paten, now in the National Museum (q.v.), Dublin. The most recent item has been dated to the ninth century A.D.

DE VALERA, EAMON (1882–1975). Born in New York (his father being a Spaniard), he was brought to Ireland in 1884 and was educated at Blackrock College and the National University of Ireland, from which he graduated in mathematics in 1904. He taught at Carysfort and Maynooth.

Traditionally regarded as a pivotal figure in the nationalist-republican movement, he joined the Irish Volunteers (q.v.) in 1913 and the Irish Republican Brotherhood as a commandant. He was one of the *Asgard* gun runners in 1914 and was active in the Easter Rising (q.v.). His resultant death sentence was commuted to life imprisonment, though he was released in 1917. He was elected republican MP for East Clare, became president of Sinn Fein (SF) with the support of Arthur Griffith (qq.v.), and was elected its MP for East Mayo in 1918 and first president of the Dáil (q.v.) in April 1919. From June 1919 to December 1920 he was in the United States, seeking financial and political support, with limited success. De Valera opposed the Anglo-Irish Treaty (q.v.), though the Dáil accepted it, and was replaced as president of the Provisional Government by Griffith. The June 1922 election confirmed popular support for the Treaty, but opposition insurgents occupied the Fourth Courts with de Valera's open support and were attacked by Provisional Government troops, giving rise to a civil war (q.v.) that lasted until 1923.

In April 1926 he formed Fianna Fail (q.v.), republicans having refused to swear the Oath of Allegiance since 1922, but acquiesced in parliamentary politics after the 1927 election. He set up *The Irish Press* newspaper in September 1931, became president of the Executive Council in 1932, though still in a minority, renounced the oath and provoked economic retaliation from Britain, remaining in office from 1933 to 1948. He framed the constitution in 1937, negotiated an economic truce by the Anglo-Irish Agreement (q.v.) of 1938, and interned IRA (q.v.) members during Ireland's World War II neutrality. With an election majority in 1957, he tried to abolish proportional representation, but the attempt was rejected by a referendum. He was effectively blind from 1952, was elected president of Ireland in 1959 and again in 1966–73, but with only a small majority. *See also* Newspapers

DEVON COMMISSION. Established on 20 November 1843 to investigate the land tenure (q.v.) system in Ireland, it reported in mid-February 1845, noting the plight of laborers and the benefits of "Ulster Custom." Ulster Custom was a tradition prevailing in the province, though not elsewhere in Ireland, that tenant farmers were given an option to renew their leases and were reimbursed by their successors for expenses incurred in making improvements to the farm during the tenancy. Its terms were broadly assimilated into the 1870 and 1881 Land Acts. The compensation it recommended for improvements was defeated in the House of Commons, and it became a mere prelude to more detailed land acts (q.v.) a generation later.

DEVOY, JOHN (1842–1928). Born in Co. Kildare, son of a smallholder, he joined the Fenians (q.v.) and later the French Foreign Legion. He was imprisoned in 1866–71, but was released on condition of living outside the UK. He went to America, led the anti-English Clan na Gael, and was ambivalent on the Invincibles' (qq.v.) murders of Cavendish and Burke in Phoenix Park. He set up the *Irish Nation* and *Gaelic American* newspapers and contributed funds to Arthur Griffith's *United Irishman* (qq.v.). In the Irish Volunteers, he split with Eamon de Valera (qq.v.) from 1919, but supported the Irish Free State after the 1921 Treaty.

DILLON, JOHN (1851–1927). Son of John Blake Dillon (q.v.), he qualified as a surgeon from the Catholic University. Elected MP for East Mayo, he joined O'Brien's "plan of campaign," supported the Land League, and led the anti-Parnell (qq.v.) movement after 1891, resigning in 1899 in favor of John Redmond (q.v.) until the latter's death in 1918. Following the defeat of the Irish Parliamentary Party (q.v.), he retired from politics.

DILLON, JOHN BLAKE (1816–66). Born in Co. Mayo. Educated first at Maynooth. He later studied mathematics and law at Trinity College Dublin, where he became a friend of Thomas Davis and C. G. Duffy. He was one of the founders of *The Nation* (qq.v.). He fled to France and then to America in 1848, after taking part in an abortive rising in Tipperary, though he had reacted against Mitchel's extremism and later that of the Fenians (qq.v.). He returned under the 1855 amnesty and became a Dublin alderman and prorepeal MP for Tipperary in 1865, but died of cholera the following year.

DISPENSARIES. Initially established by private contributions in the late 18th century to care for the health of the industrial poor by providing maternity facilities and promoting inoculation against epidemic diseases. In 1805 parliament authorized grand juries to supplement these private funds from the public purse, with the result that by 1851 every county had its own network of dispensaries, totaling 631 institutions throughout the country, to serve those communities remote from the 35 infirmaries, and 57 fever hospitals located in the main towns. *See also* Hospitals

DOWN SURVEY (CIVIL SURVEY). The survey was so named because the land measurements were "plotted down" in map form, as opposed to those of the simultaneous Civil Survey, which were merely tabulated. An outline in June 1653 was followed by detailed mapping by Sir William Petty (q.v.) in 1654 as the basis for confiscation and reallocation of land holdings after the rebellion of 1641 (q.v.).

DOWNING STREET DECLARATION (December 1993). A joint statement by the prime ministers of the UK and the Republic of Ireland (John Major and Albert Reynolds [q.v.]) on their approach to the political development of Northern Ireland (NI). The UK government pledged to uphold the democratic wish of the greater number of the people of NI on continued union with Britain or joining a sovereign united Ireland. It professed no selfish strategic interest in NI, saw its role as encouraging and facilitating agreement with full respect for the identities of both traditions, regarded self-determination as an issue for the people of Ireland in two parts, and agreed to legislate, if required. For its part, the Republic's government recognized the rights and wishes of NI people, sought self-determination by the people of Ireland as a whole, subject to the consent of an NI majority, upheld the right to equal economic and social opportunities, freedom of thought, and religion (q.v.), and aimed to achieve peaceful constitutional change through democratic institutions, undertaking to examine ways of removing obstacles.

DUBLIN. Capital and largest city of the Republic of Ireland; county borough with a population of 478,389 in 1991 and a further 546,915 residents in adjacent districts; major port on a wide bay at the mouth of the river Liffey on the fertile east coast, and longtime seat of administration for the island.

A Gaelic settlement situated at a ford (Baile Atha Cliath), serving major routeways, was developed by the Vikings from A.D. 841 as an increasingly important trading post and town. In the surrounding area Scandinavian rule was small scale, but dynastic and trading links extended Dublin's influence to northern England, and to York in particular. Partial Gaelicization occurred and brief alliances were made with Irish kings. At the battle of Clontarf near Dublin in 1014, Brian Boru (q.v.), king of Munster and high king, defeated a Leinster-Dublin force aided by Norse from the Isle of Man and the Orkneys. Despite this, Dublin prospered, having a mint and a cathedral (Christchurch, founded in 1038) within a town wall made of stone by c. 1100. The town was situated on a ridge at a harbor in a tributary of the Liffey known as Black Pool (Irish *Duibhlinn,* Norse *Dyfflin*). Dublin was captured in 1170 by an Anglo-Norman force soon after it arrived in support of the deposed Leinster king, Diarmuid MacMurrough (q.v.). Thereafter it was redeveloped by Bristol on behalf of Henry III of England as the center of administration for the lordship, due to its prominence and convenient location in relation to England and Wales. The walls were strengthened and later extended off the ridge toward the river. A stone castle was built at the harbor, and extramural areas were developed to the north across a bridge, rebuilt in 1214, where the Norse settled and the Cistercians had an abbey. To the south, it grew around a second cathedral, originally built as the collegiate church of St. Patrick by Archbishop Comyn in 1191, with other religious houses to the west and east. *See also* Viking Settlement

By the end of the 17th century medieval Dublin was rather decayed, but a new town was developed to the east on both sides of the Liffey under the strong support of the ascendancy (q.v.) parliament, which itself had a new building (now the Bank of Ireland headquarters) opposite the university, founded in 1592 on the site of an Augustinian priory. When the Irish parliament was closed by the Act of Union in 1801, this splendid era came to an abrupt end, but the streets and squares, with their parks, public and private buildings (including hospitals [q.v.], town houses of the nobility and merchants, courts of justice, and customs house) survived with varying degrees of success despite resulting economic decline that was exacerbated by Ireland's general social and political problems. Nonetheless, Dublin remained the preeminent city in Ireland, acquired another university college, and grew rapidly as the hub of the railway system in the 1840s, with important food-based industries, of which the Guinness' brewery (q.v.) is the best known. The city's population of 281,000 in 1841 increased to 381,000 by 1901, mainly as a consequence of suburban housing expansion while the core itself stagnated. *See also* Union, Act of; Railways

During the 1916 rising and in the subsequent civil war (q.v.), some damage was done to the center. Modern Dublin has remained a magnet for the rest of the republic, despite efforts at economic decentralization. The Dáil (q.v.), or parliament, meets at Leinster House (built by the earl of Kildare in 1745) and uses the restored state apartments of Dublin Castle for special functions. The former medieval city beside it was allowed to decay, but has been redeveloped recently. The city now has three separate universities (q.v.) and many other educational institutions, a thriving commercial heart, specialized industrial areas based on the port and outer suburbs, and satellite towns around earlier centers such as the outport of Dun Laoghaire. Libraries, museums, art galleries, and theaters provide cultural foci, while race courses and other sports venues attract events of local, national and international significance.

DUFFY, SIR CHARLES GAVAN (1816–1903). Born in Monaghan, the son of a shopkeeper and a farmer's daughter. After briefly attending a Presbyterian academy, he became a self-educated journalist on the *Northern Herald* in Belfast, advocating nonsectarian unity of Ireland. He moved to the Dublin *Morning Register* in 1836 and back to Belfast to the Catholic newspaper the *Vindicator* in 1839, when he also entered King's Inns. In 1841 he met Thomas Davis and John Blake Dillon (qq.v.) and from October 1842 became proprietor and editor of the weekly *Nation* as the organ of Young Ireland (qq.v.), with the aim of reestablishing an Irish parliament. He published *The Spirit of the*

Nation (1843) and *Ballad Poetry of Ireland* (1845), and he edited an inexpensive series entitled *Library of Ireland*.

He supported Daniel O'Connell (q.v.) in the aborted sedition trial of 1844, but they diverged over the Young Irelanders' support for Peel's Queen's University of Ireland and their denial of the adequacy of moral force alone. He formed the Irish Confederation (1847), but broke with John Mitchel (q.v.) over the tactic of a rent strike. Then he formed the Society of United Irishmen, which advocated an independent party to secure repeal, as opposed to Mitchel's scheme for a rebellion. Ironically, he was briefly detained after the 1848 plan for a rising, but then turned his efforts to land reform agitation and joined the Irish Tenant League to obtain the "three Fs" (fixity of tenure, fair rents, freedom for tenants to sell their interest in a holding). He became MP for New Ross at the 1852 election, in which nearly 40 percent of Irish members supported the league but failed to pursue it there. He was a staunch friend of Thomas Carlyle from 1845. *See also* Universities; United Irishmen, Society of

In October 1855 he emigrated to Australia, became a Melbourne barrister and minister of land and works, eventually rising to chief secretary (prime minister) of the state of Victoria in 1871–72. He was knighted in 1873 and was elected speaker of the Assembly (1876–80). He died in retirement in Nice, but was buried in Dublin. His books include *My Life in Two Hemispheres* (1898), *Young Ireland, a Fragment of Irish History, 1840–50* (2 vols., 1880–83), *The League of North and South: an Episode in Irish History, 1850–54* (1886), and *The Life of Thomas Davis* (1890).

Of his ten children from three marriages, two became well known in Ireland. George (1882–1951) defended Sir Roger Casement, was elected to the Dáil (1918–23), served briefly as Sinn Fein (qq.v.) representative in Paris (1919–20), and was a signatory to the Treaty in 1921. He was Irish Free State minister for foreign affairs in 1922, and a judge and president of the High Court (1936–46). Louise (1884–1969) took part in the 1916 Easter Rising in Cumann na mBan (qq.v.) and was later prominent in the Irish language education movement.

-E-

EASTER RISING (24 April–1 May 1916). While planned by the Irish (Revolutionary) Republican Brotherhood (q.v.) Military Council, the leader of the Volunteers, Eoin MacNeill (qq.v.), was not informed. There ensued a clash with Patrick Pearse (q.v.), who was under the impression that arms smuggled by the yacht *Aud* would guarantee success. In the event Sir Roger Casement (q.v.) was captured, and the *Aud* was scuttled. Despite MacNeill's orders, Pearse proceeded with a rising of about 1,500 Volunteers and 220 of Connolly's Irish Citizen Army (q.v.), settling in the General Post Office (GPO) building, from which Pearse declared in high-flown verbiage the formation of a Provisional Government of a sovereign independent republic. The declaration, incorporating the right to ownership of land, religious and civil liberty, equal rights and opportunities to all citizens, was signed by T. J. Clarke, Sean MacDiarmada, Thomas MacDonagh, Pearse, Ceannt, Connolly, and Plunkett. The insurgents took over the Four Courts, Royal College of Surgeons, several factories, railway stations, and the City Hall briefly. British reinforcements arrived from the Curragh, Belfast, and Athlone, the city center north of the river Liffey being cordoned off during Tuesday and Wednesday (April 25–26). On the Thursday the British mounted a heavy attack on the GPO building and the Four Courts, and the following day when the British commander, Sir John Maxwell, arrived the GPO was evacuated by Pearse. On 29 April Pearse surrendered unconditionally from the Moore Street pocket. Martial law was proclaimed, and courts martial were set up. Fifteen rebels were executed between 3 May and 12 May, and Casement was executed in August. Other capital sentences (97) were commuted to life imprisonment, all prisoners being amnestied by July 1917.

ECCLESIASTICAL ORGANIZATION. 1. Dioceses: the Celtic church (q.v.) had no formal territorial structure, as in the pattern of medieval parishes, but focused on monastic nuclei. Extensive territorial organization may date from Synod of Raith Bressail's (1111) 24 dioceses and the Synod of Kells' (1152) four archbishoprics at Armagh, Cashel, Dublin, and Tuam. Later, 31 dioceses functioned for the Roman Catholic Church (26 from 1968)—nine in Armagh province, seven in Cashel, six in Tuam, and four in Dublin—and 33 for the Church of Ireland (q.v.). The latter is administered by a general synod whose clerical and lay members are elected every three years. Since 1838–39 it has comprised a northern province, currently with eight bishoprics, north of a line from Dublin to Galway Bay, and a southern province with six bishoprics, the two archdioceses being Armagh and Dublin, respectively. In recent times some ancient dioceses have merged.

2. Ecclesiastical parishes date from the Anglo-Norman era, but always possessed far less real significance than in England because of the more dispersed form of settlement and greater mobility of population prevalent in early Ireland, as well as the fact that the vast majority of the population later were not communicants of the Established Church. Administratively, their functions were also complicated by the different structures established by the Church of Ireland and the Roman Catholic Church after the Reformation, so that the

two sets of boundaries seldom coincided exactly. Other nonconformist Protestant churches do not operate on such a distinct territorial basis.

After a division in the Church of Scotland in the 18th century, two seceders' synods were established in Ireland, reuniting in 1818. From 1840 the Ulster and seceding synods in Ireland combined under a single Presbyterian general assembly as its governing body with headquarters in Belfast. Its moderators are elected annually. The Methodist Church in Ireland has an annual conference of 250 representatives who elect a president; both the president and the conference are subordinate to the British Methodist conference, of which he is vice president. *See also* Religion

ECONOMY. Since independence it has been the policy of the Irish government to promote the agricultural sector, which accounted for half of total employment in the Irish Free State and 90 percent of its exports. In the general absence of large-scale, concentrated industrial raw materials or energy resources, markets for produce were essential. Yet in the 1920s and 1930s the Fianna Fail governments retreated into traditional nationalist protectionism for ideological reasons. The Tariff Commission (1926) greatly increased the number of restricted goods from 1932 to 1937, resulting in mutual retaliation measures with the UK until the 1938 Trade Agreement. Control of Manufactures Acts (1932–34) placed new firms under majority Irish control. Manufacturing declined during World War II, despite neutrality. There followed a short boom, which gave way to crisis in the 1950s, leading to high unemployment and emigration. The Department of Finance (1958) *Programme for Economic Expansion (1959–63)* favored more outward-looking policies regarding manufacturing investment and export promotion. A second program (1964–70) was replaced by a third (1969–72), which reduced tariffs and relied heavily on the Anglo-Irish Free Trade Agreement of 1965. European Community (EC) membership, effective from 1 January 1973, was approved by 83 percent of the voters in a referendum. Ireland joined the European Monetary System in 1979, though it remained closely tied to fluctuations in the UK economy. The 1985–87 Economic and Social Plan aimed at holding unemployment at about 210,000, keeping the service sector steady at about 50 percent of GDP, and reducing the primary sector in favor of manufacturing. In January 1976 the total unemployed reached 116,366, the highest since 1940. In January 1993 it exceeded 300,000 for first time. Initially, a prominent role for state bodies had been considered a realistic means of allocating scarce investment, e.g. Electricity Supply Board (1927) (q.v.), Cement (1933), Bord na Mona (1946) (q.v.), and Bord Gáis Éireann (1975) to market Kinsale gas. Public sector involvement was relaxed in the 1980s, partly in response to EC requirements.

From 1926 to 1961 the total number gainfully employed fell, and the number in agriculture declined from 51 percent to 36 percent of the total gainfully employed, although in 1982 Ireland still had twice the EC average rate employed in agriculture, at 17 percent. Between 1971 and 1981 the total labor force aged 15 and over increased by 13 percent (males by 9 percent and females by 24 percent), i.e., at a slower rate than the aggregate population growth (16%).

Table 2
Republic of Ireland: Employment by Sector, 1926–81

Year	Primary	Secondary	Tertiary	Total Employed
	%	%	%	
1926	53.6	12.8	33.6	1,220,284
1936	49.9	16.1	34.0	1,235,424
1946	47.1	16.6	36.3	1,227,745
1951	41.5	22.1	36.4	1,219,722
1961	36.9	23.5	39.6	1,052,539
1971	26.9	29.6	43.5	1,054,839
1981	17.4	30.8	51.8	1,134,798

Source: Gillmor 1985, p. 31.

Table 3
Republic of Ireland Labor Force: Occupation Groups by Region, 1981

Region	Total Labor	Agric.	Pro-ducers	Clerical	Com-merce	Serv-ice	Prof./tech.	Unempl.
		%	%	%	%	%	%	%
East	501,692	4.1	22.9	16.0	11.4	8.9	14.2	1.3
SW	188,537	18.8	24.2	8.6	10.6	7.1	11.5	1.6
SE	132,819	22.3	25.3	7.7	10.2	6.3	10.2	1.8
NE	71,118	21.4	27.0	8.1	9.8	6.0	9.7	1.6
Midwest	110,986	21.3	23.4	8.7	9.5	6.7	11.0	1.5
Donegal	41,831	22.7	23.5	5.8	8.6	6.5	9.1	3.0
Midlands	91,310	27.0	23.7	6.9	9.2	5.7	9.8	1.6
West	101,866	29.8	19.2	7.0	9.0	6.0	12.3	2.3
NW	30,963	29.5	20.6	7.0	9.0	6.3	11.4	1.6
Ireland	1,271,122	15.6	23.3	11.0	10.4	7.4	12.2	1.6

Source: Population Census of Ireland, 1981, vol. 7, Dublin, 1986.

Such general shifts reflect more detailed changes in specific occupation groups, and, given the contrasting levels of income, age, and gender composition associated with them, another concern is their varying spatial distribution throughout the country. The Eastern Planning Region held 39 percent of the total, and its composition was very different from that of any other region, especially in its low proportion in agriculture, forestry, and fishing, together with above-average shares in clerical, professional/technical, and commercial/service sectors. During 1971–81 the total numbers in agriculture declined by 31 percent, in leather working by 34 percent, in textiles and clothing by 17 percent. Laborers and unskilled declined by 16 percent. Conversely, male-dominated occupations of administration and management, electrical/electronics, building and construction, and engineering increased by 95 percent, 80 percent, 60 percent, and 49 percent, respectively. The 50-percent gain in professional and technical occupations was almost equally divided between males and females.

Nevertheless, Ireland has experienced low ranking within EC comparisons on incomes, per capita GDP, with only one-third of the population actually employed, a low economic activity rate (52%), and a high rate of natural population increase. All of these factors have been recognized by large EC subventions for infrastructural projects from its Agricultural, Social, Structural, and Regional Funds. *See also* European Union

EDGEWORTH, MARIA (1767–1849). Born in Oxfordshire, but moved with her father to his Edgeworthstown estate, Co. Longford, in 1782, the year in which the Irish parliament obtained the right to independent legislation. During a long literary life she wrote *Letters for Literary Ladies* (1795), children's stories *The Parent's Assistant* (1796), and *Moral Tales* (1801). Her best-known humorous novel was *Castle Rackrent, an Hibernian Tale, taken from facts and from the manners of the Irish squires before the year 1782* (1800). It influenced Sir Walter Scott, whom she met in 1823, to compose *Waverley* as a historical novel or a fictional social history. Her other novels, some of which dealt with Irish themes, included *Tales of Fashionable Life* (1809–12), *Belinda* (1801), *Leonora* (1806), *Harrington* and *Ormond* (1817), and *Helen* (1834).

EDGEWORTH, RICHARD LOVELL (1744–1817). An acquaintance of the scientists Joseph Banks, Erasmus Darwin, and Humphrey Davy. With James Watt and Josiah Wedgwood, he was a member of the Lunar Society of Birmingham, which was influential in Industrial Revolution developments, and a Fellow of the Royal Society. Educated at Trinity College Dublin and Oxford, he was elected to the Irish parliament in 1798. On returning to his Irish estates, he became involved in projects for the exploitation of peat resources, railway and road building (in which he may have anticipated Macadam), and balloon flight. Of his 22 children from four marriages, four died in infancy; his eldest daughter Maria completed the *Memoirs of Richard Lovell Edgeworth* after his death. His fourth wife, Frances Anne, was a daughter of Dr. Daniel Beaufort (q.v.).

EDUCATION. Despite the theoretical provision of English-language parochial and diocesan schools under Tudor Reformation legislation of 1537 (28 Hen. VIII, c. 15) and 1570 (12 Eliz. I, c. 1), by the early 19th century there were only about 37,000 pupils in 1,200 such schools in Ireland. Under the Ulster plantation, Protestant free grammar schools were established in each of the six counties by the 1620s, supplemented in the following century by voluntary charity (charter) schools that received royal and parliamentary support via their governing societies. Although they admitted Roman Catholic children, all these institutions were denounced by the Catholic clergy, and their educational impact was minimal. Renewed interest in a countrywide, nondenominational system of parish schools was promoted by Fitzherbert's parliamentary enquiry into endowed schools in Ireland. Though never published, the radical report of 1791 provided the foundation of the report produced by the British education commission (1806–12), finding practical expression in Ireland in 1816 in a parliamentary grant to the Kildare Place Society (q.v.). Until the appearance of National schools in 1831, some Catholic children received informal instruction in hedge schools (q.v.).

The Intermediate Education Act (1878) set up the Board for Secondary Education, ultimately abolished by Saorstat Eireann in 1923, while the 1926 Intermediate Education (Amendment) Act placed secondary education under a ministry, substituting junior, middle, and senior examination grades with an Intermediate Certificate for pupils aged 12–16 and a Leaving Certificate at 17–18, covering five basic subjects, including Irish. Following the recommendations of the 1926 commission, the Vocational Education Act (1930) was framed to oversee continued education beyond the age of 14. Local area committees administered about 300 vocational schools for two-year full-time courses with varying curricula to meet specific local needs, e.g., Junior Rural, Domestic Science, Technical, or Commercial schools, leading to the award of a Vocational Certificate after public examination under the ministry/department of education. One enduring difficulty for a minority was that few Protestant schools existed south of a line from Dublin to

Sligo, necessitating boarding facilities or high travel costs for children seeking a nonstate education.

The Commission on Higher Education (1960–67) established the National Science Council in 1968 which was intended to provide development advice, part of the strategy for advancing scientific and technological training being the creation of five Regional Technical Colleges and the National Institute of Higher Education at Limerick in 1972. *See also* Universities; Plantations

ELECTRICITY SUPPLY BOARD (ESB). Created under the Electricity Supply Act (May 1927) to absorb the large number of small local enterprises and supply the whole country, whenever possible, from indigenous resources. Water power was regarded as particularly significant, especially the Shannon hydroelectric station at Ardnacrusha, which became operative from 1929 under the Shannon Electricity Act (1925). Peat from Bord Na Mona (q.v.) was used as an import substitute for coal, but rural electrification was only completed in the thirty years between 1946 and the late 1970s.

EMERGENCY. In January 1940 a state of emergency was declared under the Offences against the State (June 1939) and Emergency Powers (September 1939) Acts to combat IRA (q.v.) activity that had begun in 1939 in the context of Ireland's neutrality during World War II. A blind eye was turned to British activity, but German agents were interned and their attempts to link up with the IRA were dealt with severely; 600 people were imprisoned, 500 interned, and six executed under the Emergency Powers and Treason (May 1939) Acts. Several provisions were retained under the Emergency Powers Act (September 1976 to 1994), introduced after the IRA murdered Christopher Ewart-Biggs, the British ambassador to Ireland. The Act increased penalties and gave wide powers to the Garda Siochana, but some provisions were soon repealed. In Northern Ireland the Special Powers Act (1956), introduced to combat IRA terrorism, contained far-reaching powers to order searches, internment without trial, and trial by non-jury (Diplock) courts, comparable with the Offences against the State Act in the Republic of Ireland. This legislation had to be debated for renewal by the Westminster parliament every five years until January 1996, when it was renewed for only a two-year period.

EMIGRATION. Although evident earlier, since the famines (q.v.) of 1845–49, emigration has served as a safety valve for pressures created by poverty and lack of opportunity within Ireland, its scale fluctuating with conditions at home and abroad. Passenger data from Irish ports have been collected since 1825, and statistics on travelers to the UK exist for 1852–1921 and 1939–52. Seasonal migration of male harvesters from Connacht and west Ulster to Scotland and England dovetailed two contrasting agricultural systems into an integrated labor regime. Having experienced alternative lifestyles and places, some migrants embarked on permanent moves to British industrial districts and created Irish communities in Glasgow, Liverpool, South Wales, London, and Tyneside. It has been estimated that in 1881 the number of Irish-born persons living abroad represented 60 percent of those in Ireland. After unfavorable circumstances during the 1930s economic depression, the decreasing trend of migration to Britain was reversed after World War II, but its regional orientation changed as English destinations appeared more attractive than Scottish ones in recent decades.

Table 4
Irish-Born Population of Great Britain, 1841–1991

Year	England & Wales	Scotland	Total GB
1841	289,404 (1.8%)	126,321 (4.8%)	415,725
1851	519,959 (2.9%)	207,367 (7.2%)	727,326
1861	601,634 (3.0%)	204,083 (6.7%)	805,717
1871	566,540 (2.5%)	207,770 (6.2%)	774,130
1881	562,374 (2.2%)	218,745 (5.9%)	781,119
1891	458,315 (1.6%)	194,807 (4.8%)	653,122
1901	426,565 (1.3%)	205,064 (4.6%)	631,629
1911	375,325 (1.0%)	174,715 (3.7%)	550,040
1921	364,747 (1.0%)	159,020 (3.3%)	523,767
1931	381,089 (0.9%)	124,296 (2.6%)	505,385
1951	627,021 (1.4%)	89,007 (1.7%)	716,028
1961	644,398 (1.4%)	(no data)	644,398+
1971	584,560 (1.2%)	31,260 (0.6%)	615,820
1981	579,833 (1.2%)	27,018 (0.5%)	606,851
1991	569,247 (1.1%)	22,773 (0.5%)	592,020

Source: J. A. Jackson, *The Irish in Britain* 1963, 11; *Censuses of Great Britain,* 1961–91. These figures exclude persons declaring themselves born in Northern Ireland, of whom there were over 0.24 million at each of the last four censuses.

In 1841–1925, 5.8 million Irish people went overseas, 4.7 million of them to the United States. A quota for the Irish Free State was fixed at 28,567 in1924 and at 17,853 in 1929, but it was never filled. Emigration streams often contained unusually high proportions of females and exceeded males in 1891–1921, when two-thirds of all emigrants were aged 20–24. In the period 1924–39, 68 percent of male emigrants were agricultural and construction laborers, while 64 percent of females belonged to the personal service category, reflecting the unskilled or semiskilled nature of the underlying demand.

Table 5
Irish Emigration, 1841–1960

	Total*	to USA**
1841–50	780,719	
1851–60	1,163,418	914,119
1861–70	849,836	435,778
1871–80	623,933	436,871
1881–90	770,706	655,482
1891–1900	433,526	388,416
1901–10	346,024	339,065
1911–20	150,756	146,181
1921–30	220,591	
1931–40	13,167	
1941–50	26,967	
1951–60	57,332	

Source: *Vaughan and Fitzpatrick, *Irish Historical Statistics,* pp. 261–63; **Hickey and Doherty, *A Chronology of Irish History since 1800,* p. 153.

Table 6
Emigration from Ireland by Province of Origin

	Connacht	Leinster	Munster	Ulster
1851–60	138,059	235,460	434,338	341,261
1861–70	113,676	149,838	304,105	201,240
1871–80	86,551	110,619	181,370	240,110
1881–90	161,219	138,282	252,080	216,524
1891–1900	117,750	49,552	177,236	86,455
1901–10	84,960	42,638	110,903	106,587
1911–20	33,605	22,952	36,221	57,978

Source: Vaughan and Fitzpatrick, *Irish Historical Statistics,* pp. 344–53; *Report of the Commission on Emigration and Population,* Dublin, 1954.

EMMET, ROBERT (1778–1803). A Dublin-born friend of Tom Moore at Trinity College Dublin, which he was obliged to leave in February 1798 on account of his links with the United Irishmen (q.v.). On his return to Ireland from France in 1802 he assembled arms in anticipation of a supportive French invasion. After an abortive rising in July, he was caught, tried, and executed in September.

EUROPEAN UNION (EU). In 1972 the Republic of Ireland held a referendum to ascertain opinion concerning entry to the European Community (EC). In a 71 percent turnout, 83 percent of those who voted were in favor. Ireland's accession to the Treaty of Rome took effect from 1 January 1973, when the UK also became a member. The Republic of Ireland sends 15, and Northern Ireland three, members (MEPs) to the European parliament. *See also* Referenda

Since joining the EC, Ireland has appointed seven commissioners, the first being P. J. Hillery (q.v.) (1973–76), formerly the Fianna Fail foreign minister at the time of Ireland's application for EC membership and later president of the Republic. Like two of his successors, Peter Sutherland (1985–88) and Padraig Flynn (1993–), he was given special responsibility for social affairs. Another commissioner, Ray MacSharry (1989–93), also a former Fianna Fail TD and MEP in 1984–87, held the agriculture and rural development portfolio, which was of equal concern to Ireland. In view of Ireland's special conditions a transition period offered some protection for specific economic sectors until tariffs could be removed without severe adverse consequences.

In 1987 a referendum on acceptance of the Single European Act met with only a turnout of 44 percent and a positive response of 70 percent to measures that removed remaining obstacles to open economic interaction between member states.

The third phase of Ireland's full incorporation began in 1992 when another referendum approved ratification of the (Maastricht) Treaty of European Union, which came into effect in November 1993. On that occasion public interest was again fairly low (57%) and the yes vote reached 69 percent.

Throughout Ireland's relationship with the EC ambivalent attitudes have existed among and within its political parties, while the average citizen tends to demote European issues to lower priority than national ones. Only when these apparently divergent concerns come together has popular awareness been raised. Initially, three areas of debate emerged: (1) institutional matters, such as the use of qualified majority voting in the European Council of Ministers (which was opposed by the Labour Party [q.v.]); (2) the impact of EC membership on Ireland's policy of neutrality; and (3) the effects of the Common Agricultural Policy (CAP) on the country's large farming sector and community.

The formal concern, paramount in 1972, was the existence of Article 15 in the Irish Constitution, which declared the Oireachtas (i.e., the Dáil and the Senate) as "the sole and exclusive power of making laws for the state." Despite their historical roots and essential conservatism, the two main parties were broadly for the European movement, whereas the Labour Party was against. At the 1987 referendum Labour and the trades unions reversed their former opposition to Europe, whereas it is believed that rural Fianna Fail supporters, who had previously been enthusiastic toward the potential gains from the CAP, had now become disillusioned and abstained in large numbers. By 1992, against a background of deep divisions over ratification of the Maastricht Treaty in Denmark and France, an all-party yes campaign in Ireland comfortably won the day, partly on the basis of acceptance of the principle of subsidiarity, which favored greater devolution of decision making to national parliaments. *See also* Constitution

Positions adopted by the main political parties in the Republic of Ireland have varied, though usually only in emphasis rather than principle. Fianna Fail presented itself generally as the most traditionalist group and drew much of its electoral support from rural constituencies. Consequently, it was marginally more cautious on European legislation that might infringe Irish identity, while eager to obtain safeguards for agriculture and related industries. Fine Gael, closer to the center of a political spectrum, stood on a more progressive social platform. From 1977 it was distinctly pro-European under Garret FitzGerald (q.v.), the party opting for articulate MEP candidates while firmly advocating protection of Irish interests. As in Britain in the 1970s, the Labour Party appeared on balance to be curiously reluctant to embrace wider principles and affiliations. However, by the 1980s it too had shifted in a convergence toward positive reception of EC ideas. The net result of subtle adjustments in party attitudes and the electorate's reaction to perceived trends in both policy and material benefits from Europe was that over the years 1979–94 the Fianna Fail share of the vote in European parliamentary contests declined markedly, while the fortunes of the smaller groups — Labour, Workers' Party/Democratic Left, and the Greens — improved.

There is little doubt that pragmatic considerations played a significant part in determining the outcome of such debates. The issues facing the Irish economy (q.v.) have been caused by locational peripherality in the EC, suboptimal infrastructure, and low population density. Irish representatives, often alongside their counterparts from Northern Ireland, have therefore sought to maximize the net gains available through European structural funds. Under revised funding levels and guidelines, from 1989 Ireland was identified as a priority region for receipt of financial support to promote development with the aim of reducing the disparity between its status and average conditions in the EC. A coordinated strategy was devised between the European Commission and the Irish government in the form of a 1989–93 *National Development Plan*. Of a total estimated expenditure of IR£9,500 million, some IR£3,200 million (34%) was to be provided from the EC via its Regional Development, Social, and Agricultural Funds. While some benefits are already visible, e.g., partial improvements in the road and rail networks, it is too early to assess the overall effect of the program. For the remainder of the 1990s a new *National Development Plan* is being compiled that will have to take into account greater central support for the poorest EU members and a lower share of the EU budget devoted to the CAP, both of which will have consequences for Ireland.

EVICTIONS OF TENANTS. Famine reduced the population (qq.v) significantly in the later 1840s and thereby eased the problem of land shortage to some extent, but simultaneously produced a deep sense of bitterness toward the government in general and also the attitudes of particular landlords. An immediate source of resentment was landlords' eviction of tenants unable to pay rent and demolition of their cottages. Ejectments supervised by the local constabulary peaked in 1849 (13,194) and 1850 (14,336), followed by sharp reductions over the next three years.

Table 7
Evictions of Tenants, 1846–87

1846–49	37,286
1850–59	38,639
1860–69	8,011
1870–79	5,668
1880–87	27,655

Source: Vaughan, *Landlords and Tenants in Mid-Victorian Ireland,* 1994, 230–37. Data in Hickey and Doherty are incomplete and grossly inflated for 1849–67.

Doubt exists as to the precise reliability of constabulary data due to discrepancies between ejectment decrees obtained and their actual enforcement, often as low as 7 to 10 percent. Of those allegedly evicted, in the 1850s large numbers were in fact readmitted, especially in 1849–53, and not all were removed for nonpayment of rent. The highest rates of eviction per 1,000 holdings were experienced in counties Mayo, Galway, Tipperary, Kerry, Meath, and Longford. During an upsurge in the 1880s, twice as many urban tenants were evicted as others, so that some figures are not directly relevant to the land question. In 1852 the MP for Trinity College Dublin, Joseph Napier, introduced land bills in the House of Commons, but they failed when Lord Derby's government fell. Following Sir J. C. Mathew's commission on evicted tenants (Oct. 1892–Feb. 1893), Chief Secretary Morley introduced an evicted tenants bill in April 1893, but it failed to gain a second reading in the Commons in August. Not until Birrell's Evicted Tenants Act (7 Edw. VII., c. 56) in 1907 did legislation enable land to be compulsorily purchased for them, with Congested Districts Board (q.v.) grants to reinstate them.

-F-

FAIR EMPLOYMENT AGENCY (COMMISSION). Under the terms of the Fair Employment (Northern Ireland) Act, effective from 31 December 1989, a code of practice was issued to supersede that introduced by an Act of 1976 bearing the same title. It established a new Fair Employment Commission to promote equality of opportunity and, where necessary, affirmative action to eliminate religious discrimination and to monitor employment recruitment practices in private and public sector enterprises with more than 25 employees (from 1992, enterprises with more than ten employees). All such employers are obliged by law to register with the Commission and to cooperate with its investigative procedures, e.g., by providing annual returns of the religious composition of their workforce on the basis of individual written enquiries.

Simultaneously, a tribunal was authorized to investigate specific complaints of breaches of the legislation. If the tribunal finds that an employer has practiced discrimination, it is empowered to award compensation to the victim(s) and to impose legal and economic sanctions against the offending party. Under the Disabled Persons (Employment) Acts and the Sex Discrimination (Northern Ireland) Orders of 1976 and 1988, similar requirements govern access to jobs by persons who are, respectively, either registered disabled or married females. Provision of equal pay and other benefits between genders is safeguarded under legislation passed in 1970 and 1984 and is monitored by the Equal Opportunities Commission.

FAMINES. Periodic food deficits were characteristic of Ireland, as of other peasant farming regimes in Europe, due to adverse seasonal weather conditions, wartime destruction, or crop and animal pests and diseases. Widespread shortages were experienced in 1662, 1727–29, 1739–41, 1800, and 1821–22.

From September 1845 the fungus *Phytophthora infestans,* transmitted by potatoes imported from the United States via the Low Countries, had a devastating effect on the crop, which accounted for about one-third of cultivated land in Ireland. In November the British Tory Prime Minister Peel authorized imports of Indian corn (maize) to combat famine when repeal of the Corn Laws failed. Lord John Russell's new Whig government introduced a relief employment program in March 1846, but C. E. Trevelyan sought to have the financial burden carried by landlords instead of by the state. Grain prices were forced up by demand in Europe, rents remained unpaid, evictions of tenants (q.v.) ensued, and the Poor Law and Board of Works (q.v.) found itself unable to cope with the scale of the crisis. Grain depots were opened to sell food at market prices, while charitable relief organizations funded local schemes, e.g. the Society of Friends (Quakers) under W. E. Forster (q.v.) and J. H. Tuke (q.v.) in November 1846. The Temporary Relief of the Destitute Persons (Ireland) Act operated via workhouses, but public works were run down, and widespread outbreaks of typhus, relapsing fever, oedema (dropsy), and scurvy occurred. The Board of Health was active through its fever hospitals from February 1847 to August 1850, the Irish Fever Act (10 Vict., c. 22) giving responsibility to relief committees with government funds. The Destitute Poor (Ireland) Act (10 Vict., c. 7) opened soup kitchens that fed up to three million people, and an estimated 0.75 million survived only on outdoor relief. *See also* Poor Law Commission; Hospitals

Despite another low yield in 1847, Russell insisted on collection of the poor rate. Lord lieutenant Clarendon was unable to secure more treasury finance, and the Crime and Outrage (Ireland) Act was passed in December 1847, following J. F. Lalor's (q.v.) advocacy of independence by force. The murder of Strokestown landowner Major Mahon and the increasing violence of Young Irelanders and the Irish Confederation under W. S. O'Brien and T. F. Meagher (qq.v.) led to the Treason Felony Act and suspension of the Habeus Corpus Act in 1848, as well as the arrest and trial of leading agitators. The Encumbered Estates Acts were introduced in 1848–49 to sell bankrupt properties. Cholera broke out between November 1848 and July 1849. The net result was that the island's population of 8,175,124 in 1841 declined to 6,552,385 in 1851 by a surplus of deaths over births and emigration (q.v.), initiating a trend that lasted for a century. *See also* Population

FAULKNER, BRIAN ARTHUR DEANE (1921–77). After a varied career in business and Unionist politics he was Northern Ireland's last prime minister (1971–72) and head of its only power-sharing administration (1974). He was elected to Stormont (q.v.) as MP for East Down in 1949. As a minister, he dealt with the IRA's 1959 border campaign and with new industrial development. He was responsible for introducing internment without trial in 1971 and saw the Stormont parliament closed in the violent aftermath. He failed to retain the support of most Unionists after 1974 and left politics with a life peerage in 1977; he died soon after in a riding accident.

FENIANISM. *See* IRISH (REVOLUTIONARY) REPUBLICAN BROTHERHOOD

FERGUSON, HARRY GEORGE (1884–1960). Born in Hillsborough, Co. Down, garage proprietor, inventor, and pioneer of monoplane flight in the *Bleriot,* he designed a tractor and entered into partnership with Henry Ford in 1939.

FERGUSON, SIR SAMUEL (1810–86). Born in Belfast, of Scots Presbyterian ancestry, educated at the Royal Belfast Academical Institution and Trinity College Dublin, but moved to London without taking a degree. As an outspoken cultural nationalist, during the 1840s he supported the future Young Irelanders Charles Gavan Duffy and William Smith O'Brien (qq.v.) in their efforts to restore an independent Irish parliament, but declined to write for *The Nation* and refused to take part in what he regarded as a social class war.

After his marriage to a member of the Guinness family, he withdrew from active political involvement and settled for a career as a barrister and judge, defending some of the 1848 activists against illogical charges of treason, arguing that they were merely opposing misrule in Ireland. In 1867 he was appointed Deputy Keeper of Public Records of Ireland, and he secured acceptance of the need for efficient and centralized preservation of all historical documents relating to Ireland. He strongly supported compilation of the Ordnance Survey (q.v.) Memoirs, initiated by Thomas Larcom (q.v.) as comprehensive sources of information on natural phenomena, landscape antiquities, local history, and folklore. As an amateur archeologist he corresponded with George Petrie (q.v.), and from 1863 made a particular study of fourth- to seventh-century Ogham-inscribed stones on the basis of extensive fieldwork, photography, and careful transcription, contributing papers to the *Proceedings of the Royal Irish Academy* from 1864 to 1878, which culminated in posthumous publication of his *Ogham Inscriptions in Ireland, Wales and Scotland* (1887). Having acquired a knowledge of modern Irish in the 1830s, he translated Irish literature and wrote poetry, often based on Irish mythology, publishing *Lays of the Western Gael* (1864). Though politically a unionist, within the civil service he insisted on a knowledge of the Irish language (q.v.) for entry into certain grades, a requirement that lasted for over a century. He was knighted in 1878, and in 1882 was elected president of the Royal Irish Academy (q.v.), for which he had been instrumental in obtaining government grants.

FIANNA FAIL (FF). A major political party in the Republic of Ireland, it originated as the abstentionist anti-Treaty wing of old Sinn Fein (q.v.) in 1921. Founded on 16 May 1926 by Eamon de Valera and Sean Lemass (qq.v.) as The Republican Party, its main objectives have been reunification (implicit in clauses 2 and 3 of the 1937 constitution [q.v.]), support for the Irish language (q.v.), land redistribution, protectionism, and economic self-sufficiency. Its members joined the Dáil on 11 August 1927 and set up *The Irish Press* in 1931. *See also* Newspapers

FF first held power under de Valera's leadership in 1932 and was the governing party from March 1932 to February 1948, and again in 1951–54, 1957–73, 1977–82, and 1987–94, usually without the need for a coalition. Once in office its policy was to undermine the Treaty settlement, while internally enacting a series of modest social welfare policies, though under stress because of Ireland's economic weakness in an era of global protectionism. To many, the 1937 constitution characterized the party's inherently cautious reaction to any notion of radical social change, while paying lip service to unattainable territorial goals. The government adopted a neutral stance in World War II, but its failure to achieve significant economic development in the 1950s was offset in practice by close dependence on Britain and freedom of movement between the two countries, which alleviated Irish unemployment. The cycle of stagnation was broken during Lemass's less ideological leadership, following the retirement of de Valera in 1959.

Lemass's successor, Jack Lynch (q.v.), achieved electoral gains that were overshadowed by the alleged involvement of two cabinet ministers, C. J. Haughey (q.v.) and Neil Blaney, in smuggling arms into Northern Ireland in 1970. Again the party fractured. Erratic economic policy and moral conservatism typified Haughey's abrasive administrations in the 1980s. He was forced to resign the party leadership in January 1992 and was replaced by former finance minister Albert Reynolds (q.v.), who was himself forced out in 1994 in the aftermath of judicial controversies and allegations of the government's knowledge of corrupt business deals.

British withdrawal from Northern Ireland has been a constant policy aim, although this was meant to be achieved by persuasion. Although not happy with the 1985 Anglo-Irish Agreement (q.v.), the party administered it when in government and, in a brief coalition with the Labour Party, produced the Downing Street Declaration (qq.v.) in December 1993.

FIELD, JOHN (1782–1837). Son of a Dublin theater violinist and grandson of an organist, under whom he received his early musical education, making his public debut as a pianist at the Rotunda in February 1792 at the age of nine. In 1793 the family moved to London, where he performed in a concert for the benefit of distressed Spitalfields weavers. For the years 1793–1800 he was apprenticed to Clementi, with whom he embarked on a continental tour that included concerts in Paris, Vienna, and St. Petersburg in 1802–3. In Russia his expressive keyboard playing brought immediate success in fashionable circles, and he quickly established an independent career as a performer, teacher, and composer. He married Adelaide Percheron, a former pupil, and in 1821 moved to Moscow. Over the next decade he suffered increasingly from alcoholism and cancer, traveling to London for treatment in 1831. During a subsequent European tour he became seriously ill and in September 1835 returned to Moscow, where he later died. His virtuoso solo performances greatly influenced Hummel, Chopin, and Liszt, particularly through his innovative romantic nocturnes. Moreover, his reputation in Russia is said to have been a stimulus to the development of a nationalist school of composers led by Glinka and Balakirev.

FINE GAEL (FG). Founded in 1933 as the second major political party in the Republic of Ireland, its origins lay in the pro-Treaty wing of the old Sinn Fein (q.v.) in 1921. It formed the first Irish Free State government and was known then as Cumann na nGaedheal (q.v.), from which it inherited a reactionary reputation. During World War II it reluctantly adopted Fianna Fail's (FF)(q.v.) policy of neutrality. Having lost support heavily in 1943, W. T. Cosgrave (q.v.) was replaced as leader by General Mulcahy, so clearly associated with repression of republicans in the 1920s that he was rejected as leader of the coalition government in 1948 in favor of J. A. Costello (q.v.). Subsequently, the party has formed only coalition governments, suffering electorally for its harsh economic policies in the later 1950s, and even its association with the Irish Labour Party (q.v.) did not produce a left-of-center progressive image until 1973, when it recovered power in coalition under Liam Cosgrave. It was often overshadowed by Eamon de Valera's (q.v.) anti-British republicanism, yet it was FG, under pressure from Sean MacBride (q.v.) as leader of Cumann na Poblachta, that broke the last link with the British Commonwealth by repealing the External Relations Act and declaring Ireland a republic. In the 1970s its efforts to moderate the strict legislation prohibiting sale of contraceptives failed, and an internal party crisis was intensified by a dispute with the president over the introduction of the 1976 Emergency Powers Act, which may have contributed to its defeat in the 1977 election. Under Dr. Garret FitzGerald's (q.v.) leadership, the party's electoral position revived and a coalition government with Labour was re-formed in 1981, only to be defeated on a politically inept budgetary measure in January 1982. An accommodation with Northern Ireland was more assiduously sought and resulted finally in the Anglo-Irish Agreement (q.v.) of 1985. Domestically, its reformist ideals were rebuffed twice in constitutional referenda (q.v.) on abortion and divorce, and FitzGerald resigned after the 1987 election defeat. In 1990 his successor, Alan Dukes, was replaced by John Bruton (q.v.), who, somewhat fortuitously, found himself as leader of a FG-Labour-Democratic Left coalition government in 1994 after Labour had refused to continue its alliance with FF.

FITT, GERARD (Gerry) (1926–). Born in Belfast, he served in the British merchant navy in 1941–53, including on wartime convoys to the USSR. Self-taught in law and politics, in 1958 he joined Belfast City Council as an Irish Labour member and remained until 1981, when his opposition to the hunger strike lost him the seat. In 1962 he won the Dock seat in Stormont (q.v.) from the Unionists and similarly the West Belfast seat at Westminster in 1966. There he informed the British Labour Party on Northern Ireland matters. He was a leading participant in the civil rights movement in the late 1960s and led the Social Democratic and Labour Party (SDLP) (q.v.) from its foundation until 1979, when he felt it was becoming more nationalist than socialist. He helped to form the power-sharing Executive and was its deputy chief. His strong opposition to the Provisional IRA (q.v.) resulted in attacks on his home and the loss of his Westminster seat to Sinn Fein (q.v.) in 1983. He became a life peer as Lord Fitt of Bell's Hill and was critical of the Anglo-Irish Agreement (q.v.) because of its lack of prior consultation with Unionists.

FITZGERALD, AUGUSTUS FREDERICK (1791–1874), third duke of Leinster. Eldest son of William Robert, the second duke, educated at Eton and Oxford, a fervent supporter in the House of Lords of Catholic emancipation (q.v.) and parliamentary reform, he succeeded to the Carton estate, Co. Kildare, and conducted a correspondence with Lord Stanley that led to the creation of a nondenominational National education (q.v.) system.

FITZGERALD, LORD EDWARD (1763–98), twelfth child of the first duke of Leinster. He received a military education in France after his father's death in 1773 and joined the Sussex militia in 1779, serving in America and later participating in the Canadian expedition (1788–89) that explored New Brunswick to Quebec. He was elected MP for Athy in 1783, later for Kildare (1790), and supported Henry Grattan (q.v.) in several liberal causes. In 1792, having experienced the revolutionary fervor in France with Thomas Paine, he was dismissed from the army. He became a friend of Arthur O'Connor and joined the United Irishmen (qq.v.), seeking to liaise with a French invasion in order to establish a republic in May 1798. Initially escaping arrest, he was mortally wounded in a skirmish and died in Newgate prison. His estate was forfeited under an act of attainder but was recovered in 1819.

FITZGERALD, GARRET MICHAEL DESMOND (1926–). Born in Dublin. His father was the first foreign minister of the Irish Free State. His mother was an Ulster Presbyterian. Educated in Dungarvan, Belvedere College, University College Dublin (UCD) (from which he graduated in history, French, and Spanish) and King's Inns, he became a barrister in 1947. He was awarded a doctorate and lectured in political economy at UCD from 1959. As manager of the Economist Intelligence Unit of Ireland, with wide business consultancy experience, he wrote extensively as a journalist for British and American publications and was prominent in the Irish European Movement.

He became a TD in 1969 and was a member of the Senate from 1965 to 1969. He served as minister of foreign affairs and took a close interest in Northern Ireland matters, forming good relations with all political parties except the Democratic Unionist Party (q.v.). His period in office spanned the Sunningdale Agreement (q.v.), Northern Ireland Assembly, and Convention years of 1973–77. He became leader of Fine Gael (q.v.) in 1977 and taoiseach briefly in 1981 and again in late 1982, when his concern for Northern Ireland ultimately led to the Anglo-Irish Agreement (q.v.) of 1985. He retired from active politics after losing the 1987 general election and the referendum on divorce.

FITZGERALD, LORD THOMAS (1513–37). As tenth earl of Kildare, "Silken Thomas" became deputy governor to his father, Gerald, in February 1534. On hearing rumors of his father's execution in London, he renounced his royal allegiance, attacked Dublin Castle, was defeated, and fell back on Maynooth. He sought a pardon, but was executed at Tyburn.

FITZGIBBON, JOHN (1749–1802). Born in Dublin, educated at Trinity College Dublin and Oxford, after a career as a barrister, he was MP for Kilmallock, was appointed attorney general (1783) and lord chancellor (1789–1801), was created a viscount (1793) and earl of Clare in 1795. He opposed Catholic emancipation (q.v.), repressed the Whiteboys (q.v.), and pushed the Act of Union through parliament. *See also* Union, Act of

FLIGHT OF THE EARLS (4 September 1607). Hugh O'Neill (q.v.) of Tyrone, together with Rory O'Donnell of Tyrconnell, went into permanent exile in France in the aftermath of the rebellion that briefly saw him in control of Ulster. He submitted to Mountjoy and was pardoned, but became enmeshed in family quarrels and sought Spanish help. In 1606 he mounted an attack on his son-in-law O'Cahan to confirm his own supremacy as James I's chosen ruler, independent of Mountjoy and John Davies (q.v.) in Dublin, but he was declared a traitor and consequently forfeited his property.

FORSTER, WILLIAM EDWARD (1818–86). A Quaker wool industrialist in Bradford, for which he was MP (1861–86), and Liberal chief secretary for Ireland (1880–2). During the famines (q.v.) of 1845–49 he visited Connemara with J. H. Tuke (q.v.), raising British awareness of the scale of the crisis. He promoted the Elementary Education Act (1870) and the Ballot Act (1872), but suppressed the Land League and imprisoned its leaders Michael Davitt, John Dillon, William O'Brien, and Charles Stewart Parnell (qq.v.) in 1881. When they issued their "No rent manifesto," he resigned over W. E. Gladstone's (q.v.) acceptance of the Kilmainham deal with Parnell, unwittingly making way for the succession of Lord Frederick Cavendish and T. H. Burke, who were murdered by the Invincibles (q.v.) in Phoenix Park on their arrival in May 1882.

FORTY-SHILLING FREEHOLDERS. Holders of property of this value were granted the franchise from 1793 to 1829, though Roman Catholics were not allowed to sit in parliament until 1829. Politically, they were viewed by Wolfe Tone and Daniel O'Connell (qq.v.) as little more than fodder for the landlord vote.

FRENCH, JOHN DENTON PINKSTONE (1852–1925). Commander in chief of the British Expeditionary Force in 1914, he was created a viscount as Lord French of Ypres in 1915. As lord lieutenant of Ireland from May 1918, he cracked down on Sinn Fein and the Irish Volunteers (qq.v.) in the German plot, but released nationalist prisoners after the Dáil (q.v.) was set up. He survived an IRA assassination attempt in December 1919 and declared martial law in December 1920.

-G-

GAELIC ATHLETIC ASSOCIATION (GAA). Founded on 1 November 1884 in Thurles, Co. Tipperary, by a teacher, Michael Cusack (1847–1906), with Maurice Davin as president. One of its rules, forbidding membership to the British security forces in Northern Ireland, has long been a source of sectarian antagonism, and in 1995 became the subject of debate in several branches concerning its possible removal.

GAELIC LEAGUE (CONRADH NA GAEILGE). Founded on 1 July 1893 by Eoin MacNeill (q.v.) (1867–1945), professor of history at University College Dublin from 1908. He became chief of staff of the Volunteers, though he was not in the Irish Republican Brotherhood (IRB) (q.v.) and held back from the 1916 rising, but was jailed. Elected Sinn Fein MP for the National University of Ireland in 1918, he supported the Anglo-Irish Treaty and Douglas Hyde (qq.v.) as president. When the League was infiltrated by the politically revolutionary IRB, he resigned and was replaced by Patrick Pearse (q.v.) in July 1915. He placed great stress on the status of the Irish language (q.v.). From 17 March 1899, *An Claideamh Soluis,* edited by O'Rahilly, was published as a bilingual Gaelic League weekly, adopting a controversial position on the language in relation to nationalism.

GAELTACHT. A special commission report (July 1926) defined areas, set up a special division in the Department of Lands to assist the Irish language (q.v.) and foster economic and social development in predominantly Irish-speaking areas. Its boundaries were revised in 1956 with the creation of the new department, Roinn na Gaeltachta (q.v.); from 1958 Gaeltarra Éireann provided state funding for industries, its administrative center being moved to Na Forbacha, Co. Galway, in 1969. In 1980 Údarás na Gaeltachta was formed under a cabinet minister with elected representatives as a coordinated company, making available grants to schoolchildren, agricultural incentives, housing improvements, aid for cooperatives, and tourism. These developments, however, had doubled-edged effects on the preservation of the language and population mobility. They raised an ethical issue by creating indirect or direct economic discrimination in favor of one sector of the population for cultural reasons, while almost identical facets of social and economic deprivation existed in nearby localities, which remained ineligible for assistance merely because their residents were not Irish-speaking. Further problems emerged over selection of criteria for identifying areas of need, which were not necessarily defined on purely linguistic criteria.

GALWAY (population of 48,640 in 1991). Main port and regional center of Connacht, situated on Galway Bay on the west coast, famous as a sea- and river-fishing center, and serving the Aran Islands. Created as a town by the Anglo-Norman de Burgo after the capture of an O'Flaherty stronghold, it became a royal borough in the later medieval period. Due to its isolation, its merchants, especially the 14 known as the "Tribes," whose wealth was based on its port trade, developed a large measure of independence of the Dublin administration while remaining loyal until 1642. Besieged by Cromwellian forces for ten months until its surrender in 1652, the town recovered only slowly in the 18th century and suffered badly, as did Connacht generally, during the 1840s famines (q.v.).

The town walls survive in part, as does a tower house that represents a typical merchant dwelling of the late middle ages, and part of St. Nicholas's medieval parish church. The Claddagh was formerly a distinct fishing quarter on the edge of the city, but urban redevelopment removed many of its traditional features. Galway is now an important tourist center on the eastern edge of the beautiful mountain and lake region of Connemara, with its own seaside suburb of Salthill. A university college was established in 1845 and now specializes in teaching through the medium of Irish. The cathedral was built in 1957–65. The Irish language (q.v.) has remained strong in the area served by Galway, which has a theater specializing in Irish-language productions. As a modern manufacturing center, it has concentrated on computer-related products.

GANDON, JAMES (1743–1823). Born in London, he won second prize in a competition to design the Royal Exchange/City Hall in Dublin in 1769. He declined an invitation from Princess Dashkov to go to St. Petersburg in favor of a commission to build the Custom House (1781–91) in Dublin, and went on to design some of the city's most impressive buildings, the Parliament extension (1782), the Four Courts (1785–1802), and King's Inns (1795–1809), extended by Francis Johnston (q.v.) in 1817.

GELDOF, ROBERT (BOB) FREDERICK XENON (1951–). Born in Dublin, he led the highly successful rock music group Boomtown Rats in 1975–86 and played the lead role in the 1982 film *Pink Floyd: The Wall*. In response to the famine in Ethiopia he established the charity Band-Aid in 1984, raising £8 million for relief provision, especially through Live-Aid concerts and sales of the record "Do They Know It's Christmas?" He was awarded an honorary British knighthood in 1986, the year in which his autobiography, *Is That It?,* was published.

GEORGE, DAVID LLOYD (1863–1945), first earl of Dwyfor. Brought up in modest circumstances in north Wales, he qualified as a solicitor in 1884 and became Liberal MP for the Caernarvon Boroughs (1890–1945). He spoke on the same platform as Michael Davitt (q.v.) during the election campaign of 1886 as a nonconformist Baptist displaying empathy with many Irish grievances, opposing payment of tithes (q.v.) and strongly upholding tenant farmers' rights while pursuing disestablishment of the Anglican Church in Wales and self-government for the principality. He was minister at the Board of Trade from 1905 and chancellor of the exchequer in 1908, becoming prime minister in 1916–22. He set up the Irish Convention in 1917 and negotiated the 1921 Treaty with Arthur Griffith and Michael Collins (qq.v.).

GLADSTONE, WILLIAM EWART (1809–98). British MP from 1833 to 1895. He took a prolonged and mainly constructive interest in Irish affairs. While still a student, he supported Catholic emancipation (q.v.), and in 1833 caused the Irish Church Temporalities Bill to be modified so that its funds should not be used for secular purposes. Often an intolerant high-church defender of a single state religion, he resigned from the Board of Trade in 1845 in protest at the Peel government's proposal to quadruple and make permanent the annual grant to Maynooth College, though he defended the establishment of nonsectarian university colleges and later upheld denominational education. He became an ardent free trader and leader of the Liberal Party in Britain, taking up in particular the causes of tenant rights and home rule in Ireland. In 1865 he suspended the Habeus Corpus Act in Ireland and later introduced disestablishment and disendowment of the Church of Ireland (q.v.) before becoming prime minister in December 1868. He released imprisoned Fenians to exile in 1870, introduced land bills in 1870 (belatedly based on the Devon Commission [q.v.] report, recognizing Ulster tenant right) and in April–May 1881 (setting up the Bessborough Commission [q.v.], and a land court to adjudicate rents) to ease evictions, leading to the 1886 Land Purchase Bill. He strongly enforced the law during serious unrest provoked by Parnell's "No rent manifesto" and declared the Land League (q.v.) an illegal organization. His Irish University Bill (1873) removing the religious test was defeated, as were Home Rule Bills in April 1886. They were lost by electoral defeat and in February 1893 were rejected overwhelmingly by the House of Lords. *See also* Universities

GOGARTY, OLIVER ST. JOHN (1878–1957). Born in Dublin, where his father Henry, having graduated from the College of Surgeons in 1864, practiced. Educated initially at Clongowes Wood College, he too graduated in medicine, from Trinity College Dublin in 1907, specializing in ear, nose, and throat surgery. Better known as a writer of poetry, he was a friend of W. B. Yeats, Arthur Griffith, and Michael Collins (qq.v.). He became a senator but was repelled by the ideas of Eamon de Valera (q.v.) and the reactionary, introverted Ireland of the interwar period. Having published *As I Was Going Down Sackville Street* (1937), in 1939 he retired from his home at Renvyle, Co. Galway, to New York, where he died. He was buried in Ballinakill, Connemara.

GOLDSMITH, OLIVER (1728–74). Born at Pallas, Co. Longford, son of a clergyman-farmer and a schoolmaster's daughter. Disfigured by smallpox, he attended various schools including Elphin, Athlone, and Edgeworthstown, entering Trinity College Dublin in 1744 and taking a degree in 1749. Perpetually short of money, his poverty was regularly eased by an uncle, who enabled him to study medicine at Edinburgh (1752–53) and then Leiden. In 1755–56 he traveled extensively through France, Switzerland, and Italy, sometimes paying his way by playing the flute. He failed to qualify as a surgeon in 1758 and tried to combine practicing as a physician in London with writing reviews for various magazines. The reviews brought some recognition, as did his *Enquiry into the Present State of Polite Learning in Europe* (1759). It was only after he had become a member of Dr. Samuel Johnson's circle in 1764 that his published essays, novels, plays, and verse brought success. He is best known for *The Vicar of Wakefield* (1766), *The Deserted Village* (1770), and *She Stoops to Conquer* (1773), which contain numerous characters and incidents from his own experiences, including some from Ireland.

GONNE MacBRIDE, EDITH MAUD (1866–1953). Born in Surrey, the daughter of a British army officer, who was transferred to the Curragh garrison in 1868 and lived near Dublin until his wife died in 1871. As a child she was sent to the south of France to recuperate from tuberculosis; on a later visit she met a right-wing officer, Lucien Millevoye, with whom she sought to share an active interest in freedom for Ireland and Alsace-Lorraine. She bore him two children between 1890 and 1894, but the affair ended in 1899.

Contradictory, impetuous, and theatrical, she involved herself as a campaigning orator in several political and social causes. She helped found Inghinidhe na hEireann (Daughters of Erin), an organization pledged to foster Irish culture over English culture and to obtain independence, and Cumann na nGaedheal (q.v.). She declined marriage with W. B. Yeats (q.v.), whom she first met in 1889 and who was infatuated with her, and acted in his play *Cathleen ni Houlihan.* When she walked out of the first performance of Synge's (q.v.) *In the Shadow of the Glen,* she provoked a rift with Yeats in the National Theatre.

Having formerly been prone to mysticism, she become a Roman Catholic and in 1903 married John MacBride, organizer of the anti-British Irish Brigade in the Boer War and one of the future victims of the 1916 rising. Their son Jean Seagan (Sean) (q.v.) was born in 1904. A year later she petitioned for divorce but was granted only a legal separation. She continued to live in Paris and Normandy until 1917. Having failed to secure a truce between Free State and IRA forces in the civil war (q.v.), she was ambivalent toward the 1921 Treaty until the republican surrender and Griffith's death, after which she vehemently opposed both it and the Cosgrave government. *See also* Cosgrave, William Thomas

GORE-BOOTH, CONSTANCE GEORGINA, COUNTESS MARKIE-VICZ, (1868–1927). Born in London, but educated on the Lissadell estate, Co. Sligo, she studied painting at the Slade in 1893 and in Paris from 1898 to 1900. She married the Polish Count Casimir Dunin-

Markievicz. She lived in Dublin from 1903, becoming active in the Gaelic League and the Abbey Theatre (qq.v.) circle. She formed the United Arts Club in 1907. She joined Sinn Fein (SF) in 1908 and Maud Gonne's (qq.v.) Inghinidhe na hEireann, founding Na Fianna for boys in 1909. She was imprisoned to 1917 and became a Roman Catholic on her release. In 1918 she was elected as the first woman MP, but adopted a SF abstentionist stance. She became a member of the Dáil (q.v.) and minister of labour in 1919, opposed the Treaty, was rearrested for republican activity in 1923, and joined de Valera's Fianna Fail (qq.v.) party in 1926.

GOVERNMENT OF IRELAND, ACT (for the better), 23 December 1920. It excluded six of the nine Ulster counties from its provisions, effectively creating two states in Ireland, and recognized two parallel parliaments. After the election 124 Sinn Fein (q.v.) members in the south boycotted the Dáil (q.v.) in June 1921.

GRATTAN, HENRY (1746–1820). Born in Dublin, educated at Trinity College Dublin and the Middle Temple. MP for Charlemont in 1775 and opposition leader, he achieved repeal of restrictive trade acts, sought legislative independence via the Dungannon Convention (1782), and repeal of the Declaratory Act (q.v.). He was an advocate of Catholic emancipation (q.v.), but saw little hope of parliamentary reform. He retired in 1797 but returned as MP for Wicklow in 1798 to oppose the Act of Union and later sat for Dublin in the Westminster parliament. *See also* Union, Act of

GRAVES, CHARLES (1812–99). Born in Dublin, graduating from Trinity College Dublin (TCD) in 1836. He became a Member of the Royal Irish Academy (q.v.) (1837) and eventually its president (1861). A mathematician specializing in cones, he became a professor at TCD (1843), was awarded a DD degree in 1851, and was successively appointed dean of Dublin Castle Chapel (1860), dean of Clonfert (1864), and bishop of Limerick (1866–99). Elected Fellow of the Royal Society in 1880, he wrote poetry, interpreted Ogham inscriptions, and promoted a translation of the Brehon laws (q.v.) (1851).

GRAVES, ROBERT JAMES (1796–1853). Entered Trinity College Dublin at the age of 15, obtained his B.A. degree in 1815 and B.Med. in 1818, then toured Europe until 1820, sketching in the Alps in the company of J. M. W. Turner. He received his licentiate at the College of Physicians, joined the Meath Hospital, then founded Park Street (Lincoln Place) Medical School with Arthur Jacob (q.v.). In 1827 he became King's Professor at the Institutes of Medicine at Dublin University where he taught physiology. He moved to Galway in 1822 to combat famine fever after several doctors there had died. He obtained additional experience during the 1832 Dublin cholera outbreak, and in 1847 he was a vocal critic of official measures to overcome epidemics, emphasizing the need to combat fevers with sound nutrition. He went on to make notable contributions to the understanding of the hyperthyroid gland and neurology, in addition to using lead acetate to combat Asiatic cholera. He published *A System of Clinical Medicine* (1843), was president of the College of Physicians in 1843–45, and was elected Fellow of the Royal Society and Member of the Royal Irish Academy.

GREGORY, LADY AUGUSTA (1852–1932). Born at Roxborough, Co. Galway, she met W. B. Yeats in 1898 and with him formed the Irish Literary Theatre (qq.v.), and held salons at Coole Park, Gort, her late husband's estate. She became codirector of the Abbey Theatre with Yeats and J. M. Synge (q.v.) in 1904, and wrote comedy plays with lively, realistic rural dialogue. Her account *Our Irish Theatre* appeared in New York in 1913, and her *Journals* for the years 1916–30 were published posthumously under the editorship of Lennox Robinson, a director and manager of the Abbey.

GRIFFITH, ARTHUR (1871–1922). Born in Dublin, he worked in South African goldmines and fought in the Boer War. He edited the *United Irishman* (1898–1906) and in 1900 founded Cumann na nGaedheal (qq.v.), advocating passive resistance to British rule and a national assembly in Dublin, though not necessarily political independence. He participated in the Gaelic League and joined the Irish (Revolutionary) Republican Brotherhood (qq.v.) in 1893. In 1904 he published essays entitled *The Resurrection of Hungary,* a discussion of the Austro-Hungarian dual-monarchy model of equal but separate nation-states. He wanted a return to the 1782 position of a Dublin-based sovereign, national, bicameral legislature. He founded Sinn Fein (q.v.), along with the newspaper of the same name, in 1906 as a constitutional movement for Irish economic independence, and was involved in the Volunteers' German gun-running incident to Howth in 1913. He stayed aloof from the 1916 Easter Rising (q.v.). With the party overrun by Eamon de Valera (q.v.) as vice-president, he led negotiations with Britain on the Anglo-Irish Treaty (q.v.) in 1921. He replaced de Valera as president when the latter opposed the Treaty, but died suddenly in August 1922.

GRIFFITH, SIR RICHARD JOHN (1784–1878). Born in Dublin, son of the MP for Askeaton, Member of the Royal Irish Academy (q.v.), and owner of an estate in Co. Kildare, where he was an innovative landlord. He attended school at Portarlington, joined the Royal Irish Regiment of Artillery, but retired in 1801 after one year. He studied natural sciences in London and mining geology in various localities in England and Wales, moving to Edinburgh in 1805 to study geology at the university. In May 1809 he was commissioned by the Royal Dublin Society (q.v.) to survey the Leinster coalfield, was elected mining engineer (1812–29), and traveled through Ireland to survey bogs in 1809–13. He became inspector general of His Majesty's mines in Ireland (1812), compiled a geological map of the country (1835–1839), and was involved in public works (roads and bridges) in Munster after the 1822 famine. He was head of the Ordnance Survey's (q.v.) boundary survey in 1825, a key figure in the Geological Society (1831–78), and a railway commissioner in 1836. In 1827 he was appointed commissioner of the General Survey and Valuation of Rateable Property, although work did not begin until the first maps became available in Coleraine in May 1830; surveys of townlands were completed in the 1840s and tenements in 1853–65. He was chairman of the Board of Works (q.v.) in 1850–64 and was created a baronet in 1858. *See also* Famine; Railways

GUINNESS' BREWERY. Occupying a four-acre site at St. James' Gate on James' Street and Thomas Street, Dublin, it developed into the fifth largest brewery in the UK by 1865 and the leading city industry, being extended to the Liffey in 1873. By 1900 it was the largest in the world, producing 5 percent of the total volume of UK beer, and two-thirds of Irish output. Exports of porter and stout began about 1825, expanding at a remarkable rate to the end of the century, cargoes being sent from the Liffey wharf by barge to the North Wall quays. The brewery used mostly Irish barley malt, transported to Dublin along direct railway links and the Grand Canal, which also provided water for the industrial process.

GUINNESS, ARTHUR (1725–1803). A brewer in Leixlip in 1756, who leased the James's Gate premises in December 1759. His early charitable involvement included donations to St. Patrick's Cathedral and to the first Sunday school in 1786. Later he became a member of Dublin City Council. One of his sons, also named Arthur (1768–1855), became a prominent merchant, a director (1808), deputy governor (1818) and finally governor (1820) of the Bank of Ireland. Deeply religious and strongly influenced by the Methodists Wesley and Whitefield, he supported Catholic emancipation (q.v.) in the 1820s and parliamentary reform in 1831, but resisted Daniel O'Connell's (q.v.) later more extreme radical position in demanding repeal of the Union. He developed flour mills at Kilmainham (q.v.), which his father had set up in 1782, using the Grand Canal to bring in grain and developing trade with Bristol, London, and Liverpool.

GUINNESS, SIR ARTHUR EDWARD (1840–1915). Son of Sir Benjamin (q.v.), MP in 1868–69 and 1874–80. He funded the rebuilding of Marsh's library and the Coombe Lying-in Hospital to serve one of the poorest parts of Dublin, where he was also active in constructing artisan housing. A president of the Royal Dublin Society (q.v.), in 1880 he was created Baron Ardilaun of Ashford, where he undertook an afforestation program. That year, in another benefaction, he presented St. Stephen's Green park to the city of Dublin. *See also* Hospitals

GUINNESS, SIR BENJAMIN LEE (1798–1868). Son of the younger Arthur Guinness, lord mayor of Dublin in 1851, Conservative and Unionist MP for Dublin (1865), having declined an invitation to stand as a candidate in 1851. By then he had become fearful of the nationalist republican movement in anticipation of the 1867 Fenian rising. He funded the restoration of St. Patrick's Cathedral in 1861–65 and was awarded a baronetcy in 1867. He bought the estate of Ashford, Co. Mayo. His daughter Anne married William Plunket, Archbishop of Dublin.

GUINNESS, SIR EDWARD CECIL (1847–1927). He was approached by Isaac Butt (q.v.) in 1874 to stand as a parliamentary candidate on the Conservative Home Rule ticket, but was in fact a staunch Unionist. He became deputy lieutenant of the city of Dublin; his business partnership with Sir A. E. Guinness (q.v.) was dissolved in December 1876. He lost his seat at the 1885 election, and was created first earl of Iveagh in 1891. Iveagh House on St. Stephen's Green, Dublin, purchased by Sir Benjamin Guinness (q.v.) in 1856, was presented with its gardens to the government in 1939 and is now the headquarters of the Department of Foreign Affairs.

-H-

HAMILTON, REV. JAMES ARCHIBALD (1747–1815). Born near Athlone, educated by the headmaster of Armagh Royal School, and at Trinity College Dublin in 1765. He received divinity degrees in 1784, took holy orders, and was rector of Derryloran (1780–90) before becoming dean of Cloyne (1804). At Cookstown he set up an observatory, and in 1791 Lord Rokeby appointed him astronomer at Armagh, where he made important observations on the transit of Mercury. His papers are preserved in the Royal Irish Academy (q.v.), to the *Transactions* of which he contributed articles on astronomy between 1794 and 1807.

HAMILTON, SIR WILLIAM ROWAN (1805–65). Born in Dublin and educated by a clergyman uncle at Trim, he was a talented linguist who taught himself mathematics. He entered Trinity College Dublin in 1823, was appointed professor of astronomy there in 1827 and superintendent of Dunsink Observatory, where he spent all his working life as a mathematician. He became Astronomer Royal for Ireland and was knighted in 1830. He was an honorary member of the St. Petersburg Academy and became a world authority on quaternions, publishing *Lectures on Quaternions* (1853) and *Elements of Quaternions* (1866). Hamiltonian functions are common to optics, mechanics, and modern quantum theory. He was a friend of Maria Edgeworth (q.v.), Wordsworth, and Southey.

HARLAND, SIR EDWARD JAMES (1831–95). Born in Scarborough, Yorkshire, he served his apprenticeship at Robert Stephenson's works in Newcastle and became a Tyne shipyard manager in 1853. The following year he moved to Belfast and entered into an industrial partnership with G. W. Wolff in 1862. He received a baronetcy and was mayor of Belfast, and its MP (1889–95).

HAUGHEY, CHARLES JAMES (1925–). Born in Castlebar, Co. Mayo, though his parents with a strong republican tradition were from Co. Londonderry. He obtained B.Comm. and B.L. degrees from University College Dublin, joined Fianna Fail (FF) (q.v.), and married the daughter of former FF taoiseach Sean Lemass (q.v.). He was elected TD for Dublin North-East in 1957 and became a government minister in 1961. In 1970 he figured at the center of gun-running allegations and was dismissed as minister for finance. In 1977 he became taoiseach and worked for closer links with the UK over Northern Ireland, an approach endorsed by the UK in 1980, but opposed by fearful Unionists. Haughey supported imprisoned hunger-strikers, and relations with UK became soured. His later pro-Argentinian stance during the Falklands Islands crisis exacerbated the situation. In opposition he supported the New Ireland Forum, but opposed the Anglo-Irish Agreement (qq.v.). In government again, but without a majority, he operated the agreement, although he altered the related extradition arrangements in favor of the Irish courts. While dealing firmly with financial difficulties at home, he made overtures to Unionists, which were cautiously welcomed by the Official Unionist Party (q.v.).

HEALLY, TIMOTHY MICHAEL (1855–1931). Born in Bantry, left the Christian Brothers School, Fermoy, at 13 and became a railway clerk in Newcastle and a correspondent for *The Nation*. He was elected MP for Wexford in 1880, for Monaghan in 1883, and then for South Londonderry in 1885. A barrister specializing in land law, although a protegé of Charles Stewart Parnell (q.v.), he opposed him after the divorce scandal and was expelled from the Irish Parliamentary Party (q.v.) in 1902. He was MP for North Louth (1891–1910), and for North-East Cork (1910–18), resigning in favor of a Sinn Fein (q.v.) prisoner candidate. He was appointed first governor general of the Irish Free State (1922–28).

HEANEY, SEAMUS (1939–). Born near Bellaghy, educated at Derry and the Queen's University of Belfast, where he lectured in English (1966–72) and then moved to Co. Wicklow and resumed teaching. He became professor of rhetoric and oratory at Harvard in 1988 and professor of poetry at Oxford (1989–94). He has been acclaimed as an outstanding Irish poet of his generation and was awarded the Nobel Prize for Literature in December 1995. His published poetic works include *Death of a Naturalist* (1966), *Door into the Dark* (1969), *Wintering Out* (1972), *North* (1975), *Field Work* (1979), *Station Island* (1984), *Selected Poems 1965–75* (1980), *Preoccupations: Selected Prose, 1968–1978* (1980) and *The Spirit Level* (1996).

HEARTH TAX. This source of revenue was collected in England only between 1660 and 1689 because it fell most heavily on the poor. It continued in Ireland from December 1662 until 1793 under the Hearth-tax Act (14 & 15 Chas II, c. 17). The rate payable by tenants was two shillings per annum on fixed chimneys, stoves, and hearths, with exemptions for the very poorest. Its eventual abolition led to improvements in peasant dwellings. Incidentally, it provided the basis for an approximate indication of population totals by providing lists of houses in specific localities. Considerable doubt has been expressed as to the reliability of population calculations based on hearth money returns in view of avoidance of payment, especially in remote districts, fraud on the part of collectors, and incomplete totals of exempted premises, with the result that reported figures are generally considered underestimates. *See also* Population

HEDGE SCHOOLS. Beginning in the 17th century, these schools became widespread in the 18th century, offering rudimentary education (q.v.) for Roman Catholics discriminated against by the penal laws (q.v.). While much respected locally, they were conducted, often in secret, by poorly qualified peripatetic teachers who were paid by individual parents, sometimes in kind. With the repeal of inhibiting legislation in 1782–93, they were able to occupy rural buildings on a more regular basis, but textbooks were usually scarce. Nevertheless, English and Irish were taught, augmented in the very best examples with classics, mathematics, geography, and history. They became less necessary with the success of the Kildare Place Society (q.v.) and ceased operating after introduction of the National schools system in 1831.

HENRY, AUGUSTINE (1857–1930). Born in Cookstown, educated at Cookstown Academy and the Queen's Colleges of Galway and Belfast, from which he graduated in medicine. He served as a customs official in China (1881–1900), collecting plants for Kew Gardens, and became a Fellow of the Linnean Society in 1888. He studied forestry at Nancy and was appointed reader at Cambridge in 1908 and professor of forestry at the College of Science, Dublin, in 1913. His foremost published work was the seven-volume *Trees of Great Britain and Ireland* with H. J. Elwes.

HENRY, PAUL (1876–1958). Son of a Belfast Baptist minister, educated at the Royal Belfast Academical Institution and the Belfast School of Art. He drew from the age of five and at 15 decided to become an artist, moving to Paris in 1900–1901, where he met Edith Somerville (q.v.) and Violet Florence Ross, the future Countess Markievicz (q.v.), Whistler, Charles Sibley (who advised rejection of existing artistic conventions), J. M. Synge and W. B. Yeats (qq.v.). He set up a school in London, was influenced by Cézanne, Gauguin, and Van Gogh. He spent the years 1912–19 at Keel, Achill Island, which provided tonal inspiration for his best-known landscape paintings of Co. Mayo and Connemara. He was elected to the Royal Hibernian Academy in 1929, but became blind from 1945.

HERVEY, FREDERICK AUGUSTUS (1730–1803), fourth earl of Bristol, educated at Westminster School and Cambridge. During a tour of the continent he witnessed the eruption of Vesuvius in 1766 and became interested in natural history, visiting Dalmatia and investigating disappearing rivers in Istria in 1777–79. He claimed to have been the first to discover basalt flows at the Giant's Causeway, Co. Antrim. From royal chaplain (1763), he rose to be bishop of Cloyne (1767) when his brother, George (1721–75), was viceroy. His reclamation of bog there brought him into conflict with local inhabitants. Translated to Derry in February 1768, he set up a fund for retired clergy, constructed churches, roads, and river bridges, improved farming, and built mansions at Downhill and Ballyscullion. He succeeded to the earldom in 1779 and thereafter became known as "the Earl Bishop." He opposed tithes (q.v.) and favored parliamentary reform and Catholic emancipation from the penal laws. Nevertheless, he voted for the Act of Union. He joined and led the local Irish Volunteers in February 1782–83 after the Dungannon convention, which enhanced his popularity with Presbyterians. He was awarded the freedom of Derry and Dublin. Many of his treasures were seized in Italy in 1798, and all his personal papers were ultimately lost or destroyed. *See also* Union, Act of

HEWITT, JOHN HAROLD (1907–87). Born in Belfast and educated at Methodist College and the Queen's University of Belfast, from which he also received an M.A. degree (1951) for a thesis on "Ulster Poets, 1800–1870." He worked in Belfast Museum and Art Gallery (1930–57), becoming its deputy director and keeper of art in 1950. He was art critic of the *Belfast Telegraph* and *Irish Times*. An active participant in socialist politics, he was a founder and literary editor of the *Irish Democrat* (1937). In 1957 he was appointed director of the Herbert Art Gallery and Museum, Coventry, returning to Belfast when he retired in 1972. He traveled extensively in Europe, at first with his radical schoolmaster father to Belgium and France, then with his wife in Spain, Italy, and Greece, and later to Yugoslavia, Russia, and central Asia. *See also* Newspapers

Heavily influenced as a student by the writings of William Morris and Upton Sinclair, his poetry was first published in left-wing periodicals in the 1920s. He went on to produce a selection of the *Poems of William Allingham* (1967), edited *Rhyming Weavers and Other Country Poets of Antrim and Down* (1974), *Art in Ulster* (1977), and several volumes of poetry. His *Collected Poems* (edited by Frank Ormsby) appeared in 1991, and *Ancestral Voices: The Selected Prose of John Hewitt* (edited by Tom Clyde) in 1987. He was awarded the Gregory Medal of the Irish Academy of Letters (1984), of which he had been vice-president in 1975. His poetry is permeated by profound regional sensitivities, yet is simultaneously universal in its themes. The author's status as a father figure of modern Ulster writing has been recognized by, among others, Seamus Heaney (q.v.).

HIGGINS, WILLIAM (1763–1825). Born in Co. Sligo and educated at Magdalen and Pembroke Colleges, Oxford. Apparently independently of his contemporary John Dalton, he revived the Greek (and Robert Boyle's) atomic theory of matter in contrast to phlogiston theory, which focused on the role of combustion in chemical reactions. As a chemist with the Irish Linen Board, he developed a cheaper bleaching process. He was professor of chemistry at the Royal Dublin Society (q.v.). *See also* Boyle, Robert

HILLERY, PATRICK JOHN (1923–). Born in Miltown-Malbay, Co. Clare, educated at Cashel, and graduated in medicine at University

College Dublin. After a career as a medical officer, he became Fianna Fail (q.v.) TD for Clare from 1959. He held a series of ministerial posts—Education (1959–65), Industry and Commerce (1965–66), Labour (1966–9), and Foreign Affairs (1969–73). He made an unofficial visit to west Belfast in 1970, which was regarded by the UK as discourteous. Having led negotiations that culminated in Ireland's entry into the European Community (EC), as Commissioner for Social Affairs in 1973–76 and vice-president of the Commission, he was instrumental in setting up the EC's office in Belfast. He was president of the Republic of Ireland from 1976 to 1990. *See also* European Union

HOBSON, BULMER (1883–1969). Born in Holywood, Co. Down, and educated at Friends' School, Lisburn. Already influenced by nationalist ideas, in 1900 he set up a youth debating club in Belfast that led to the formation of the Protestant National Society. He joined the Gaelic League in 1901 and became a member of the Gaelic Athletic Association (qq.v.) in Co. Antrim, soon leaving it to establish Na Fianna Éireann, which was developed with Countess Markievicz (q.v.) from 1909 as a quasi-military scouts' organization. He was briefly a member of Arthur Griffith's Cumann na nGaedheal (qq.v.), but in 1905 founded the republican Dungannon Clubs, for which he wrote a manifesto. After promoting the cause of Sinn Fein (SF)(q.v.) in America in 1907, he helped merge the Dungannon Clubs with Cumann na nGaedheal. He was vice-president of SF, leaving in 1910 after a policy rift with Griffith. He became a member of the Irish Republican Brotherhood's (IRB) Supreme Council, and secretary of the Irish Volunteers (q.v.), helping in the Howth gun-running incident. Having broken with the more extremist members of the IRB in 1914, with Eoin MacNeill he opposed the Easter Rising (qq.v.) in 1916. Subsequently, he retired from active politics and published the first volume of *A Short History of the Irish Volunteers* (1918) and *The Life of Wolfe Tone* (1919).

HOME GOVERNMENT (RULE) ASSOCIATION. Founded in 1870 by Isaac Butt (q.v.), a leading barrister and former Unionist who was influenced by the suffering that he witnessed during the famine years. He defended T. F. Meagher (q.v.) at his trial. The group attracted cross-cultural support, even from former Young Ireland members and some Fenians (qq.v.). It sought a Dublin-based parliament with local jurisdiction at a time when Gladstone (q.v.) was interested in resolving the Irish problem, and the notion of total independence espoused by the Fenians seemed impossible. In the 1872 election, the first held under secret ballot, the movement won over half the Irish seats and sought to achieve its aims by persuasion. The Association was superseded by the Home Rule League in 1873, alongside the Home Rule Confederation of Great Britain, which was intended to tap the feelings of an increasing Irish element of the mainland population. However, the organization had been infiltrated by the Irish Republican Brotherhood/Fenians (q.v.) by 1877, and Isaac Butt was replaced by Charles Stewart Parnell (q.v.). Adopting a more obstructionist policy, Parnell became leader of the party after Butt's death in 1879.

In 1886 Gladstone introduced a Home Rule Bill, comparable to the one that operated in Northern Ireland after 1921. Gladstone's bill was in line with a tradition then developing in Canada and elsewhere. An upper parliamentary chamber was designed to safeguard minority Protestant interests. Defections from the ruling Liberal Party brought about its defeat, but it was seen as a landmark. Gladstone continued to support home rule actively and got his second bill through the House of Commons in 1893, but it was defeated in the House of Lords. Parnell's fall complicated matters in Ireland too. Home rule became an issue again in 1906 when the Liberals were returned to power and John Redmond (q.v.) had reunited the Irish party. By 1910 the Liberals were dependent on Redmond's party for support. A Home Rule Bill was passed in 1912, which could only be held up in the House of Lords until 1914. In the interval, opposition in Ulster was intensified and found sympathy with Conservatives in Britain generally, while in Ireland criticism of Redmond grew. The outbreak of war put the whole matter in abeyance and by 1918 a different scenario existed, the ultimate result of which was partition and two different constitutional arrangements.

HONOURABLE THE IRISH SOCIETY, THE. A body, comparable with the East India Company, set up in 1610 to administer the Londonderry part of the Ulster plantation on behalf of the City of London Livery Companies, as a standing committee of the Common Council of the City of London. It was composed of the governor (a former mayor), his deputy, and 24 assistants. Through local agents it developed the towns of Londonderry and Coleraine. It is now largely a charitable body. *See also* Derry/Londonderry; Plantations

HOSPITALS. The need to treat wounded soldiers gave rise to the first hospital in Ireland, founded by Charles II at Kilmainham (q.v.) in 1680, later supplemented by the Royal Military Infirmary in Phoenix Park (1788). The earliest civilian institution was the Charitable Infirmary founded in Dublin in 1718 by six surgeons, but already in December 1710 Dr. Richard Steevens, son of an Athlone clergyman, had made a bequest for the building of a hospital for the poor. It opened in July 1733, incorporating a large collection of books bequeathed by a trustee, Dr. Edward Worth. Mercer's Hospital was named after Mary Mercer, the daughter of a Fellow of Trinity College and philanthropist who in 1734 gave her St. Stephen's Street house as an infirmary. It lacked endowments other than the profits of a state lottery and the proceeds from concerts, one of which was the first performance of Handel's *Messiah* in April 1742. Mercer's closed in 1983. In 1745 Dr. Bartholomew Mosse (1712–59) founded the charitable Hospital for Poor Lying-in Women in George's Lane (South Great George's Street), Dublin, which received finance from the Irish parliament. By 1748 sufficient funds had been secured to move to the city's north side, where in 1751–57 the Rotunda was built, which is still a leading institution. In 1756 the earl of Meath established a hospital for his estate workers that became the Co. Dublin Infirmary in 1774, the year that saw the first House of Industry Hospital (St. Lawrence's). There followed Cork Street Fever Hospital (1804) and Sir Patrick Dun's (1814), his original bequest to fund teaching at the Royal College of Surgeons (RCS) having been modified by parliament.

The RCS had been founded in 1784 under the leadership of the United Irishman William Dease and RCS professors founded the City of Dublin Hospital in 1832. Dr. Charles Johnson and Sir Henry Marsh set up the Pitt Street Institution for the Diseases of Children in 1822, and the National Children's Hospital (Harcourt Street) was opened in 1884. The Coombe Lying-in Hospital (1829) was followed by the Sisters of Charity at St. Vincent's Hospital (1835), and the Adelaide in 1839. Outside the capital, Cork Hospital was founded in 1721.

Several early hospitals in Dublin also acquired teaching functions. By 1876 the King's and Queen's College of Physicians was open to men and women licentiates, and the faculty of medicine at Queen's College Cork and Queen's College Galway began admitting students in 1849. However, Sir Andrew Horne, opposing the admission of women to Fellowship of the College of Surgeons, hoped the proposal would be rejected "not only unanimously but unanimously with a large majority." Under the Irish public health legislation (9 Vict., c. 6) (1846), a new Central Board of Health required Poor Law (q.v.) guardians to provide fever hospitals and dispensaries in their unions, and thereafter ad hoc government grants in support of charitable foundations became more regular.

Numerous Irish clinicians and surgeons have made distinguished contributions to advances in medical science, among them R. J.

Graves, Arthur Jacob, William Stokes, Sir William Whitla, and Sir William Wilde (qq.v.).

HUME, JOHN (1937–). Born in Derry, he taught there, having been awarded an M.A. degree in history at Maynooth. He first came to political prominence in the civil rights movement in 1968 and was elected to the Stormont (q.v.) parliament for the Foyle constituency in 1969, urging the creation of a social democratic party and unseating the Nationalist Party leader, Edward McAteer (qq.v.). He helped create the Social Democratic and Labour Party (q.v.) in 1970 and became its leader in 1979. Elected to the Northern Ireland Assembly in 1973, he was involved in the Sunningdale Conference and headed the Commerce Department in the ensuing power-sharing Executive. Thereafter he lobbied actively in Ireland, Europe, and the United States for a peaceful accommodation in Northern Ireland. In 1979 he was elected Member of the European Parliament, joining the socialist group there, but often cooperating with Ian Paisley (q.v.) and the Official Unionist Party member on economic development matters. His assessment that Unionists were no longer interested in power sharing and his desire to strengthen the Irish dimension led ultimately to the creation of the New Ireland Forum (q.v.) in Dublin. In 1983 he became a Westminster MP for the new Foyle constituency, the first non-Unionist in that area. While welcoming the Anglo-Irish Agreement (q.v.) of 1985, he did not lead his party into devolution talks until 1988. In 1985, and again in 1988, he sought unsuccessfully to bring about a Provisional IRA (q.v.) cease-fire by direct talks with them or Sinn Fein (q.v.), incurring the wrath of Unionists and the doubts of others, including Republic of Ireland ministers. His second attempt to negotiate a cease-fire on the part of the IRA in 1994 was more successful. When that cease-fire collapsed in February 1996, he again met their leadership with Gerry Adams (q.v.) to seek its reinstatement. *See also* Sunningdale Agreement; Ulster Unionist Party

HYDE, DOUGLAS (1860–1947). Born in Castlerea, Co. Roscommon, son of the local rector, educated at Trinity College Dublin. A great linguist, from 1892 he studied Irish, folklore, and poetry, wrote translations, and became first president of the nonsectarian, apolitical Gaelic League (q.v.). He resigned in 1915 because of its politicization. He was appointed first professor of modern Irish at University College Dublin (1909–32), was a member of the Senate in 1925–26, and was unanimously elected president of Ireland in 1937–45. His most famous works include *Beside the Fire* (1889), *Love Songs of Connacht* (1893), *Religious Songs of Connacht* (1906), and *A Literary History of Ireland* (1899).

-I-

INTERNATIONAL FUND FOR IRELAND. Set up in 1986 to back the Anglo-Irish Agreement (q.v.) by providing money for economic development in deprived localities of Northern Ireland and border areas of the Republic of Ireland. The main contributor was the United States, but "old Commonwealth" and European Union (q.v.) countries also participated. The fund is administered by an independent board based in Belfast.

INVINCIBLES. A terrorist splinter organization encouraged by a London group in late 1881 to create a cell whose purpose was to attack high-ranking government officials. Several leaders were Land League (q.v.) members, and were condemned as renegades by the Fenians and Charles Stewart Parnell (qq.v.). They plotted unsuccessfully to assassinate W. E. Forster (q.v.) and were implicated in the murders of members of several landed families outside Dublin after the killing of Lord Frederick Cavendish and T. H. Burke in May 1882. Initial inability to discover the culprits led to the introduction in July of special powers under the Prevention of Crime Act (45 & 46 Vict., c. 25), but a combination of careful detection, trickery, and betrayal led to five members being tried, convicted, and executed in 1883 for the Phoenix Park murders. The society collapsed in Ireland as its shadowy leaders fled to America.

IRISH AGRICULTURAL ORGANISATION SOCIETY. Founded in April 1894 "to improve the condition of the agricultural population of Ireland by teaching the principles and methods of co-operation as applicable to farming and allied industries." While unaware of similar developments abroad, the leaders—Lord Monteagle, Fr. Finlay, and Sir Horace Plunkett (q.v.)—capitalized on the experience of small cooperative creameries that had been active since 1891, at least in the Limerick area. By 1900 the society's shareholding membership had increased from 1,650 to 46,000 and the number of affiliated agricultural, dairy, and poultry societies from 33 to 298. Extended ownership of livestock was paralleled by improved quality of cattle and pig breeds, with the help of the Royal Dublin Society (q.v.) and with more effective marketing of bacon, butter, and eggs.

IRISH CHRISTIAN BROTHERS. Founded as the Institute of the Brothers of the Christian Schools of Ireland by the Kilkenny-born merchant Edmund Ignatius Rice (1762–1844). He set up a boys' school at Mount Sion, Waterford, in 1803. In 1820 he was appointed Superior

General by Pope Pius VII, moved to Cork at the invitation of the bishop, and to Dublin in 1812. The organization originally provided elementary education outside the National system for children of poorer families. *See also* Education

IRISH CITIZEN ARMY. Created on 23 November 1913 by James Larkin and James Connolly (qq.v.) to occupy the time of the unemployed during a lockout and defend themselves against the Dublin Metropolitan Police and employers. From its center at Liberty Hall, it published *The Irish Worker;* its general secretary was Sean O'Casey (q.v.). Under Connolly it became overtly political and aimed to take over land for the people and establish a workers' republic. They were close to, but more radical than, the Irish Volunteers and joined the Easter Rising (qq.v.) in 1916, attacking the General Post Office and Dublin Castle. They were encouraged by Countess Markievicz (q.v.) not to accept the Treaty but to aid the Irregulars, i.e. Republicans, in the civil war (q.v.).

IRISH FOLKLORE COMMISSION. Established in 1927 as An Cumann le Béaloideas Éireann, to preserve oral tradition. In collaboration with the Royal Irish Academy (q.v.) it set up the Irish Folklore Institute, which has produced the journal *Béaloideas* since 1927.

IRISH LANGUAGE. Irish is one of the Goidelic family of Celtic languages, which seems to have reached western Britain some eight centuries before the Ogham-inscribed stones of the fifth century A.D. During the 18th and 19th centuries its use suffered from the lack of a formal primary education system and the everyday socioeconomic pressures to acquire a knowledge of English. Between the Act of Union and the Great Famine all estimates suggest that only about half the total population could speak Irish, although in rural communities in the western peninsulas that proportion often reached three-quarters. Thereafter, the pattern was one of continued reduction in the number of Irish speakers and steady westward retreat of the language frontier as anglicization progressed with the help of a mix of demographic, economic, and cultural factors. Since independence a conscious attempt has been made to revive the language after its collapse, partly induced by massive emigration and despite the activities of the Gaelic League (qq.v.) in the later 19th century. A government ministry of the Irish language was set up in 1921. In 1922 the Irish Free State made it a compulsory subject in National schools, and from 1925 an obligatory qualification for entry to certain civil service grades. The 1937 constitution declared it to be the country's first official language.

Table 8
Republic of Ireland: Irish-Language Speakers Aged 3 and Over

Year	Irish	%	Total Population (aged 3+)
1926	540,802	19.3	2,802,452
1936	666,601	23.7	2,806,925
1946	588,725	21.2	2,771,657
1961	716,420	27.2	2,635,818
1971	789,429	28.3	2,787,448
1981	1,018,413	31.6	3,226,467
1991	1,095,830	32.5	3,367,006

Table 9
Irish-Speakers by Province (Number and Percentage), 1926–91

	1926	1936	1946	1961	1971	1981	1991
Connacht	174,234	183,082	154,187	148,708	137,372	155,134	162,680
	33.3	36.7	33.2	37.6	37.2	38.8	40.2
Leinster	101,102	183,378	180,755	274,644	341,702	473,225	511,639
	9.4	15.9	15.1	22.2	24.5	28.2	28.8
Munster	197,625	224,805	189,395	228,726	252,805	323,704	352,177
	21.6	25.2	22.0	28.7	30.6	34.6	36.5
Ulster	67,841	75,336	64,388	64,342	57,550	66,350	69,334
(part)	23.9	28.3	26.0	31.4	29.5	30.8	31.3

The only age-groups with more than 50 percent Irish speakers in 1971, 1981, and 1991 were 10–14 and 15–19, a clear reflection of the state's education policy in secondary schools. Curiously, among postschool populations the only consistent growth in knowledge of Irish in the most recent decade has occurred among those aged over 35, and especially those aged over 55. The continuing significant decline in the use of the Irish language with increasing age is shown in Table 10 on the following page.

Whereas in 1971 the Irish-speaking population of the seven-county Gaeltacht areas totaled 55,440 (83%), in 1981 it was 58,026 (77%). The Gaeltacht Areas Order, 1974, extended such areas in counties Kerry and Waterford. As defined by the 1956 and 1982 Gaeltacht Areas Orders, the Gaeltacht areas had a population of 83,430 in 1986 and 83,238 in 1991, suggesting that whereas the number of citizens who had learned the language at school had increased, those living in defined favored districts had stagnated or even decreased, mainly as a result of demographic aging and the out-migration of younger elements.

Table 10
Irish Speakers as a Percentage of the Total in Specific Age-groups

Age-group	1971	1981	1991
3–4	5.5	4.9	4.6
5–9	27.6	27.8	27.3
10–14	50.6	50.8	50.9
15–19	51.5	51.0	54.8
20–24	37.0	40.0	38.6
25–34	29.4	32.8	29.2
35–44	27.2	30.0	31.9
45–54	23.4	28.3	29.5
55–64	14.7	22.9	25.7
65+	9.6	13.0	18.5

Source: Census of Population of Ireland 1981, vol. 6, Irish Language, Dublin, 1985; Census 91: Summary Report, Dublin, 1994.

IRISH LITERARY THEATRE. Formed late in 1898 as an offshoot of the Irish National Literary Society by W. B. Yeats with Lady Gregory (qq.v.) and Edward Martyn, producing Douglas Hyde's (q.v.) Irish-language play *Casadh an tSúgáin* (1901). They declined to see literature used as propaganda, as advocated by Arthur Griffith (q.v.) and Moran, and in 1902 joined the Fay brothers to create the Irish National Theatre Society, which later spawned the Abbey Theatre (q.v.). The Ulster Literary Theatre dates from 1904, but it never established a permanent base.

IRISH MANUSCRIPTS COMMISSION. Founded in 1928 under Eoin MacNeill (q.v.) to report and publish surviving Irish historical and literary manuscripts. From 1930 it has published *Analecta Hibernia*.

IRISH NATIONAL LEAGUE. Emerged in October 1882, with William O'Brien (q.v.) as secretary, as an arm of the Home Rule Party under Charles Stewart Parnell (q.v.) in Westminster. Its immediate roots lay in the Land League (q.v.). It received financial support from local clergy and the United States, but was declared illegal for incitement in July 1887. It fell apart by 1891 in the wake of the Parnell divorce scandal.

IRISH NATIONAL LIBERATION ARMY. An illegal republican paramilitary group formed in 1975 as part of the Irish Republican Socialist Party, a breakaway group from Sinn Fein/IRA (of which Bernadette Devlin was the best-known member). It had a reputation for ruthlessness, both in its terrorist activities, mostly bombings that resulted in loss of life, and its relations internally or with other republicans. In 1986 a new faction developed known as the Irish People's Liberation Organisation.

IRISH PARLIAMENTARY PARTY (IPP, Nationalist Party). Initially a vague association, sharing the ideals of Butt's Home Government (Rule) Association (q.v.)/League of self-government for Ireland. After 56 of its candidates were elected in 1874, it fought against absorption by other parties and against the Fenianism of Charles Stewart Parnell, who initiated the "Land War" (qq.v.). In 1880, when Parnell narrowly took over the chairmanship from the moderate William Shaw, 61 were elected, but split in January 1881. It supported the Conservatives in the election of 1885, when it first received the approval of the Catholic hierarchy led by Archbishop Croke of Cashel; 86 were elected and held the balance between Liberals and Conservatives, but the IPP felt let down by Conservative inaction on home rule and transferred its support to W. E. Gladstone (q.v.) in January 1886, leading to the first Home Rule Bill in April. In July 1886 it had 85 candidates elected, but was again divided by violence in Ireland and the Parnell divorce case, Parnell eventually being forced out by Gladstone and the Catholic hierarchy.

The party split in December 1890 when a majority followed Justin McCarthy, who was succeeded by John Dillon in 1896, but reunited under John Redmond (qq.v.) in 1898. Periodically fragmented by personal feuds, and with only marginal opposition from the Fenians/Sinn Fein, it succeeded in having progressive legislation passed at Westminster, e.g., the Irish Universities Act (1908), and in obtaining recognition of tenant rights. Liberal Prime Minister Asquith promised full self-government for Ireland in 1909, when 70 were elected, plus 11 Independent Nationalists, whose help after 1910 enabled success of the Parliament Act, removing the House of Lords' veto on Commons legislation. A consequence was the passage of the third Home Rule Bill in 1912 and the abortive Buckingham Palace Conference in July 1914 when Redmond and Dillon confronted Sir James Craig and Sir Edward Carson (qq.v.). World War I put home rule on hold, after which it became derailed by the 1916 uprising, the introduction of conscription, the death of Redmond (1918), the rise of Sinn Fein, and the formation of the Dáil (q.v.) in January 1919.

IRISH REPUBLICAN ARMY (IRA). Four phases may be identified in the emergence of the organization. (1) Originally owing allegiance to the Irish (Revolutionary) Republican Brotherhood (IRB) (q.v.) as the putative government of a republic in the 1860s, the illegal force absorbed the Irish Volunteers (q.v.) in 1916 to create (2) the new IRA as defenders of the nascent state in the Anglo-Irish war of 1919, prior to the signing of the Anglo-Irish Treaty. After the Treaty was signed in December 1921, the organization split, with Michael Collins (q.v.) and Harry Boland leading the pro-Treaty regular army (3) of the Irish Free State (IFS), and Liam Lynch leading the Irregulars, (4) who opposed the IFS troops during the civil war (q.v.) until surrendering on the orders of Eamon de Valera and Frank Aiken (qq.v.) in 1923.

The remnant under Sean MacBride (q.v.) that rejected the constitutional Sinn Fein movement was outlawed by W. T. Cosgrave, but became reconciled to Fianna Fail (qq.v.) by 1933. Some were assimilated into the regular army and the Garda Siochana. The IRA was again banned by de Valera in 1936, as extremists led by Sean Russell declared war on Britain and Northern Ireland in 1939. As they had done in the 1860s, they sought American Clan na Gael (q.v.) support for a bombing campaign in the UK, the worst example of which occurred in Coventry. Those activities brought about passage of the Special Powers Act in Northern Ireland and the Treason and Offences against the State Acts in the Republic, followed by the Emergency Powers Act, which led to internment of known IRA members during World War II.

After that stage MacBride's followers proceeded to form Clann na Poblachta in 1946 and entered government in the coalition of 1948–51. Meanwhile, a renewed campaign of violence under Cathal Goulding and Ruari Ó Bradaigh, conducted from 1956 to 1962, failed. Consequently, a more Marxist political stance was promoted by Tomás Mac-Giolla, with activists sheltering Northern Ireland Civil Rights Association (NICRA) (q.v.) marches until another upsurge began in 1969 with a full resumption of armed action. Early in 1970 yet another schism developed. A southern faction sought to establish socialist objectives, with the Official IRA, based in Gardner Street, Dublin, clashing with its northern nationalist counterparts led by Sean MacStiophan (John Stevenson), Ó Bradaigh, and Daithi Ó Conaill (David O'Connell) as the Provisional IRA (q.v.), based in Kevin Street. In 1979 the latter rejected a papal appeal to stop the violence and in 1986 reconstituted themselves as abstentionist Republican Sinn Fein. They rejected the Downing Street Declaration (q.v.) and fought to undermine it. Throughout the 1994–95 cease-fire, and subsequently, they have firmly declared that the IRA will never give up its weapons, thus creating an apparently permanent impediment to acceptance of Sinn Fein as a party committed exclusively to nonviolent democratic politics.

IRISH (REVOLUTIONARY) REPUBLICAN BROTHERHOOD (IRB). Formed under American pressure on 17 March 1858 in Dublin by a group generally connected with the 1848 rising, including James Stephens (q.v.), T. C. Luby, and Jeremiah O'Donovan Rossa's Phoenix Society, with a parallel Fenian movement, Clan na Gael (q.v.) in New York. It accepted Davis's doctrine of nationality, but believed also that Britain would never concede independence. Condemning all other means as futile, it concentrated on the single narrow aim of creating an independent Irish republic by force, seeking support among working people. Never more than a minority element in Ireland itself, by drawing on support from emigrés it attempted to broaden the political issue. The organization was subdivided into secret cadres, or "circles," with subordinate command structures. It was opposed by the Roman Catholic Church, being officially denounced in 1863, again in 1865 by Archbishop Cullen and in 1869 by Pope Pius IX, though not necessarily by parish priests. Its newspaper, *The Irish People,* was short-lived (1863–65). Stephens and Luby were arrested in September 1865. The former escaped to America where he was deposed as leader of the Fenian Brotherhood by his rescuer, Thomas J. Kelly, who was sent to organize a rising in March 1867. That lacked popular support and proved little more than an inept gesture leading to the trial and execution of some activists, the so-called "Manchester martyrs." When Kelly and Timothy Deasy, who had been arrested as Fenians, were themselves rescued from custody, a police sergeant was killed. Despite some dubious evidence, William Allen, Michael Larkin, and Michael O'Brian were soon charged with and convicted of complicity in the murder and were publicy executed in Manchester, coining the phrase "Manchester Martyrs." An eccentric Fenian invasion of Canada was routed in two days in June 1866. *See also* Cullen, Cardinal Paul

In 1873 the IRB was reorganized with a new tactic of winning election to Westminster and then obstructing parliamentary business, while using the IRA as its military arm. Fenians still in the Irish Parliamentary Party (q.v.) were expelled from the IRB Supreme Council in 1877, cutting them off from constitutional activity. The IRB regained some influence in the "New Departure" of the National (Land) League of 1882. It supported the extremist statements of Charles Stewart Parnell in 1890, infiltrated the Gaelic Athletic Association (qq.v.) in 1884, and was active in the 1798 centenary commemorations. Ultimately, it was taken over by Arthur Griffith's Cumann na hGaedheal and Hobson's (qq.v.) Dungannon Clubs, which led to the formation of Sinn Fein (SF) and the Irish Volunteers (qq.v.) (later IRA) in 1913.

Its practical role in the 1916 rising is still a matter of debate, though it grasped World War I as the long-awaited opportunity and was revitalized by new members drawn from the Gaelic League, such as Patrick Pearse (qq.v.). After the rising's failure the IRB was reestablished in 1917 by Collins as secretary and Thomas Ashe (qq.v.) as president of the Supreme Council. In 1918 it controlled SF election candidates, but was overtaken during the Anglo-Irish war (q.v.) by the IRA, following the declaration of a republic. The Supreme Council favored the Anglo-Irish Treaty in 1921, and the organization split during the civil war (q.v.) and dissolved in 1924. Its residual funds contributed to the erection of a Wolfe Tone (q.v.) memorial in 1967.

IRISH SOCIALIST REPUBLICAN PARTY. A small minority group, with a parallel Irish Socialist Federation in New York, formed in 1896 by James Connolly (q.v.). He was committed to Marxist notions of public ownership of land, means of production, distribution, and exchange.

IRISH VOLUNTEERS. Formed on 25 November 1913 under the leadership of Eoin MacNeill, Patrick Pearse (qq.v.), and Thomas MacDonagh as a parallel to the Ulster Volunteer Force, augmented by Gaelic Athletic Association, Sinn Fein, and Gaelic League (qq.v.) members.

-J-

JACOB, ARTHUR (1790–1874). Studied at Dr. Steevens' Hospital under Abraham Colles, the College of Surgeons, Edinburgh University, and London. Having first been an anatomy demonstrator at Trinity College Dublin under James Macartney, he set up a private Park Street medical school and was professor of anatomy and physiology at the College of Surgeons (1827–67). He founded the Opthalmic Hospital in Pitt (Balfe) Street in 1829 until the opening of the Royal City of Dublin Hospital in Baggot Street (1832). He was founder/editor of the *Dublin Medical Press.*

JOHNSTON, FRANCIS (1761–1829). Born in Armagh and was sent to Dublin for architectural training in 1779–84 by Archbishop Richard Robinson. He succeeded Thomas Cooley as the primate's architect in 1784, and was subsequently responsible for buildings that adopted classical/castle styles in design, including Charleville, Co. Offaly, and the Chapel Royal in Dublin Castle. His church architecture is characterized by the inclusion of steeples, among them St. Peter's, Drogheda, St. Andrew's and St. George's, Dublin. In 1805 he became architect of the Board of Works (q.v.) and Civil Buildings. His commissions in the capital included the Bank of Ireland (the former parliament building, 1802), the General Post Office (1814–18), the Richmond penitentiary (1812–16), and the Royal Hibernian Academy (1824). While in Belfast he designed the Lunatic Asylum (1829).

JOYCE, JAMES AUGUSTINE ALOYSIUS (1882–1941). Born in Dublin, educated at Clongowes Wood and Belvedere Colleges, before entering University College Dublin to study languages and philosophy. In 1904 he moved to Zurich with Nora Barnacle, whom he eventually married in 1931, and taught English in Pula and Trieste. A voluntary exile from Ireland after 1912, his work was nevertheless rooted in

Dublin, albeit in a totally different social and cultural milieu from that of the Irish Literary Movement, which he scorned. His main works were *Dubliners* (1914), *A Portrait of the Artist as a Young Man* (1916), *Ulysses* published in Paris (1922), stream-of-consciousness tales of a single day, "Bloomsday 1904," and *Finnegan's Wake* (1939).

JOYCE, PATRICK WESTON (1827–1914). Born in Co. Limerick and educated in hedge schools (q.v.), he became a teacher in Clonmel. He was selected to help reorganize the National school system in 1856. He graduated from Trinity College Dublin in 1861 and was principal of the Training College, Dublin (1874–93). He published *Origin and History of Irish Names of Places* (1869), *Ancient Irish Music* (1873), and several school history texts. He was president of the Royal Society of Antiquaries of Ireland.

JUSTICES OF THE PEACE. *See* Magistrates/Justices of the Peace

-K-

KANE, SIR ROBERT (1809–90). Son of a Dublin industrial chemist, he studied at Trinity College Dublin, in Paris, and in Berlin. He then turned to medicine, becoming a licentiate of the College of Physicians in 1831 and a Fellow in 1842. He was employed at the Meath Hospital, having been awarded a prize for his research into typhus fever. As professor of chemistry at the Apothecaries' Hall (1831–45), he received the gold medal from the Royal Irish Academy (RIA) (q.v.) in 1843 for research into compounds of ammonia, publishing *Elements of Practical Pharmacy* (1831) and *Elements of Chemistry* (2 vols., 1841–43). As professor of natural philosophy at the Royal Dublin Society (q.v.) (1834–47), his lectures led to publication of his *Industrial Resources of Ireland* (1844). He proposed the creation of an Irish technical museum, and in 1847 became director of the Museum of Irish Industry (later the Royal College of Science), where his interest in economic geology, parallel to the new Geological Survey under Thomas Oldham and Thomas Larcom's (q.v.) Ordnance Survey (q.v.), initiated a soil mapping program at the RIA in 1848, itself related to Sir Richard Griffith's (q.v.) land valuation. He investigated university education in Europe and was president of Queen's College Cork from 1845 until 1873, when he was appointed commissioner of national education, and then vice-chancellor of the Royal University of Ireland in 1880. He was a member of the Central Board of Health and of a commission investigating the causes and relief of famine in 1845. He was knighted in 1846, elected Fellow of the Royal Society (1849), secretary to the RIA council (1842), and its president (1877).

KEARNEY, PEADAR (1883–1942). Author of the "Soldier's Song" (1907), which was adopted by the Irish Volunteers (q.v.) and then as the Irish national anthem in 1926.

KEATING, SEAN (1889–1977). Born in Limerick, he lived on the Aran Islands after 1910. He was elected to the Royal Hibernian Academy in 1923 and later became its president (1949–62). He exhibited widely from 1914 to 1975 and was professor of painting at the National College of Art.

KELLS (CEANANNUS MOR). A Co. Meath market town, famous as the site of an early Christian monastery. The date of its original foundation is unknown, but Columban monks from Iona built a new monastery as their chief center by A.D. 807. Its most important treasures include the *Book of Kells,* possibly the finest surviving illuminated Latin gospel book, which was housed at the monastery until 1654 when it was transferred to the library of Trinity College Dublin; the richly decorated Crozier of Kells, now in the British Museum; and a group of four finely carved, tenth-century, stone high crosses in the graveyard, where there is also a round tower and a tiny stone-roofed church of the Irish Romanesque period. There is another high cross in the town, which was developed by the Anglo-Normans and became one of the walled towns defending the frontier of the Pale (q.v.). Close by near the Blackwater river is the 18th-century Headford House, designed by Robert Adam for the earl of Bective, who was influential in Kells's later development.

KILDARE. A market, garrison, and cathedral town (population 4,200 in 1991) on the southern edge of the Curragh, Co. Kildare, the largest open area (5,000 acres) in Ireland, covered with glacial sands and used for sheep grazing, horse racing, and a military camp. Kildare monastery, founded in the fifth/sixth century, was unusual in having a woman, St. Brigid (ob. c. A.D. 521–526), as its founder and maintaining a double structure with abbess and abbot/bishop. It became the most prominent institution in Leinster and was subjected to many attacks by the Vikings and the Irish kings. The center of a diocese since 1111, the town was developed by the Anglo-Normans, who rebuilt its cathedral. It survives in the same style (though "restored") as St. Brigid's (Church of Ireland). A fine round tower with Romanesque doorway, remains of a high cross, and a small house associated with a tradition of perpetual fire are all in the graveyard. In the market square is Kildare castle, a 15th-century tower house successor to Strongbow's castle. Lord Edward Fitzgerald (q.v.), whose family acquired the manor in the 14th century and took its title from it, lived in adjacent Kildare Lodge. The town suffered in the

16th- and 17th-century wars; remains of two monastic houses survive nearby, the Franciscan possessing the Kildare burials and Knights Hospitaller. The headquarters of the Irish National Stud is at Tully House, where the gardens were laid out in Japanese style in 1906. *See also* Viking Settlements

KILDARE PLACE SOCIETY (1811). The Protestant Society for Education of the Poor in Ireland provided nondenominational education though it received state support. Partly for that reason it was suspected of Church of Ireland (q.v.) bias by Roman Catholics led by Daniel O'Connell (q.v.), who was a minority member of its board of governors. Dissatisfied by the Society's apparent help for other Protestant societies in 1820, he resigned and began a campaign, buttressed by the Catholic hierarchy, against its work. The Society maintained a training college for primary school teachers (1814–78) under the Church Education Society and the General Synod's education committee. *See also* Education

KILMAINHAM. An important ford on the river Liffey; site of a seventh-century Celtic monastery commemorated in its name. After the Reformation the lands of a priory and a hospital of St. John of Jerusalem, founded before1176 by Strongbow, became a royal deer park and later Phoenix Park. On the priory site itself the Royal Hospital for old and disabled soldiers was built in 1680–87 to a design by Sir William Robinson, surveyor general of Ireland. Other buildings were added in the 19th century, and it became the headquarters of the Civic Guard in 1925–49; recently it has been restored for use as a cultural venue. Nearby is Kilmainham jail, in use from 1796 until 1924, where prominent patriots were incarcerated, including McCracken, Emmet, O'Brien, Parnell, and Pearse (qq.v.). It is now a museum. Also nearby is Islandbridge Park of Remembrance (designed by Lutyens on a site where Viking graves were found), dedicated to the memory of Irishmen who died in World War I.

KING, WILLIAM (1650–1729). Born in Antrim into a family that had migrated from Aberdeenshire. From school in Dungannon he entered Trinity College Dublin (TCD) in 1666, graduating in 1670, and was ordained as a deacon by Bishop Mossom of Derry (1671) and as a priest by Archbishop Parker of Tuam (1674). Having been provost of Tuam (q.v.), he accompanied Parker to Dublin, being appointed chancellor of St. Patrick's Cathedral. He was a founding member of the Dublin Philosophical Society in 1683. In 1687 he became embroiled in a theological dispute with Peter Manby of Derry, a convert to Catholicism. As dean of St. Patrick's in 1688 he became more strongly whiggish and Orangeist, and was arrested for anti-Jacobite statements immediately before the outbreak of war in Ireland. While bishop of Derry (1691), he wrote a firm justification of the revolution of 1688, restored churches, opposed Presbyterians' and other dissenters' leases of London Company lands, and supported the provision of Gaelic-speaking clergy for Scots Highlanders settled in Inishowen and the teaching of Irish at TCD. Yet he voted for penal legislation in 1695. He strove for the independence of the Irish administration and argued against taxation of the clergy without their consent. His primary work, *De Origine Mali* (1702, though not translated into English until 1729) expounded the doctrine of free will. He succeeded Narcissus Marsh (q.v.) as archbishop of Dublin (1703), again improving the provision of clergy and places of worship in collaboration with Jonathan Swift (q.v.), with whom he was not always on good terms. In 1719 he came into conflict with government over his opposition to the Toleration Act (6 Geo. I, c. 5) and rejected political preferment of Englishmen to the church in Ireland. He left huge sums to charities, endowed a lectureship in divinity at TCD, and at his own request was buried without a memorial. His letters provide valuable insights into contemporary Ireland.

KIRWAN, RICHARD (1733–1812). Born in Co. Galway, educated at Poitiers and St. Omer. He intended to join the priesthood, but returned to Ireland to inherit family estates in 1755, only to be imprisoned for his wife's debts. He was called to the Bar but practiced for only two years, having conformed to the Established Church in order to do so. During a ten-year stay in London he met several eminent scientists, was elected Fellow of the Royal Society in 1780 and in 1782 received the Society's Copley Medal for his early chemical research. He produced the first table of specific heats and worked on acid-alkali reactions. His breadth of interest in industrial activity, soil chemistry, and weather are reflected in his published works, including *Elements of Mineralogy* (1784), *An Estimate of the Temperatures of Different Latitudes* (1787), which formed the basis of studies of atmospheric circulation and winds, *Essay on Phlogiston Theory* (1787), and *Geological Essays* (1799), the latter following a criticism of James Hutton's theory of the earth. For health reasons he retired to Dublin, but continued to be an active scientist, being president of the Royal Irish Academy (RIA) (q.v.) from 1799 to 1812. He added to its collection of minerals valuable specimens purchased from Marburg. Having founded the Dublin Library Society in 1791, his own second library survives at the RIA, the first having been stolen by privateers and taken to Salem, Massachusetts. Having traveled extensively since his youth, he was a great linguist and many of his researches were translated into other European languages. *See also* Higgins, William

KNOWTH (Co. Meath). The location of the most important passage tomb complex yet excavated in Ireland. The mound itself measures 80–95 meters in diameter and nearly ten meters in height. Its structure incorporates corbelling, decorated orthostats, and kerb stones. Finds included bone antler pins, pendants, beads, and a flint mace head. Seventeen other tombs exist, all of which have been plundered, although Neolithic pottery, flints, and Beaker pots have been discovered in the vicinity. *See also* Boyne, River

-L-

LABOUR PARTY (LP). Except for a brief period in the late 1980s, it has been the third largest political party in the Republic of Ireland, having been formed in 1912 in Clonmel by James Connolly and James Larkin (qq.v.), who were its early leaders. After ultimately deciding not to take part in the 1918 election because of its special circumstances, it avoided nationalist issues. With 21 percent of electoral support it attended the first Dáil as the main opposition, while Fianna Fail (FF) (q.v.) remained abstentionist. It joined with the Irish Trades Union Congress until 1930 and helped FF to power in 1932, forsaking socialist objectives for a pronationalist stance in a rift that reappeared in the 1940s. The rift was not resolved until the party decided to adopt an independent, left-of-center approach from 1960 onward. Its members remained sharply divided on the tactic of entering coalition governments, but it joined with Fine Gael (q.v.) on five occasions (1948–51, 1954–57, 1973–77, 1982–87, and 1994–) and with FF only in 1992–94, when its leader, Dick Spring (q.v.), first became tanaiste and foreign minister, playing a major part in formulating the Downing Street Declaration (q.v.).

The party was successful in promoting the presidential candidacy of a former member, Mary Robinson (q.v.), in 1990. Its leaders have been Thomas Johnson, Thomas O'Connell (1927–32), William Norton (q.v.)(1932–60), Brendan Corish (1960–77), Frank Cluskey (1977–81), Michael O'Leary (1981–82), and Dick Spring (1982–). Its policies and personnel should not be confused with either the British or the Northern Ireland Labour Party (q.v.).

LABOURERS' COTTAGES AND ALLOTMENTS ACT. This Act (45 & 46 Vict., c. 60) (August 1882) provided subsidized cottages with half an acre of land at low rents, the scheme being administered by Poor Law (q.v.) guardians. The permitted size of allotments was increased to one acre in 1892, thereby offering formerly landless rural families improved prospects of gaining income.

LALOR, JAMES FINTAN (1807–49). Son of an MP-farmer from Co. Laois. He wrote letters to *The Nation* (q.v.) in 1847 on land reform, advocating land for the people, having already argued to Peel that concessions on that issue would remove agitation for repeal of the Act of Union. He had, nevertheless, believed in the use of force as a means of securing independence. He assumed control of the *Irish Felon* a month after the *United Irishman* (q.v.) was suppressed in May 1848 and was arrested in July, but was released on grounds of deteriorating health. *See also* Union, Act of

LAND ACTS. During the postfamine era it was widely accepted that all aspects of the land tenure (q.v.) system in Ireland required urgent attention. Some landlords' abuses of power over economically pressured tenants, aggravated by massive social inequalities of agricultural land distribution, fueled broader political agitation, gave rise to civil unrest, and led to atrocities against individuals. After three pieces of legislation in 1860 which paved the way for better rural housing, in August 1870 W. E. Gladstone (q.v.) introduced his first land act, which proved largely ineffective against evictions. However, for the first time it did indicate government sympathy for tenants by extending Ulster custom, or "tenant right," as yet undefined in law, to the other provinces by providing security of holding for tenant farmers and requiring landlords to pay compensation for improvements and lease alterations, though only for those tenants not in arrears of rent.

Successive bad harvests culminated in 1878–79 in an Irish (Revolutionary) Republican Brotherhood campaign led by Michael Davitt (qq.v.) and in the formation of the Irish National Land League. With Parnell's political participation, the league attracted wider internal support than previously, as well as financial help from America. The "Land War" (1879–82) (q.v.) emerged as a popular movement manifested in mass demonstrations at agrarian evictions, with practical support for those families involved. In response to the Richmond and Bessborough Commissions' (qq.v.) reports, Gladstone introduced the second Land Act (August 1881), incorporating the "three Fs" and creating a Land Commission and land courts. The former provided money for tenant purchases on 35-year loans, but were not applicable to those in arrears of rent, an issue that was tackled in August 1882 in the wake of the so-called "Kilmainham treaty," by a commission that enabled small arrears to be canceled if tenants had paid the 1881 rent and part-paid another two years, with the balance being supplied from the Church Surplus Fund.

By reducing rents by almost 20 percent, the acts encouraged landlords to sell to tenants, especially when the 1885 (Ashbourne) and 1887 (Cadogan) Acts greatly increased state-aided land purchase, further facilitating the development of peasant ownership by providing for 49-year purchase on loan. That facility was especially taken up in Ulster where 25,400 occupiers acquired 942,600 acres of land (an average of 37 acres). Full peasant proprietorship became even more of a reality under the Balfour Act (1891) when government offered £33 million for land purchase. Simultaneously, the most severe problems of the smallest holdings along the west coast were dealt with by creating the Congested Districts Board (q.v.). After the operation of the 1881 and 1885 Acts had been scrutinized by the Cowper Commission (Oct. 1886–Feb. 1887), and the 1896 (Balfour) Act resulted in the sale of 47,000 holdings to tenants of bankrupt estates, the 1903 (Wyndham) Act saw the virtual abolition of landlordism through compulsory purchase. Tenants became owners of consolidated farms, in consideration for which the original proprietors were given a bonus on top of the purchase price. The act forbade subdivision or mortgaging of the new holdings. A fund of £28 million was allocated for this purpose, with twice that sum being paid in arrears by 1908; it applied to an area of seven million acres. Meanwhile, hundreds of evicted tenants were restored to their holdings.

By 1922 approximately 11 million acres had already been purchased, leaving three million acres. From July 1923 the Land Commission took over administration of the Congested Districts Board and the Estates Commission. A month later compulsory sale of all remaining land was authorized, pre-1911 rent levels were reduced by 35 percent, the vendor was to be compensated with 14 years' rent plus state-funded expenses and a 10 percent bonus. Arrears incurred before 1920 were canceled, while those accumulated since then were reduced. Squatters' rights were recognized, but subtenanting was forbidden. Finally, in October 1933 the Fianna Fail government, which had collected reduced annuities but not paid them to the British Exchequer, canceled all pre-1930 arrears, amounting to £4.6 million, and abolished fixed tenures.

Land Improvement Act (23 Vict., c. 19) 1860

Landed Property (Ireland) Improvement Act (23 & 24 Vict., c. 153), 1860 (Napier)

Landlord and Tenant Law Amendment (Ireland) Act (23 & 24 Vict., c. 154), 1860 (Deasy)

Landlord and Tenant (Ireland) Act (33 & 34 Vict., c. 46), 1870

Landlord Law (Ireland) Act (44 & 45 Vict., c. 49), 1881

Arrears of Rent (Ireland) Act (45 & 46 Vict., c. 47), 1882

Purchase of Land (Ireland) Act (48 & 49 Vict., c. 73), 1885 (Ashbourne)

Land Law (Ireland) Act (50 & 51 Vict., c. 33), 1887 (Cadogan)

Purchase of Land (Ireland) Act (54 & 55 Vict., c. 48), 1891 (Balfour)

Land Law (Ireland) Act (59 & 60 Vict., c. 47), 1896 (G. W. Balfour)
Irish Land Act (3 Edw. VII., c. 37), 1903 (Wyndham)
Evicted Tenants (Ireland) Act (7 Edw. VII., c. 56), 1907 (Birrell)
Irish Land Act (9 Edw. VII., c. 42), 1909 (Birrell)
Land Law (Commission) Act, 1923 (Irish Free State)
Land Act, 1923 (Irish Free State)
Land Act, 1933 (Irish Free State)
See also Evictions of Tenants

LAND LEAGUE. Formed in Dublin on 21 October 1879 by Davitt (q.v.), Brennan, Kettle, and with Charles Stewart Parnell (q.v.) as president. It was supported by the Irish (Revolutionary) Republican Brotherhood, the Fenians, and the Irish Parliamentary Party with funds from the American Clan na Gael (qq.v.). It became associated with violent action on the model of secret societies (q.v.). Its constitution declared, "The land of Ireland belongs to the people of Ireland, to be held and cultivated for the sustenance of those whom God decreed to be the inhabitants thereof." Cultivators' rights were considered to be superior to those of landowners, the principles advocated by J. F. Lalor (q.v.), including action to protect tenants and the abolition of landlordism as an immoral and unjust system. The League was intent on securing Ulster custom, namely, the "three Fs" (fair rent, free sale, and fixity of tenure), though more radical elements wanted to create a freeholding peasantry. In their demands supporters of the League were joined by laborers against farmers, and a few Catholic leaders such as Archbishop Croke of Cashel. Publicity and press support was sharpest from Parnell's *United Ireland*. Boycott tactics were adopted after a rally held in Ennis in September 1880, with the ostracism policy of John Dillon (q.v.).

The Bessborough and Richmond Commissions (qq.v.) (January 1881) led to Gladstone's Land Act (1881), which was opposed by Parnell (but not by his party), who advocated nonpayment of rent and was thus condemned by moderates. The League was suppressed, Parnell was imprisoned, and the subsequent unrest culminated in the Phoenix Park murders of Cavendish and Burke. Most tenants acquiesced in fair rent assessments.

LAND TENURE. As elsewhere in Europe during the 19th century, the myriad issues related to the ownership, occupancy, and use of agricultural land represented some of the most acute problems facing state governments. First, the small size and physical fragmentation of farms constrained potential economic viability under prevailing technological practice, itself retarded by tenant indebtedness, meager provision of credit, slow rates of capital accumulation, and low investment in buildings and equipment or higher quality livestock breeding and maintenance. In 1892 holdings under 25 acres (10 hectares) constituted 85 percent of all farms in Ireland, but occupied only 25 percent of the land. In contrast, large farms, on which innovative methods could be introduced and from which adequate profits might be obtained, were unevenly spread geographically, the imbalance favoring eastern, predominantly grain-producing regions, in contrast to the pastoral smallholdings that characterized the west.

Second, an economic structure often associated with underdeveloped countries prevailed, insofar as there existed high overall dependency on agriculture, in this case exacerbated by the absence of significant quantities of modern industrial raw materials and fuel resources, which could have sustained more widespread, manufacturing-based, urban settlement away from the mainly east coast ports.

Third, regionally differentiated demographic pressure on agricultural resources intensified from the later 18th century onward under the force of accelerated population growth rates, brought about by a combination of higher nuptiality, increased marital fertility, and improved life expectancy as the impact of epidemic diseases began to be curbed.

Fourth, social disparities revolved around the distribution of landed property in which a cultural regime institutionalized religious and political cleavages between groups of estate owners (sometimes absentees who devolved decision making to their agents), farm tenants, cottiers, and landless laborers, each with its own outlook that contrasted with those of the others. Tensions between rival interests or individuals frequently erupted into isolated instances or more coordinated campaigns of violence against people and property as specific real or perceived grievances became absorbed into wider struggles for power.

The net result of successive pieces of legislation was that between 1841 and 1901 units of up to 15 acres decreased from 563,235 (81%) to 217,273 (42%). Meanwhile, in 1841–91 the agricultural population declined from 1,844,000 to 937,000 and the number of farm laborers and male servants fell from 1,229,000 to 258,000. The share of the total population dependent on agriculture was reduced from 62 percent to 49 percent between 1841 and 1881, partly by overseas emigration and partly by assimilation of rural people into urban employment through internal migration. Simultaneously, the aggregate population of Ireland and its rate of growth had both been reduced by famine and the initial effects of the demographic transition. *See also* Population; Emigration

"LAND WAR." A term applied to periods of agrarian unrest in 1879–82. In a context of agricultural depression and poor harvests, especially in Connacht, many tenants' rents went unpaid. Consequently, landlords slid into bankruptcy and resorted to evictions of tenants (q.v.). In April 1878 the earl of Leitrim was murdered in Fanad, Co. Donegal, anti-Protestant disturbances occurred in Connemara, leading to Charles Stewart Parnell's (q.v.) Mayo meetings and agitation, boycotts, formation of the National Land League in October 1879, and the murder of Viscount Mountmorres in Co. Galway in September 1880. Despite passage of the second land act in 1881, the Land League (q.v.) refused to call off the agitation as peasant ownership was still not conceded. All the leaders, including Parnell, were arrested in October, but as the situation threatened to get out of control a deal was struck. The "Kilmainham Treaty" (1882) saw the release of the prisoners and the end of the "land war," with a new administration installed in Dublin under Lord Frederick Cavendish and T. H. Burke. They were assassinated immediately, and the whole process was jeopardized. But W. E. Gladstone (q.v.) kept faith over tenant arrears, and other land acts (q.v.) followed. *See also* Evictions of Tenants; Leitrim, Earl of

LANSDOWNE, third MARQUIS OF (Henry Petty-Fitzmaurice) (1780–1863). Educated at the Universities of Edinburgh and Cambridge; Whig MP for Clane, Co. Kildare. Initially he supported Catholic emancipation (q.v.), was interested in economic measures, including abolition of the Corn Laws, helped in the House of Lords with famine relief, and was considered a good landlord in counties Kerry and Limerick. He was a patron of Thomas Moore.

LANYON, SIR CHARLES (1813–89). Born in Eastbourne, he was apprenticed as a civil engineer to Jacob Owen at the Board of Works (q.v.) in Dublin, and married his daughter. After passing the first public examinations for entry to the profession in Ireland, he was appointed county surveyor of Kildare in 1835 and transferred to Co. Antrim in 1836, assuming responsibility for the building of the coast road from Larne to Portrush. His architectural designs incorporated varied styles and may be seen in numerous public buildings in Belfast (including the Queen's College, the Court House, the Custom House, the Queen's and Ormeau bridges). He became mayor of Belfast in 1862, a harbor commissioner, and a Conservative MP in 1866–68. He was president of the Royal Institute of Architects of Ireland (1862–68) and supervised construction of most railway lines in the Belfast and Northern Counties network. *See also* Railways

LARCOM, SIR THOMAS AISKEW (1801–79). Educated at the Royal Military Academy, Woolwich, he served in the Royal Engineers, joined Thomas Colby at the Ordnance Survey (OS)(q.v.) in 1824, and went to Ireland in 1826. After completion of the triangulation, he became Colby's assistant at Mountjoy, Phoenix Park, producing fine county maps, but more importantly conceiving of the OS memoirs as compendia of all relevant data on the country's parishes. The first memoir completed, and the only one to be published at the time, was that for Templemore (Londonderry) in 1837; the unpublished series passed to the Royal Irish Academy (q.v.). From 1836 maps of 67 towns were prepared for municipal reform.

In 1841 Larcom was census commissioner, classifying occupations, agricultural statistics, investigating the Irish Society in 1842, and the Queen's Colleges in 1845. As Commissioner of Public Works immediately before the great famine, he drew on his experience with Sir Richard Griffith (q.v.) on roads and other relief works, and headed the Poor Law Commission (q.v.) of enquiry, becoming deputy chairman of the Board of Works (q.v.) (1850) and sitting on boundary commissions, etc.

From 1853 to 1868 he was undersecretary for Ireland and a friend of Thomas Drummond. He acquired a reputation for being humane, impartial, and just. He supported the Irish National Society's educational system for the working class, and the Queen's Colleges. His administration witnessed a great decline in reported criminal offences, but an upsurge in American-promoted Fenianism (q.v.) in the 1860s. He became a Knight Commander of the Order of the Bath in 1860 and retired from public life in 1868, having published William Petty's Down Survey (qq.v.) in 1861 for the Irish Archaeological Society and having been a founder of the *Journal of the Statistical and Social Inquiry Society of Ireland.*

LARKIN, JAMES (1876–1947). Born in Liverpool, but raised by his grandparents in Newry. He organized strikes of the National Union of Dockers in Liverpool and Belfast and set up the Irish Transport and General Workers Union in Dublin in 1909, which led to the lockout of 1913. In 1920–23 he was imprisoned in America for agitation. On his return to Ireland he was expelled from the union for excessive radicalism. Consequently, he founded the Workers' Union of Ireland. He was elected to the Dáil (q.v.) in 1927–32, 1937–38, and 1943–44. *See also* Connolly, James; Trades Unions

LARMOR, SIR JOSEPH (1857–1942). Born in Magheragall, Co. Antrim, and educated at Queen's College Belfast and St. John's College, Cambridge. He was appointed Professor of Natural Philosophy at Queen's College Galway in 1880, and Lucasian Professor of Mathematics at Cambridge (1903). He enunciated the formula for the radiation of energy from an accelerated electron and explained the effect of the magnetic field in splitting the spectrum. He was elected Fellow of the Royal Society in 1892, acted as secretary of the Society (1901–12), was knighted in 1909, and became MP for Cambridge University (1911–22).

LAVERY, SIR JOHN (1856–1941). Born in Belfast, he was orphaned while young and was brought up in Scotland. Having studied art in Glasgow, London, and Paris, his artistic career took off in 1888 when he was commissioned to paint Queen Victoria's visit to the Glasgow Exhibition. Becoming widely known as a portrait painter, he was knighted in 1918 and was elected to the Royal Academy in 1921.

LECKY, WILLIAM EDWARD HARTPOLE (1838–1903). Born in Dublin, son of a magistrate of Scottish extraction, who owned property in Carlow and Queen's County; educated at Armagh, Cheltenham, and Trinity College Dublin (TCD) (1856–59). He traveled extensively on the continent, wrote *Leaders of Public Opinion in Ireland* (1861), and a *History of Rationalism* (2 vols., 1865), which brought immediate fame and the company of eminent politicians and literati. His main work was an eight-volume *History of England in the Eighteenth Century* (1878–90), much of it devoted to Irish leaders. He supported disestablishment of the Church in Ireland and the 1870 land act, but opposed home rule. He was in favor of a Roman Catholic university and admired Horace Plunkett's (q.v.) agricultural measures. From 1895 to 1902 he was MP for Dublin University, his maiden speech in the House condemning Irish imprisonments under the Treason Act of 1883. He became a Privy Councillor in 1897, one of the first members of the British Academy (1902), and was awarded the Order of Merit in 1902. From 1871 he lived in London, but when he died his ashes were interred in Dublin, where his widow endowed a chair of history at TCD.

LEGAL SYSTEMS. The Courts of Justice Act (April 1924) set up a hierarchy in the Irish Free State consisting of several elements.

The Supreme Court, under the chief justice with four senior judges and the president of the High Court ex officio, receives appeals and considers constitutional matters relating to Dáil and Senate bills.

The Court of Criminal Appeal, comprising a judge of the Supreme Court and two judges of the High Court, hears appeals forwarded from the Central Criminal Court, the Circuit Court, and the Special Criminal Court.

The High Court has a president and sixteen other judges, each sitting alone in individual cases; it becomes the Central Criminal Court when trying serious criminal cases under a High Court judge and jury.

Eight Circuit Courts, under 18 judges, handle all cases except murder and treason, with a judge and 12-person jury for criminal cases, and receive appeals from District Courts.

Twenty-three District Courts, under 46 judges, process lesser civil and criminal cases. The Special Criminal Court is constituted under three judges, sitting without a jury, for cases where normal procedures are considered inadequate to uphold justice and public order.

In Northern Ireland, the Supreme Court comprises the High Court's Lord Chief Justice, and the Court of Appeal is made up of the Lord Chief Justice with two Lord Justices of Appeal, above county and magistrate's courts, which deal with routine minor cases.

LEITRIM, EARL OF (William Sidney Clements) (1806–78). Born in Dublin, MP for Leitrim (1839–47). From 1854 he owned the Milford estate, Co. Donegal, on which he resisted granting tenant right even after the 1870 land act. His murder, the three perpetrators of which were never punished, prefaced the so-called "land war" (q.v.) of 1879.

LEMASS, SEAN FRANCIS (1899–1971). Born in Ballybrack, Co. Dublin, he was a member of the Irish Volunteers with Eamon de Valera in the Easter Rising (qq.v.). As a Republican in the civil war (q.v.), he was interned in 1922–23 and was elected TD for Dublin city (1925–69). A founding member of Fianna Fail (q.v.), he became tanaiste to de Valera in 1945, and taoiseach from June 1959 until November 1966. During that period he initiated more amicable relations with Northern Ireland politicians, notably the Unionist prime minister, Terence O'Neill (q.v.). He promoted state agencies such as Bord na Mona and Aer Lingus (qq.v.) until adopting a free trade policy in 1965.

LESTER, SEAN (1888–1959). Born in Carrickfergus and educated at Methodist College Belfast, he wrote for *Freeman's Journal* before becoming a diplomat and Irish representative at Geneva in 1929. As League of Nations commissioner in Danzig, he protested against Nazi persecution in 1936. He was secretary-general of the League of Nations from 1940 until its collapse in 1945.

LIMERICK. County borough with a population of 52,000 in 1991. A port, industrial (food, especially bacon and milling, clothing), and regional center for southwest Ireland. The Vikings established an urban settlement in the tenth century on an island where the Shannon river system, which they used to launch raids into the middle of Ireland, enters its estuary. As a prosperous Hiberno-Norse town, it became the capital of the O'Brien kings of Thomond (q.v.). Despite a siege in 1175, it was not fully absorbed into Anglo-Norman Ireland until 1197. In the 13th century its walls were strengthened and extended, a large castle was built, in addition to a bridge to give access to Clare (Thomond) and Connacht, and royal charters were granted. Another walled town was created beyond the island in the 14th century and both were subjected to prolonged, but ultimately successful, sieges in the 17th century. The Treaty of Limerick (commemorated by a large stone at the bridge) brought the Jacobite-Williamite war to an end in 1691.

Little of the elaborate defences survive except for degraded stretches and the castle, which long served as a garrison center and is now a museum. St. Mary's (Church of Ireland) Cathedral nearby dates from 1176. Being the least "restored" of the original cathedrals, it still contains many features from its long history, of which the late 15th-century choir stalls, containing the only medieval carved misericords surviving in Ireland, are among the most interesting. There are remains of the 13th-century Dominican friary which, like many of Limerick's churches, has been rebuilt in later times.

Newtown Pery was added in the late 18th century on land beyond the town boundary by a group of merchants wishing to free themselves from the governing clique and from the physical restraints imposed by the densely settled walled areas. In contrast, it is characterized by a grid plan of wide streets lined by fine Georgian terraces and individual buildings such as the 1784 house of Edmond Pery, who owned the land, and the 1805 town hall. St. John's (Roman Catholic) Cathedral is a Gothic Revival building (1856–61) that contains important pre-Reformation treasures, including the only surviving Irish medieval crozier. In recent years a university has been created, the riverside areas of both old towns have been redeveloped, and the city has grown considerably since the establishment of the Shannon Free Airport Development Area on the Clare side.

LOCAL GOVERNMENT. During the 18th and 19th centuries the expenditure of funds, collected as the county cess, was administered locally through presentments approved by grand juries, themselves selected by county high sheriffs who were responsible for the constabulary, jails, appointing justices of the peace (JPs), allocating subscriptions to maintain infirmaries and dispensaries (q.v.), and drawing up plans for other public works. Beginning in 1836, committees of JPs and ratepayers debated such schemes at the barony level, thereby creating greater accountability. County surveyors were appointed to achieve improved technical competence, while full-time paid resident magistrates supervised the conduct of petty sessions.

Elizabethan Poor Law did not extend to Ireland, which had no system of parish relief. Statutory provision for poorhouse corporations in each county did exist from 1772, though few were actually created, with the result that the majority of Ireland's poor faced a choice between relying on charity, emigrating in search of work, or facing utter destitution. In the context of Poor Law reform in England in 1834, pressure mounted for the standard framework to be applied to Ireland. A parliamentary commission under Archbishop Whately conducted a detailed investigation of the problems, reporting in 1836. Its recommendations included the establishment of a Poor Law Commission (q.v.) to oversee emigration of those displaced by farm amalgamation, formation of subordinate boards to undertake public works for the able-bodied, and care for those who were not. However, in July 1838, after taking further advice from Sir George Nicholls, Lord John Russell extended the new English legislation to Ireland under the Poor Relief Act (1 & 2 Vict., c. 56). Parishes were grouped into 130 Poor Law Unions, although by 1845 only 118 possessed a workhouse regulated by an elected board of guardians. From 1851 these unions were subdivided into dispensary districts where local committees of Poor Law guardians, JPs, and ratepayers held additional responsibility for maintaining public health. In August 1872 the Poor Law Commission was transformed into the Local Government Board for Ireland (33 & 36 Vict., c. 69), revising boundaries of districts within which more diverse functions were operated, especially after the 1898 act.

Meanwhile, dissatisfaction with the activities of archaic urban corporations led to the 1840 Municipal Corporations Act (3 & 4 Vict., c. 108), which introduced a £10 householder franchise while leaving only ten of the former 60 boroughs intact. A further 40 or so later opted for more limited administration by commissioners under legislation dating from 1828 and 1854 (9 Geo. IV, c. 82 and 17 & 18 Vict., c. 103). *See also* Administrative Divisions; Emigration; Whately, Richard

LONDONDERRY. *See* Derry/Londonderry

LOUGH GUR. On a site lying southeast of Limerick city, Neolithic dwellings and burials dating from 2000–1500 B.C. have been discovered. Originally found when the lake was drained in the 19th century, antiquities include megalithic tombs, a wedge-shaped gallery grave, stone circles (one of them being the largest in Ireland), an Early Christian fort and houses, a field system, a ring fort, a former lake dwelling, and late Neolithic/Bronze Age pottery. *See also* Introduction

LYNCH, JOHN MARY (Jack)(1917–). Born in Cork, he began as a civil servant and was called to the Bar in 1945. He served as Fianna Fail (q.v.) TD for Cork constituencies from 1948 to 1981, first becoming a minister in 1951. He was taoiseach in 1966–73 and continued to forge links, begun by his predecessor, with Northern Ireland (NI) politicians. During the early years of the "troubles" his comments of solidarity with NI Roman Catholics were perceived as unhelpful at the least, while later his cross-border security measures were regarded as inadequate. In 1978 he tried unsuccessfully to persuade the UK government to join the European Monetary System at the same time as the Republic of Ireland in order to avoid problems in cross-border currency matters. He resigned as taoiseach in 1979 and as a TD in 1981.

-M-

McATEER, EDWARD (1914–86). Born in Coatbridge, Scotland, son of an Irish-speaking migrant laborer from Fanad, Co. Donegal. He became Stormont (q.v.) MP for Mid-Derry in 1949 and then for Foyle in 1953. He led the Nationalist Party (q.v.) in Northern Ireland from 1964, but lost his seat to John Hume (q.v.) in February 1969. He retired in 1970 after failing to win a Westminster seat.

MacBRIDE, SEAN (1904–88). Son of John MacBride and Maud Gonne (q.v.). As a teenager he joined the IRA (q.v.), in which he was very prominent until 1938, being arrested in 1927 and accused of assassinating the minister of justice, Kevin O'Higgins. He became leader of the republican party, Clann na Poblachta, serving as a TD in 1947–57. Trained later as a lawyer, he served as minister for external affairs in the coalition government of 1948–51, though he abandoned his colleague Noel Browne (q.v.) in the latter's "Mother-and-child" health scheme, which brought down the government and caused his expulsion from Clann na Poblachta, which itself collapsed in the ensuing election.

Subsequently, MacBride became a diplomat, serving as UN assistant secretary-general and as commissioner in Namibia in 1973–74. In 1977 he tried in vain through intermediaries to get an agreement between loyalist and IRA paramilitaries. Despite his background, he opposed Provisional IRA (q.v.) policy. He was awarded the Nobel Peace Prize in 1974 and the Lenin Peace Prize in 1977. In 1985 he gave his name to a set of principles proposing stricter rules against religious discrimination in jobs in Northern Ireland, which influenced American industrial investment there.

McCORMACK, JOHN (1884–1945). Born in Athlone, he studied singing in Italy and made his operatic debut as a tenor at Covent Garden in 1907, performed in New York, Chicago, and Boston in 1903–9, toured Australia with Dame Nellie Melba in 1911, and subsequently performed as a concert soloist. He was made a papal count in 1928 for his Catholic charity work. A U.S. citizen from 1919, he died in Dublin.

McCRACKEN, HENRY JOY (1767–98). Born to Huguenot parents in Belfast, where he managed a cotton factory at the age of 22. With Thomas Russell he helped form the Society of United Irishmen in

Belfast in 1791. Later he commanded the rebels in Antrim, for which he was hanged in July 1798. *See also* United Irishmen, Society of

MacDONNELL, Jacobite earls of Antrim. The family, of Scottish origin, held the title from 1620, having settled in Ulster in the 15th century. The second earl Randal (1609–83) was a royalist Catholic leader who bypassed the viceroy Thomas Wentworth (q.v.) in dealing with Ireland and almost provoked the rebellion of 1641 (q.v.) by promoting the Catholic Irish as a force to resist Scots Presbyterians antagonized by Charles I. They invaded Scotland in 1644 and were subjected to retaliation.

McDONNELL, SORLEY BOY (1505–90). Born in Ballycastle, Co. Antrim, a clan chieftain who expelled the English from Carrickfergus in 1552 and became embroiled in a feud with Shane O'Neill (q.v.). He ruled northeast Ulster with Scots allies to 1586.

McDYER, Canon JAMES DANIEL (1911–87). Born in Glenties, Co. Donegal, a Catholic priest on Tory Island and Glencolumbkille (1951–71). He developed a cooperative to create employment in knitting, vegetable- and fish-processing, and tourism. The cooperative also worked to improve local water and electricity supplies, to build surfaced roads, and to establish a folk museum.

MacENTEE, SEAN (1889–1984). Born in Belfast, he joined the Irish Volunteers in the Easter Rising (qq.v.). He received a death sentence that was commuted to life imprisonment. He was released under amnesty in 1917. He became Sinn Fein (q.v.) MP for Monaghan in 1918, opposed the Anglo-Irish Treaty (q.v.) as an antipartitionist, and was imprisoned by the Irish Free State. A founding member of Fianna Fail (q.v.), he represented Dublin as a TD (1927–69), was minister of finance and tanaiste (1959–65). His daughter married Conor Cruise O'Brien (q.v.).

MacGONIGAL, MAURICE (1900–79). Landscape painter, professor of painting at the National College of Art in succession to Sean Keating (q.v.), and president of the Royal Hibernian Academy (1962–78).

MacHALE, JOHN (1791–81). The fifth son of a Mayo innkeeper, he attended a local Irish-language school and Maynooth College in 1807. Ordained in 1814, he lectured in theology until being appointed coadjutor bishop of Killala in 1825. As early as January 1820 he had written against coeducation of Catholics and Protestants, e.g. in Kildare Place Society (q.v.) schools. In 1831 he protested to Lord Grey at proposals for nondenominational education in the new National schools system, despite the Catholic hierarchy's favorable response to the idea, also arguing for abolition of tithes (q.v.), and repeal of the Act of Union. No doubt because of these views, despite government opposition, he was translated to the archbishopric of Tuam (q.v.) in 1834. There he provoked several internal controversies, including complaints of nepotism, and later even deposing his own nominee, the Dominican O'Finan, to Killala in 1835. What has been described as his "inflexible devotion to his principles" (*DNB*) resulted in a vehement outburst against illegitimate children in 1840. He opposed the Queen's Colleges as "godless" and quarrelled with Archbishop Cullen over the invitation to John Henry Newman (qq.v.) to become rector of the Catholic University, regarding him as an unwanted Englishman. His broader anti-English stance was, however, praised by Daniel O'Connell (q.v.). He prepared a catechism in Irish (1840) and translated Homer's *Iliad* (1844–71), though both his style of English and understanding of Irish poetic meters drew adverse comment. He voted against acceptance of the doctrine of papal infallibility at the Vatican Council in 1870. *See also* Union, Act of

MacLIAMMOIR (originally Willmore), MICHEAL (1899–1978). Born in Cork, studied art at the Slade School, London, and around Europe. He turned to acting and designing on his return to Ireland in 1927, forming the Gate Theatre with Hilton Edwards. *See also* Theaters

MacMURROUGH, DIARMUID (1110–71). Succeeded his father as king of Leinster c. 1126, abducted the wife of O'Ruairc of Breifne, was banished, and invited the Normans under Henry II and Richard de Clare (Strongbow) to help restore him to power. With Pope Adrian IV's approval he returned to Ireland in May 1169; his daughter Aoife married de Clare in 1170. *See also* Anglo-Norman Invasion

MacNEILL, (John) EOIN (1867–1945). Born in Glenarm, Co. Antrim, educated at St. Malachy's, Belfast, and the Royal University. He helped Douglas Hyde form the Gaelic League (qq.v.) and edited its *Gaelic Journal*. He became chief of staff of the Irish Volunteers, but rejected the 1916 Easter Rising (qq.v.) as futile. He countermanded mobilization of the Irish Citizen Army (q.v.) for Easter Sunday in opposition to Patrick Pearse, James Connolly, (qq.v.) et al. He was arrested, but amnestied in 1917. He was elected TD for the National University to 1927, and he supported the Anglo-Irish Treaty (q.v.). As chairman of the Irish Manuscripts Commission (q.v.)(1927) and professor of early Irish history at University College Dublin, he published *Phases of Irish History* (1919) and *Celtic Ireland* (1921).

MAGEE, (née Stewart) MARTHA MARIA (?–1846). Widow of the Rev. William Magee, she made a bequest to establish a college for the training of Irish Presbyterian ministers. The site eventually chosen in 1865 developed as Magee College, Londonderry. In 1968 it became a campus of the New University of Ulster. *See also* Universities

MAGISTRATES/JUSTICES OF THE PEACE. Created in 1603 in Ulster, they conducted local courts of Quarter and Petty Sessions to deal with crime and other infringements of law, to authorize expenditure, and supervise grand juries. At first they were predominantly unpaid gentry, with barristers' assistance in the early 19th century, but were reformed under Thomas Drummond in 1835–40 into a paid nonsectarian magistracy.

MAHAFFY, SIR JOHN PENTLAND (1839–1919). Born near Vevey, Switzerland, the youngest of seven children of a Donegal clergyman whose wife's family owned land in Monaghan. Until 1848 he lived in Lucerne and Bad Kissingen, Bavaria, where his father was chaplain. He returned to Ireland and in 1855 took a degree at Trinity College Dublin (TCD), of which he was elected a Fellow in 1864. His earliest scholarly publications were on Kant and Descartes, but he forsook philosophy for classics and became TCD's first professor of ancient history (1869–99). He served as provost from 1914 to 1919 and was knighted in 1918. Some of his books have become dated, while others retain their original quality of learning and insight: *Prolegomena to Ancient History* (1871), *Greek Social Life from Homer to Menander* (1874), *History of Classical Greek Literature* (1880), *The Story of Alexander's Empire* (1887), *Greek Life and Thought from Alexander to the Roman Conquest* (1887), *The Greek World under Roman Sway* (1890), *Problems in Greek History* (1892), *Flinders Petrie Papyri* (3 vols., 1891–94), *The Empire of the Ptolomies* (1895), and *An Epoch in Irish History, 1591–1660* (1904). A man of broad cultural and recreational interests, he was founding president of the Georgian Society and president of the Royal Irish Academy (q.v.)(1911–16). Fluent in German and French, and vehemently antinationalist, he commended a Swiss confederation model, embodying autonomy for Ulster, to the Irish Convention in 1917.

MALACHY, ST. (1094–1148). Abbot of Bangor, bishop of Connor in 1124, and reformist archbishop of Armagh from 1132. He introduced the Roman liturgy for the Celtic, separated Down and Connor dioceses, and set up an Augustinian priory at Downpatrick. A friend and admirer of St. Bernard, he traveled to Clairvaux and Rome in 1139 and established an abbey at Mellifont (q.v.) for the Cistercians. He died at Clairvaux and was canonized in 1190.

MALTON, JAMES (c. 1750–1803). Son of Thomas Malton (1726–1801), he came to Ireland in 1785 with his father and his brother, also named Thomas, as a draftsman to work for the architect James Gandon (q.v.) on the Customs House. He is best known for his architectural drawings and views, published in *A Picturesque and Descriptive View of the City of Dublin* (1797).

MARKIEVICZ, COUNTESS. *See* GORE-BOOTH, CONSTANCE GEORGINA

MARSH, NARCISSUS (1638–1713). Born in Wiltshire and educated at Oxford (1655–58), he was ordained in 1662 and became chaplain to the Lord Chancellor Clarendon. Appointed as provost of Trinity College Dublin (1679–83) with the support of James Butler, duke of Ormond, he deplored the ignorance of undergraduates, among whom he fostered the teaching of Irish by a converted Catholic priest. Together they collaborated on Robert Boyle's (q.v.) translation of the Old Testament into Irish. In 1683 he became bishop of Ferns and Leighlin, was forcibly expelled in 1689, and fled to St. Asaph in north Wales as vicar of Gresford. He returned in 1690 after the battle of the Boyne. *See also* Boyne, River

Marsh was consecrated archbishop of Cashel (1691). He revived regular preaching by a formerly lax clergy and was translated to Dublin (1694), where he appointed Jonathan Swift (q.v.) to the chapter of St. Patrick's Cathedral (1700), near which he had built the first public library in Ireland (1701–4), which still bears his name. For it he purchased the collection of the late Bishop Stillingfleet, adding his own books. Moving to Armagh in 1703, he restored tithes (q.v.) and repaired churches in that diocese. He was six times a lord justice of Ireland in the years 1699–1711.

MASON, WILLIAM SHAW (1774–1853). Born in Dublin, he graduated from Trinity College Dublin (1796), and became secretary to the Commissioners of Public Records in 1810. He was invited to compile a model *Statistical Account or Parochial Survey of Ireland drawn up from the communications of the clergy* (1814–19) by Sir Robert Peel, for whom he also prepared a catalogue, *Bibliotheca Hibernicana* (1823). His broader interest in the collection of statistical information found expression in his *Survey, Valuation and Census of the Barony of Portnahinch* (1821), and he was responsible for the conduct of the first census of Ireland in 1821. *See also* Census of Population

MEAGHER, THOMAS FRANCIS (1823–67). Born in Waterford, son of a merchant MP and mayor of the city. Educated by the Jesuits at Clongowes Wood College, Kildare, and Stoneyhurst, Lancashire. On returning to Ireland he abandoned a career in law for reform politics through the Repeal Association and was prominent in the Young Ireland (q.v.) Movement. In the Irish Confederation he made speeches upholding the right to violence as a means of obtaining radical change and was arrested on a charge of sedition. After being released on bail and visiting France, he toured the country with William O'Brien (q.v.), making preparations for war. He was said to have proposed the tricolor as the national flag, and was arrested after the rising in 1848. Found guilty of treason, but with a recommendation for mercy, his death sentence was commuted to deportation to Van Diemen's Land, where he was transported in July 1849. Having escaped to America, with John Mitchel (q.v.), he founded the *Citizen* in New York in 1854, explored Central America in 1857, and took part in the American civil war on the Union side. After becoming colonel of the Irish brigade and participating in the battles of Bull Run, Richmond, and Fredericksburg, he was wounded and resigned. Appointed temporary governor of Montana in 1866, he accidentally drowned in the Missouri river.

MELLIFONT. Founded in 1142 by St. Malachy (q.v.), as the first Cistercian abbey in Ireland on land granted by Donogh O'Carroll, with Irish monks from Clairvaux and elsewhere. Its church was consecrated in 1157 and later sent out daughter houses in the 13th century. The abbey was plundered by local inhabitants in 1494, and was finally dissolved in 1539. Some of its fine architectural features have survived.

MITCHEL, JOHN (1815–75). Son of a Dungiven Presbyterian minister and educated at Newry and Trinity College Dublin. He wrote for *The Nation* and founded *The United Irishman* (qq.v.), advocating passive resistance by farmers. Convicted of sedition in 1848, he was transported to Bermuda and then Van Diemen's Land. He escaped to America in 1853 with T. F. Meagher (q.v.). Unlike Meagher, Mitchel supported the Confederacy in the civil war. He became MP for Tipperary and in 1854 published *Jail Journal,* in which he recounted his experiences as an exile. *See also* Newspapers

MOLYNEAUX, SIR JAMES HENRY (1920–). He became Unionist MP for South Antrim at Stormont (q.v.) in 1970 and led the (Official) Ulster Unionist Party (q.v.) from 1974 until his resignation in 1995. His approach at Westminster was neutral rather than close to the Conservatives, as previously, and he used his limited power to extract more parliamentary seats for Northern Ireland from the Callaghan Labour government, eventually obtaining a Select Committee on Northern Ireland at Westminster in 1994. He held the Lagan Valley seat at Westminster from 1983. His relations with Rev. Ian Paisley and the Democratic Unionist Party (qq.v.) varied over the years, depending on the nature of the political issue. They became close following the 1985 Anglo-Irish Agreement (q.v.) when they jointly led the "Ulster Says No" campaign and temporarily withdrew from Westminster and from contact with government ministers. He was awarded a knighthood in the 1996 New Year's Honours List.

MONASTERBOICE. A sixth-century monastery near Drogheda, Co. Louth. Vikings who had occupied the site were expelled by King Domhnall of Tara (q.v.) in A.D. 968. The National Monument complex consists of two small churches, a round tower, and the well-preserved carved stone High Cross of Muiredach, as well as the Tall Cross. A third cross also survives, though partly damaged. *See also* Viking Settlements

MONASTICISM (medieval). By the 11th century, after the devastation of the Norse raiding period, contact was resumed with continental Christianity. The reform movements were welcomed as a means of restructuring the Irish church and reviving its inherent monastic tradition. Augustinian (by 1126 at Armagh [q.v.]) and Benedictine (by 1127 near Downpatrick) orders, including the Cistercians (by 1142 at Mellifont [q.v.]), were in the forefront of this development. From the early 12th century a series of synods established an episcopal system alongside the monastic one, while practice was standardized on European lines. A leading figure in this process was St. Malachy (q.v.), who represented the Irish bishops at Rome.

Most of the surviving Celtic monasteries became houses of the Augustinian Canons Regular. Some church construction, known as Romanesque, has survived from this period, showing stylistic contacts beyond Ireland and a native peculiarity in its simplicity and small scale, even in buildings intended as cathedrals, e.g., at Cashel. In time the great orders imported the grander style of European Gothic and this type of church construction gathered pace under the Anglo-Normans with parish churches and cathedrals, particularly in the towns. The number of new priories or abbeys also increased and was joined in the 13th century by those of the mendicant orders, the Dominicans and the Franciscans. The Observant movement among these orders arrived in Ireland in the 15th century, the first house at Quin, Co. Clare, dating from before 1433. It set the pattern for what was a largely west of Ireland development. By that time laxity was besetting Christianity in Ireland, as elsewhere in mainland Europe.

MOORE, GEORGE AUGUSTUS (1852–1933). Born in Co. Mayo and educated in Birmingham. He went to Paris in 1873 to paint, but when his estate income declined, he returned to London to become a writer.

In *A Drama in Muslin* (1884) and *Parnell and His Island* (1887), he cast a harsh realist's eye on social and economic divisions in late 19th-century Ireland. From 1901 to 1911 he participated in the Dublin literary and theatrical revival with Lady Gregory, W. B. Yeats (qq.v.), and Edward Martyn, writing *The Untilled Field* (1904, published unsuccessfully in an Irish translation in 1902), and the autobiographical *Hail and Farewell* (1911–14). Non-Irish themes were treated in *Esther Waters* (1894) and *Heloise and Abelard* (1921).

MUNICIPAL GALLERY OF MODERN ART. Set up in Parnell Square, Dublin, in 1908, until the government donated Charlemont House to the city in 1927. It opened in 1933 after renovation. It currently houses the Sir Hugh Lane collection, with emphasis on post-1860 artists, and some works on loan from the National Gallery, London.

MUSEUMS. The first geological collections were assembled in Belfast as part of J. E. Portlock's work in the Ordnance Survey (OS)(q.v.), but were transferred to Dublin in 1840. When the scale and breadth of the first OS memoir was realized by the exchequer, geological, archeological, and other specimens collected by the surveyors were retained. Further work was discouraged because of the high cost, and exhibits were not put on public view. The Museum of Economic Geology grew out of the Geological Survey, leading to the Museum of Irish Industry, forerunner of the College of Science. Responsibility for the Geological Survey was removed to the Commissioners of Woods and Forests in 1843, then to the Department of Science and Art from 1853 until 1905, when it passed to the Department of Agriculture and Technical Instruction. In 1856 a new building for the Natural History Museum was commissioned on Leinster Lawn. In 1877 an act was passed enabling the state to acquire its lands for the Dublin Museum of Science and Art, with the National Gallery and natural history section facing the National Library (q.v.) and Metropolitan School of Art. The museum itself initially housed collections of classical and Irish antiquities, Irish and oriental decorative architecture and sculpture, geology, and natural history, as well as domestic crafts and industrial products.

Although the Ulster Museum, Belfast, dates from 1821, the Ulster Folk and Transport Museum, established by statute in 1958, represents a more modern concept in cultural preservation, namely, the creation of a center for traditional material culture and folklore research modeled on the 1891 Skansen open-air museum, Stockholm, and the Welsh Folk Museum near Cardiff. Re-creation of the totality of economic and social life has been attempted by assembling characteristic buildings and their contents, combined with live displays of past crafts. Originally proposed in 1947 as an adjunct of Belfast Municipal

Museum, it later expanded to embrace the whole province and was relocated at Cultra, Co. Down, where the prototype of the world's oldest tramway, from the Giant's Causeway to Bushmills, Co. Antrim, is preserved. Similarly, the Ulster-American Folk Park, near Omagh, focuses on the Mellon house and depicts vernacular buildings from both countries, together with portrayals of the emigrant experience.

Other thematic museums include the Irish Agricultural Museum at Johnstown Castle, Co. Wexford, the Famine Museum at Strokestown House, Co. Roscommon, which commemorates the great famine, and the Irish Linen Centre at Lisburn, Co. Antrim, which received the Gulbenkian "Museum of the Year" Award in 1995.

Among multiperiod exhibitions are those at Bunratty Castle and Folk Park, and Creggaunowen prehistoric settlement reconstructions at Quin, both in Co. Clare, and Muckross, Killarney.

More specialist collections are contained in some of the few surviving 18th-century mansions such as Castletown House at Celbridge, Co. Kildare; Florence Court, Enniskillen; Mount Stewart, Co. Down; Castle Coole, Enniskillen; Westport House; the 19th-century O'Conor Don home, Clonalis House, Castlerea; and the Sir Alfred Beit art collection at Russborough, Blessington. The homes of several eminent politicians have also been converted into personal museums, e.g., Parnell's at Avondale, Co. Wicklow, and O'Connell's at Derrynane, Co. Kerry. Numerous properties have been taken over by An Taisce (1948) in the Republic of Ireland and The National Trust in Northern Ireland to conserve Ireland's physical and natural heritage.

Most larger municipalities have established their own local or regional museums, art galleries, and heritage centers, some of which possess broader national or international significance.

-N-

NATION, THE. Newspaper founded on 15 October 1842 by the moderate C. G. Duffy for the Young Ireland (qq.v.) movement. Its main contributors were editor Thomas Davis and J. B. Dillon (qq.v.), who fostered an awareness of Irish identity and emphasized the right to independence, but remained nonsectarian. All three had previously collaborated on the Dublin *Morning Register* (1824–43). The paper supported the Repeal Association and Daniel O'Connell (q.v.), until he rejected violence in 1846, and the creation of an Irish parliament. In 1845–47 John Mitchel (q.v.) was its lead writer. In 1858 it published a letter (aimed at the Irish Revolutionary Brotherhood [IRB] [q.v.]) from W. S. O'Brien warning against membership of secret societies (qq.v.). It supported the Queen's Colleges, disestablishment of the church, and Charles Stewart Parnell and the Land League (qq.v.) in the 1880s. It became anti-Parnellite after the divorce issue surfaced.

NATIONAL EDUCATION SYSTEM. "National" schools began to be created late in 1831, 40 years before W. E. Forster's (q.v.) act provided for compulsory primary education in England and Wales, under the supervision of an unpaid board of commissioners drawn from various professions. Routine administration was left in the hands of local managers, usually clergy of appropriate denominations. Grants from central funds met the greater part of the cost of buildings, staffing, and publishing approved textbooks, which also came to be used in England. By 1870 pupil enrollment in 6,800 new primary schools had risen tenfold to 1 million, and financial aid had multiplied correspondingly. Chief secretary Edward Stanley had intended that the National schools system should give preference to projects leading toward a nondenominational, indeed religiously integrated, network in which the prime purpose was secular teaching, with religious instruction being kept entirely discrete. Regrettably, these ideals were overrun by demands for rapid implementation and, with the exception of Church of Ireland schools, sectarian clerical control was soon imposed at the local level. Paradoxically, it was the Anglican clergy who later boycotted the National system and in 1839 established the Church Education Society as an alternative, though this faded within two decades. In effect, by 1870 the "national" system had assumed a narrower connotation as parallel but separate denominationally-based structures became entrenched. *See also* Education; Kildare Place Society

NATIONAL GALLERY OF IRELAND. Under an act of 1854 (17 & 18 Vict., c. 99) provision was made for a national gallery of paintings, sculpture, and fine arts. On 29 January 1859 the foundation stone was laid, and the building designed by Sir Charles Lanyon was formally opened by the earl of Carlisle (qq.v.) exactly five years later. It was extended in 1903 and 1964. The initial financing was provided by the rail entrepreneur William Dargan (q.v.) as a gift to the 1853 Great Exhibition. The collection includes works by European masters as well as Irish art, and it has benefited from bequests from the countess of Milltown, Sir Arthur Chester Beatty (q.v.), Hone, Shaw, and Lane. It now encompasses the Vaughan collection of Turner watercolors and Byzantine-Russian icons.

NATIONAL LIBRARY OF IRELAND. Now located on Kildare Street, Dublin, it emerged in 1877 from the transfer of the Royal Dublin Society (q.v.) library to the state following the recommendation of a parliamentary commission in 1836. Initially administered by the Department of Science and Art, after 1900 it came under the Department of Agriculture and Technical Instruction, and is now administered by the Arts and Culture division of the Department of the Taoiseach. Its holdings had been considerably augmented by the Joly Collection in 1863, and it automatically receives all printed works either written by Irish authors or published in Ireland. Physically it is linked with the nearby Genealogical Office, formerly situated in Dublin Castle, which preserves records of the former Office of Arms from 1552. Photographic material includes the famous Lawrence, Clonbrock, Poole, and Morgan Collections, and there are also very extensive holdings of newspapers (q.v.), pamphlets, maps, topographical prints and architectural drawings, portraits and music.

NATIONAL MUSEUM. Established originally on Kildare Street, Dublin, in 1877 as the National Museum of Science and Art, it contains prehistoric and protohistoric treasures of Ireland, most notably the Tara brooch, the Ardagh chalice (q.v.), and the Cong cross, together with displays of Irish glass, silver, and lace. *See also* Museums

NATIONALIST PARTY. Derived from the old Irish Parliamentary Party (q.v.), it was the main antipartition party until the advent of the civil rights movement in 1968–69. In the 1960s under the leadership of Edward McAteer (q.v.), who represented constituencies in Co. Londonderry at Stormont (q.v.), a less clerical and more radical base was developed and the party became the official opposition. The Social Democratic and Labour Party (q.v.) was formed to some extent out of its ranks.

NAVAN FORT (Emhain Macha). Situated near Armagh (q.v.), this earthwork has an external diameter of 87 meters and consists of a set of banks and ditches on a drumlin. According to tradition, it was the capital of King Conchobar of the *Tain* legend. Archaeological excavations have revealed finds of La Tène style and form. The inner ring fort, investigated in 1863, yielded Iron Age material. It contains a mound from the Neolithic period, after which a ditch and succession of structures of late Bronze and early Iron Age were added. Pig remains are common, suggesting a more wooded landscape at the time of occupation. An interpretive heritage center was opened in 1994. *See also* Introduction

NAVIGATION ACTS (October 1651, September 1660, April 1671, July 1685). These acts variously required the exclusive use of English ships to carry imports from Ireland to Britain. They also prohibited the direct importation of goods from British colonies to Ireland and channeled trade through Dublin at the expense of other ports. *See also* Cattle Acts

"NEW ENGLISH." Overwhelmingly Protestant settlers from the first decades of the 16th century, as distinct from medieval immigrants whose descendants were often Roman Catholic, they constituted a relatively small minority. They were most strongly represented in counties Wicklow, Wexford, Cork, Armagh, Antrim, and Londonderry after the "flight of the earls" (q.v.), when they were joined by Scottish Presbyterian colonists. The Roman Catholic Irish viewed the English element, predominantly Church of Ireland (q.v.), as an oppressive ascendancy (q.v.), primarily because of penal enactments by the English parliament and its implementation of agrarian policy toward tenants of all origins. However, they often chose to ignore progressive and liberal strands that, for example, favored and fought for Catholic emancipation (q.v.), parliamentary independence, economic development, educational freedom, and intellectual toleration. Many of the political and social movements of the 19th century were in fact initiated and promoted by members of the so-called Protestant ascendancy.

NEWGRANGE. A cruciform passage grave, 13 meters high and 103 meters in diameter, with corbeled vaulting, and incised decoration on some orthostats. Its 24-meter-long entrance passage is aligned to the sun at dawn on the winter solstice. Quartz pebbles covering the mound were brought from the Wicklow Mountains near Dublin. Its existence has been documented since at least 1699, and excavations have found flint flakes, together with Beaker pottery that may be dated to c. 2500 B.C. *See also* Boyne, River

NEW IRELAND FORUM. A conference of the four main nationalist parties (Fianna Fail, Fine Gael, Irish Labour Party, and Social Democratic and Labour Party), largely at the instigation of John Hume (qq.v.). It held its first meeting in Dublin in May 1983 with the aim of working out an agreed approach to a Northern Ireland political settlement. It produced a report in 1984 that detailed a nationalist historical analysis and a set of options—a unitary 32-county state, under federal, or joint Republic of Ireland and UK authority. Although unacceptable to Unionists and the UK government, it was influential in establishing the "Irish dimension" of the Northern Ireland problem.

NEWMAN, JOHN HENRY (1801–90). Educated at Trinity College, Oxford, he became tutor and Fellow of Oriel, as well as leader of the evangelical Oxford Movement. He was ordained as an Anglican in 1824, but resigned in 1843 and joined the Roman Catholic Church in 1845. He was ordained into the priesthood in 1847 and became a cardinal in 1879. He held discussions with Archbishop Cullen (q.v.) at Armagh in 1850 on the possibility of founding a Catholic University in Ireland. Newman was appointed its rector in November 1851, although the university itself did not come into being until May 1854. Archbishop John MacHale (q.v.) of Tuam and other nationalist clergy opposed the appointment of English staff to the university, and Newman resigned in November 1858. His autobiography, *Apologia Pro Vita Sua,* was published in 1864 and *The Idea of A University Defined* in 1873. *See also* Universities

NEWSPAPERS. Printing in Dublin may be traced to c. 1550. Only from 1617 did the London Company of Stationers extend its activities to Ireland, initially with a monopoly of government publishing. Presses began to function for news and propagandist purposes after 1643 in Waterford, Cork, and Kilkenny. The first weekly newspaper (1659) was short-lived, yet religious and political controversy, together with increasing literacy and demand for information, prompted rapid growth in printing after the Restoration (1660). This growth led to the more regular, though still brief, appearance of Robert Thornton's *Dublin News-Letter* (1685), the same publisher's Williamite *Dublin Intelligence* (1690), and the first provincial journal, the Cork *Idler* (1715), followed closely by the *Limerick Newsletter* (1716) and the Waterford *Flying Post* (1729). Francis Joy's *Belfast News-Letter and General Advertiser* began publication on 1 September 1737, though no issues survive prior to 9 January 1738. Liberal until the 1790s, but conservative after 1800, it is now the oldest continuous daily paper (from 1855) in Ireland.

Most early newspapers were content to reprint items from London issues and identifiably Irish content was meager, so they appealed mainly to a narrow Dublin circulation. Financially, they often survived by acting as the establishment's gazette, deriving income from printing official notices and reports. Whereas Saunders' *News-Letter* (1755–1879) relied mainly on advertising, from the outset other journals took strong political stands and often suffered because of that. The Belfast *Northern Star* (1792–97) was the paper of the United Irishmen, and *The Nation* (q.v.) (1842–48, 1849–91) was specifically created for the Young Ireland movement (q.v.); consequently both had a restricted, if scattered, readership. In contrast, provincial papers like the *Londonderry (Derry) Journal,* founded in 1772 by George Douglas, catered to a more compact regional audience over three counties (Donegal, Londonderry, Tyrone) in their news items and advertising, as did the *Londonderry Sentinel* (1829–1974, now the *Sentinel*) and *Londonderry Standard* (1936–88, *Derry Standard* to 1964). A wider sphere is served from Belfast by the *News Letter* (1737–1962/1989–) and *Irish News* (1891–), though their coverage of Irish matters broadly diverges along political lines, while the *Belfast (Evening) Telegraph,* (1870–1918–) reaches more of the entire northern community through its advertising.

From 1785 the *Public Register and Freeman's Journal (and Daily Commercial Advertiser,* from 1805) (1763–1924) was almost an official mouthpiece. After 1810 it became more independent, supporting Catholic emancipation, repeal of the Union, the Land League, Home Rule, John Redmond and the Irish Parliamentary Party (IPP), and finally the Anglo-Irish Treaty (qq.v.) in 1921. Its premises were destroyed by the IRA in March 1922, after which it became assimilated into the *Irish Independent,* now the largest-circulation daily (144,000). The latter had been initiated by Charles Stewart Parnell (q.v.), with a nucleus of Irish (Revolutionary) Republican Brotherhood (q.v.) supporters, as the *Irish Daily Independent* in December 1891, after the IPP had split. Later controlled by Redmond on the former printing site of *The Nation,* its financial problems necessitated merger with *The Daily Nation* in 1900, and it took its present title from 1905, producing a Sunday edition since 1907. It supported Fine Gael (q.v.) in the interwar period, and now tends to have a professional, middle-class readership.

On the other political flank, the *Irish Press,* created in September 1931 by Eamon de Valera for Fianna Fail (qq.v.), has a modest circulation (39,000 in 1994), with a Sunday edition from 1949 and an evening edition since 1954. Of the other main national daily papers, the *Cork Examiner* (1841–) now commands the fourth-largest morning circulation (52,000), especially in the southwest. Having earlier merged with *Faulkner's Dublin Journal* (1725–1825), for much of its history *The Irish Times* (1859–) was viewed as being allied to the ascendancy (q.v.). In recent decades it has assumed a more international, liberal outlook, and it is certainly no longer pro-Unionist. Its daily circulation in the 1970s was the fourth largest, but in 1994 was second (93,000).

NORTHERN IRELAND CIVIL RIGHTS ASSOCIATION (NICRA). Formed in Belfast in 1967, it was based on the National Council for Civil Liberties in London, having Noel Harris, a trade unionist, as its first chairman. Its primary aims were (1) reform of the Northern Ireland electoral system, which was significantly different from that operating in the rest of the UK; (2) creation of structures to prevent and deal with discrimination in public bodies; (3) fair allocation of public housing; (4) repeal of the Special Powers Act; and (5) disbanding of the Ulster Special Constabulary (q.v.). Its first protest march was held in Dungannon in August 1968. The second march in Derry in October led to clashes with the police and made an international impact when it was shown on television. The Cameron inquiry reported that the police action had been unjustified and that there was no evidence that NICRA was a front for the IRA (q.v.), though some of its members were involved. During the period when internment without trial was being practiced, NICRA organized a civil disobedience campaign. When that ended, the body ceased to have a prominent role, as most of its aims had been satisfied through a series of reforms.

NORTHERN IRELAND LABOUR PARTY (NILP). Formed in 1923–24, its support came mainly from the Belfast area. Its best years were 1958–65 when it had four MPs at Stormont (q.v.). Its trades-union support in Northern Ireland was not very strong; neither was assistance from the British Labour Party. What support it did have waned following the formation of the Social Democratic and Labour Party, and it gradually lost all influence. In 1987 it and other minor labor groups became part of Labour '87, which had fraternal but no direct links with either the Irish or the British Labour Party, the latter having persistently declined to accept members from, or to organize in, Northern Ireland.

NORTON, WILLIAM (1900–63). Born in Dublin. A trades unionist, secretary of the Post Office Workers' Union (1924–48), he was elected TD for Co. Dublin (1926–27) and then for Kildare (1932–63). He led the Labour Party (q.v.) in the Republic of Ireland from 1932, becoming tanaiste in the first coalition government of 1948–51 and in 1954–57.

-O-

O'BRIEN, CONOR CRUISE (1917–). Historian, academic, diplomat, and writer. Educated at Trinity College Dublin, by which he was awarded a doctorate. He moved from the Irish civil service to the United Nations Organization, serving in Katanga in 1961, later becoming vice-chancellor of the University of Ghana (1962–65) and a professor at New York University (1965–69). He was elected as a Labour Party (q.v.) TD in 1969 and became a minister (1973–77), banning paramilitary broadcasts on Radio Telefís Éireann (q.v.). He has always held strongly individualistic views on Northern Ireland, based on his belief that repeated calls for a united Ireland are counterproductive. Those opinions, and his interpretation of their historical background, are concisely presented in *Ancestral Voices: Religion and Nationalism in Ireland* (1994). He regarded the Northern Ireland Civil Rights Association as being too easily highjacked by the IRA, and he was critical of the Anglo-Irish Agreement (qq.v.). He was editor in chief of *The Observer* newspaper in London (1978–80).

O'BRIEN, MURROUGH (1614–74). A Spanish soldier in Italy, vice president of Munster in 1640, and its governor after the death of his father-in-law, St. Leger, in 1642. In 1645 he became president of Munster after expelling Roman Catholics from Cork, Kinsale, and Youghal. He was created earl of Inchiquin in 1654. He converted to Roman Catholicism and was granted a large estate after the Restoration.

O'BRIEN, WILLIAM (1852–1928). Born in Mallow, Co. Cork, educated at Queen's College Cork, edited *United Ireland* for the Land League (q.v.) from 1881. He was elected MP for Mallow in 1883, and with John Dillon (q.v.) initiated the "plan of campaign" (1886–91), which was condemned by the pope. He became anti-Parnellite in 1891 and set up the United Irish League to reunite the party by 1900. He sought conciliation with Unionists under the All-for-Ireland League (q.v.) in 1910. He wrote a Fenian novel, *When We Were Boys* (1890), *Recollections* (1906) and *The Irish Revolution* (1928).

O'BRIEN, WILLIAM SMITH (1803–64). Born in Co. Clare, educated at Harrow and Cambridge, Conservative MP for Ennis in 1825 and for Co. Limerick in 1835. By 1844 he supported repeal of the Union. A leader of Young Ireland, he broke with Daniel O'Connell (qq.v.) to set up the Irish Confederation in March 1848. He was captured after an abortive uprising and received a death sentence, which was commuted to life imprisonment in Tasmania (1849–54), but he was pardoned in 1856. He died in Bangor, Caernarvonshire.

O'CASEY, SEAN (1880–1964). Born in Dublin, the youngest of 13 children of a Protestant Church Missions Society clerk. Largely self-taught, he worked as a laborer until 1926. He was influenced by the socialist James Larkin and by the pacifist Francis Sheehy-Skeffington (qq.v.). He was briefly involved with the Irish Citizen Army (q.v.), but was fundamentally antimilitant and did not take part in the Easter Rising (q.v.). He taught himself Irish, joined the Gaelic League, and was encouraged by Lady Gregory to offer plays to the Abbey Theatre (qq.v.). There followed *The Shadow of a Gunman* (1923), *Juno and the Paycock* (1924), and *The Plough and the Stars* (1926), which caused a riot in the theater at its first performance. In 1927 he quarrelled over Abbey business with W. B. Yeats (q.v.), who had proclaimed him a genius. He then left Ireland and spent the rest of his life in England with his wife, the actress Eileen Carey. He also wrote stories and a six-volume autobiography (1939–54). His later plays were less successful.

Ó CEALLAIGH (O'KELLY), SEAN THOMAS (1883–1966). Born in Dublin, he became active in the Gaelic League (q.v.) and the Celtic Literary Society with Arthur Griffith and Maud Gonne (q.v.). After joining the Irish Republican Brotherhood, he was a founder member of Sinn Fein (qq.v.) in 1905, manager of *An Claidheamh Soluis,* general secretary of the Gaelic League (1915), and was interned in England after the Easter Rising (q.v.). He was elected as a Sinn Fein MP in 1918, became *Dáil Cean Comhairle* in 1919, opposed the Anglo-Irish Treaty, was a founder of Fianna Fail (qq.v.) in 1926, and vice president of the Executive Council in 1932. He was president of Ireland in 1945–52 and 1952–59.

O'CONNELL, DANIEL (1775–1847). Born in Cahirciveen, Co. Kerry, but was raised in Derrynane by an uncle. Educated in St. Omer and Douai in 1791, he was horrified by the excesses of the French Revolution and the 1798 rising's violence. He entered Lincoln's Inn, read widely in philosophy and economics, became a barrister in Munster, and opposed the veto on the appointment of Roman Catholic bishops. After a rift with Henry Grattan (q.v.) he set up the Catholic Association to achieve emancipation by constitutional means. He was victorious in the 1828 Clare election, after which Catholic emancipation (q.v.) was won from Peel in April 1829 on the basis of the £10 franchise. He turned to full-time political activity on the issues of repealing the Union and creating a fully representative Irish parliament. He was elected lord mayor of Dublin in 1841 in an atmosphere of increasing radicalism after the Suppression of Disturbances (Ireland) Act of 1833 and the growing power of the Irish group at Westminster. Following the organization of "monster meetings," such as that at Tara, he was charged with conspiracy after the banned Clontarf meeting in October 1843. He died in Genoa en route to Rome.

O'CONNOR, ARTHUR (1763–1852). Irish MP (1791–95), an extreme United Irishman (q.v.) under strong French influence, linked to Lord Edward FitzGerald (q.v.). After the 1796 Antrim incitement led to repression, he was arrested and released. He joined the Napoleonic army in 1804 and attempted another rising from exile in 1810.

O'CONNOR, FEARGUS EDWARD (1794–1855). Born in Co. Cork, educated at Portarlington and Trinity College Dublin. Elected repeal MP for Cork in 1832–35, he became involved in a rift with Daniel O'Connell (q.v.). He was active in the north of England, founding the *Northern Star* (1837) and the "People's Charter" (the basis of the Chartist movement in Britain) (1838). He led the 1840s "National Land Campaign" to give workers smallholdings. He was elected MP for Nottingham in 1847, but was declared insane in 1852.

O'CONNOR, FRANK (Michael Francis O'Donovan)(1903–66). Born in Cork, son of an army bandsman and an orphaned domestic servant. At school he was taught by Daniel Corkery. He left at 14 and was employed as a railway messenger boy. As a republican during the civil war (q.v.), he was interned for a year. After working as a librarian, he met W. B. Yeats and George Russell (qq.v.). Through them he found a positive outlet for his literary interests and talent. His first short stories were published in 1931 as *Guests of the Nation*. He collaborated with Yeats as an Abbey Theatre (q.v.) director in 1935–39, also writing a biography of Michael Collins (q.v.) entitled *The Big Fellow* (1937). He lived in the United States in 1939–60, lectured at Trinity College Dublin, and published an autobiography, *An Only Child* and *My Father's Son*. His translations from the Irish, *The Midnight Court* (1946) and *Kings, Lords and Commons* (1961), among other books, were banned in Ireland. With David Greene he edited *A Golden Treasury of Irish Poetry: A.D. 600 to 1200*.

O'CONOR, KING FELIM (Fedlimid Ó Conchobair) (?–1265). Son of Cathal Crobderg Ó Conchobair, he was installed as king of Connacht by Richard de Burgh in 1230, but was captured and deposed in favor of his kinsman Aed the following year. In a feud for control of Connacht he killed Aed in 1233 and recovered his title after attacking Norman castles at Rindown and Galway. Renewed campaigns by the justiciar and de Burgh reestablished a Norman presence, and, having submitted to the crown, Felim was granted the five king's cantreds of Connacht in 1237. By that time the Gaelic kingdom was effectively dead and de Burgh was supreme. Another Felim did battle with the Anglo-Normans from 1310 and died in 1316 as the last O'Connor king of Connacht.

Ó DALAIGH, CEARBHALL (1911–78). Born in Bray, graduated in Celtic studies at University College Dublin, studied law at King's Inns, and was Irish-language editor of *The Irish Press*. Having practiced as a barrister, he was attorney general in 1946–48 and 1951–53. He became chief justice in 1961. He was appointed president of Ireland in succession to E. H. Childers (q.v.) on 19 December 1974, but became involved in a dispute over the 1976 Emergency Powers Act after referring it to the Supreme Court; he resigned on 2 October that year.

O'DOHERTY, SIR CAHIR (1587–1608). Lord of Inishowen, a Derry alderman and a member of the jury who pronounced the earls of Tyrone and Tyrconnell guilty of treason in 1607. He led a revolt in which Governor Paulet of Derry was killed in April 1608 and the garrison massacred. He himself was killed at Kilmacrenan in July.

O'DONNELL, (RED) HUGH ROE (c. 1571–1602). Son of Hugh, Lord of Tyrconnell, he was taken hostage by Perrott in 1587 and held in Dublin Castle until 1591, when he escaped to Donegal with the sons of Shane O'Neill (q.v.). As chief of the O'Donnells in May 1592, he overran Sligo and Connacht. With Hugh O'Neill (q.v.) he defeated and killed Sir Henry Bagenal at the Yellow Ford near Armagh in August 1598. He tried to link up with Spanish forces and Tyrone's army at Kinsale on Christmas Eve 1601, but was heavily defeated by Mountjoy. He went to Philip III of Spain for further help but died, possibly poisoned, at Simancas. He was buried in Valladolid.

O'DONOVAN, JOHN (1809–61). Born in Co. Kilkenny. Both parents died when he was young, and he was brought up by his brother in Dublin from 1817. He joined the staff of the Irish Record Office in 1826 and studied the Irish language, archaeology, and historical documents under the supervision of the Galway historian James Hardiman. In 1829 he joined George Petrie at the Ordnance Survey to investigate the Royal Irish Academy's (qq.v.) collection of Irish manuscripts for townland place-name evidence. Ultimately, 50 volumes of place-names were published, edited by Fr. M. O'Flanagan. He contributed many articles to the *Dublin Penny Journal* and *Irish Penny Journal,* and wrote an *Irish Grammar* (1845). Called to the Bar in 1847, he edited and translated the *Annals of the Four Masters* (6 vols., 1848–51), for which he received the Academy's Cunningham Medal. He translated ancient Irish laws and poetry for the Irish Archaeological Society (which he founded in 1840 with E. Curry) and the Celtic Society, though they were not published in his lifetime.

O'FAOLÁIN, SEAN (John Whelan)(1900–91). Born in Cork, son of a Royal Irish Constabulary (q.v.) officer, educated at University College Cork. He joined the IRA (q.v.), and was an active Republican in the civil war (q.v.), rejecting the Anglo-Irish Treaty (q.v.). Later, influenced by Daniel Corkery, he became a teacher and a writer. His *Midsummer Night Madness* (1932) and *Bird Alone* (1936) were banned in Ireland. He was founder and first editor of a leading Irish literary journal, *The Bell* (1940), struggling against unthinking censorship. He wrote biographies of Daniel O'Connell, Countess Markievicz, and Hugh O'Neill, earl of Tyrone (qq.v.). *See also* Censorship of Publications

OFFICIAL IRA. The prefix dates from 1970 when the republican movement split into "Official" and "Provisional" wings, on the issue of parliamentary action. Each had its military section, the IRA (q.v.), and its political party, Sinn Fein (q.v.). The Officials have not been openly active since a cease-fire in 1972. Prior to that they were responsible for some horrific incidents and many deaths. They lost out to the originally less numerous Provos because of their more political approach, in contrast to the more practical outlook of the latter, who built up support via local defense units. Periodically, the two sections clashed violently.

O'FIAICH, TOMAS (1923–92). Born in Cullyhanna, Co. Armagh, educated at Maynooth and University College Dublin. A history lecturer, he wrote a biography of *St. Oliver Plunkett* (q.v.), and became vice president and later president of St. Patrick's College Maynooth. He was appointed Roman Catholic archbishop of Armagh in 1977, and a cardinal in 1979. He died suddenly while on a pilgrimage to Lourdes.

O'FLAHERTY, LIAM (1896–1984). Born on Inishmore, Aran Islands, educated at Blackrock College and University College Dublin. He served in the British army in 1915–17, joined the Communist Party (q.v.) in 1921, and moved to London to write in 1922. His most popular works were *The Informer* (1925), *Skerret* (1932), *Famine* (1937), and a collection of stories, *Duil* (1953).

"OLD ENGLISH." The term applied in post-Reformation times to early Catholic settlers or those assimilated into the native population—"English of Irish birth." Most of them derived from the Anglo-Normans based in Dublin and other urban nuclei, such as Galway, and the Pale (qq.v.). Their ancient title to land was questioned by the policies of confiscation and regrant during the plantation (q.v.) era. Traditionally royalist, many joined the native Confederacy to preserve their lands.

O'NEILL, HUGH (1550–1616), earl of Tyrone. Born in Dungannon, but was raised by Sir Henry Sidney in Ludlow and London. He returned to Ireland in 1568, rescued Spanish Armada (q.v.) survivors in Inishowen in 1588, and eloped with Sir Henry Bagenal's sister in 1591. He rebelled in 1595, defeating Bagenal in 1598. He parleyed with Essex at Dundalk in 1599, but reneged after Essex's execution, provoking Mountjoy's campaign in 1600. However, numerous chiefs deserted him for Sir Henry Docwra, and he was forced to retreat after the fiasco at Kinsale in 1601. He surrendered to Mountjoy at Mellifont in March 1603, unaware that Queen Elizabeth had died a week earlier. He fled to Rome in September 1607. *See also* Blount, Charles; Flight of the Earls

O'NEILL, OWEN ROE (c. 1590–1649). He served in the Spanish army in the Netherlands and elsewhere until returning to Ireland in 1642 to form the Catholic Confederacy, negotiated with Lord Deputy Ormond (q.v.) and Rinuccini. His troops were victorious over Monro at the battle of Benburb in June 1646. Having been declared a traitor by the Confederacy in 1648, he arranged a treaty with Ormond in October 1649, but died the following month.

O'NEILL, SIR PHELIM (c. 1604–53). Dungannon member of the 1641 Irish parliament, and commander of Irish forces until Owen Roe O'Neill (q.v.) took over. He fought on until he was betrayed in 1652. He was executed for treason in March 1653.

O'NEILL, SHANE (1530–67). Eldest son of Conn, first earl of Tyrone. He became clan chief in 1559, but was not acknowledged by the English, who accepted his illegitimate brother, Matthew. He attacked the Scots MacDonnells in the Glens of Antrim, Armagh, and the Pale, captured Sorley Boy McDonnell (qq.v.), and was murdered by them at Cushendun.

O'NEILL, TERENCE (1914–90). Born in London, with ancestors on both sides of the Ulster divide—the ancient family of O'Neill and the later English planter, Arthur Chichester (q.v.). Educated at Eton, he served in the army in World War II. In 1946 he was elected to Stormont (q.v.) as Unionist MP for Bannside, and worked in the ministry of finance, eventually becoming party leader and prime minister of Northern Ireland in 1963–69. He quickly developed a reformist course, in which meetings with the Republic's taoiseach were the most evident feature. This angered some Unionist colleagues, and Rev. Ian Paisley (q.v.) started to campaign against him. The Ulster Volunteer Force (q.v.) was formed on the loyalist side, and Northern Ireland Civil Rights Association (NICRA) (qq.v.) marches started among nationalists. O'Neill announced a five-point reform program in response to several NICRA demands, and called an election. This led to bitterness within his own party, and did not give a clear mandate. He resigned in April 1969 and became Baron O'Neill of the Maine.

ORANGE ORDER. Founded in 1795 in Loughgall, Co. Armagh, after the so-called "battle of the Diamond" between Protestants and Catholics over the latter's attempts to hold armed demonstrations. Its name refers to William, Prince of Orange, whose victory over James II at the battle of the Boyne in 1690 signaled the end of a long period of religious wars in Europe. Supported by the gentry, its members began to dominate the northern yeomanry until it was disbanded in 1803, whereas further south Catholic Defenders and United Irishmen (q.v.)

infiltrated the militia, leading to direct conflict in the 1798 rebellion. *See also* Boyne, River

It revived as a popular organization in the 1820s when its public profile was threatened by Lord Lieutenant Arthur Wellesley's (q.v.) policies on law enforcement and the rise of Daniel O'Connell's (q.v.) Catholic Association. Both institutions were dissolved by Peel in 1825. Thereafter, Orangemen regrouped in political forms as Brunswick Clubs. After Catholic emancipation (q.v.) in 1829, Orangeism revived again in Ulster, twice partly provoked by O'Connell, to rival processions held by Ribbonmen (q.v.), which reached a peak in 1848–49. Its Grand Lodge was reinstated twice (1828 and 1846). The movement was further stimulated by the growth of Fenianism (q.v.) in the 1860s, both in Ireland and in North America, and experienced a change in composition as it attracted middle-class Presbyterians, hitherto discouraged.

It is now the largest Protestant organization with about 100,000 active members and branches in the Republic of Ireland, parts of Great Britain, and overseas. The organization comprises local branches or lodges, and the main event is the annual march and demonstration on 12 July, the anniversary (New Style, Gregorian calendar) of the Boyne battle. The senior branch is known as the Royal Black Institution. The Home Rule movement of the later 19th century encouraged a more political, pro-Union stance within the Order. The Unionist Party developed out of a group of Orangemen who became Westminster MPs in 1886, and a close connection remains. The defense of civil and religious liberty is part of the Order's aims, but the Northern Ireland Civil Rights Association (NICRA) (q.v.) was seen as only republican or communist inspired. More recently the Order has been active in the opposition to the Anglo-Irish Agreement (q.v.). *See also* Home Government (Rule) Association

ORDNANCE SURVEY (OS). On 21 June 1824 (6 Geo. IV, c. 99) parliament authorized a survey on a scale of six inches to one mile to establish an accurate inventory of taxable property. Lieutenant Colonel Thomas Colby was appointed to conduct the trigonometrical survey in Ireland, and he chose Mountjoy House, Phoenix Park, Dublin, as his base. Primary triangulation was completed in 1858, the baseline being located on the shore of Lough Foyle in Co. Londonderry in 1827. In July 1825, Richard Griffith (q.v.) was appointed head of the boundary department to identify and plot the limits of parishes and townlands, followed in 1830 by a valuation of lands. Lieutenant T. A. Larcom (q.v.) became head of the survey in 1828, producing the first more extensive verbal survey memoir for Templemore parish (Londonderry), in 1837. The manuscript originals of these memoirs, containing much geological, contemporary economic, and antiquarian material, are preserved at the Royal Irish Academy (q.v.). Many volumes have been published for the first time in recent years under the auspices of the Institute of Irish Studies at The Queen's University of Belfast. From 1830 Irish place-name material was collected and standardized in anglicized forms, notably by John O'Donovan (q.v.), subsequently professor of Celtic at Belfast.

The datum for altitudinal observation and recording was the low-water mark at Poolbeg Lighthouse, Dublin, from 1843 until 1958, when it was changed to mean sea level at Malin Head. Town plans on larger scales were compiled from 1840. These contain useful information on the extent and nature of urban development in the mid-19th century. In 1924 the OS Dublin was transferred from the Department of Agriculture to the Department of Finance, and a similar administrative change occurred at the OS of Northern Ireland in 1933. In 1947 an Archaeological Branch was set up in the OS Dublin to produce a survey of megalithic tombs throughout the island. The Placenames Branch, formed in 1955, embarked on systematic publication of correct townland name volumes.

ORMOND, TWELFTH EARL OF. *See* BUTLER, James

O'TOOLE, ST. LAWRENCE (1130–1180). Educated at the monastery of Glendalough, of which he became abbot in 1153. Consecrated archbishop of Dublin in 1162, he assembled an army to recapture Dublin from the earl of Pembroke (Strongbow) in 1170. He was canonized in 1225.

-P-

PAISLEY, REV. IAN RICHARD KYLE (1926–). Born in Armagh, the son of a Baptist minister. In 1951 he founded a Free Presbyterian church in Belfast and began political activity in 1963 with a protest march over use of the Union flag in Belfast to show respect on the death of the pope. When it was banned, the march became the first loyalist activity to suffer under the Special Powers Act. The closer links with the Republic of Ireland fostered by Northern Ireland's Prime Minister Terence O'Neill (q.v.) drew forth further, often noisy and abusive protests. He denied any connection with the Ulster Volunteer Force (q.v.), but set up two groups that were later involved in counterdemonstrations to the civil rights marches, the Ulster Constitution Defence Committee and the Ulster Protestant Volunteers. He was imprisoned for six months after blocking off the town center of Armagh in November 1968.

He regarded O'Neill's subsequent resignation a result of his activities and won O'Neill's Bannside seat for Stormont (q.v.) at the ensuing by-election, followed soon by the Westminster parliamentary seat of North Antrim. In 1971 he formed the Democratic Unionist Party (DUP) (q.v.). Not having been included in the conference, he attacked the Sunningdale Agreement (q.v.) Assembly. After the 1974 loyalist strike began, he was active in the United Ulster Unionist Council. He supported the Convention and appeared at times to favor some form of partnership government. His strike call in 1977 failed, and his relations with other Unionists became strained. The Scarman report on the disturbances of 1969 reproved Paisley's provocative verbal style but considered that he "neither plotted nor organized the disorders," although he raised tension thereby.

Paisley headed the poll in the first (and all later) European Community (EC) parliamentary elections, campaigning against the EC on economic and religious (its allegedly anti-Protestant bias) grounds. He continued to protest through the 1980s on the government's attitude toward security matters and on well-known constitutional and religious concerns. In 1981 he briefly produced an armed force of 500 that was later claimed to have grown to 20,000. At the end of 1981 the United States withdrew his visa on the grounds of "divisive" statements and actions. His alternative trip to Canada early in 1982, however, achieved the desired media coverage.

His suspicions of the motives of Westminster governments regarding Northern Ireland policy and their contacts with government of the Republic, which were often expressed forcibly and sometimes resulted in temporary suspension from the House of Commons, made him favor devolution. He cooperated with the Official Ulster Unionist Party (q.v.) toward this end from time to time, notably in 1987–89. Thus he worked within the Assembly, but objected strongly to the Anglo-Irish Agreement (q.v.) because of its intrinsic Irish dimension. During another upsurge in IRA terrorism in 1988 he called for restoration of capital punishment, as he did in 1993 when loyalist murder squads were active. When Official Ulster Unionists adopted a conciliatory position on talks with the Haughey (q.v.) government in Dublin in 1992, the DUP did not join them. Bitter personal criticism of James Molyneaux (q.v.) froze relations between the two parties. A recurring theme in Paisley's attacks on successive British Conservative governments' policy vis-à-vis Dublin has been real or imagined fear of a sellout to the Republic's objectives as expressed in clauses 2 and 3 of its constitution (q.v.) (the territorial claim on the six Ulster counties). Such apprehensions seemed to be confirmed by interpretations of the Downing Street Declaration (q.v.). They were reinforced in November 1993 when it was revealed that British officials had been in secret (and often denied) contact with Sinn Fein/IRA for several years. In January 1994 Paisley sought, unsuccessfully, a UK referendum on the future status of Northern Ireland. His wife, daughter, and son have all been active alongside him in Northern Ireland politics at various times.

PALE, THE. An area settled by medieval English invaders in the east-center of Ireland, focused on Dublin, Kildare, Louth, and Meath, was given precise territorial limits c. 1495. It was extended to Waterford, Wexford, and Tipperary in the 14th century. Minor parallel pales existed in the early 17th century around the cities of Cork, Galway, Limerick and Waterford (qq.v.), in reality as spheres of English culture, broadened by plantations of "New English" (qq.v.).

PARNELL, CHARLES STEWART (1846–91). Born at Avondale, Co. Wicklow, son of a pronationalist Protestant landowner, and educated in Somerset and at Magdalene College, Cambridge. He was elected MP for Meath in 1875 and joined Isaac Butt's (q.v.) Home Rule Party, succeeding him as leader. He was invited by Michael Davitt to preside over the Land League (qq.v.) in 1879, but was arrested in October 1881 after violence during the "land war" (q.v.) and Boycott incidents. While in prison he negotiated the 1882 "Kilmainham treaty" with W. E. Gladstone, intended to lead to implementation of the 1881 land act under a new chief secretary, Cavendish, who was murdered in Phoenix Park on his arrival on 6 May. During the 1885 election campaign he argued for legislative independence for Ireland, but Gladstone's 1886 Home Rule Bill was defeated by Conservatives and Unionists, and the government fell. In 1887 *The Times* implicated Parnell in crime on the basis of what were later proved to be forged letters. Parnell's innocence was vindicated by a special commission report in 1890, but any restoration of public approval was destroyed by the O'Shea divorce affair. He was abandoned by Gladstone and lost the confidence of his own party shortly before his death. *See also* Boycott, Captain Charles Cunningham; Land Acts

PARSONS, SIR CHARLES ALGERNON (1854–1931). Younger son of the third earl of Rosse, himself a noted astronomer, he was educated at Birr, Trinity College Dublin, and Cambridge University. In 1884 he invented a high-speed steam turbine at Armstrong's engineering works in Newcastle-upon-Tyne, and in 1889 he set up his own factory on Tyneside, subsequently contracted by the admiralty. He bought and transferred to Tyneside the Dublin firm of Sir Howard Grubb, who had made his father's telescope and went on to build Europe's largest telescope in 1931 (74-inch diameter). He was elected Fellow of the Royal Society in 1898, was made a Companion of the Bath (1904) and a Knight Commander of the Bath (1911). He was awarded the Order of Merit in 1927.

PARSONS, WILLIAM (1800–67), third earl of Rosse (1841). Born in York, educated at Trinity College Dublin and Magdalen College, Oxford. He was MP for King's County (1831–34). He improved Herschel's reflecting telescope and published his experimental methods in 1828–30. In 1842–45 he constructed a telescope with a diameter of six feet. It was the world's largest until 1915, though not the most useful because of its unwieldiness. Nevertheless, it did reveal the spiral structure of the "Milky Way" system, and led to the discovery of new nebulae in 1848–78. He was president of the Royal Society (1849–54), a member of the Imperial Academy of St. Petersburg (1853), and was active in relief of the 1846–47 famine.

PATRICK, ST. (?–c. A.D. 490) According to his Latin *Confessions,* he was captured from Britain at the age of 16 by Irish raiders and spent some time as a shepherd on Slemish, Co. Antrim. A supposed disciple of St. Germanus of Auxerre, his mission was to convert the Irish to Christianity. Tradition gives the place of his death as Saul, Downpatrick, Co. Down, and its supposed date, 17 March, is celebrated as Ireland's national day. Many legendary events and places are associated with St. Patrick's life, including the shamrock emblem and his banishment of snakes from Ireland. Numerous pilgrimage sites include Croagh Patrick, Co. Mayo, and St. Patrick's Purgatory, Co. Donegal.

PEARSE, PATRICK HENRY (1879–1916). Born in Dublin, educated at a Christian Brothers school and the Royal University of Ireland. He joined the Gaelic League (q.v.), edited *An Claidheamh Soluis,* lectured at University College Dublin, and founded the bilingual St. Enda's school, Rathmines, Dublin, in 1908. He participated in a meeting in September 1914 to plan an Irish rebellion. He was a member of the Irish (Revolutionary) Republican Brotherhood's (q.v.) Supreme Council, of its three-man military committee (1915), and of the committee of the Irish Volunteers (q.v.). He commanded republican forces in the 1916 uprising and authorized the surrender on 29 April. He was tried by court martial, found guilty of treason, and shot.

PENAL LAWS (1657–1734). The Convicting, Discovering, and Repressing of Popish Recusants Act (26 June 1657) required the Oath of Abjuration, renouncing papal supremacy and the doctrine of transubstantiation, to be sworn, on penalty of confiscation of two-thirds of one's property. Under Oliver Cromwell (q.v.) "recusants," i.e., noncommunicants of the Protestant Established Church, were equally regarded as Roman Catholics. An Act of 24 December 1691 debarred Catholics from public office in Ireland and from taking up seats in the Irish parliament. In the face of a threat to the Crown from Catholic Jacobites, reaction set in against James II's pro-Catholic policies. Two acts of September 1695 imposed a prohibition on sending children abroad for a Catholic education, and its teaching in Ireland (7 Will. III, c. 4), while Catholics were forbidden to bear weapons or to own a horse worth more than £5 (7 Will. III, c. 5). From January 1699 they were forbidden to practice law (10 Will. III, c. 13) and in 1704 to buy land or to act as guardians to estate heirs (2 Anne, c. 6). It should not be overlooked that the sacramental test was also imposed on Dissenters. In May 1728 Roman Catholics were disenfranchised in law (1 Geo. II, c. 9), though in effect most were already excluded by the property qualification. In 1734 converts to the Established Church were precluded from educating their children in their mother's faith if she was a Catholic, or from becoming justices of the peace if married to a Catholic (7 Geo. II, c. 6). They were also restricted in leaseholding. By the 1770s there was growing impatience with these laws among rising Roman Catholics and equally among liberal Protestants, with the result that relief from disabilities relating to land ownership, to the activities of Catholic clergy, and to education was granted under acts of 1772, 1778, and 1782.

PETRIE, GEORGE (1789–1866). Born in Dublin, son of the portrait painter James Petrie, of Scottish ancestry, who made likenesses of several leaders of the 1798 rebellion. Educated at Samuel Whyte's school, as were Tom Moore and R. B. Sheridan (q.v.), and at the Dublin Society's art school. He became a landscape artist and antiquarian illustrator, a prominent figure in the Royal Hibernian Academy from 1828, an academician and its librarian (1830), and later its president. In 1842 he edited the *Dublin Penny Journal,* having contributed to the *Irish Penny Journal* since 1832. He was elected to the council of the Royal Irish Academy (RIA) (q.v.) in 1829. He secured many notable antiquities for its collections, including the *Annals of the Four Masters.* He worked in the Ordnance Survey in 1833–46 and published a study of Tara (1837)(qq.v.) for which he was awarded a gold medal. He received another for his comprehensive *Essay on the Origin and Uses of the Round Towers in Ireland,* published in 1845 as part of his *Ecclesiastical Architecture of Ireland.* His research was encouraged by William Stokes (q.v.), who wrote his biography in 1868, and E. R. W. Quin, the future earl of Dunraven. He collected Irish inscriptions and traditional music, and was himself a violinist. His antiquarian collection was purchased by the state for the RIA.

PETTY, SIR WILLIAM (1623–87). Professor of anatomy at the University of Oxford (1650). As a physician with Oliver Cromwell's (q.v.) army in Ireland, he conducted a survey in 1654, published *Hiberniae Delineatio* (1685), calculated populations from mortality statistics, the hearth tax, and poll tax lists. He asserted that Ireland had lost 36 percent of its population by war in the years 1641–53. He proposed redrawing parish boundaries to place people nearer parish churches. He was a transport and trade enthusiast on specialized production and advocated immigration to Ireland from Britain to raise cultural and economic standards.

PLANTATIONS. English occupation of Ireland had progressed since the Anglo-Norman invasion (q.v.) in the 12th century. Yet by the middle of the Tudor period it was at best tenuous and essentially restricted to the eastern third of the country centered on Dublin, with an outlier beyond Limerick in Kerry. From 1534 the English monarchy, seeking to impose the religious Reformation and exert greater political control, undertook more assertive direct administration of affairs in Ireland. A pivotal mechanism in this change was the process of planned land settlement by new colonists. To counteract rebellion and raiding, some lands, held of the Crown by Irish chieftains or suppressed monastic houses, were confiscated and reallocated to loyal "New English" (q.v.)—the policy of "surrender and regrant." Elsewhere, territories were granted wholesale, fortifications were erected, and planter tenants of varied ethnicity were introduced. By the 1550s part of Leinster was already well settled by the English, e.g. Kildare, Meath, Wicklow, Queen's County (Laois), and King's County (Offaly). In Wexford freeholders with less than 100 acres were expropriated and turned into leaseholders, surplus land being allocated to new planters, a strategy that often created an ethnic division between landowners and tenants.

In Munster the Fitzgeralds revolted in 1569 and when peace was restored in 1584 the forfeited and depopulated Desmond lands were resettled in chief grants (seignories) of 4,000–12,000 acres by "New English" from northwestern and southwestern England, among the greatest being Sir Walter Raleigh in Co. Waterford. By the end of the century some 4,500–5,000 English males had settled. However, the scale of grants proved too large, and the infrastructure to protect colonists was inadequate. Consequently, many localities required resettling after 1603–25.

The plantation of Ulster was rooted in the urban bridgeheads of Carrickfergus (the Chichester [q.v.] nucleus), Coleraine, Downpatrick, and Londonderry. After the "flight of the earls" (q.v.) and confiscation of the lordship of Tyrone, six counties were declared free to be colonized in 1608, with new titles to land in blocks of 1,000–2,000 acres. The London Companies were given Londonderry. Scots entrenched in north Antrim and north Down received formal grants in 1604–5. Many settlers fled or were killed during and after the rebellion of 1641 until Oliver Cromwell (qq.v.) restored order in 1652. *See also* Derry/Londonderry

Access to Connacht was improved by the 1567 bridge over the Shannon at Athlone. Planned private settlement appeared in Roscommon in the 1570–80s. Further west, numerous revolts deterred new tenants. The native residents of Connacht, especially the earls of Clanricard in Galway, resisted Thomas Wentworth's (q.v.) later effort to secure royal control in 1635–37, but it too was subjected to resettlement of Cromwellian deportees.

The net result of the policy over three generations was initial devastation of extensive areas, disruption and reduction of the indigenous population, restructuring of tenurial patterns, implantation of new colonists, and transformation both of the settlement system and ethnic distributions as bases for economic and political recovery.

PLUNKETT, SIR HORACE CURZON (1854–1932). Educated at Eton and Oxford, he spent a decade in Wyoming before returning in 1889 to agricultural cooperative work in Ireland. A member of the Congested Districts Board (q.v.) in 1891, he was MP for South Dublin in 1892–1900. He helped establish the Department of Agriculture and Technical Instruction, of which he was vice president in 1899–1906. He supported home rule within the Commonwealth, and founded the Irish Dominion League. He was elected Fellow of the Royal Society in 1902, and he became a member of the Irish Free State senate in 1922.

PLUNKETT, ST. OLIVER (1629–81). Born in Co. Meath and educated at the Irish College, Rome. In 1647 he settled Jesuits at Drogheda seminary and was appointed archbishop of Armagh in 1669. The "Popish Plot" (1678) led to his arrest for conspiracy to armed rebellion in 1679, and he was executed at Tyburn in July 1681. He was canonized in 1975.

POOR LAW COMMISSION. Set up in September 1833. It reported that nearly 2.4 million people in Ireland existed in severe need, many surviving on irregular agricultural wages at 6–12 pence per day. As a partial response, it suggested organized and subsidized emigration, the creation of a Board of Improvement to carry out land reclamation, and a Board of Works (q.v.) to oversee model schools for agriculture and gainful labor activity. In 1838, with the approval of many Catholics, the English poor law system was extended to Ireland, despite the opposition, for different reasons, of Daniel O'Connell and Archbishop Whately (qq.v.).

It created 130 poor law unions, each focused on a market town, maintaining state-built workhouses for indoor relief only. The system was completed in 1840–46. Boards of guardians or ratepayers were constituted in each union, financed equally by tenants and landlords, the underpinning property valuation being later amended to ease the burden on poor tenants. The famine (q.v.) totally undermined this system of finance and revealed the inadequacy of outdoor relief. The 1847 Poor Law Extension Act created another 32 unions and separated all from the British poor law administration. In 1848 over 2 million people received relief, as did a similar number in 1849.

Poor law unions were divided in 1847 into 2,049 electoral divisions, the populations of unions averaging nearly 63,000. Their valuations were not conducted systematically, and therefore varied locally in size until Richard Griffith's (q.v.)(1848–65) primary valuation survey for calculating property rates. *See also* Administrative Divisions; Local Government

POPULATION. Great controversy has revolved around the supposed precensus number of inhabitants, average family size, and rates of population increase in Ireland. Sir William Petty (q.v.) estimated that the population of 17th-century Ireland was 1.1 million, of whom he believed 0.8 million to be Irish/Catholic, 0.2, English, and 0.1, Scots (or one member of the Established Church for every two Dissenters). Those aggregate figures were calculated on the basis of 0.2 million hearths, with 5.5 persons each. Half a century later Arthur Dobbs calculated a population of 2.3 million, based on 0.38 million houses and an average of six persons per household. None of these figures are wholly reliable, and indeed even the first two censuses were subject to statistical and clerical error. Accurate data cannot be presented for the whole country before 1841, but all authorities agree that the population had probably increased quite rapidly during the second half of the 18th century.

D. A. Beaufort's (q.v.) *Memoir of a Map of Ireland* (1792) asserted that Ireland's population had nearly trebled since 1700 to about four million, a figure accepted as an initial basis for deciding on the number of MPs for the proposed Union parliament in 1798. Very imperfect efforts were made to take a census (q.v.) in 1813. The first attempt at a systematic, comprehensive enumeration was completed in 1821 under W. S. Mason (q.v.). Records of non-Catholic marriages were kept from 1845 by William Donnelly, the first holder of the recently created office of registrar general, which was responsible for preserving records of all births, marriages, and deaths from 1864. The development of precisely enumerated aggregate and provincial totals at census dates is shown below:

Table 11
Aggregate and Provincial Census Totals

Year	Connacht	Leinster	Munster	Ulster	Ireland
1821	1,110,229	1,757,492	1,935,612	1,998,494	6,801,827
1831	1,343,914	1,909,713	2,227,152	2,286,622	7,767,401
1841	1,418,859	1,973,731	2,396,161	2,386,373	8,175,124
1851	1,010,031	1,672,738	1,857,736	2,011,880	6,552,385
1861	913,135	1,457,635	1,513,558	1,914,236	5,798,564
1871	846,213	1,339,451	1,393,485	1,833,228	5,412,377
1881	821,657	1,278,989	1,331,115	1,743,075	5,174,836
1891	724,774	1,187,760	1,172,402	1,619,814	4,704,750
1901	646,932	1,152,829	1,076,188	1,582,826	4,458,775
1911	610,984	1,162,044	1,035,495	1,581,696	4,390,219
1926	552,907	1,149,092	969,902	1,556,652	4,228,553
1936*	525,468	1,220,411	942,272	1,560,014	4,248,165
1951	471,895	1,336,576	898,870	1,624,173	4,331,514
1961**	419,465	1,332,149	849,203	1,642,566	4,243,383
1971	390,902	1,498,140	882,002	1,743,269	4,514,313
1981	424,410	1,790,521	998,315	1,762,355E	4,975,601
1991	423,031	1,860,949	1,009,533	1,810,042	5,103,555

*1937 for Northern Ireland
**9 April for Republic of Ireland, 23 April for Northern Ireland
E: Estimate for Northern Ireland

Long-term effects of the mid-19th century famines (q.v.), through heavy mortality, delayed marriage, and external migration, are clearly displayed in the totals for each province. By 1961 Connacht had declined heavily to only one-third of its 1821 total. Leinster's population was also reduced by one-third from its 1841 peak, but recovered to its 1870s levels by the 1950s. Munster fell by two-thirds from its peak in the early 19th century. Ulster, like Leinster, lost only one-third from its 1841 peak, though this aggregate masks a contrast between the Republic of Ireland and Northern Ireland sections of the province. Whereas the Republic section had lost half of even its 1881 population by 1961, and one-third in 1926–71, the Northern Ireland area began to recover from its 1890s nadir by 1926, and by 1991 it was almost back to its 1831 total.

The 1981 Northern Ireland population census suffered from underenumeration as a consequence of an ill-judged campaign of noncompliance by some nationalists, but estimates have been calculated of those who declined to complete the schedules. Any residual anomalies relate primarily to Roman Catholic communities and thus possess a regional component too. In 1991 the number of inhabitants in the whole island exceeded five million for the first time in over a century, but was still fewer than the total recorded in 1881.

In 1841 17 percent of Ireland's people lived in towns. By 1891 that proportion had risen to 26 percent, by 1926 to 32 percent, and by 1966 to 49 percent. In 1981, apart from Dublin and Dun Laoghaire, Cork, Limerick, and Waterford, there were 17 towns with populations of 10,000 to 40,000 and a further 35 with 5,000 to 10,000 inhabitants. The Greater Dublin Area housed 915,115, or 27 percent, of the country's total residents. In contrast to all urban categories, country districts were characterized by a deficit of females. Using settlements with over 2,000 inhabitants as an indicator of urbanization, in 1841 less than 14 percent of the country's population was urban; by 1891 it had almost doubled to over 26 percent, and by 1911 that share had increased to 33 percent. Superficially, Leinster was the most urbanized province throughout this period, but the high figure is distorted by the inclusion of Dublin within that total. The imbalance, and Ulster's real preeminence in this field, is illustrated by the fact that throughout the postpartition era Northern Ireland's urban population exceeded 50 percent, whereas that figure was reached in the Republic only in the later 1960s.

POYNINGS' LAW. An act (10 Hen.VII, cc. 9/11), named after Lord Deputy Sir Edward Poynings (1459–1521). In 1494 parliament introduced enactments to achieve removal of Yorkist support in Ireland, extending all previous English legislation there. All the Irish parliament's bills or amendments were to be approved by the Privy Council, having been submitted to the lord deputy for prior vetting. The 1720 Declaratory Act (q.v.) gave the English parliament authority over the Irish parliament until its repeal in 1782.

PRAEGER, ROBERT LLOYD (1865–1953). Born in Holywood, Co. Down, son of a linen merchant, educated at the Queen's College Belfast. He was founding editor of *The Irish Naturalist*. From 1893 to 1924 he worked at the National Library of Ireland (q.v.), of which he became chief librarian in 1920. He conducted surveys of Lambay and Clare Islands, published *Flora of County Armagh* (1893), *The Botanist in Ireland* (1934), *The Natural History of Ireland* (1950), and *The Way That I Went. An Irishman in Ireland* (1939). He was president of the Royal Horticultural Society of Ireland in 1940, a founder and president of the Geographical Society of Ireland (1937) and of the Royal Zoological Society of Ireland. He was also president of the Royal Irish Academy (1931) (q.v.), its librarian, and editor of its *Proceedings* from 1903.

PROGRESSIVE DEMOCRATS. The Republic of Ireland's newest political party, it was founded in 1985 by the former minister Desmond

O'Malley with other Fianna Fail (FF) and some Fine Gael (qq.v.) dissidents. It put forward radical ideas on a revised constitution, both with regard to Northern Ireland and to social and religious matters in the Republic. At first it overtook the Labour Party (q.v.) in popularity, but later joined in coalition with FF in 1989–92. O'Malley was succeeded as leader by Mary Harney late in 1993.

PROVISIONAL IRISH REPUBLICAN ARMY (PIRA, Provos). Formed in 1969 as a result of a split in the IRA (q.v.) army council regarding recognition of the Westminster, Dublin, and Stormont (q.v.) governments, and changing the traditional policy of abstentionism and armed force (the Officials in favor, Provos against). The split was mirrored in the political wing, Sinn Fein (SF) (q.v.), in 1970. The Official SF leaned toward a Marxist approach (in 1982 it became the Workers' Party [q.v.]) while the Provisional SF concentrated on a campaign aimed at British withdrawal from Northern Ireland, initially seeking a federal solution. During the next 25 years PIRA became the main element in the Northern Ireland political violence. It caused many deaths and much damage to buildings, mostly in Northern Ireland but also in Great Britain, and less often at British army installations in mainland Europe. Its tactics often changed for security reasons and for the publicity value of new events.

The PIRA developed a grassroots approach in the early days and thus gained popularity in some Belfast housing estates as defenders and enablers. Money, arms, and explosives were acquired illicitly, mostly from abroad and via the Republic, and activists were trained secretly. Following mounting violence, the Stormont government introduced internment without trial for 350 of the original 450 activists and sympathizers arrested. By 1972 there were 900 internees. This policy was unsuccessful in reducing the level of terrorist activity, and it alienated many law-abiding Roman Catholics, thus increasing support for the Provos. The declared aim of the violence was to force British withdrawal and thus achieve a united Ireland. The proroguing of the Stormont parliament was not regarded as a measure sufficient to warrant a permanent cease-fire, except by the Officials who then dropped out of the action. Secret talks were held with the Westminster government, fruitlessly, and the violence reached a new intensity; in July 1972 alone 74 civilians and 21 security personnel were killed, and about 200 explosions and 2,800 shooting incidents occurred due to Provo activity. Moreover, some areas of Belfast and Derry had been so dominated by the Provos as to become "no-go" areas for the security forces. In addition, loyalist assassinations increased. The "no-go" areas were reclaimed by the army, but few terrorist leaders were apprehended.

Over the following years the violence continued, with only the level and the details varying. There were internal feuds and punishment attacks, both of which resulted in deaths and severe injuries. Gradually the problem was internationalized. As the atrocities have been reported on television, the PIRA has received support from "unfriendly" governments such as Libya and the Basque terrorist movement in Spain. The Czech commercial explosive Semtex was widely used. The security forces in both Northern Ireland and the Republic had their successes, and many activists were imprisoned by the courts. Nevertheless, few high-ranking leaders have been caught or have died in action.

There were also occasional attempts, all ultimately unsuccessful, to start a dialogue with a view to halting the violence, particularly as discrimination against Roman Catholics was made illegal and the futility of trying to force a united Ireland, as well as the legacy of bitterness produced by violence, were plain to see. This remained the position until 1994. The political wing, Provisional Sinn Fein, sought to supplant the Social Democratic and Labour Party (q.v.) as the main voice of nationalists and gave up its traditional abstentionist approach, taking up its seats at local council level, if not at Westminster. A cessation of hostilities was announced in 1994, but bombings were resumed in London in February 1996.

PUBLIC RECORD OFFICE OF IRELAND (PROI). During the 18th and early 19th centuries Irish government archives were dispersed among several technically unsatisfactory repositories: the courts, the medieval Bermingham (Record) Tower in Dublin Castle, the Registry of Deeds at the Four Courts, the State Paper Office, and the Parliamentary Record Office, often under the part-time supervision of enthusiastic but poorly paid deputies for the formal, appointed custodians. In 1810, following the report of a select committee to examine British public records, the Irish Record Commission was established with W. S. Mason (q.v.) as its secretary. Its paid subcommissioners began arranging, transcribing, and indexing original documents with a view to publication. In 1830 the work of the commission was divided between the Record Tower and the Registry of Deeds. Two subsidiary sections comprised the Rolls Office, under George Hatchell, and the future Landed Estates Record Office. Two years later, most financial records from the latter were placed in the Custom House under the supervision of W. H. Hardinge. After several abortive attempts to consolidate Irish official archives, PROI was set up under the Public Records (Ireland) Act 1867, and collections were transferred to a new building at the Four Courts. The first deputy keeper was Samuel Ferguson (q.v.). During the civil war (q.v.) in 1921 the Four Courts building, occupied by insurgents, was bombarded and partially destroyed by fire, resulting in irreplaceable loss of thousands of historic documents. Subsequently, some of its functions were devolved to local and municipal institutions, or Irish Manuscripts Commission, National Library of Ireland (qq.v.), Representative Church Body, Royal Irish Academy (q.v.), the State Paper Office and Genealogical Office in Dublin Castle, and Trinity College. Under a 1986 act the National Archive was established as the main central repository with its headquarters at Bishop Street, Dublin.

The Public Record Office of Northern Ireland (PRONI), now located in Balmoral Avenue, Belfast, was created in 1923 as the repository for both government and private archives, the former being normally subject to a 30-year confidentiality rule. In addition to documents from government departments relating to Northern Ireland, it holds originals or copies of records of other public bodies, churches, schools, estates, and industrial and commercial firms.

-Q-

QUIN, WINDHAM THOMAS WYNDHAM (1841–1926), fourth earl Dunraven and Mount-Earl (1871). Born in Adare, Co. Limerick, educated in Rome and at Christ Church, Oxford. A yachtsman and horse breeder, he was responsible for the 1903 land act (q.v.). A federalist, he also published *The Irish Question* (1880).

-R-

RADIO (TELEFÍS) ÉIREANN (RTÉ). The state broadcasting company in the Republic of Ireland, which began as Radio 2RN (its call sign) on 1 January 1926. It was known as Radio Éireann from 1932. It was controlled from January 1953 by a five-person council (enlarged to nine in 1960), appointed by the minister for post and telegraphs. At present its radio programs are broadcast in stereo on three VHF networks, including one (Raidió na Gaeltachta) specifically for Irish-language services. Television transmissions were added at the end of December 1961. In 1973 it became embroiled in a wrangle with the government over the broadcast of an interview with a Provisional IRA leader, despite a restriction order imposed in 1971. A second television channel was opened in 1978, and an Irish-language service is planned to commence in 1996.

RAILWAYS. The first line was built in 1831–34 from Dublin to the ferry port of Kingstown (Dun Laoghaire). Acts for making lines from Belfast to Armagh and Dublin to Drogheda were passed in 1836, when a Royal Commission under Thomas Drummond was also set up to investigate railway construction in Ireland. However, it was not until the later 1840s that the networks expanded very far beyond the two main cities. The standard gauge was fixed uniquely at five feet, three inches in 1846. In February 1847 Lord George Bentinck failed to secure passage of an act enabling public money to be spent on construction. Development thus proceeded in a piecemeal private manner. Separate webs of narrow-gauge light railways served local industrial enterprises. The 1888 Railway and Canal Traffic Act replaced the commission created under the 1873 Regulation of Railways Act, one of its five members, the lord chancellor, being responsible for Ireland. Directors of rail companies were not allowed to acquire canal interests. A Royal Commission was invited to investigate the feasibility of developing resources by means of a rail system at minimal cost. Its report advocated state investment because Irish conditions could not guarantee a sufficient volume of traffic to interest private companies in competition. In fact, many small private ventures were allowed to proceed, the initial number of 30 having been reduced to 17 main companies by 1900. At that date they operated 93 percent of the total track. Ireland possessed almost the same length of lines and the same population as Scotland in 1901. But Irish railways had only one-quarter of the latter's receipts, reflecting the contrasting nature of the two countries' natural resources and population distributions. The five most important companies in Ireland included: (1) Great Southern and Western (1844)—Dublin to Cork 1855, Waterford, Athlone 1859; (2) Great Northern (formerly Ulster Railway)(1876)—Belfast to Lisburn 1839, Portadown 1842, Armagh 1848, Dundalk-Drogheda (already linked to Dublin 1844–49); Portadown to Omagh/Enniskillen/Ballyshannon 1858–68; (3) Midland Great Western (1845)—Dublin to Mullingar 1848, Athlone/Galway 1851, Longford 1855, Sligo 1862, Westport 1866 (it also owned the Royal Canal); (4) Waterford, Limerick and Western—merged with the Great Southern and Western in 1900; (5) Belfast and Northern Counties (1845)—Belfast to Ballymena 1848, Coleraine 1855 (the Bann Bridge was opened to rail traffic in 1860); Londonderry to Enniskillen 1854; and Belfast-Larne 1862.

Unfortunately, the network began to be constructed in a period of declining population. Early attention was paid to linking large urban centers with key tourist locations, e.g., the Giant's Causeway and Portrush, Achill, Recess, and Killarney. Between 1871 and 1900, the track length increased from 1,988 to 3,183 miles (80 percent of it single track), while receipts for passenger and mail (especially third class) and goods (especially minerals) increased by about two-thirds and three-quarters, respectively. During the same period passenger numbers increased from 15.5 to 27.6 million, despite a sharply reduced population, i.e., the average annual number of journeys per head of population rose from 2.9 to 6.2.

By 1898 canals (q.v.) carried 0.7 million tons of freight, whereas the railways transported 5.1 million tons. Under the 1924 Railways Act all 27 companies within the confines of the Irish Free State were amalgamated as the Great Southern Railways Co., subsequently operating under CIE (q.v.) from 1945. In Northern Ireland in 1948 the Ulster Transport Authority was established, and in 1967 its rail component became Northern Ireland Railways.

REBELLION OF 1641. A struggle in England between King Charles I and parliament provided the context of the rebellion, as well as grievances in Ireland related to religion and land due to Protestant colonists' being favored over indigenous Roman Catholics. Help, especially from the pope and Cardinal Richelieu, was sought in Europe through the many Irish soldiers and priests there. The revolt began on 23 October, 1641, with an attempt to seize Dublin Castle. It failed due to treachery, but a general rising occurred in Ulster, where the most recent plantation (q.v.) had been. It resulted in many deaths, most new settlers having to flee for their lives. The "Old English" of the Pale (qq.v.) reluctantly gave their support, but the rising spread to Munster. A Scottish force was sent to Ulster in April 1642 to regain control. By August 1642 the civil war began in England, and Ireland was not brought under control until Cromwell (q.v.) could afford to go there in 1649. Meanwhile, in October 1642 the Irish Confederates had set up a parliament in Kilkenny that was dominated from November 1645 by the Papal Nuncio, Cardinal Rinuccini. After Ormond (q.v.) had negotiated a peace with the confederates in March 1646, Rinuccini imposed pressure on a synod in Waterford to interdict places and excommunicate individuals supporting the truce. A similar process was invoked against those accepting a truce with Lord Inchiquin, who had earlier (1648) abandoned the royalists for the Parliamentarian side. Many exiled Irish professional soldiers returned, including Owen Roe O'Neill (q.v.), to fight three different forces: Irish loyal to the king led by Ormond, Parliamentarians who gradually grew in strength, and a Scots force sent originally by king and parliament.

REDMOND, JOHN EDWARD (1856–1918). Born in Co. Wexford, son of an MP, educated at Trinity College Dublin. He became a clerk in the House of Commons and qualified as a barrister. He was elected as Parnellite MP for New Ross in 1881, for Waterford 1891–1918, and leader of the Irish Parliamentary Party (q.v.) in 1900. He was also a member of the land conference that gave rise to the 1903 (Wyndham) land act.

REFERENDA. Under article 50 of the 1922 constitution (q.v.), any proposed amendment to it was subject to a referendum, in which positive acceptance could only be achieved if a majority of registered electors voted, and that any such amendment received the support of either a majority of the electors or a two-thirds majority of those who actually voted. Other provisions exist for a referendum to be called by a petition of electors on issues that had not been discussed in the Oireachtas, or to resolve conflict over legislation between the Dáil (q.v.) and the Senate. In the former case, such an initiative was undertaken by anti-Treaty Fianna Fail in 1927 on the issue of the oath of allegiance to the Crown, shortly before the Dáil abolished that particular referendum option. However, similar provisions for referenda were contained in the 1937 constitution and 18 have subsequently been held, the first being to approve that constitution. Turnout has been below 66 percent on 12 occasions and below 50 percent on four.

Two Fianna Fail (q.v.) attempts to abolish proportional representation, and thereby reduce the electoral significance of smaller opposition parties, were defeated in 1959 and 1968.

In December 1972, 84 percent favored removal of clauses 1.2 and 1.3 of article 44, which recognized the special status of the Roman Catholic church. In May 1972 accession to the EEC was approved by 83 percent. In December 1972, 85 percent supported lowering the voting age to 18. In September 1983 a motion seeking to amend article 44 by defending the right to life of the unborn child was approved by 67 percent.

In June 1986 it was proposed to amend article 41 (effectively prohibiting divorce) by permitting dissolution of marriage, provided evidence was produced that a marriage had failed, that such a breakdown had continued for at least five years, and that there was no reasonable possibility of reconciliation. Legal dissolution would be granted subject to adequate provision having been made for the dependent spouse and any dependent child. The proposal was rejected by 63 percent of electors in a poll of 63 percent.

Voting on three amendments was held on the same day in November 1992 against a background of extreme confusion over the case of a 14-year-old alleged rape victim prevented from traveling to Britain to have an abortion; the case related to the right to information and possible abortion in the Republic of Ireland. The latter, on the grounds of a threat posed to the mother's life, was defeated by 65 percent, but the other two motions were approved by 62 percent and 60 percent, respectively.

In November 1995, 50.2 percent voted to remove the ban on divorce, subject to similar safeguards as in 1986, although the result was contested in the courts by defeated opponents.

RELIGION. The disparity whereby Roman Catholicism claims proportionally two and a half times as many adherents in the Republic of Ireland as in Northern Ireland reflects the more successful plantation (q.v.) of Ulster with British Protestants in the late 16th and 17th centuries, as well as the province's 19th-century industrialization, which resulted in considerable internal migration. The Reformation had found little indigenous positive response in Ireland, and its identification with the Tudor monarchy provided just as little attraction. Politically, Catholicism came to be seen as a reinforcement of national identity, with the distinction being useful in attracting outside interest from Rome, France, and Spain. When the turmoil of the 17th-century wars ended, legislation, known collectively as the penal laws (q.v.), was introduced, limiting the rights of Roman Catholics and also Dissenters in order to boost the "Established" Anglican Church. This proved counterproductive, imposing further strains on loyalty to the Crown, particularly among the Roman Catholic upper classes. Priests operated only unofficially in clandestine ways, as did hedge schools (q.v.), and it was not until the end of the 18th century that proper church buildings were allowed. Most were located on the edges of already built-up towns or at cross roads in the countryside. Although many of them were remodeled as imposing edifices later, their locations have often stayed the same. Diocesan reforms were introduced to counter lax performance of clerical duties, and consequently of public religious observance and behavior. This attempt to establish stricter discipline coincided with efforts to wean the uneducated peasantry away from traditional folk beliefs and customs. Among the prime movers was the "Ultramontanist" Archbishop Cullen (q.v.) of Armagh who sought to impose papal authority on a church vacillating between negligence, subservience to the state, and alignment with religious and political nationalism, as in the case of Archbishop John MacHale (q.v.) of Tuam. Church going in large numbers on Sunday mornings and on major feast days remains a noticeable feature of life in the Republic of Ireland, although the number of purely nominal adherents has grown recently with increasing levels of urban-based sophistication and the questioning of the church's traditional teachings on social issues.

Seminaries for home and foreign needs have increasingly experienced difficulties in finding recruits. Religious orders reappeared or were founded during the 19th century, particularly to provide schools, and these too have come under some strain. Nonetheless, state education in the Republic remains essentially religiously based. In Northern Ireland specifically Roman Catholic schools, though administratively separate, receive state funding.

Protestantism, for historical reasons, is strongest in Northern Ireland, where over 50 percent of the population regard themselves as

Protestant. In the Republic Protestants now account for only 3 percent of the population, concentrated mainly in major cities, especially Dublin. Protestant churches are a common feature throughout the island, partly as a relic of the Church of Ireland's ubiquitous parochial system. Like those of other denominations both in towns and the countryside, some of these parish churches are now derelict, closed, or used for other purposes, but many operate in grouped parishes. While the Church of Ireland remains the largest Protestant church in the Republic, it is less dominant in Northern Ireland, where Presbyterianism is strongest, and other groups associated with the industrialization period, such as Methodists, are also active. Under pressure from nonconformist sects, Anglicanism in 19th-century Ireland was subjected to reformist criticism from within and demands for disestablishment (1869) from without, resulting in improved personnel and practice.

Modern Irish Protestantism is characterized by diversity, so that groups of Quakers, Unitarians, Baptists, and numerous evangelical "gospel-based" churches exist. The association with education is less strong than in the case of the Roman Catholic Church, though it is often influential all the same. Politically, many Protestants in Northern Ireland support the Union because of an affinity with the rest of the UK. They dislike some Roman Catholic doctrines and the perceived pervasiveness of the Roman Catholic Church in political and social affairs in the Republic. In the later 18th century Dissenters generally were antiestablishment because of some of the penal laws, and Ulster Presbyterians in particular were in the forefront of early republican movements in Ireland.

Conflict between sectarian groups over the past two centuries has often been simplistically portrayed as having essentially religious roots, whereas neither theological discord nor regular church observance is characteristic of active participants in civil strife. Like most forms of fermented disorder, the causes have always been complex and may be traced to isolated incidents or to the formation of rival secret societies (q.v.) to combat local economic or social injustice in the 18th century, only later becoming permeated by ideological and political beliefs. At that stage the involvement of clerical personalities of diverse persuasions frequently proved inflammatory, especially after Catholic emancipation (q.v.) in 1829. At official levels open disagreements arose concerning interfaith marriages, nondenominational (integrated) schooling, higher education, legal aspects of social behavior, civil rights, attitudes toward political violence, constitutional status, and party politics.

In 1831–34 Catholics were calculated as constituting 80 percent of the population of Ireland, virtually the same as Sir William Petty's (q.v.) mid-17th century estimate. This declined to 74 percent by 1901.

Table 12
Percentage Share of Denominational Adherence, 1961–91

	Republic of Ireland	Northern Ireland
ROMAN CATHOLIC		
1961	94.9	34.9
1971	95.4	31.4
1981	95.0	28.0*
1991	93.8	38.4
CHURCH OF IRELAND		
1961	3.7	23.1
1971	3.3	22.0
1981	2.8	19.0
1991	2.4	17.7
PRESBYTERIAN		
1961	0.7	29.0
1971	0.5	26.7
1981	0.4	22.9
1991	0.4	21.3
METHODIST		
1961	0.2	5.0
1971	0.2	4.7
1981	0.2	4.0
1991	0.1	3.8

*This anomalously low figure resulted from the refusal of some Roman Catholics to answer the census question on religious affiliation.

In the Republic of Ireland a significant increase occurred between 1981 and 1991 both in the number declaring themselves to belong to no religion and in the number not responding to that census question. In the Republic even in 1991 members of the Church of Ireland, despite their small absolute numbers, were proportionally overrepresented in the professions, in business, and among the class of substantial farmers.

In Northern Ireland in 1961–91, the total population increased by 11 percent, and the number of Roman Catholics increased by 22 percent. Members of the Church of Ireland, however, decreased by 15 percent, Presbyterians by 18 percent, and Methodists by 17 percent. The 1981 Roman Catholic figure could be 150,000 higher than that enumerated, raising its share to about 37 percent of the total. *See also* Census of Population

Among non-Christian communities, Jews were formerly prominent in the professional and business life of both Dublin and Belfast. In 1991 there remained only 1,600 Jews in the Republic, their number having decreased by 25 percent since 1981; in Northern Ireland there were 500 Jews, with a similar rate of decrease as in the Republic since 1981.

REYNOLDS, ALBERT (1932–). Born in Co. Roscommon. He began as
a clerk with the state transport company CIE (q.v.), became a dance-
hall and nightclub proprietor, and was a county councillor in Longford
in 1975–79. In 1977 he was elected Fianna Fail (q.v.) TD, was appointed minister for posts and telegraphs in 1979, then minister for industry and energy (March–Dec. 1982), and minister for industry and
commerce in 1987–88. He succeeded Ray MacSharry as minister for
finance in November 1988, but was dismissed by Taoiseach Charles
Haughey (q.v.) after challenging for the party leadership in November 1991. Three months later he defeated Haughey and was himself
elected taoiseach in February 1992. Subsequently, he was sustained in
office by the Labour Party (q.v.), but at the cost of granting six cabinet posts to the minority partner in the coalition.

He expressed a wish to see the 1920 Government of Ireland Act re-
opened for negotiation, but declined to move on articles 2 and 3 of the
Republic's constitution (q.v.), by which the Republic laid claim to the
territory of the whole island. Nevertheless, during his brief period in
office he concluded the Downing Street Declaration (q.v.) with British
Prime Minister John Major. After widespread concern over the Fianna
Fail government's relationship with certain commercial companies
and alleged misuse of subsidies in the beef-processing industry, a crisis emerged in the coalition over the proposed appointment of controversial attorney-general Whelehan as president of the High Court. The
tanaiste Dick Spring (q.v.) withdrew Labour Party support from the
government, and Reynolds was forced to resign as taoiseach. He was
then replaced as Fianna Fail party leader by Bertie Ahern.

RIBBONMEN. Localized Ribbon Societies appeared about 1805–7 in
defense of Catholic tenant farmers, sometimes anti-Orangeist and sectarian, but equally opposing payment of tithes (q.v.) and dues to the
Roman Catholic clergy. Four periods of special activity may be identified—1814–16, 1821–23, 1831–34, and 1850–51 in counties Armagh and Down—emphasizing the economic roots of unrest, e.g.,
concerns over the reduced operation of conacre, pressurizing cottiers
and laborers who were seeking cheap potato plots, and evictions (q.v.)
for rent arrears in the wake of poor harvests, etc. Central and southern
foci of their activities were in counties Kilkenny, Limerick, Monaghan, Queen's County, Roscommon, and Tipperary. Members swore
oaths of loyalty to each other, wore identifying ribbons, and participated in rituals. They organized themselves into small lodges, the
masters of which met in a hierarchy of committees, implying a national structure and a set of objectives. Having been excommunicated,
the society officially changed its title in 1825 to St. Patrick's Fraternal Organisation, or St. Patrick's Boys. It was regarded by the au-

thorities as seditious, anti-English, and anti-Protestant, and it operated under various local names: Carders in Connacht, Caravats in Cork, Limerick, Kilkenny, and Tipperary, Shanavests, and Rockites. It had no quasi-national or ideological underpinnings, but usually concentrated on resolving specific injustices. *See also* Secret Societies

RICHMOND COMMISSION (1881). Set up by Disraeli in August 1879 to investigate agricultural conditions in Ireland, it reported the failures of the 1870 land act, noting that agrarian unrest in Ireland was rooted in general poverty. The "land war" (q.v.) was attributed to bad weather, failure of the potato crop, the hunger for land forcing up rents, and excessive subdivision of holdings. Among its recommendations was the promotion of migration and emigration (q.v.) as a safety valve, while the Carlingford minority report advocated the adoption of the "three Fs."

RIGHTBOYS. Like the Whiteboys, secret societies (qq.v.) that emerged in Munster in the autumn of 1785, taking their name from their sworn allegiance to "Captain Right." Initially an anti-tithe protest, the movement broadened to include opposition to Catholic clergy dues. It spread into Leinster by means of recruiting at Sunday mass in a peak of unrest in 1786. The mostly nonviolent campaign appeared to seek redress through the force of public opinion, with even Lord Lieutenant Rutland persuading British Prime Minister Pitt to formulate a scheme for tithe commutation, a course also advocated without success by Grattan (q.v.) in 1787–89. The movement died out after 1787 with the increased enforcement of tithe (q.v.) collection under supervision.

ROBINSON (née de Vere), MARY TERESA WINIFRED (1944–). Born in Ballina, Co. Mayo. Educated at the Sacred Heart Convent, Mount Anville, Dublin, and at Trinity College Dublin (TCD), King's Inns and Harvard, she practiced as a barrister. She was particularly concerned with European Union law and human rights cases, and was Reid Professor of Constitutional and Criminal Law at TCD (1969–75). A former Labour Party (q.v.) senator for Dublin University and law lecturer (1975–90), she was the first woman to be elected president of Ireland (1990). In keeping with that nonexecutive office, she has since remained aloof from party political issues, while making known her support for causes such as improved women's welfare and status in the Republic of Ireland and reconciliation between religious groups in both parts of the island. In May 1993 she was received by Queen Elizabeth at Buckingham Palace, the first-ever meeting between British and Irish heads of state.

ROBINSON, THOMAS ROMNEY (1792–1882). Born in Dublin, educated at Bruce's Academy, Belfast, and Trinity College Dublin. He was rector of Carrickmacross and astronomer at Armagh (1823–82). He was elected Fellow of the Royal Society in 1856, was awarded the Society's Gold Medal in 1862, and invented the cup anemometer for measuring wind velocity. He was a friend of William Parsons (q.v.), earl of Rosse, and helped set up his telescope at Birr.

ROINN NA GAELTACHTA. A department of state set up by the Gaeltacht Areas Order in 1956 to promote the culture, society, and economy of Gaeltacht (q.v.). Apart from preserving the Irish language and reversing long-term population decline, its objectives included housing improvements, provision of tourist accommodation, public amenities, land improvement, and development of horticulture and cooperatives. Gaeltarra Eireann was established as a statutory board in 1958 to operate, or to cooperate with, private industries in the fields of investment, production, and marketing, especially textiles.

ROSS, MARTIN. *See* Somerville, Edith Anna Oenone

ROYAL DUBLIN SOCIETY (RDS). Established privately on 25 June 1731 as "The Dublin Society for improving Husbandry, Manufactures, and other useful Arts" (and later "and Sciences"), its founders were drawn from the Anglo-Irish ascendancy (q.v.) (doctors, clergymen, landowners, and parliamentarians). Like other regional societies in Britain, it offered premiums for land drainage and reclamation, introduction of new crops, tree planting, creation of botanical gardens, fisheries, demonstrations of experimental farm equipment, and mineral exploration. The Society received its charter in 1750, revised it in 1866, and adopted the prefix from 1820, having become partly state-funded from 1761. It established an academy that led to the School of Art. Industries—linen, glass, paper, pottery—were also encouraged, and in 1771 it sponsored breweries and good malt distilleries to discourage heavy consumption of cheap spirits. Initially it disseminated its findings through the *Dublin Newsletter*. After its first session in Trinity College Dublin, the society subsequently met at various venues, its headquarters being at Leinster House from 1815 until 1924 when that building was finally transferred to the Free State government. In 1800 it initiated 24 county statistical surveys similar to those undertaken by the Board of Agriculture in Britain.

In the same year there was a move to set up a less theoretical, more practical Farming Society at Summerhill under John Foster and the marquess of Sligo, the institution receiving a royal charter in 1815. This too was state funded until 1828, its work then reverting to the

RDS. In 1877 the Royal Irish Academy (q.v.) declined a merger with the RDS, which absorbed the Royal Agricultural Society in 1886. Richard Griffith (q.v.), appointed as the RDS mining engineer, compiled a geology map and initiated a trigonometrical survey as the forerunner of the Ordnance Survey (q.v.). Its School of Science applied to Mining and the Arts became the precursor of the Royal College of Science (1865). From 1868 the Society developed an annual horse show, held from 1877 at its Ball's Bridge premises, and this enterprise was extended to other agricultural livestock shows.

The RDS still holds regular lecture and concert series, publishes journals and monographs, and operates a members' library. Its valuable county statistical surveys included volumes for Antrim (J. Dubourdieu, 1812), Armagh (C. Coote, 1804), Cavan (C. Coote, 1802), Clare (H. Dutton, 1810), Cork (H. Townsend, 1810), Donegal (J. McParlan, 1802), Down (J. Dubourdieu, 1802), Dublin (J. Archer, 1801), Galway (H. Dutton, 1824), Kildare (T. J. Rawson, 1807), Kilkenny (W. Tighe, 1802), King's (C. Coote, 1801), Leitrim (J. McParlan, 1802), Londonderry (G. V. Sampson, 1802), Mayo (J. McParlan, 1802), Meath (R. Thompson, 1802), Monaghan (1801), Queen's (C. Coote, 1801), Roscommon (I. Weld, 1832), Sligo (J. McParlan, 1802), Tyrone (J. McEvoy, 1802), Wexford (R. Fraser, 1807), and Wicklow (R. Fraser, 1801); the manuscript for Tipperary is in the National Library (q.v.). The Society's *Proceedings* have been published since 1764.

ROYAL IRISH ACADEMY (RIA). Founded in 1785 by the earl of Charlemont to "advance the studies of science, polite literature and antiquities." It receives a state grant and publishes its *Transactions* (1786–1907), now *Proceedings* (1830–). Its library houses the largest collection of Irish manuscripts, some dating from the sixth century. The most important early items are the *Cathach* or *Psalter of St. Columba* (A.D. 560–660), *Stowe Missal* (*c.* A.D. 800), *Domnach Airgid* (*c.* A.D. 900), *Lebor na hUidre* (1106), *Book of Lecan* (early 15th century), *Leabhar Breac* (1408–11), *Book of Ballymote* (14th–15th century), *Book of Fermoy* (15th century), *Book of Hy-Many* (14th–15th century), and *Annals of the Four Masters* (17th century). In addition, a research library accommodates some 40,000 books and 2,600 periodicals, current issues largely being obtained by worldwide exchanges with other learned societies.

ROYAL IRISH CONSTABULARY (RIC). In 1814 Sir Robert Peel introduced the Peace Preservation Act (54 Geo. III, c. 131), which superseded legislation of 1787–92 concerning small part-time constabularies in each barony, the lord lieutenant having authorized local magistrates to dispatch special constables to areas periodically designated as being in a state of disturbance. In practice their use was limited by the fact that, unlike deployment of the army, the cost was borne locally. By August 1822 the Irish Constabulary Act (3 Geo. IV, c. 103) had set up a permanent force of about 4,500 inspectors, chief constables, and subconstables to control growing violent unrest. In 1836 Drummond's Constabulary Act (6 & 7 Will. IV, c. 13) created a centralized unitary professional police force of up to 14,000, which was consciously removed from sectarian direction or influence and performed a range of administrative duties, such as collecting statistics.

Following its success in suppressing the Irish (Revolutionary) Republican Brotherhood (q.v.), from 12 September 1867 it became known as the RIC, having assimilated the revenue police ten years earlier. The Belfast and Derry city police were absorbed in 1865 and 1870, respectively, but the Dublin Metropolitan Police (DMP) remained a separate unit. Even as Catholics, its officers were targeted by republicans in 1916, when it was supplemented by the Black and Tans and the Auxiliaries (qq.v.). After independence in the south, the Garda Siochana (Guardians of the Peace, Civic Guards) was set up as an unarmed police force in 1922, women officers being recruited from 1958. In the north the Royal Ulster Constabulary (q.v.) was created on 1 June 1922.

ROYAL SOCIETY OF ANTIQUARIES OF IRELAND (RSAI) (1849). Growing out of the Kilkenny Archaeological Society, it was founded by Rev. James Graves to preserve ancient monuments, the Irish language, and Irish customs. It received its royal charter in 1912.

ROYAL ULSTER CONSTABULARY (RUC). The impartiality of the police force was questioned by 1969, but the main criticism concerned lack of suitable backup support during the civil disturbances of that year, which were investigated by the Scarman tribunal. Its image was reformed by British Home Secretary James Callaghan, and its paramilitary structure, which had survived from its origins as part of the Royal Irish Constabulary (q.v.), was removed. The head of the City of London police was put in charge, and the force was remodeled along the lines of the police in Great Britain. A police authority, representing all sections of community, was created to monitor its duties and operations. As republican disorder escalated, the size of the force grew from 3,531 in 1970 to 8,236 regular officers, with 2,987 full-time and 1,659 part-time reservists in 1987. Since the mid-1970s the RUC has held the main role of peacekeeping, with the army as backup. Individual officers and police stations have frequently been targets of Provisional IRA (q.v.) shootings and bombings. The Anglo-Irish Agreement (q.v.) established a communications hot line between the Garda Siochana and the RUC, and cooperation between the two organizations has improved. A Police Complaints Commission was set up for Northern Ireland in 1988.

RUNDALE. A traditional system of joint landholding involved periodic reallocation of plots of land to ensure equal access to varying resources of unfenced cultivation strips and common grazing areas. The inherent fragmentation and morcellation of units was seen by outside observers as wasteful of energy. As a result, many progressive landlords attempted reform and the consolidation of farms in the mid-19th century, resulting in the creation of "striping" and geometric "ladder farms," which characterize many upland margin landscapes today.

RUSSELL, GEORGE WILLIAM ("AE") (1867–1935). Born in Lurgan, Co. Armagh, and educated at Rathmines and the Metropolitan School of Art. He met W. B. Yeats and Lady Gregory (qq.v.), wrote poetry and essays, edited Horace Plunkett's (q.v.) *Irish Homestead* (1897) and *Irish Statesman* (1923–30) for the Irish Agricultural Organisation Society (q.v.). He vigorously opposed the introduction of censorship (q.v.) in 1929, while deploring the low level of education and related lack of literary interest in Ireland.

RUSSELL, SIR WILLIAM HOWARD (1820–1907). Born in Tallaght, Co. Dublin, his father a Protestant business agent and his mother from a Roman Catholic farming family. His parents moved to Liverpool in search of greater prosperity, and he was brought up by his grandparents. He converted from Catholicism and studied classics at Trinity College (TCD) (1838–41), but took no degree. Having been admitted to the Middle Temple he was called to the Bar in 1850, but did not practice regularly.

Taking employment with the London *Times,* he was sent to Ireland to report on the 1841 election and the 1843 repeal campaign, attending "monster meetings" and having good-humored brushes with Daniel O'Connell (q.v.). After a short spell with the *Morning Chronicle* (1845–48), he returned to *The Times,* his first foreign assignment being to cover the Schleswig-Holstein war (1850). With the outbreak of the Crimean War (1854), his Gallipoli and Varna dispatches, severely critical of the war's administration under Lord Raglan, simultaneously brought immediate public recognition and also official disfavor. His dispatches also promoted humanitarian aid through the work of Florence Nightingale's nursing corps. He coined the phrase the "thin red line" in reference to the British infantry at Balaclava. His subsequent career as a correspondent extended to the Indian Mutiny (1858), the American civil war (1861–62), in which he expressed strong antislavery views and favored the Union cause, the Franco-Prussian War (1870), the Zulu War in South Africa (1879), and the 1882 Egyptian revolt.

He was awarded an honorary LL.D. by TCD after the Crimea, and was the founding editor of the *Army and Navy Gazette* (1860). He was a friend of Dickens and Thackeray, accompanied Edward, Prince of Wales (the future King Edward VII), on Near Eastern (1869) and Indian (1875–6) tours. He published his diaries of those experiences, together with accounts of visits to Canada and South America. He was knighted in 1895 and became a Companion of the Victorian Order in 1902.

-S-

SARSFIELD, PATRICK (1655?–93). Born in Lucan, Co. Dublin, the family estates having been sequestrated by Oliver Cromwell (q.v.), but retrieved in 1660. In 1685 he fought for James II against the Duke of Monmouth at Sedgemoor, after fighting with him abroad. He went to Ireland with James II in 1689, represented Co. Dublin in the Irish parliament, expelled William of Orange's forces from Connacht, and participated in a minor capacity at the battle of the Boyne (1690). After defeat he took his troops into exile in France after the 1691 treaty to serve with the Irish Brigade of Louis XIV. He was made earl of Lucan in 1691 in recognition of his action at the siege of Limerick, though the true significance of his role has since been debated. He was mortally wounded at the battle of Landen. *See also* Boyne, River

SECRET SOCIETIES. In 1763, two years after Whiteboy (q.v.) attacks in Munster, Protestant members of Hearts of Oak societies (Oakboys) mounted similar disturbances in northwest Ulster which were equally condemned by the establishment. By 1769 another group, Hearts of Steel, or Steelboys, began to operate in Ulster, allegedly protesting against Roman Catholics offering higher rents for tenancies. They were countered by short-lived legislation (11 & 12 Geo. III, c. 5) in 1772–74, like the Tumultuous Risings Act of 1766 (5 Geo. III, c. 8) introduced against the Whiteboys.

Economic and sectarian motives evidently ran in tandem in such affrays when political unrest was increasing, partly in response to wider intellectual ferment in Europe. In Ireland specifically, recurrent clashes between Protestant Peep-O'-Day Boys searching for arms and Catholic Defenders in the 1780s led to the formation of Brunswick Clubs, which in turn presaged the establishment of the Loyal Orange Institution in Co. Armagh in 1795 to meet the threat of nonconstitutional Jacobinism and republican upheaval spreading from France. Partisan allegiances were, however, blurred during the rebellion of the United Irishmen (q.v.) in 1798. Orangeism also became widespread in England under the duke of Cumberland in 1828–35, and in Ireland it had been counteracted in the 1780s and 1790s by the Defenders spreading south. These and numerous agrarian protest groups in the 19th century usually responded to perceived local injustices. In many cases secrecy was modeled on the rituals of Masonic lodges, including initiation ceremonies, sworn oaths, and passwords and signs. Their activities to redress grievances were mainly violent and sporadic. From the 1760s they ceased to be gangs of rootless will-o'-the-wisp marauders and developed more within the communities they aimed to serve or protect.

Conflict of belief, loyalty, and mode of action emerged between politically motivated societies, on the one hand, and the state, the civil and criminal law, and especially the Church, on the other. At a later stage the Royal Irish Constabulary (q.v.) and Dublin Metropolitan Police forbade membership, except of Freemasons, to their officers. The same conflict applied to Orangeism, inherently political in its integral links with the Protestant Crown, early leaders often being clergy of the Established Church. A peak of official Catholic opposition to such organizations in Ireland was reached under Archbishop Paul Cullen during outbursts of Fenianism (qq.v.) in the 1860s, fed by papal phobias about socialism, nationalism, the overthrow of established order, and the swearing of oaths, which had all featured in a fundamental rift between church and state in revolutionary Italy in 1848–60. Cullen's stance was, however, undermined in rural areas, especially by Archbishop John MacHale (q.v.) of Tuam. Fenianism as such was condemned by Rome only in 1870, though later Archbishop Walsh of Dublin was more conciliatory toward the Irish (Revolutionary) Republican Brotherhood (q.v.) nationalists. In 1916 most senior clergy remained equivocal or ambivalently silent. When they did object to republicanism, it was largely on grounds of using force and undermining the Irish state.

SETTLEMENT, ACT OF (14 & 15 Chas. II, c. 2)(July 1662). Lands confiscated before 23 October 1641 were held by the Crown until competing claims were resolved. The 1642 parliament having by-passed the royal prerogative of allocating forfeited land, seven commissioners confirmed grants to the Adventurers (q.v.) and to soldiers prior to 7 May 1659. It also reviewed compensation claims made by those expropriated via the Court of Settlement. Those found not guilty of participation in the rebellion were to be reinstated, unless their property was situated in towns, when equivalent areas were found for them outside town limits. In 1665 the Act of Explanation (17 & 18 Chas. II, c. 2) ironed out inconsistencies, confirming that Cromwellian beneficiaries should relinquish one-third of their allocations in order to reinstate Roman Catholics. The Settlement Act itself was repealed by King James II in 1689, though it had never been fully implemented.

SHAW, GEORGE BERNARD (1856–1950). Born in Dublin, son of a merchant, educated at Wesley School. He moved to London in 1874, met the socialists Sidney and Beatrice Webb, and joined the Fabian Society in 1884. Book reviewer and art critic, he wrote witty, thought-provoking Ibsenite plays from 1892: *Mrs. Warren's Profession* (1893), *Arms and the Man* (1894), *Candida* (1894), *The Devil's Disciple* (1901), *John Bull's Other Island* (1904) for Yeats's Irish Literary Theatre, *Man and Superman* (1903), *Major Barbara* (1907), *Pygmalion* (1913), and *Saint Joan* (1924). He was awarded the Nobel Prize for Literature in 1926.

SHEEHY-SKEFFINGTON, FRANCIS (1878–1916). Born in Co. Cavan, he helped edit *The Nationalist* in 1905, wrote the *Life of Michael Davitt* (1908), and edited the *Irish Citizen* in 1912. He became vice-chairman of the Irish Citizen Army (q.v.) in 1913 in the belief that its purpose was to defend workers from the police. He abandoned it when it became overtly military. He was shot as a witness of an unlawful killing, for which the perpetrator was later court-martialed. His widow, Hanna, was an active campaigner for women's suffrage in Ireland and founding secretary of the Irish Women's Franchise League (1908).

SHERIDAN, RICHARD BRINSLEY (1751–1816). Born in Dublin, grandson of a friend of Dean Swift, and son of Thomas Sheridan, actor-manager of the Theatre Royal, and Frances Chamberlaine, a dramatist. He never returned to Dublin after leaving Whyte's school in 1759. His best-known plays were *The Rivals* (1775) and *The School for Scandal* (1777). He later bought out David Garrick in the Drury Lane Theatre, London. He was MP for Stafford (1780–1812), opposed the Act of Union regarding the 1782 parliament as an irrevocable agreement, and vigorously defended freedom of the press. *See also* Union, Act of; Swift, Jonathan

SINN FEIN (SF)("We Ourselves"; members often deny the implication of the "Ourselves alone" translation). Founded in November 1905 on the basis of (1) Arthur Griffith's (q.v.) policy statement of republicanism and independence and (2) rejection of imposed laws. The SF League was derived from the Dungannon Clubs and Cumann na nGaedheal (q.v.). Entering election politics, it represented a potential rival to the Irish Parliamentary Party (q.v.) if it did not achieve home rule. Sinn Fein capitalized on the 1916 Easter Rising (q.v.) for propaganda and support. It won initial victories at North Roscommon, Longford, and Kilkenny in 1917, and the party's tenth Ard-fheis (annual conference) saw Eamon de Valera (q.v.) installed as its president. At the 1918 election abstentionist SF candidates won 73 seats to John Redmond's six and set up the Dáil (qq.v.). Always stronger in rural areas, it supported the IRA (q.v.) in the 1919–21 war, but was split—essentially between supporters of Michael Collins and de Valera/Lemass—over acceptance of the Anglo-Irish Treaty (qq.v.). In 1922 the anti-Treaty faction won 36 seats, pro-Treaty candidates 58, and others 34. Sinn Fein won only five seats in 1927. It currently operates as a legitimate party in the Republic of Ireland and Northern Ireland, but until 1994 its access to television and radio broadcasting in both jurisdictions was constrained by special legislation (in the Republic from 1973 and in Northern Ireland from 1988). In general elections its share of the vote has usually been only 10 to 14 percent. In recent years Provisional IRA violence was recognized as a constraint on Provisional SF's growth, and there was an effort to limit at least civilian casualties. The personnel of both organizations are close, if not coincident.

SOCIAL DEMOCRATIC AND LABOUR PARTY (SDLP). Formed in Northern Ireland in August 1970, absorbing most of the Nationalist, National Democratic, and Republican Labour parties and campaigners involved in civil rights. Its aims were civil rights, a just distribution of wealth, and the promotion of understanding between North and South in Ireland with a view to eventual unity through consent. It withdrew from Stormont (q.v.) and promoted a civil disobedience campaign involving nonpayment of rents and rates. It favored a Northern Ireland Assembly elected by proportional representation within a system of joint Republic of Ireland and UK sovereignty, and was willing to cooperate in the power-sharing Executive. It had four seats and its leader, Gerry Fitt (q.v.), was deputy chief executive. The succeeding years saw various initiatives of its own, to revive some form of power sharing and to keep the "Irish dimension" to the fore. It tends to get about 20 percent of first preference votes, but faces opposition of varying intensity from Sinn Fein (q.v.). Its relationship with Unionists is often fraught, depending on the extent to which it seems to relate to politicians in Dublin. It has held one of the three Northern Ireland European parliamentary seats since 1979. Fitt resigned on the grounds that the party was becoming less socialist and more nationalist. Under John Hume (q.v.) it did not attend the 1982 Assembly, but promoted the New Ireland Forum (q.v.) in Dublin and sought support in Europe and the United States. It welcomed the Anglo-Irish Agreement (q.v.) and hoped it would lead to interparty talks. In 1996 a few of its leaders called for a simplistic referendum in Ireland on the popular desire for peace and immediate all-party talks, without specifying the practical issues surrounding the questions to be posed. It revived political conflict aroused by such an expression of contrasting views, or the precise purpose and structure of the talks, while simultaneously ignoring other severe obstacles to progress, such as the need for decommissioning illegally held paramilitary groups' weapons and explosives. This tactic, combined with Hume's continued meetings with Adams and the IRA following the renewed bombing campaign in Britain, tended to reinforce Unionists' beliefs that the SDLP was too readily aligning itself with Sinn Fein/IRA demands.

SOLEMN LEAGUE AND COVENANT (28 September 1912). Sir Edward Carson (q.v.) obtained 218,000 signatories in Ulster against home rule, with a further 229,000 women supporters, "convinced that Home Rule would be disastrous to the material well-being of Ulster as well as of the whole of Ireland, subversive of our civil and religious freedom, destructive of our citizenship, and perilous to the unity of the Empire." They pledged themselves to defend "our cherished position of equal citizenship in the United Kingdom and to use all means which may be found necessary to defeat the present conspiracy to set up a Home Rule Parliament in Ireland . . . to refuse to recognize its authority."

SOMERVILLE, EDITH ANNA OENONE (1858–1949). Born in Corfu, but brought up in Skibbereen and educated at Alexandra College, Dublin, she studied painting in London and Paris. From 1886 she collaborated with her cousin Violet Florence Martin (1862–1915), who took the literary name of "Martin Ross" from the family home, Ross House, Co. Galway, in writing *The Real Charlotte* (1894), *Experiences of an Irish R.M.* (1899–1908), *In Mr. Knox's Country* (1915), and *The Big House of Inver* (1925). Their stories offer humorous, frequently sharp depictions of the rural Anglo-Irish ascendancy's (q.v.) relations with each other and their tenants. Their *Irish Memories* (1917) include letters written by Maria Edgeworth (q.v.) to their great-grandfather.

SPANISH ARMADA. After encounters in the English Channel, the fleet commanded by the duke of Medina Sidonia was driven to the west via northern Scotland by severe weather. Sites of more than 20 wrecks have been located around the Irish coast from the Giant's Causeway to the Dingle peninsula. The most famous are the *Girona* off north Antrim, the *Santa Maria de la Rosa*, Blasket Islands, and *la Trinidad Valencera* off Donegal. Marine archeologists have recovered numerous spectacular finds from the vessels, some of which are now exhibited at the Ulster Museum.

SPRING, DICK (1950–). Educated at the Christian Brothers School in his home town of Tralee and at Trinity College Dublin as a lawyer. Having represented Kerry at Gaelic football and Ireland at rugby, he was elected Labour TD for North Kerry in 1981. He held junior portfolios in the ministries of justice, and environment and energy in 1982–87 before becoming tanaiste in 1982 under Garret FitzGerald (q.v.) and cooperating closely with him over the Anglo-Irish Agreement (q.v.). As leader of the Labour Party (q.v.) in the Republic since 1982, the party's electoral success in 1992 put him in a strong bargaining position when Albert Reynolds (q.v.) was in need of a coalition partner. In a deal worked out in January 1993 Spring managed to have himself appointed not only tanaiste in the new administration but also minister of foreign affairs, thereby including within his remit responsibility for overseeing policy on Northern Ireland. He supported Reynolds in discussions leading to the Downing Street Declaration (q.v.), but caused widespread unease and resentment in the UK when he asserted unilaterally that in the absence of Unionist agreement the British and Irish governments would impose their own solution.

At successive Anglo-Irish intergovernmental conferences he has sought to present a forceful yet conciliatory stance that has sometimes appeared inconsistent. In November 1990 he suggested the possibility of a review of articles 2 and 3 of the Republic's constitution in relation to the territorial claim to Northern Ireland, but has not raised the issue since. He has also been wrong-footed occasionally by seeming unaware of the detailed content of parallel discussions between Sinn Fein and John Hume (qq.v.).

STEPHENS, JAMES (1824–1901). Born in Kilkenny. He worked as a railway engineer, joined Young Ireland (q.v.), and participated in the 1848 uprising. He structured the Irish (Revolutionary) Republican Brotherhood/Fenians (q.v.) along military lines, and he founded *The Irish People* (1863–65) with T. C. Luby. He sought American funding for an armed rising, which he declared for 1865. It never took place. He was arrested but escaped from Dublin to France and was replaced in 1866 as head of the Fenians in America.

STOKES, WILLIAM (1804–78). Son of the United Irishman Whitley Stokes (who held the chair of medicine at Dublin University and the College of Surgeons, and was Donegall Professor of Mathematics). His father, an evangelical and an advocate of providing the Irish scriptures for the population in 1806, wrote *Observations on the Population and Resources of Ireland* (1821). He was a physician at the Meath Hospital in 1818. William also studied medicine in Dublin and Edinburgh, published a treatise on the stethoscope immediately after graduating in

1825, joined R. J. Graves (q.v.) at the Meath Hospital in 1826, and wrote textbooks on diseases of the lungs (1837) and the heart (1854). He was president of the Royal Irish Academy (q.v.) in 1874, and he wrote a biography of the archaeologist George Petrie (q.v.) in 1868.

STORMONT. Synonymous with the parliament of Northern Ireland, although the building at Stormont Castle on the outskirts of Belfast was not ready until 1932. Under the 1920 Government of Ireland Act (q.v.), the parliament consisted of a 52-seat House of Commons and 26-member Senate, 24 elected with the two city mayors (the representative from Londonderry was suspended in April 1969). Throughout its history Stormont's House of Commons was dominated by the Unionist Party, their members fluctuating between 42 in 1938 and 34 in 1962. Nationalists who held 11 seats in 1929 had only six in 1969, reflecting the growth of Republican Labour, Northern Ireland Labour Party (NILP), and Independents. *See also* Ulster Unionist Party

The Stormont parliament was abolished by the Northern Ireland Constitution Act in July 1973 and was replaced by a 78-seat Assembly elected from multiple-member constituencies by proportional representation. Of those elected in 1973, 50 were Unionists of various parties with 61 percent of first preference votes, 19 Social Democratic and Labour Party (SDLP)(22%), eight Alliance Party (9%), and one NILP candidate. In 1982 the balance was very similar, except that Alliance had gained two seats and the SDLP had lost five to Sinn Fein.

Northern Ireland voters also send 18 members to the Westminster parliament; in 1992 these were 13 Unionists, three SDLP, and two Sinn Fein.

SUNNINGDALE AGREEMENT (6–9 December 1973). Named after the location in Berkshire where British and Irish government representatives and Northern Ireland Assembly Executive members sought to clarify relationships. It agreed that there would be "no change to the status of Northern Ireland within the United Kingdom until a majority of the population support it," revived the Council of Ireland idea, and envisaged close cooperation between Northern Ireland and the Republic of Ireland on law and order. It failed to secure support from extremists or Fianna Fail (q.v.) and failed to stabilize the immediate situation, though its ideas were built upon later.

SWIFT, JONATHAN (1667–1745). Born in Dublin, educated at Kilkenny and Trinity College Dublin. He became secretary to Sir William Temple in Surrey, where he was tutor to Esther Johnson, celebrated in his later writings as "Stella." He is believed to have married her in 1716. He was ordained and appointed prebend of Kilroot, Co. Antrim, returning to Ireland in 1699 as vicar of Laracor, Co. Meath. He was disappointed at not receiving the deanery of Derry. After his first great satire, *A Tale of a Tub* (1704), he briefly changed his political stance to become a Tory pamphleteer in London (1710–13). He returned to Dublin as dean of St. Patrick's Cathedral in April 1713, followed by the tubercular "Vanessa," Esther Vanhomrigh, who died ten years later. Profoundly sympathetic to the plight of the Irish poor and antagonistic to rack-renting landlords, he fiercely opposed England's restrictive colonial trade policy toward Ireland, which caused ruin among its woollen weavers. *Drapier's Letters* (1724) scourged those responsible for corrupt official debasement of Irish copper coinage. *Gulliver's Travels* (1726) received supreme acclamation for its bitter satire of the conduct of English public life. He was the center of a brilliant circle of literary men, including Joseph Addison, John Arbuthnot, William Congreve, John Dryden, John Gay, Alexander Pope, and Sir Richard Steele. His circle also included the foremost ecclesiastical and political figures of his day. From his bequests St. Patrick's hospital for the insane was established in Dublin.

SYNGE, JOHN MILLINGTON (1871–1909). Born at Rathfarnham, Dublin, the son of a barrister and a Church of Ireland rector's daughter. He studied languages and history at Trinity College Dublin, then attended the Royal Irish Academy of Music. In Paris in December 1896 he met W. B. Yeats (q.v.), who encouraged him to seek inspiration among the Gaelic peasantry of the Aran Islands, which he did in 1898. He reacted against Yeats's sources of romantic legend, and his own plays were rooted in the reality and everyday speech of country life, set in cottage kitchen, shebeen, or lane, far from both polite society and urban squalor. His best-known works are *Riders to the Sea* (1902), *The Shadow of the Glen* (1904), *The Playboy of the Western World* (1907), *The Tinker's Wedding* (1907), *The Well of the Saints* (1905), and *Deirdre of the Sorrows* (1909). Several of his humorous plays offended the aspiring guardians of a new puritan Irish tradition, but were defended by Yeats who compared Synge's achievement to that of Robert Burns in Scotland. His journal *The Aran Islands* (1902) was illustrated by Jack B. Yeats (q.v.).

-T-

TALBOT, RICHARD (1630–91). Born in Malahide. He defended Drogheda against Oliver Cromwell (q.v.) in 1649, returning from exile after the Restoration to receive lands for his services. He was James II's commander in Ireland from 1685, supplanting Protestants in all offices. He was made earl of Tyrconnell in 1685, appointed viceroy in February 1687, commanded a cavalry regiment at the battle of the

Boyne (q.v.), and took the defeated army to France. In 1691 he returned to Limerick (q.v.), where he died.

TARA. A pre-Christian site near Navan, Co. Meath, associated with the goddess Maeve and the paramount O'Neill kings since at least the sixth century. By the eighth century its subordinate territories had fragmented, and it had declined as a religious-royal center, though its legendary status became enhanced. The whole site consists of complex earthworks around a low hill, including a Neolithic passage grave, with evidence of subsequent Bronze Age burials, a 300-meter-radius Iron Age defensive ditch partly cut into rock, several ring forts, and a carved stone pillar. *See also* Introduction

TENANT LEAGUE. Founded in August 1850 by C. G. Duffy (q.v.) and Frederick Lucas, it was intended to relate to the whole of Ireland, but Ulster withdrew. Archbishop Croke suggested a written pledge among members not to bid for holdings brought onto the market by ejectments of tenants, in order to secure the "three Fs." The question of rents preoccupied the minds of small tenants, whereas security of tenure was paramount for the larger ones, who wanted a pressure group in parliament to obtain "tenant right." It led to the election of 50 members to the Commons in 1852 and to the formation of the Irish Parliamentary Party (q.v.) in September 1852. That year the Napier land bill granting compensation to evicted tenants was introduced, but it failed when the earl of Derby's administration fell. Later the movement lost the support of the Roman Catholic Church and disintegrated by 1855. It was revived by the Land League (q.v.) in 1873.

THEATERS. The Abbey Theatre has always represented the focus of dramatic life in Dublin because of its associations with all the great literary figures of the Gaelic revival at the turn of the century. In addition the city hosts other performing companies, which evolved distinctively. The Gaiety Theatre in South King Street opened in 1871 with a performance of Goldsmith's (q.v.) *She Stoops to Conquer*. It hosted Christmas pantomimes from 1873, and from 1900 it was the home of the Irish Literary Theatre (q.v.), becoming the venue for the Dublin Grand Opera Society from 1941.

The Dublin Gate Theatre Studio was formed in 1928 by Hilton Edwards and Micheal MacLiammoir (q.v.). It became a limited company in 1929 and moved from its Peacock site to the Rotunda Building, Cavendish Row, designed by Richard Johnston and James Gandon (q.v.). It was funded by the earl of Longford, undertook foreign tours from 1935, and in 1969 was offered a government subsidy that enabled it to operate a six-month season.

The Lyric Theatre Company grew out of the Dublin Verse Speaking Society founding by Austin Clarke and Robert Farren. At first it focused on Clarke's verse dramas.

THOMOND. The ancient Irish kingdom of the O'Brien dynasty, centered on Limerick (q.v.) and composed of the later counties of Clare, Limerick, and the northern parts of Cork and Kerry.

TITHES. The procedure whereby one-tenth of the annual increase from the profits of lands, stock, and crafts was collected for the upkeep of the church. It originally dates from the time of King Henry II, but in practice was not applied outside the Dublin area until the late 16th century. It was particularly resented in Ireland because only a small minority (about one-tenth) of the population belonged to the Established Church. Even in the early 18th century landlords too resisted collection of tithes, to such an extent that levies were removed from pastureland, thus exerting greater pressure on cottiers' and smallholders' cultivated plots. By the 19th century complaints became open warfare, arrears developed, and tithe farmers were targeted by mobs. In 1838 the Tithe Rent-charge Act (1 & 2 Vict., c. 109) commuted its assessments into a rent charge levied on the head landlord, and the problem subsided.

TONE, THEOBALD WOLFE (1763–98). Born in Dublin, educated at Trinity College Dublin and the Middle Temple. Strongly influenced by French Revolutionary ideas, he helped to form the Society of United Irishmen in 1791 and agitated for the Catholic Relief Act (1793). Though a Presbyterian, he became assistant secretary of the Catholic Committee in 1792. He was exiled to America and to France. In December 1796 he led an army from France, and again in September 1798, to Lough Swilly. He was captured at Buncrana and was tried before a court martial. He was convicted of high treason, but committed suicide before he could be hanged. *See also* United Irishmen, Society of

TRADES UNIONS. The Irish Trade Union Congress (ITUC) was formed in Dublin in 1894. It remained apolitical until 1910, when James Larkin and James Connolly (qq.v.) joined it to the Irish Labour Party (LP). The ITUC-LP was formed in 1912. It was an all-Ireland body, and many of its affiliated unions were branches of British unions, a feature that created strains as Irish politics changed. In the 1920s and 1930s it was dominated by William O'Brien of the Irish Transport and General Workers Union. He split the movement in 1945 by forming the Congress of Irish Unions out of fear of Communist infiltration. The split was healed in 1959 with the formation of the Irish Congress of Trade Unions (ICTU). Among the foremost women leaders was the suffragette Louie Bennett (1870–1956), founder of the Irish Women Workers' Union, and president of the ITUC in 1932.

TUAM. The Co. Galway site of a fifth/sixth-century monastery of St. Jarlath, a 12th-century cathedral and archbishopric during Tuam's period as a center of the O'Conor kings of Connacht. It did not feature prominently in the Anglo-Norman period. One 12th-century high cross survives by the rebuilt cathedral (Church of Ireland), as does another in the town center.

TUKE, JAMES HACK (1819–96). A Quaker from York, Tuke traveled to Ireland with W. E. Forster (q.v.) with relief in the 1845 famine. After that he published his very influential *A Visit to Connaught in 1847,* which exposed the horrors of the people's suffering. He visited Ireland again during the 1880–82 famine when Forster was chief secretary for Ireland and in 1885–86, promoting emigration as well as adoption of the "three Fs." He gave practical assistance to the poor as adviser to the Congested Districts Board (q.v.). His other publications included *Achill and the West of Ireland: Report of the Distribution of the Seed Potato Fund* (1886), and *The Condition of Donegal* (1889). *See also* Famines

-U-

ULSTER DEFENCE ASSOCIATION (UDA). Formed in September 1971 to coordinate loyalist vigilante groups (defense associations) in the Belfast area, it soon became the largest Protestant paramilitary organization with a working-class composition, without MPs or clergymen. Estimates of its membership have varied from 10,000 to 40,000. It has been associated with violence, most often through its military wing, the illegal Ulster Freedom Fighters (UFF), which was formed in 1973. Its purpose is to protect loyalist protests, usually by strongarm measures. Intermittently it has also tried to seek a long-term political solution by approaches to the Social Democratic and Labour Party (q.v.) and others, although its preferred option seems to have been independence for Ulster. It recognizes a Gaelic element in the Ulster identity, yet it was closely involved with the Vanguard movement in the early 1970s and from time to time with the Ulster Volunteer Force (q.v.). Its biggest operation, in concert with other worker or paramilitary groups, was the loyalist strike of 1974, which brought down the power-sharing Executive. UFF activities have been largely sectarian murders of Roman Catholics (allegedly those with IRA connections) or attacks on their property, including churches, often as retaliatory measures for IRA action. Arms have sometimes been acquired illegally through sympathizers in Scotland and funds often through racketeering and possibly from sources abroad, such as Libya. Intermittent internal feuds have produced violent results for individual members. It opposed the Anglo-Irish Agreement (q.v.) and took part in demonstrations, but left most of the protests to politicians, later issuing *Common Sense,* a policy document (1987) that found wide support because of its sensitivity to identity and minority issues. The 1988 British broadcasting ban applied to both UDA and UFF, which sponsored the Ulster Loyalist Democratic Party in 1981 for political developments.

ULSTER DEFENCE REGIMENT (UDR). This regular regiment was formed in 1970 as a locally raised and largely part-time force within the British army structure, as suggested by the Hunt Report, to be a replacement for the B Specials (Ulster Special Constabulary) (q.v.). Its initial success in attracting 18 percent Catholic membership was not sustained, and since 1978 it has been a mere 3 percent. Nationalists have criticized it for bias, and some members have been convicted of terrorist-related offences. Nevertheless, it proved its impartiality during the 1977 loyalist strike, and its local knowledge has always been highly regarded in security circles. By 1988 its complement reached 6,300, nearly half of whom were full-time personnel. Thus it became the largest regiment in the army and was later merged with the Royal Irish Regiment. *See also* Army, British

ULSTER SPECIAL CONSTABULARY (B Specials). A largely part-time, locally based force in Northern Ireland, formed in 1920 to combat the IRA (q.v.). The Scarman tribunal criticized its training and emphasized its capacity to raise tension when deployed. In 1969 there were about 10,000 members. The Hunt Report of 1969 recommended abolishing it, and in 1970 it was replaced by the Ulster Defence Regiment (UDR) (q.v.).

ULSTER UNIONIST PARTY (Official Unionist Party, OUP). The largest political organization in Northern Ireland and the party of government in the Stormont parliament (q.v.) from 1921 to 1972. The party was formed from members of the Orange Order (q.v.) to oppose home rule in the late 19th century. Until the period of Terence O'Neill's (q.v.) leadership in the late 1960s, it was a broad coalition of left and right that was united by a commitment to maintain the union with Great Britain and a devolved parliament at Stormont. Factions developed out of O'Neill's attempts at reform in Northern Ireland and out of the shock that resulted from the closure of Stormont, fragments of unionist parties developing or individuals leaving for the Alliance Party or Democratic Unionist Party (DUP) (qq.v.). The connection with the British Conservative (and Unionist) Party was largely ignored, and the Sunningdale Agreement (q.v.) produced further divisions. The Westminster MPs, as elected in 1974, were overwhelmingly anti-reform and in Northern Ireland most, as Official Unionists, backed the loyalist strike that brought down the power-sharing Executive, whose chief was the former party leader Brian Faulkner (q.v.). They sought other solutions in combination with the DUP and Vanguard, as the United Ulster Unionist Council (UUUC). When those were unacceptable to the UK government they sought, unsuccessfully, their own accommodation with the Social Democratic and Labour Party (SDLP) (q.v.) in 1976. The UUUC grouping collapsed under divergent opinions regarding vigilante organizations, although it has worked closely with the DUP in opposition to the Anglo-Irish Agreement (q.v.) and other developments.

The party was restructured as the landed gentry element became less important than the working and middle classes. Under James Molyneaux's (q.v.) leadership the Unionist Party at Westminster played a more independent role, seeking maximum influence wherever it lay. Support for the Labour government led to increased representation at Westminster and the Boundary Commission in 1978. It has often criticized security policy (one of its MPs, Rev. Robert Bradford, was murdered in 1981), and it has sought to confine contacts with Dublin to a strictly personal, friendly level rather than a structured, cooperative one. Party members were doubtful about the 1982 Assembly and used the Falklands Islands problem to highlight the differences between Northern Ireland and Republic of Ireland instincts. They therefore opposed the Anglo-Irish Agreement (q.v.), again in alliance with the DUP. To some extent their resentment at having been excluded from its development fueled their innate suspicion. Their MPs withdrew from Westminster, and the party declined to have any contact with government ministers. By 1988 relations resumed as the Anglo-Irish Agreement remained intact and talks took place about the way forward. The Downing Street Declaration (q.v.) received a guarded welcome, but an accommodation with Sinn Fein/IRA remains anathema. They were very dubious about the 1994–95 cease-fire becoming effective without the Unionist position being seriously compromised.

ULSTER VOLUNTEER FORCE (UVF). An illegal loyalist paramilitary force. In 1966 it revived a name used for "Carson's army," the Unionist body set up in 1912 to oppose home rule by force. Most of it formed the 36th (Ulster) Division in the British army after 1914 and suffered severe losses at the battle of the Somme in 1916. In 1966 it threatened war against the IRA (q.v.) and opposed Prime Minister Terence O'Neill's (q.v.) reforms. It has been illegal for most of the time since 1972, when it probably had 1,500 members (including some ex-soldiers), but it has organized underground. Operating like the IRA, it specialized in murdering republican activists or their associates. Many of its members have been imprisoned, 26 alone after a single trial in 1977. Its scale was reduced, probably to a core in Belfast, with some residual support in Scotland. Further problems arose as a senior member turned "supergrass" (informer) in the early 1980s and as illegal arms from abroad were seized. The Volunteer Political Party appeared briefly in 1974 as its political wing.

UNION, ACT OF (1801). Ireland possessed its own parliament from 1295, achieving legislative independence from 1782 to 1800 under Henry Grattan (q.v.). However, its strategic and political relationship with Britain was complicated by the French revolutionary wars and the United Irishmen's (q.v.) rising in 1798. Despite the government's intense lobbying, bordering on corruption, of Irish members to promote Union, opposition to it was growing. In January 1799 George Ponsonby's amendment to maintain the Irish parliament's independence was defeated by one vote. The following day the opposition succeeded in having the "Union paragraph" deleted from the Lord Lieutenant Cornwallis's address, framed by Chief Secretary Castlereagh (q.v.). Nevertheless, within a week, at Westminster the British prime minister, William Pitt, easily secured passage of measures leading toward Union. Pitt tried to obtain the support of the Roman Catholic Archbishop Troy of Dublin by promises of emancipation, while giving a guarantee to the Established Church and the Presbyterians, most of whom opposed it or were neutral. In January 1800 Grattan, the marquis of Downshire, Earl Charlemont, and others mobilized electoral opinion against the government's relentless, if inept, pro-Union campaign. Yet by February, shadowed by hints of intervention by Downshire's militia, Castlereagh obtained from the alarmed Dublin parliament a majority of 43 in support of the principle of Union. The Irish Commons overruled Grattan's objections, brittle opposition crumbled, and both parliaments eventually voted in favor. A flush of peerages ensued. Faced with King George III's refusal to countenance Catholic emancipation (q.v.), Pitt resigned in February 1801. On 1 August 1800 the act received the royal assent (40 Geo. III, c. 38). It contained eight articles:

1. that on 1 January 1801 the kingdoms should be united as the United Kingdom of Great Britain and Ireland;

2. that the succession to the Imperial Crown and its dominions should continue according to existing laws;

3. that there should be a single parliament;

4. that the House of Lords should have 28 secular life peers and four spiritual representatives elected in rotation by the peers of Ireland, and the Commons, 100 Irish members, two from each county (64), two each from the cities of Cork and Dublin, 31 from the other 116 boroughs, and one from Trinity College. Electoral laws should be the same as in England;

5. that there should be a single Protestant episcopal church, called the United Church of England and Ireland, as an essential and perpetual part of the Union;

6. that all Irish subjects should have equal economic entitlements with British citizens regarding bounties and freedom of trade;

7. that debts incurred before Union should be met through separate exchequers as hitherto, but for 20 years UK expenditure should be shared by Ireland and Great Britain in a ratio of 2:15; thereafter, Ireland's contributions to combined expenditure would be periodically determined by the UK parliament on the basis of averaged values of their respective imports and exports;

8. that all existing laws and courts were confirmed.

Opposition mounted under Daniel O'Connell (q.v.) and the Repeal Association from 1830 and later by the Irish Parliamentary Party (q.v.), which was prepared to remain in the UK, whereas the Irish Republican Brotherhood and Sinn Fein (qq.v.) wanted total independence and called a Dáil (q.v.) in 1919.

UNITED IRISHMAN (February–May 1847). John Mitchel's (q.v.) newspaper sought to provoke a radical armed rising over the land issue, advocating nonpayment of rent and boycotts. The newspaper was revived by Arthur Griffith (q.v.) as a weekly from March 1899 to 1906, becoming a mouthpiece of Cumann na nGaedheal (q.v.), aiming at self-government from 1904. It was also the title of an IRA/Sinn Fein monthly that appeared in 1948 and of Official Sinn Fein (q.v.) after the 1970 schism. *See also* Newspapers

UNITED IRISHMEN, SOCIETY OF. Founded in Belfast on 14 October 1791, with a parallel organization in Dublin on 9 November. A Protestant reformist group that was greatly influenced by French and American revolutionary ideals. It aimed at achieving parliamentary reform through peaceful means and at securing common rights for all Irishmen, irrespective of sectarian belief, though Wolfe Tone (q.v.) wanted an independent republic on the French model. As it became more militant and conspiratorial, it began losing its constitutional members. Finally it was suppressed and went underground as a secret organization in 1794–95. Administering or taking its oath became a capital offense under the Insurrection Act (1796). At the same time it sought narrower Catholic support from Defenders, Oakboys, and Steelboys and mounted an ill-conceived uprising in 1798. It was destroyed by the futile revolt of Robert Emmet (q.v.) in 1803. The society, increasingly organized in a hierarchical structure of small military cells, became part of the mythology of Irish republicanism and was in some ways a model for nationalist republicans like Davis, Connolly, Mitchel, and the Irish (Revolutionary) Republican Brotherhood (qq.v.) in the mid-19th century, culminating in the 1916 Easter Rising (q.v.). *See also* Secret Societies

UNIVERSITIES. Trinity College Dublin (TCD) was granted a charter by Queen Elizabeth I in 1591 with the intention that it would give rise to other colleges to disseminate English liberal education and Protestant reformist culture, which it did with distinction until Hobart's Catholic Relief Act (1793), which inter alia permitted Catholics to seek degrees.

The 1845 Colleges (Ireland) Act (8 & 9 Vict., c. 66) established nondenominational colleges of higher education at Belfast, Cork, and Galway. From 1850 they were opposed by the Roman Catholic hierarchy, which in 1854 set up the Catholic University of Ireland (CUI) with John Henry Newman (q.v.) as its rector. In 1875 a synod at Maynooth effectively extended the ban on Catholic attendance at the Queen's Colleges to TCD too. The Royal University was founded in 1879 as an examining body to allow students of CUI to obtain degrees, hitherto not recognized by the state. From October 1883 the Catholic University, now renamed University College Dublin (UCD), was administered by the Society of Jesus (Jesuits).

The 1908 Irish Universities Act (8 Edw. VII, c. 38) dissolved the former Royal University and Queen's College Belfast, replacing them with the National University of Ireland (NUI) and The Queen's University of Belfast (QUB), respectively. The former comprised four constituent colleges, UCD, University College Cork (UCC), University College Galway (UCG) and St. Patrick's College, Maynooth, which had been founded in 1795 as a Roman Catholic seminary. TCD houses a legal deposit library, which receives every work published in UK and Ireland, and also contains many valuable Irish medieval illustrated manuscripts, the most famous of which are the *Book of Kells, Book of Armagh* and *Book of Durrow.*

In September 1960 the Republic's minister for education appointed Cearbhall Ó Dálaigh (q.v.), as chief justice, to chair a commission on higher education, which reported in March 1967. It recommended that separate university status be granted to UCC, UCD, and UCG and that further third-level education provision be made available in new Dublin and Limerick colleges. TCD was to remain independent of this system, and the over-arching Commission for Higher Education was to control financial allocation. A month later the government announced that TCD and UCD would in fact be merged, but no action was taken due to fierce opposition and the death of the minister, D. O'Malley, in 1968. However, rationalization of courses was agreed between the two Dublin universities in 1970.

In 1965 the Lockwood Committee on Higher Education in Northern Ireland proposed the creation of a New University of Ulster (NUU) at Coleraine, to incorporate Magee University College, Londonderry, opening in 1968. In 1984, as a consequence of the Chilver Report, NUU was merged with the Ulster (College) Polytechnic at Jordanstown, near Belfast, to form the University of Ulster, with four campuses—Coleraine, Londonderry, Jordanstown, and Belfast.

USSHER, JAMES (1581–1656). Born in Dublin and entered Trinity College Dublin (TCD) in 1594. Although he held Calvinistic views, he was appointed bishop of Meath (1621) and then archbishop of Armagh (1625). A royalist in the English Civil War, he was translated to Carlisle in 1642. From a literal study of Old Testament chronology he calculated the date of the Creation at 4004 B.C., a belief that was widely accepted until Charles Darwin and others in the mid-19th century produced evidence of much longer evolution of life forms. Ussher's extensive library was bequeathed to TCD.

-V-

VIKING SETTLEMENTS. These were coastal in location, ranging from Limerick (q.v.) on the Shannon estuary in the southwest to Carlingford in the northeast. Vikings attacked Irish monastic centers frequently from A.D. 795. Initially the Viking camps were probably staging posts that developed to serve a wide-ranging trading system as the Scandinavian peoples gained dominance of the European seaways in the ninth century and turned their attention from raiding to peaceful colonization and commerce. One of the earliest occupation sites, dating from A.D. 841, later grew into the fortified town of Dublin (q.v.) and became the focus of an extensive Norse kingdom that included York in northeastern England. Viking settlements in Ireland were entirely urban oriented, except at Dublin where they also held a narrow strip of coastal territory to the north and south. Their main legacy is twofold: (1) the names of coastal features, for example, islands such as Lambay and inlets such as Strangford; and (2) port towns like Waterford, Wexford, and possibly Cork (qq.v.), which were a new but enduring element in the Irish scene. In time some developed into essentially Hiberno-Norse towns, their Viking settlers becoming Christian and intermarrying with their Irish neighbors, while their leaders formed political alliances with the local Irish kings and took part in their wars. They remained distinctive until after the Anglo-Norman invasion (q.v.)(1169). Their ports proved to be valuable fulcrums for the resulting economic development of southeastern Ireland.

-W-

WATERFORD (Port Lairge). County borough with 40,300 inhabitants in 1991. An industrial (food, iron, printing, glass) city and regional focus for southeastern Ireland. As a port on the river Suir it was founded by the Vikings in the tenth century, ten kilometers from the sea on a significant south-coast estuary. It became one of the Vikings' most important trading centers and developed its own diocese independent of the Irish Church. Though fortified, it fell to an Anglo-Norman siege in 1170. Its continuing importance was acknowledged when it became a town reserved to the Crown in the following year. In fact, for many travelers, kings and commoners alike, Waterford was their point of entry to Ireland and one of its key cities in the medieval period. A distinctive feature remains its long river quay. Its walls were improved and extended on several occasions, withstanding numerous sieges, including a prolonged one during the Cromwellian period. Parts of the walls, with towers attached, survive; one, Reginald's Tower, is now a museum. In the 18th century Waterford became a leading center for glass production, which was revived in 1947. The medieval Christchurch Cathedral (Church of Ireland) was rebuilt in 1770 and further redesigned in 1891. The Mall and a number of fine buildings elsewhere in the town, including the Bishop's Palace, the City Hall (incorporating a theater and art gallery) and Theatre Royal, and the Holy Trinity Cathedral (Roman Catholic), also originated in the 18th century. A number of Waterford men were prominent in the struggle for Catholic Ireland, the most notable being the Franciscan Luke Wadding (1588–1657) and Thomas Meagher (q.v.). The Irish Christian Brothers' (q.v.) teaching order was founded there in 1806 by Edmund Rice, a prosperous merchant.

WELLESLEY, ARTHUR (1769–1852). Born in Dublin, son of the earl of Mornington, aide to the lord lieutenant from 1787 to 1793. He became MP for Trim in the Irish parliament of 1790–95, supported granting the franchise to Roman Catholics, was knighted in 1804, and was secretary for Ireland in 1807–9. He was military commander against the Napoleonic armies in the Peninsular War (1809), and as field marshal was created Duke of Wellington. He was appointed ambassador to Paris and played a pivotal role at the Congress of Vienna. His military reputation climaxed in the defeat of Napoleon at Waterloo in June 1815. He became British prime minister in 1818, and with Sir Robert Peel was responsible for Catholic emancipation (q.v.) in 1829.

WENTWORTH, THOMAS (1593–1641), earl of Strafford. Having been lord deputy in Ireland in 1632–41, he was charged with treason for misgovernment there. During his era of "thorough" government, he played off the Old English against the New English, led by Richard Boyle (qq.v.) of Cork, to enforce the will of Charles I in the absence of parliament. He acquired vast estates in counties Wicklow and Kildare, but he offended the earl of Clanricard in the Galway resettlement. He was awarded an earldom in 1640, and he built up an independent army to rival the Scots. He was later executed.

WESTMINSTER REPRESENTATION. After the English civil war and the Commonwealth, the Irish parliament was restored for the period 1660–1801. After the Union 100 seats at Westminster were allocated to Irish members, the number being increased to 105 in 1832, reduced to 103 in 1885, and restored to 105 in 1918. "Forty-shilling freeholders" (q.v.) were enfranchised in 1793, but no Roman Catholic members were allowed to take up their seats until emancipation (1829), when the freehold property qualification was raised to £10, thereby augmenting the electorate from about 37,000 to 92,000. That figure was further increased, especially outside the boroughs, to 163,000 by the 1850 Representation of the People Act (13 & 14 Vict., c. 69). Similarly, another act of 1868 (31 & 32 Vict., c. 49) reduced the borough property qualification to £4 and included lodgers, so that by 1884 the electorate numbered about 738,000. In 1918 the franchise was widened to include all males over the age of 21 and females over 30 (7 & 8 Geo. V, cc. 64/65). As a result of these democratic concessions and the consequent shift in political opinion and power, in 1835 the party composition was 37 Conservatives, 34 Liberals, and 34 Repealers. By 1918 abstentionist Sinn Fein candidates won 73 seats and formed the Dáil (q.v.). *See also* Stormont; Union, Act of

WEXFORD (Loch Garman). Industrial (food, agricultural machinery) town, population 9,500 in 1991, and small seaport on Wexford Harbour at the southeastern corner of Ireland. Its origins as a port are

Norse. It was the first of their walled towns to fall to the Anglo-Normans, who added a castle and strengthened the defenses, parts of which survive with towers. The medieval street plan is largely intact and forms the nucleus of the modern town; remains of some of the medieval churches are interspersed through it. The small, restored 18th-century theater is the venue for the international Wexford Opera Festival held each autumn.

WHATELY, RICHARD (1787–1863). Born in London, schooled near Bristol, and educated at Oxford. Three years after graduating he became a Fellow of Oriel in 1811. After taking divinity degrees and serving as a parish clergyman in Suffolk, he became principal of St. Alban Hall, Oxford, in 1825 with John Henry Newman (q.v.) as his deputy, influencing him by his *Letters on the Church* (1826). He became Drummond Professor of Political Economy in 1829. Discussion of the division of labor featured prominently in his lectures, which were published in 1831.

He moved to Dublin reluctantly as Protestant archbishop, being consecrated in October 1831. As head of the commission on non-denominational education, with his Roman Catholic counterpart, Archbishop Daniel Murray, he prepared unorthodox scriptural texts for schools. They offended fellow Protestants, as did his later decision to approve granting state aid to Catholic clergy and to St. Patrick's College Maynooth in 1845. Catholics objected to his school lesson guides of 1838, but only after Archbishop Cullen's (q.v.) succession. Withdrawal of the guides led to Whately's resignation in July 1853.

Never a profound theologian, he did hold firm anti-Calvinist views and initially tried to develop religious teaching in Trinity College (TCD), but he failed to set up a separate theological hall in the college. As an Anglican, he opposed anti-tithe agitation and disapproved of tithe commutation in 1838. As an antievangelical, he strongly resisted Newman's Oxford Movement. Although a supporter of Catholic emancipation (q.v.), in 1851 he established the Society for Protecting the Rights of Conscience to help Catholic converts under pressure from their clergy. In addition to attempting educational reforms through the National schools system, he chaired the Poor Law Commission (q.v.) (1833–36). He resolutely opposed outdoor relief in Ireland, even during the famine (q.v.), while nevertheless contributing generously to relief. On penal matters, he rejected transportation of convicts as a futile reaction to crime. Many of his opinions were rational and rooted in his faith in the capacity of political economy to resolve problems. He established a chair in that discipline at TCD. Favoring a plural property-based vote rather than parliamentary reform in the 1830s, his liberalism made him averse to the obligatory swearing of oaths in parliament. He was a founder of the Statistical Society of Dublin (1847) and the Society for Promoting Scientific Inquiries into Social Questions (1850). He wrote *Logic* (1826), *Rhetoric* (1828), and he edited *Paley's Moral Philosophy* (1859) and *Bacon's Essays* (1856). He also published texts on economics and the British constitution. Distinctly ahead of his time, though somewhat impractical, in 1851 he proposed adoption of a universal currency. He was often a lord justice in place of the viceroy, and was elected vice-president of the Royal Irish Academy (q.v.) in 1848.

WHITEBOYS (or LEVELLERS, Buachaillí Bána). A secret society (q.v.) that appeared in Tipperary and Limerick between 1761 and 1762 and then spread to other Munster counties — Cork, Kilkenny, and Waterford. Members were sworn to mutual loyalty by oaths and identified by white shirts. They opposed enclosure of common grazing lands, tithes (q.v.), the imposition of marriage fees, insecurity of tenure, and tolls. Their intimidation, arson, and atrocities were condemned by the Catholic bishops, including Archbishop Troy of Dublin, who excommunicated participants. Their violence was also condemned by landlords anxious to distance themselves from attempts to encourage wider disorder or rebellion. Lord Lieutenant Halifax considered the outbreaks as being nonsectarian and fundamentally economic in their causes, though anti-Catholic feeling was active during the war with France and Austria.

WHITELAW, REV. JAMES (1749–1813). Born in Co. Leitrim and educated at Trinity College Dublin. He was rector of various Dublin parishes in the Liberties where he sought to relieve the poverty of the Coombe weavers and to provide education. His *Essay on the Population of Dublin in 1798* (1805), based on his own fieldwork (which he pursued despite the risk of disease), was the first attempt to assess the size of the city's population. He collaborated with John Warburton, keeper of records at Dublin Castle, in writing a history of Dublin, which was completed by Robert Walsh in 1818.

WHITLAW, SIR WILLIAM (1851–1933). Born in Monaghan and educated at Queen's College Belfast, receiving an M.D. degree from Queen's University of Ireland in 1877. He held licentiates from the Royal College of Physicians Edinburgh, the Royal College of Surgeons Dublin, and the Apothecaries' Hall Dublin. As medical officer of the Royal Victoria Hospital, Belfast, he published *Elements of Pharmacy, Materia Medica and Theraputics* (1882), *Dictionary of Medical Treatment* (1892), and a two-volume *Manual of Practice and Theory of Medicine* (1908). He was knighted in 1902, endowed the

Medical Institute in 1903, and became pro-chancellor of The Queen's University of Belfast and MP for the University (1918–22).

WILDE, OSCAR FINGAL O'FLAHERTIE WILLS (1854–1900). Son of Sir William Wilde (q.v.), he was born in Dublin and educated at Portora Royal School, Enniskillen, Trinity College Dublin, and Magdalen College, Oxford. His wit became proverbial, notably through his plays *The Picture of Dorian Gray* (1891), *Lady Windmere's Fan* (1892), *A Woman of No Importance* (1893), *An Ideal Husband* (1895), *The Importance of Being Earnest* (1895), and *Salomé* (1894). Some of his works were banned, and he succumbed to the scandal of his friendship with Lord Alfred Douglas, son of the marquis of Queensberry. He was convicted of homosexual practices and imprisoned in 1895, resulting in *The Ballad of Reading Gaol* (1898).

WILDE, SIR WILLIAM ROBERT WILLS (1815–76). Born in Castlerea, Co. Roscommon, and educated at Dr. Steevens' Hospital and the Royal College of Surgeons (1837). He acted as personal physician to a wealthy businessman on a cruise to Egypt and became interested in subtropical eye diseases, later writing a two-volume *Narrative of a Voyage to Madeira, Teneriffe and along the Shores of the Mediterranean* (1840). He founded a dispensary for the poor, established the Mark Street Hospital (1844) for eye and ear ailments, and edited the *Dublin Journal of Medical Science* from 1845. As a friend of George Petrie (q.v.), he catalogued the Royal Irish Academy's (q.v.) antiquities (published in three volumes, 1858–62), acted as medical commissioner for the 1841 Irish census, wrote *The Beauties of the Boyne* (1849) and *Lough Corrib, its Shores and Islands* (1867). He was knighted in 1864 and lived in semi-retirement under the shadow of a libel action brought by a former patient.

WORKERS' PARTY (WP). From 1970 a republican Marxist-socialist party in Northern Ireland and the Republic of Ireland, known until 1982 as Official Sinn Fein (q.v.) and then the Republican Clubs. In the Republic it supported the Fianna Fail (q.v.) minority government. In Northern Ireland it was declared illegal from 1967 to 1973. It has had very limited success at local elections in Northern Ireland. It refused to take part in the New Ireland Forum (q.v.) in Dublin, but declared "reluctant" approval for the Anglo-Irish Agreement (q.v.). It denies having links with terrorists. In the Republic the shift toward a democratic socialist platform, as distinct from previous echoes of authoritarian European parties, caused a schism in 1992. When the more pragmatic views of Proinsias De Rossa were not wholeheartedly accepted, he and six other TDs formed the new party, the Democratic Left (DL). From 1992 it participated in the Fine Gael-Labour-DL coalition, occupying one seat in cabinet.

-Y-

YEATS, JACK BUTLER (1871–1957). Born in London, the youngest of five children of John B. Yeats (q.v.). Between the ages of 8 and 17 he enjoyed a Sligo upbringing with his grandparents, returning to London in 1888 to study art. He returned to live in Co. Wicklow and Dublin in 1910, published *Life in the West of Ireland* (1912), and changed from being an illustrator to a painter in oils, developing a characteristic flair for use of color. He was elected to the Royal Hibernian Academy in 1915.

YEATS, JOHN BUTLER (1839–1922). Born in Co. Down, son of a village rector, he was educated in the Isle of Man and at Trinity College Dublin. He inherited his father's estate in Kildare in 1862 and studied painting in London in 1867. He was elected to the Royal Hibernian Academy in 1892. He held numerous exhibitions in Britain, Ireland, and America, where he spent the last 14 years of his life, publishing collections of essays and biographical memoirs. Several of his portraits are displayed in the National Gallery of Ireland (q.v.).

YEATS, WILLIAM BUTLER (1865–1939). Born in Dublin, eldest son of John B. Yeats (q.v.). From 1865 to 1880 the family lived in London, where he studied at the Metropolitan School of Art (1884–85). He contested traditional views that Irish identity was framed by the language and encouraged contemporary literature written in English, alongside writings of the romantic Irish folklore/legend genre, through the National Literary Society (1892) and by his own verse plays, *The Wanderings of Oisin* (1889), *The Celtic Twilight* (1893), and *The Land of Heart's Desire* (1894). He met and was captivated by Maud Gonne in 1889 and joined the Irish Republican Brotherhood (qq.v.). He met Lady Gregory (q.v.) in 1897 and during periods of poor health spent summers at her home in Galway. The founding of the Irish Literary Theatre (1899) (q.v.) added a new element, drama, to the literary renaissance, exemplified in *The Countess Cathleen* (1899), *Diarmuid and Grainne* (1901), and *Cathleen Ni Houlihan* (1902). He formed the Irish National Theatre with Lady Gregory as codirector (and later J. M. Synge [q.v.]), producing *On Baile's Strand* (1904) and *The King's Threshold* (1904). He wrote four volumes of poetry, *The Wild Swans at Coole* (1919), *Michael Robartes and the Dancer* (1921), *The Tower* (1928), and *The Winding Stair* (1933). He moved to Galway in 1922 and received the Nobel Prize for Literature in 1923. He published a three-volume autobiography: *Reveries over Childhood and Youth* (1915), *The Trembling of the Veil* (1922), and *Dramatis Personae* (1936). The savagery of the 1919–21 war grieved him deeply, not least because he felt that he had been partly responsible, through his poetry, for the upsurge in nationalism. He was a member of the Irish Free State Senate (1922–28). He died at Rocquebrune near Monaco, and his remains were returned in 1948 to be buried at Drumcliff, near Sligo.

YELVERTON'S ACT (July 1782). This act (21 & 22 Geo. III, c. 47) repealed the Declaratory Act of 1720 by amending Poynings' law (qq.v.). It deprived the lord lieutenant of the right to initiate or modify Irish parliamentary bills to be sent to Westminster. This ultimately led to legislative independence under the Renunciation Act (23 Geo. III, c. 28) in 1783.

YOUNG IRELAND. This Protestant liberal group emerged after Daniel O'Connell's (q.v.) failed repeal of the Union campaign with its twin Catholic and nationalist preoccupations around 1842 through publication of *The Nation*. Young Ireland's anti-English advocacy of force through Sarsfield Clubs alienated O'Connell, as did its reliance on a romanticized historical idealization of resistance. In 1846 a nonconstitutional faction, led by Thomas Meagher, John Mitchel, and William Smith O'Brien (qq.v.), set up the Irish Confederation, which ended with the 1848 rising fiasco.

Appendix A
Viceroys: Lords Lieutenant of Ireland,
1640–1921

1640	Thomas Wentworth, Earl of Strafford
1641	Robert Sydney, Earl of Leicester
1643	James Butler, Marquis of Ormond
1646	Philip Sidney, Viscount Lisle
	[1647 Parliamentary Commissioners]
1648	James Butler, Marquis of Ormond
1649	Oliver Cromwell
1650–60	Commissioners of Civil Affairs
	[1658 Henry Cromwell as Commander in Chief]
1660	George Monck, Duke of Albermarle
1662	James Butler, Duke of Ormond
1669	John, Baron Robartes
1670	John, Baron Berkeley
1672	Arthur Capell, Earl of Essex
1677	Duke of Ormond
1685	Henry Hyde, Earl of Clarendon
1687	Richard Talbot, Duke of Tyrconnell
1692	Henry, Viscount Sidney
1700	Lawrence Hyde, Earl of Rochester
1703	Duke of Ormond
1707	Thomas Herbert, Earl of Pembroke
1708	Thomas, Earl of Wharton
1710	Duke of Ormond
1713	Charles Talbot, Duke of Shrewsbury
1714	Charles Spencer, Earl of Sunderland
1717	Charles, Viscount Townshend
1717	Duke of Bolton
1720	Charles Fitzroy, Duke of Grafton
1724	John, Baron Carteret
1730	Lionel Cranfield Sackville, Duke of Dorset
1737	William Cavendish, Duke of Devonshire

1745	Philip Dormer Stanhope, Earl of Chesterfield
1746	William Stanhope, Earl of Harrington
1750	Duke of Dorset
1755	Marquis of Hartington (Duke of Devonshire)
1757	John Russell, Duke of Bedford
1761	George Montague-Dunk, Earl of Halifax
1763	Hugh Percy, Duke of Northumberland
1765	Thomas Thynne, Viscount Weymouth
1765	Francis Seymour-Conway, Earl of Hertford
1766	George William Hervey, Earl of Bristol
1767	George, Viscount Townshend
1772	Simon, Earl Harcourt
1776	John Hobart, Earl of Buckinghamshire
1780	Frederick Howard, Earl of Carlisle
1782	William Henry Cavendish Bentinck, Duke of Portland
1782	George Nugent-Temple-Grenville, Earl Temple
1783	Robert Henley, Earl of Northington
1784	Charles Manners, Duke of Rutland
1787	Earl Temple (Marquis of Buckingham)
1789	John Fane, Earl of Westmorland
1794	William Wentworth Fitzwilliam, Earl FitzWilliam
1795	John Jeffreys Pratt, Earl Camden
1798	Charles, Marquis Cornwallis
1801	Philip Yorke, Earl of Hardwicke
1806	John Russell, Duke of Bedford
1807	Charles Lennox, Duke of Richmond
1813	Charles, Viscount Whitworth
1817	Charles Chetwynd Talbot, Earl Talbot
1821	Richard Colley Wellesley, Marquis Wellesley
1828	Henry William Paget, Marquis of Anglesey
1829	Hugh Percy, Duke of Northumberland
1830	Marquis of Anglesey
1833	Marquis Wellesley
1834	Thomas Hamilton, Earl of Haddington
1835	Constantine Henry Phipps, Earl of Mulgrave
1839	Hugh Fortescue, Viscount Ebrington
1841	Thomas Philip de Grey, Earl de Grey
1844	William A'Court, Baron Heytesbury
1846	John William Ponsonby, Earl of Bessborough
1847	George William Frederick Villiers, Earl of Clarendon
1852	Archibald William Montgomerie, Earl of Eglinton
1853	Edward Granville Eliot, Earl of St. Germans
1855	George William Frederick Howard, Earl of Carlisle
1858	Earl of Eglinton

1859	Earl of Carlisle
1864	John, Baron Wodehouse
1866	James Hamilton, Marquis/Duke of Abercorn
1868	John Poyntz Spencer, Earl Spencer
1874	Duke of Abercorn
1876	John Winston Spencer Churchill, Duke of Marlborough
1880	Francis Thomas de Grey Cowper, Earl Cowper
1882	Earl Spencer
1885	Henry Howard Molyneux Herbert, Earl of Caernarvon
1886	John Campbell Hamilton Gordon, Earl of Aberdeen
1886	Charles Stewart Vane-Tempest-Stewart, Marquis of Londonderry
1889	Lawrence Dundas, Earl of Zetland
1892	Robert Offley Ashburton Milnes, Baron Houghton
1895	George Henry Cadogan, Earl Cadogan
1902	William Humble Ward, Earl of Dudley
1905	Earl of Aberdeen
1915	Ivor Churchill Guest, Baron Wimborne
1918	John Denton Pinkstone French, Viscount French
1921	Edmund Bernard Talbot, Viscount FitzAlan

Appendix B
Chief Secretaries of Ireland, 1798–1920

1798	Robert Stewart, Viscount Castlereagh
1801	Charles Abbot
1802	William Wickham
1804	Sir Evan Nepean
1805	Sir Nicholas Vansittart/Charles Lang
1806	William Elliot
1807	Sir Arthur Wellesley
1809	Robert Dundas/William Wellesley-Pole
1812	Robert Peel
1818	Charles Grant
1821	Henry Goulbourn
1827	William Lamb
1828	Lord Francis Levenson Gower
1830	Sir Henry Hardinge/Lord Stanley
1833	Sir John Cam Hobhouse/Edward John Littleton
1834	Sir Henry Hardinge
1835	Viscount Morpeth
1841	Lord Eliot
1845	Sir Thomas Freemantle
1846	Earl of Lincoln/Henry Labouchere
1847	Sir William Somerville
1852	Lord Naas
1853	Sir John Young
1855	Edward Horsman
1857	Henry Arthur Herbert
1858	Lord Naas
1859	Edward Cardwell
1861	Sir Robert Peel
1865	Chichester Parkinson-Fortescue
1866	Lord Naas
1868	John Wilson-Patten/Chichester Parkinson-Fortescue
1870	Marquis of Hartington
1874	Sir Michael Edward Hicks Beach

1878	James Lowther
1880	William Edward Forster
1882	Lord Frederick Cavendish/Sir George Otto Trevelyan
1884	Henry Campbell-Bannerman
1885	Sir William Hart Dyke
1886	William Henry Smith/John Morley/Sir Michael Hicks Beach
1887	Arthur James Balfour
1891	William Lawies Jackson
1892	John Morley
1895	Gerald William Balfour
1900	George Wyndham
1905	Walter Hume Long/James Bryce
1907	Augustine Birrell
1916	Henry Edward Duke
1918	Edward Shortt
1919	James Ian Macpherson
1920	Sir Hamar Greenwood

Appendix C
Presidents of Ireland, 1938–1997

1938–45   Douglas Hyde
1945–59   Sean T. O'Kelly
1959–73   Eamon de Valera
1973–74   Erskine H. Childers
1974–76   Cearbhall Ó Dálaigh
1976–90   Patrick J. Hillery
1990–97   Mary T. W. Robinson

Appendix D
Prime Ministers and Deputy Prime Ministers of Eire/Republic of Ireland, 1937–1997

	Taoiseach	Tánaiste
1937–38	E. de Valera	S. T. O'Kelly
1938–43	E. de Valera	S. T. O'Kelly
1943–44	E. de Valera	S. T. O'Kelly
1944–48	E. de Valera	S. T. O'Kelly/S. F. Lemass (1945)
1948–51	J. A. Costello	W. Norton
1951–54	E. de Valera	S. F. Lemass
1954–57	J. A. Costello	W. Norton
1957–59	E. de Valera	S. F. Lemass
1959–61	S. F. Lemass	S. MacEntee
1961–65	S. F. Lemass	S. MacEntee
1965–66	S. F. Lemass	F. Aiken
1966–69	J. M. Lynch	F. Aiken
1969–73	J. M. Lynch	E. Childers
1973–77	L. Cosgrave	B. Corish
1977–79	J. M. Lynch	G. Colley
1979–81	C. J. Haughey	G. Colley
1981–82	G. M. D. FitzGerald	M. O'Leary
1982F–N	C. J. Haughey	R. MacSharry
1982–87	G. M. D. FitzGerald	D. Spring
1987–89	C. J. Haughey	B. Lenihan
1989–92	C. J. Haughey	B. Lenihan/J. Wilson (1990)
1993–94	A. Reynolds	D. Spring
1994–	J. Bruton	D. Spring

Appendix E
Prime Ministers of Northern Ireland, 1921–1972

June 1921–40	Sir J. Craig
November 1940–43	J. M. Andrews
May 1943–63	Sir B. Brooke (Viscount Brookeborough)
March 1963–69	T. M. O'Neill
May 1969–71	J. D. Chichester-Clark
March 1971–72	A. B. D. Faulkner

Appendix F
Secretaries of State for Northern Ireland, 1972–1997

Mar.1972–Nov.1973	William Whitelaw (Conservative)
Dec.1973–Feb 1974	Francis Pym (Conservative)
Mar.1974–Sept.1976	Merlyn Rees (Labour)
Sept.1976–May 1979	Roy Mason (Labour)
May 1979–Sept. 1981	Humphrey Atkins (Conservative)
Sept.1981–Sept.1984	James Prior (Conservative)
Sept.1984–Sept. 1985	Douglas Hurd (Conservative)
Sept. 1985–July 1989	Tom King (Conservative)
July 1989–Apr. 1992	Peter Brooke (Conservative)
Apr. 1992–Apr. 1997	Sir Patrick Mayhew (Conservative)
May 1997–	Marjorie Mowlam (Labour)

Appendix G
Church of Ireland Archbishops of Armagh and Primates of All Ireland

1747–64	George Stone (1708–64)
1765–94	Richard Robinson (1709–94)
1795–1800	William Newcome (?–1800)
1800–22	Hon. William Stuart (1755–1822)
1822–62	Lord John George Beresford (1773–1862)
1862–85	Marcus Gervais Beresford (1801–85)
1886–93	Robert Bent Knox (1808–93)
1893–96	Robert Samuel Gregg (1834–96)
1896–1911	William Alexander (1824–1911)
1911–20	John Baptist Crozier (1853–1920)
1920–38	Charles Frederick D'Arcy (1859–1938)
1938–38	John Godfrey Fitzmaurice Day (1874–1938)
1938–59	John Allen Fitzgerald Gregg (1873–1961)
1959–69	James McCann (1897–1983)
1969–80	George Otto Simms (1910–91)
1980–86	John Ward Armstrong (1915–87)
1986–	Robert (Robin) Henry Alexander Eames (1937–)

Appendix H
Roman Catholic Archbishops of Armagh and Primates of All Ireland

1749–58	Michael O'Reilly (?–1758)
1758–87	Anthony Blake (?–1787)
1787–1818	Richard O'Reilly (?–1818)
1819–32	Patrick Curtis (1740–1832)
1832–35	Thomas Kelly (?–1835)
1835–49	William Crolly (1780–1849)
1850–52	Paul Cullen (1803–78)
1852–66	Joseph Dixon (1806–66)
1867–69	Michael Kieran (?–1869)
1870–87	Daniel MacGettigan (1815–87)
1887–1924	Michael Logue (1840–1924)
1924–27	Patrick O'Donnell (1856–1927)
1928–45	Joseph MacRory (1861–1945)
1946–63	John Francis D'Alton (1883–1963)
1963–77	William Conway (1913–77)
1977–92	Tomás Séamus O'Fiaich (1923–92)
1992–96	Cahal Brendan Daly (1917–)
1996–	Sean Brady (1939–)

Bibliography

Among the many paradoxes pervading Irish history is the fact that while Ireland possesses some of the earliest and most artistic manuscript works in Europe, high levels of mass literacy did not characterize the country's indigenous culture until the present century. Consequently, although the quality of its creative literature has been recognized by the award of Nobel Prizes to four of its writers (Beckett, Heaney, Shaw, and Yeats), broad expanses of Ireland's past are silent from the point of view of extant documentary records. That dearth of reliable objective data sometimes allowed political animosity, economic backwardness, social upheaval, and cultural divergence to contribute to a tendency for the writing of Irish history to be colored more by partisan views than it was sustained by sound reasoning and profound scholarship. However, intellectual rigor and dynamism are increasingly questioning long held stereotyped opinions, helping to dispel erroneous belief or unbalanced interpretation.

In compiling this bibliography a primary consideration has been to include the most recently published books and articles up to the end of 1995, but simultaneously to set them alongside earlier works that have contributed to our understanding of a particular theme or topic or epitomize a special viewpoint. The presence—or absence—of a specific item should in no sense be taken to indicate endorsement or rejection of the stance adopted by any author or group. Considerations of space required overlooking many useful publications of only local interest, which may in any case be traced in other cited references. As in the main text, the overriding concern has been to offer a representative selection, strands of which may be pursued at leisure by the individual reader. It is important to note that no theme or category is self-contained and that related items may be located in other sections.

Contents

1. Chronologies
2. Bibliographies
3. Thematic guides to sources
4. Biographical dictionaries
5. Maps and atlases
6. Statistics
7. Periodicals

8. Contemporary historical accounts
9. General texts, collected essays, and historiography
10. Archaeology
11. Language
12. Literature, drama, and theater
13. Art, architecture, and music
14. Press and publishing
15. Agriculture, land ownership, and rural society
16. Development
17. Trade
18. Industry
19. Labor
20. Transport and communications
21. Towns
22. History: Pre-Norman
23. History: Medieval
24. History: The Tudor-Stuart Plantations
25. History: The Great Famine
26. History: Postfamine
27. History: Twentieth Century
28. Government
29. Law
30. Politics
31. Geography
32. Regional studies
33. Education
34. Religion
35. Population
36. Emigration
37. Health and medicine
38. Science
39. Traditional culture and folklore
40. Women in Irish society
41. Economic, political, and social protest movements

1. Chronologies

Bew, P., and G. Gillespie. *Northern Ireland: A Chronology of the Troubles, 1968–93*. Dublin: Gill and Macmillan, 1993.

Deutsch, R. *Northern Ireland: A Chronology of Events, 1968–73*. Belfast: Blackstaff, 1973.

Doherty, J. E., and D. J. Hickey. *A Chronology of Irish History since 1500*. Dublin: Gill and Macmillan, 1989.

Keesing's Record of World Events. Cambridge/Harlow: Longmans. Published monthly.

Moody, T. W., F. X. Martin, and F. J., Byrne, eds. *A Chronology of Irish History to 1976: A Companion to Irish History.* Part I. Oxford: Oxford University Press, 1982.

2. Bibliographies

Asplin, P. W. A. *Medieval Ireland c. 1170–1495: A Bibliography of Secondary Works.* Dublin: Royal Irish Academy, 1971.

Blessing, P. J. *The Irish in America: A Guide to the Literature and Manuscript Collections.* Washington, D.C.: Catholic University of America Press, 1992.

Doyle, D. N. "The Regional Bibliography of Irish America, 1800–1930: A Review and Addendum." *Irish Historical Studies* 23 (1983): 254–83.

Eager, A. R. *A Guide to Irish Bibliographical Material: A Bibliography of Irish Bibliographies and Some Sources of Information.* 2d ed, rev. and enl. London: Greenwood, 1980.

Edwards, J. R. *The Irish Language: An Annotated Bibliography of Sociolinguistic Publications, 1772–1982.* New York/Belfast: Garland/Blackstaff, 1983.

Ferguson, P. *Irish Map History: A Select Bibliography of Secondary Works, 1850–1983, on the History of Cartography in Ireland.* Dublin: University College, Department of Geography, 1983.

Hickman, M. J., ed., and Hartigan, M., comp. *The History of the Irish in Britain: A Bibliography.* London: The Irish in Britain History Centre, 1986.

Kernowski, F., C. W. Spinks, and L. Loomis, eds. *A Bibliography of Modern Irish and Anglo-Irish Literature.* San Antonio, Tex.: Trinity University Press, 1976.

MacLysaght, E. *A Bibliography of Irish Family History.* Dublin: Irish Academic Press, 1982.

Murray, J., A. Ford, J. I. McGuire, S. J. Connolly, F. O'Ferrall, and K. Milne. "The Church of Ireland: A Critical Bibliography, 1536–1992." *Irish Historical Studies* 28 (1993): 345–84.

Ó Danachair, C. *A Bibliography of Irish Ethnology and Folk Tradition.* Cork: Irish Book Centre, 1978.

Shannon, M. O. *Modern Ireland: A Bibliography on Politics, Planning, Research, and Development.* London: Greenwood, 1981.

Shannon, M. O. *Irish Republic.* World Bibliographical Series 69. Santa Barbara, Calif./Oxford: Clio, 1986.

―――. *Northern Ireland.* World Bibliographical Series 129. Santa Barbara, Calif./Oxford: Clio, 1991.

White, S. "Soviet Writings on Irish History, 1917–80: A Bibliography." *Irish Historical Studies,* 23 (1982): 174–86.

3. Thematic Guides to Sources

Browne, V., ed. *The Magill Book of Irish Politics*. Dublin: Magill, 1982.

Church of Ireland Directory, Dublin: Styletype Publishing, annually.

de Brun, P., and M. Herbert. *Catalogue of Irish Manuscripts in Cambridge Libraries*. Cambridge: Cambridge University Press, 1986.

Edwards, R. W. D., and M. O'Dowd. *Sources for Modern Irish History, 1534–1641*. Cambridge: Cambridge University Press, 1985.

Ellis, P. B. *A Dictionary of Irish Mythology*. Oxford/London: Constable, 1987.

Encyclopedia of Northern Ireland Labour Law and Practice. 3 vols. Belfast: Labour Relations Agency, 1983.

Falley, M. D. *Irish and Scotch-Irish Ancestral Research: A Guide to the Genealogical Records, Methods, and Sources in Ireland*. 2 vols. Evanston, Ill.: privately printed, 1961.

Finnegan, R., and J. Wiles. *A Guide to Irish Official Publications, 1972–92*. Dublin: Irish Academic Press, 1994.

Flackes, W. D. *Northern Ireland: A Political Directory, 1968–79*. Dublin/New York: Gill and Macmillan/St. Martin's Press, 1980.

Flackes, W. D., and S. Elliott. *Northern Ireland: A Political Directory, 1968–88*. Belfast: Blackstaff, 1989.

———. *Northern Ireland: A Political Directory, 1968–1993*. Belfast: Blackstaff, 1994.

Flanagan, L. *A Dictionary of Irish Archaeology*. Dublin: Gill and Macmillan, 1992.

Griffith, M. "The Irish Record Commission, 1810–30." *Irish Historical Studies,* 7 (1944): 17–28.

Harbison, P. *Guide to the National Monuments of Ireland*. Dublin: Gill and Macmillan, 1992.

Hayes, R. J., ed. *Manuscript Sources for the History of Irish Civilisation*. 11 vols. Boston/Dublin: G. K. Hall, 1965; also *First Supplement, 1965–75,* 3 vols., 1979.

———. *Periodical Sources for the History of Irish Civilisation*. 9 vols. Boston/Dublin: G. K. Hall, 1970.

Helferty, S., and R. Refaussé, eds. *Directory of Irish Archives*. Dublin: Irish Academic Press, 1993.

Hickey, D. J., and J. E. Doherty. *A Dictionary of Irish History since 1800*. Dublin: Gill and Macmillan, 1980.

Hogan, R. ed. *A Dictionary of Irish Literature*. London: Greenwood, 1979.

Hudson, K., and A. Nicholls. *The Cambridge Guide to the Museums of Britain and Ireland*. Cambridge: Cambridge University Press, 1987.

Irish Catholic Directory. Manchester: Gabriel Communications, 1991.

Kenney, J. F. *Sources for the Early History of Ireland: Vol. 1, Ecclesiastical*. New York, 1929. Reprint, New York: Octagon, 1967.

Killanin, Lord, and M. V. Duignan, eds. *The Shell Guide to Ireland*. London: Ebury, 1967. Rev. ed., Dublin: Gill and Macmillan, 1989.

Lindsay, D., and D. Fitzpatrick. *Records of the Irish Famine: A Guide to Local Archives, 1840–1855*. Dublin: Irish Famine Network, 1993.

Maltby, A., and J. Maltby. *Ireland in the Nineteenth Century: A Breviate of Official Publications*. Oxford: Pergamon, 1979.

Maltby, A., and B. McKenna. *Irish Official Publications, 1922–1972*. Oxford: Pergamon, 1980.

Mitchell, B. *Guide to Irish Parish Registers*. Baltimore: Genealogical Publishing, 1988.

Munter, R. L. *A Handlist of the Irish Newspapers, 1685–1750*. London: Bowes and Bowes, 1960.

Newman, P. R. *Companion to Irish History, 1603-1921*. Oxford/New York: Facts on File, 1991.

Nolan, W. *Tracing the Past: Sources for Local Studies in the Republic of Ireland*. Dublin: Geography Publications, 1982.

O'Day, A., and J. Stevenson, eds. *Irish Historical Documents since 1800*. Dublin: Gill and Macmillan, 1992.

O'Toole, J. *Newsplan: Report of the Newsplan Project in Ireland* [an inventory of library holdings of Irish newspapers in the British Isles]. London/Dublin: British Library/National Library of Ireland, 1992.

Popplewell, S. ed. *Irish Museums Guide*. Dublin: Ward, 1983.

———. *Exploring Museums: Ireland*. London: HMSO, 1990.

Prochaska, A. *Irish History from 1700: A Guide to Sources in the Public Record Office*. London: British Records Association, 1986.

Reid, N. *A Table of Church of Ireland Parochial Records and Copies*. Naas: Irish Family History Society, 1994.

Ryan, J. G. *Irish Records*. Salt Lake City, Utah/Dublin: Ancestry Publishing, 1988.

Trench, B., et al., eds. *Magill Book of Irish Politics: Election February 1987*. Dublin: Magill, 1987.

Weir, A. *Early Ireland: A Field Guide to the Stone Monuments of Ireland*. Belfast: Blackstaff, 1980.

4. Biographical Dictionaries

Boylan, H. *A Dictionary of Irish Biography*. Dublin: Gill and Macmillan, 1988.

Brady, A. M., and B. Cleeve. *A Biographical Dictionary of Irish Writers*. Mullingar: Lilliput, 1985.

Cleeve, B. *Dictionary of Irish Writers*. Cork: Mercier, 1967.

Crone, J. S. *A Concise Dictionary of Irish Biography*. Dublin: Kraus, 1970.

Dictionary of National Biography. 32 vols. Oxford/London: Oxford University Press, 1963–96.

Loeber, R. "Biographical Dictionary of Engineers in Ireland, 1600–1730." *Irish Sword* 13 (1977–79): 30–44; 106–22; 230–55; 283–314.

———. *A Biographical Dictionary of Architects in Ireland, 1600–1720*. London: Murray, 1980.

Newman, K. *Dictionary of Ulster Biography*. Belfast: Queen's University, Institute of Irish Studies, 1993.

Strickland, W. G. *A Dictionary of Irish Artists*. 2 vols. Dublin, 1913. Reprint, Shannon: Irish University Press, 1969.

Wallace, M. *100 Irish Lives*. Newton Abbot: David and Charles, 1983.

Webb, A. *A Compendium of Irish Biography*. Dublin: Gill, 1878. Reprint, New York: Lemma, 1970.

5. Maps and Atlases

Andrews, J. H. *History in the Ordnance Map*. Dublin: Ordnance Survey, 1974.

Andrews, J. H., and A. Simms, eds. *Irish Historic Towns Atlas*. Dublin: Royal Irish Academy:

1. Kildare (J. H. Andrews), 1986
2. Carrickfergus (P. Robinson), 1986
3. Bandon (P. O'Flanagan), 1988
4. Kells (A. Simms and K. Simms), 1990
5. Mullingar (J. H. Andrews and K. M. Davies), 1992
6. Athlone (H. Murtagh), 1995
7. Maynooth (A. A. Horner), 1995

Compton, P., ed. *Northern Ireland: A Census Atlas*. Belfast: Gill and Macmillan, 1978.

Edwards, R. *An Atlas of Irish History*. London: Methuen, 1986.

Hajducki, S. M. *A Railway Atlas of Ireland*. Newton Abbot: David and Charles, 1974.

Haughton, J. P., et al., eds. *Atlas of Ireland*. Dublin: Royal Irish Academy, 1979.

Hayes-McCoy, G. A., ed. *Ulster and Other Irish Maps, c. 1600*. Dublin: Irish Manuscripts Commission, 1964.

Horner, A. A., J. A. Walsh, and J. A. Williams, eds. *Agriculture in Ireland: A Census Atlas*. Dublin: University College, Department of Geography, 1984.

Horner, A. A., J. A. Walsh, and V. P. Harrington, eds. *Population in Ireland: A Census Atlas*. Dublin: University College, Department of Geography, 1987.

Mitchell, B. *A New Genealogical Atlas of Ireland*. Baltimore: Genealogical Publishing, 1986.

Wagner, H. *Linguistic Atlas and Survey of Irish Dialects*. Dublin: Institute for Advanced Studies, 1958.

The respective Ordnance Surveys produce the following scales:
1:1000 (OS Dublin only) for urban areas with more than 1000 residents.
Irish grid 1:1250 county series (50.69 inches to one mile).
Irish grid 1:2500 (25.34 inches to one mile).

Irish grid 1:10560 (six inches to one mile, since 1986 being replaced by the 1:10000 series).

1: 63360 (approx. one inch to one mile, being replaced by the 1:50000 series) Map of Monastic Ireland, OS Dublin, 1964.

Map of Medieval Dublin, OS Dublin, 1978.

OS Dublin and OSNI also publish county indexes for all scales and street maps of the larger individual towns at various scales, e.g., Dublin at 1:20000, Cork at 1:15000, Greater Belfast at 1:12000, Limerick/Waterford at 1:9000, and place-name gazetteers.

6. Statistics

Black, R. D., ed., *Centenary History of the Statistical and Social Inquiry Society of Ireland.* Dublin, 1947.

Central Statistics Office, *Census of Agriculture,* Dublin.

Central Statistics Office, *Census of Population,* Dublin.

Central Statistics Office, Department of Health, *Vital Statistics* (quarterly), Dublin.

Central Statistics Office, *Economic Series* (monthly), Dublin.

Central Statistics Office, *Statistical Bulletin* (quarterly), Dublin.

Central Statistics Office, *Statistical Abstract* (annual), Dublin.

Digest of Statistics of Northern Ireland, Belfast: HMSO.

Kirwan, F. X., and J. W. McGilvray. *Irish Economic Statistics.* Dublin: Institute of Public Administration, 1983.

McGilvray, J. W. *Irish Economic Statistics.* Dublin: Institute of Public Administration, 1977.

Registrar General of Northern Ireland. *The Northern Ireland Census.* Belfast: HMSO.

Vaughan, W. E., and A. J. Fitzpatrick, eds. *Irish Historical Statistics: Population 1821–1971.* Dublin: Royal Irish Academy, 1978.

Walker, B. M., ed. *Parliamentary Election Results in Ireland, 1801–1922.* Dublin: Royal Irish Academy, 1978.

———. *Parliamentary Election Results in Ireland, 1918–92.* Dublin/Belfast: Royal Irish Academy/Queen's University, Institute of Irish Studies, 1992.

7. Periodicals

Administration (1953–)

Analecta Hibernica (1930–)

Archaeology Ireland (1987–)

Archivium Hibernicum (Irish Historical Records) (1912–)

Bealoideas (1927–)

Carloviana, Journal of the Old Carlow Society (1947–)

Clogher Record (1953–)

Decies, Journal of the Old Waterford Society (1976–)
Dublin Historical Record (1938–)
Economic and Social Review (ESR) (1969–)
Eighteenth Century Ireland (1987–)
Eire-Ireland (1966–)
Friends Historical Society Journal (1903–)
Galway Archaeological Society Journal (1900–)
Hermathena (1873–)
Historical Studies: Papers Read before the Irish Conference of Historians (1958–)
Irish Ancestor (1969–)
Irish Archives Bulletin (1971–)
Irish Ecclesiastical Record (IER) (1864–1968)
Irish Economic and Social History (IESH) (1974–)
Irish Genealogist (1936)
Irish Geography (IG) (1944–)
Irish Historical Studies (IHS) (1938–)
Irish Journal of Agricultural Economics and Rural Sociology (IJAERS) (1968–1991)
Irish Jurist (1965–)
Irish Political Studies (IPS) (1986–)
Irish Sword (1949–)
Irish Texts Society (1899–)
Irish University Review (IUR) (1970–)
Journal of the Cork Historical and Archaeological Society (1892–)
Journal of the Galway Archaeological and Historical Society (1900–)
Journal of the Kerry Archaeological and Historical Society (1908–)
Journal of the County Kildare Archaeological Society (1891–)
Journal of the County Louth Archaeological (and Historical) Society (1904–)
Journal of the Royal Society of Antiquaries of Ireland (JRSAI) (formerly *Journal of the Kilkenny Archaeological Society*) (1849–)
Journal of the Statistical and Social Inquiry Society of Ireland (JSSISI) (1861–)
Journal of the Waterford and South East of Ireland Archaeological Society (1894–)
North Munster Antiquarian Society Journal (1936–)
Peritia (1982–)
Proceedings of the Royal Irish Academy (PRIA), Section C (1902–)
Quarterly Bulletin of the Irish Georgian Society (1958–)
Saothar: Journal of the Irish Labour History Society (1975–)
Seanchas Ard Mhacha: Journal of the Armagh Diocesan Historical Society (1953–)
Studia Celtica (SC) (1966–)
Studia Hibernica (SH) (1961–)

Studies: An Irish Quarterly Review (1912–)
Ulster Folklife (UF) (1955–)
Ulster Journal of Archaeology (UJA) (1853–)
Ulster Local Studies (1975–)

8. Contemporary Historical Accounts

A very useful classified list of published tours in Ireland is contained in H. J. Heaney's unpublished typescript, "Tourists in Ireland, 1800–1850: An Annotated Bibliography." Submitted in part completion of Fellowship of the Library Association in 1967.

Bennett, W. *Narrative of a Recent Journey of Six Weeks in Ireland.* London: Gilpin, 1847.

de Latocnaye, B. *Promenade d'un français dans l'Irlande, 1796–7.* Translated by J. Stevenson. Dublin: M'Caw, Stevenson, and Orr, 1917. Facsimile ed., Belfast: Blackstaff Press, 1984.

Foster, T. C. *Letters on the Condition of the People of Ireland.* London: Chapman and Hall, 1846.

Gorst, G. *A Narrative of an Excursion to Ireland.* London, 1825. Reprint, London: Charles and Skipper, 1925.

Gough, J. *A Tour in Ireland in 1813 and 1814.* Dublin: Gough and Co., 1817.

Hall, Mr. and Mrs. S. C. *Ireland: Its Scenery, Character, etc.* 3 vols. London: Virtue, 1841–43.

Hill, Lord George. *Facts from Gweedore.* Dublin, 1846. Facsimile ed., Belfast: Queen's University, Institute of Irish Studies, 1971.

Inglis, H. D. *A Tour throughout Ireland in the Spring, Summer, and Autumn of 1834.* 2 vols. London: Whitaker, 1835.

Kane, R. *The Industrial Resources of Ireland.* Dublin: Hodges and Smith, 1844. Facsimile ed., Shannon: Irish Universities Press, 1971.

Kohl, J. G. *Ireland, Scotland, and England.* London: Bruce and Wild, 1844.

Larkin, E., trans. and ed. *Alexis de Tocqueville's Journey in Ireland, 1835.* Dublin/Washington, D.C.: Wolfhound/Catholic University of America Press, 1990.

Lewis, S. *A Topographical Dictionary of Ireland.* 2 vols. London: S. Lewis and Co., 1837. Facsimile ed., Port Washington/London: Kenniket, 1970.

McVeagh, J., ed. *Richard Pococke's Irish Tours.* Dublin: Irish Academic Press, 1994.

Martineau, H. *Letters from Ireland.* London, 1852. Facsimile ed., New York: Garland Publishers.

Mason, W. S. *A Statistical Account or Parochial Survey of Ireland: Drawn up from the Communications of the Clergy.* 3 vols. London/Dublin: Longman, Hurst, Rees, Orme, and Brown/Cumming and Mahon, 1814–19.

Moody, T. W., and R. Hawkins, eds. *Florence Arnold-Forster's Irish Journal.* Oxford: Clarendon Press, 1988.

Noel, B. W. *Notes of a Short Tour through the Midland Counties of Ireland in the Summer of 1836.* Nisbet, 1837.

Reid, T. *Travels in Ireland in the year 1822.* London: Longman, 1823.

Smyth, G. L. *Ireland Historical and Statistical.* 3 vols. London: Whitaker, 1844–49.

Snell, K. D. M., ed. *Alexander Somerville: Letters from Ireland during the Famine of 1847.* Dublin: Irish Academic Press, 1994.

Stokes, G. T. *Pococke's Tour in Ireland in 1752.* Dublin, 1891.

Thackeray, W. M. *An Irish Sketch-book, 1842.* London: Smith and Elder, 1843. Facsimile ed., Oxford/Belfast: Oxford University Press/Blackstaff, 1925/85.

Thomson, D., and M. McGusty, eds. *Irish Journals of Elizabeth Smith, 1840–50,* Oxford: Clarendon, 1980.

Tuke, J. H. *A Visit to Connaught in the Autumn of 1847.* London: Charles Gilpin, 1847.

Wakefield, E. *An Account of Ireland: Statistical and Political.* 2 vols. London, 1812.

Young, A. *A Tour in Ireland . . . in the Years 1776, 1777, and 1778.* 2 vols. London, 1780. Reprint, Belfast: Blackstaff, 1983.

9. General Texts, Collected Essays, and Historiography

Bartlett, T., and D. W. Hayton, eds. *Penal Era and Golden Age: Essays in Irish History, 1690–1800.* Belfast: Ulster Historical Foundation, 1979.

Bartlett, T., R. O'Dwyer, G. O'Tuathaigh, and C. Curtain. *Irish Studies: A General Introduction.* Dublin: Gill and Macmillan, 1988.

Beckett, J. C. *A Short History of Ireland.* London: Hutchinson, 1979.

———. *The Making of Modern Ireland.* London: Knopf, 1966.

Boyce, D. G., and A. O'Day, eds. *Making of Modern Irish History: Revisionism and the Revisionist Controversy.* London: Routledge, 1996.

Bradshaw, B. Nationalism and Historical Scholarship in Modern Ireland, *Irish Historical Studies,* 26 (1989): 329–51.

Brady, C., ed. *Interpreting Irish History: The Debate on Historical Revisionism.* Dublin: Irish Academic Press, 1994.

Canny, N. *Kingdom and Colony: Ireland in the Atlantic World, 1560–1800.* Baltimore/London: Johns Hopkins University Press, 1988.

Canny, N., and A. Pagden, eds. *Colonial Identity in the Atlantic World, 1500–1800.* Guildford/Princeton, N.J.: Princeton University Press, 1988.

Cosgrove, A., and D. MacCartney, eds. *Studies in Irish History Presented to R. Dudley Edwards,* Dublin: University College, 1979.

Cullen, L. M. *Life in Ireland.* London: Batsford, 1968; new ed., 1979.

Curtis, E. *A History of Ireland.* London: Methuen, 1961.

Dickson, D. *New Foundations: Ireland, 1660–1800.* Dublin: Helicon, 1987.

Donnelly, J. S., and K. Miller, eds. *Irish Popular Culture, 1650–1850.* Dublin: Irish Academic Press, 1995.

Doyle, D. N., and O. D. Edwards, eds. *America and Ireland, 1776–1976: The American Identity and the Irish Connection.* London: Greenwood, 1980.

Drudy, P. J., ed. *Ireland: Land, Politics and People.* Cambridge: Cambridge University Press, 1982.

Foster, R. F. *Modern Ireland, 1600–1972.* London: Allen Lane/Penguin, 1988/89.

———, ed. *The Oxford Illustrated History of Ireland.* Oxford: Oxford University Press, 1989.

Hoppen, K. T. *Ireland since 1800: Conflict and Conformity.* London/New York: Longman, 1989.

James, F. *Lords of the Ascendancy.* Dublin: Irish Academic Press, 1994.

Lee, J. J., ed. *Irish Historiography, 1970–79.* Cork: Cork University Press, 1981.

Lyons, F. S. L., and R. A. J. Hawkins, eds. *Ireland under the Union: Varieties of Tension. Essays in Honour of T. W. Moody.* Oxford: Oxford University Press, 1980.

McDowell, R. B. *Ireland in the Age of Imperialism and Revolution, 1760–1801.* Oxford: Oxford University Press, 1979.

MacLysaght, E. *Irish Life in the Seventeenth Century.* Dublin: Irish Academic Press, 1979.

Meenan, J., and D. A. Webb, eds. *A View of Ireland,* Dublin: British Association for the Advancement of Science, 1957.

Moody, T. W., ed. *Irish Historiography, 1936–70.* Dublin: Irish Committee of Historical Sciences, 1971.

Moody, T. W., and F. X. Martin, eds. *The Course of Irish History.* Cork: Mercier Press, 1967. (Revised and enlarged edition, 1995.)

Moody, T. W., F. X. Martin, and F. J. Byrne, eds. *Early Modern Ireland, 1534–1691.* Oxford: Oxford University Press, 1976.

O'Tuathaigh, G. *Ireland before the Famine, 1798–1848.* Dublin: Gill and Macmillan, 1972.

Roebuck, P., ed., *Plantation to Partition: Essays in Ulster History in Honour of J. L. McCracken.* Belfast: Blackstaff, 1981.

Vaughan, W. E., ed. *Ireland under the Union. Vol. 1, 1801–1870.* Oxford: Clarendon Press, 1989.

10. Archaeology

Barry, T. B. *The Archaeology of Medieval Ireland.* London: Methuen, 1987.

Briggs, C. S. "Stone Resources and Implements in Prehistoric Ireland: A Review." *Ulster Journal of Archaeology,* 51 (1988): 5–20.

Brindley, A. L. *Archaeological Inventory of County Monaghan.* Dublin: Stationery Office, 1986.

Cuppage, J. *Archaeological Survey of the Dingle Peninsula.* Ballyferriter: Oidhreacht Chorca Duibhne, 1986.

de Valera, R., and S. Ó Nuallain. *Survey of the Megalithic Tombs of Ireland.* Vol. 4. Dublin: Stationery Office, 1982.

218 • Bibliography

Dunlevy, M. "A Classification of Early Irish Combs." *Proceedings of the Royal Irish Academy,* 88C (1988): 341–422.

Edwards, N. *The Archaeology of Early Medieval Ireland.* London: Batsford, 1990.

Eogan, G. *The Hoards of the Irish Later Bronze Age.* Dublin: University College, 1983.

————. *Knowth and the Passage Tombs of Ireland.* London: Thames and Hudson, 1986.

Flanagan, L. N. W. *Ireland's Armada Legacy.* Dublin: Gill and Macmillan, 1988.

Grogan, E., and G. Eoghan, "Lough Gur Excavations by Sean P. O'Riordain: Further Neolithic and Beaker Habitations on Knockadoon." *Proceedings of the Royal Irish Academy,* 87C (1987): 299–506.

Halpin, A. "Irish Medieval Swords c. 1170–1600." *Proceedings of the Royal Irish Academy,* 86C (1986): 183–230.

Hamlin, A. "The Archaeology of the Irish Church in the Eighth Century." *Peritia* 4 (1985): 279–99.

Herity, D. "Irish Decorated Neolithic Pottery." *Proceedings of the Royal Irish Academy,* 82C (1982): 247–404.

Herity, M. *Irish Passage Graves.* Dublin: Irish University Press, 1974.

————. "The Finds from Irish Court Tombs." *Proceedings of the Royal Irish Academy,* 87C (1987): 103–281.

Herity, M., and G. Eogan, *Ireland in Prehistory.* London: Routledge, 1977.

Ireland, A. "The Royal Society of Antiquaries of Ireland, 1849–1900." *Journal of the Royal Society of Antiquaries of Ireland,* 112 (1982): 72–92.

Kelly, M. J. *Early Ireland: An Introduction to Irish Pre-history.* Cambridge: Cambridge University Press, 1989.

Lacy, B., et al. *Archaeological Survey of County Donegal: A Description of the Field Antiquities from the Mesolithic Period to the 17th century A.D.* Lifford/Dublin: Donegal County Council, 1983.

Macalister, R. A. S. *Ireland in Pre-Celtic Times.* Dublin, 1921. Reprint, New York: Arno, 1976.

————. *The Archaeology of Ireland.* London, 1928. Reprint, London: Milford House, 1973.

Mallory, J. P., and T. E. McNeill. *The Archaeology of Ulster from Colonisation to Plantation.* Belfast: Queen's University, Institute of Irish Studies, 1991.

Murray, H. "Documentary Evidence for Domestic Buildings in Ireland c. 400–1200 in the Light of Archaeology." *Medieval Archaeology* 23 (1979) 81–97.

O'Kelly, M. J. *Newgrange: Archaeology, Art and Legend.* London: Thames and Hudson, 1982.

O'Kelly, M. J., and C. O'Kelly. "The Tumulus at Dowth, County Meath." *Proceedings of the Royal Irish Academy* 83C (1983): 135–90.

Ó Nuallain, S. "Irish Portal Tombs: Topography, Siting and Distribution." *Journal of the Royal Society of Antiquaries of Ireland,* 113 (1983): 75–105.

————. "Stone Rows in the South of Ireland." *Proceedings of the Royal Irish Academy,* 88C (1988): 179–256.

O'Riordain, S. P. *Tara: The Monuments on the Hill.* Dundalk: Dundalgan, 1954.

O'Riordain, S. P., and G. Daniel. *Newgrange and the Bend of the Boyne.* London: Thames and Hudson, 1964.

————. *Antiquities of the Irish Countryside.* London: Methuen, 1979.

Raftery, B. *La Tene in Ireland.* Marburg: Wasmuth, 1984.

Reeves-Smith, T., and F. Hammond, eds. *Landscape Archaeology in Ireland.* Oxford: British Archaeological Reports 116, 1983.

Richardson, H. "Derrynavlan and Other Early Church Treasures." *Journal of the Royal Society of Antiquaries of Ireland,* 110 (1980): 92–115.

Ryan, M., ed. *The Illustrated Archaeology of Ireland.* Dublin: Town House and Country House, 1991.

Scott, B. G., ed. *Studies on Early Ireland: Essays in Honour of M. V. Duignan.* Belfast: Association of Young Irish Archaeologists, 1982.

Wallace, P. F. *The Viking Age Buildings of Dublin: Medieval Dublin Excavations, 1962–81.* Vol. 1. Dublin: Royal Irish Academy, 1992.

Woodman, P. C. *The Mesolithic in Ireland.* Oxford: British Archaeological Reports 58, 1978.

————. *Excavations at Mount Sandel, 1973–77.* Belfast: HMSO, 1985.

————. "Problems in the Colonisation of Ireland." *Ulster Journal of Archaeology,* 49 (1986): 7–17.

11. Language

Adams, G. B., ed. *Ulster Dialects: An Introductory Symposium.* Belfast: Ulster Folk and Transport Museum, 1964.

————. "The Validity of Language Census Figures in Ulster, 1851–1911." *Ulster Folklife* 25 (1979): 113–22.

Fitzgerald, G. "Estimates for Baronies of Minimal Level of Irish-Speaking amongst Successive Decennial Cohorts: 1771–1781 to 1861–1871. *Proceedings of the Royal Irish Academy,* 84C (1984): 117–55.

Hindley, R. *The Death of the Irish Language: A Qualified Obituary.* London: Routledge, 1990.

MacAodha, B. S. "Aspects of the Linguistic Geography of Ireland in the Early Nineteenth Century." *Studia Celtica* 20–21, (1994): 205–20.

Ní Chatháin, P. "Sir Samuel Ferguson and the Ogham Inscriptions." *Irish University Review,* 16 (1986): 159–69.

Ó Cuiv, B., ed. *A View of the Irish Language.* Dublin: Stationery Office, 1969.

Robinson, P. "The Scots Language in Seventeenth-Century Ulster." *Ulster Folklife,* 35 (1989): 86–99.

Stockman, G. "The Sounds of Ulster Irish: A guide for Non-Irish Speakers." *Ulster Folklife,* 40 (1994): 39–48.

12. Literature, Drama, and Theater

Adams, M. *Censorship: The Irish Experience*. Dublin: Irish Academic Press, 1968.

Allingham, H., and D. Radford. *William Allingham: Diary*. London: Macmillan, 1907. Reprint, with an introduction by G. Grigson, Fontwell, Sussex: Centaur, 1967.

Bieler, L., with F. Kelly. *The Patrician Texts in the Book of Armagh*. Dublin: Institute for Advanced Studies, 1979.

Carlson, J. *Banned in Ireland: Censorship and the Irish Writer*. London: Routledge, 1990.

Clark, W. S. *The Early Irish Stage: The Beginnings to 1720*. Oxford: Oxford University Press, 1954. New ed., London: Greenwood, 1973.

Cowell, J. *No Profit but the Name: The Longfords and the Gate Theatre*. Dublin: O'Brien, 1989.

Donoghue, D., ed. *W. B. Yeats: Memoirs*. London: Macmillan, 1972.

Dorgan, T., ed. *Irish Poetry since Kavanagh*. Dublin: Four Courts Press, 1995.

Dunne, T. "The "Morbid Anatomy" of Anglo-Ireland: New Approaches in Literary History." *Irish Economic and Social History,* 14 (1987): 71–79.

Durkan, M. J. "Seamus Heaney: A Checklist for a Bibliography." *Irish University Review,* 16 (1986): 48–76.

Egan-Buffet, M., and A. J. Fletcher. "The Dublin *Visitatio Sepulcri* Play." *Proceedings of the Royal Irish Academy*. 90C (1990): 159–241.

Foot, M. *The Pen and the Sword: A Year in the Life of Jonathan Swift*. London: Macgibbon and Kee, 1957.

Gregory, Lady. *Coole*. Dublin, 1931. Reprint, Dublin, Irish Academic Press, 1971.

Hadfield, A., and J. McVeagh. *Strangers to That Land: British Perceptions of Ireland from the Reformation to the Famine*. Gerrards Cross, Bucks.: Colin Smythe, 1994.

Harmon, M. *Sean O'Faolain: A Critical Introduction*. Dublin: Wolfhound, 1984.

———, ed. *The Irish Writer and the City*. Gerrards Cross, Bucks.: Colin Smythe, 1984.

———. *Sean O'Faolain: A Life*. London: Constable, 1994.

Harrington, J. P. *The English Traveller in Ireland*. Dublin: Wolfhound, 1991.

Harvey, C. B. *Contemporary Irish Traditional Narrative: The English Language Tradition*. Berkeley/Oxford: University of California Press, 1992.

Hayton, D. W. "From Barbarian to Burlesque: English Images of the Irish c. 1660–1750." *Irish Economic and Social History,* 15 (1988): 5–31.

Henderson, G. *From Durrow to Kells*. London: Thames and Hudson, 1987.

Herr, C., ed. *For the Land They Loved: Irish Political Melodramas, 1890–1925*. Syracuse, N.Y.: Syracuse University Press, 1991.

Hughes, A. J. "Deirdre Flanagan's 'Belfast and the Place-names therein,' in Translation." *Ulster Folklife,* 38 (1992): 79–97.

Kelly, J., ed. *The Collected Letters of W. B. Yeats.* 3 vols. Oxford: Clarendon, 1986–94.

Kinahan, F. "Armchair Folklore: Yeats and the Textual Sources of *Fairy and Folk Tales of the Irish Peasantry.*" *Proceedings of the Royal Irish Academy,* 83C (1983): 253–67.

Kohfeldt, M. L. *Lady Gregory: The Woman behind the Irish Renaissance.* London: Deutsch, 1985.

Laurence, D. H., and N. Grene, eds. *Shaw, Lady Gregory and the Abbey: A Correspondence and a Record.* Gerrards Cross, Bucks.: Colin Smythe, 1993.

Leersen, J. T. *Mere Irish and Fior-Ghael: Studies in the Idea of Irish Nationality, Its Development and Literary Expression prior to the Nineteenth Century.* Amsterdam/Philadelphia: John Benjamins, 1986.

Lloyd, D. *Nationalism and Minor Literature: James Clarence Mangan and the Emergence of Irish Cultural Nationalism.* Berkeley/London: University of California Press, 1987.

McCormack, W. J. *Sheridan Le Fanu and Victorian Ireland.* Oxford: Oxford University Press, 1980.

McHugh, R., and M. Harmon. *Short History of Anglo-Irish Literature from Its Origins to the Present Day.* Dublin: Wolfhound, 1982.

Madden, R. R. *The History of Irish Periodical Literature from the End of the 17th to the Middle of the 19th Century.* 2 vols. London, 1867. Reprint, Hildesheim: Johnson Reprint, 1984.

Maume, P. *"Life That Is Exile": Daniel Corkery and the Search for Irish Ireland.* Belfast: Queen's University, Institute of Irish Studies, 1993.

Maxwell, D. E. S. *A Critical History of Modern Irish Drama, 1891–1980.* Cambridge: Cambridge University Press, 1984.

Meyer, K. *Selections from Ancient Irish Poetry.* London: AMS, 1959.

Mikhail, E. H. *Sean O'Casey and His Critics: An Annotated Bibliography, 1916–1982.* Metuchen, N.J./London: Scarecrow, 1985.

Nokes, D. *Jonathan Swift: A Hypocrite Reversed. A Critical Biography.* Oxford: Oxford University Press, 1985.

Ó Cuiv, B. "Medieval Irish Scholars and Classical Latin Literature." *Proceedings of the Royal Irish Academy* 81C (1981): 239–48.

———. "Observations on the Book of Lismore." *Proceedings of the Royal Irish Academy,* 83C (1983): 269–92.

Ormsby, F., ed. *The Collected Poems of John Hewitt.* Belfast: Blackstaff, 1991.

Owens, C. D., and J. N. Radner, eds. *Irish Drama, 1900–1980.* Washington, D.C.: Catholic University of America Press, 1990.

Saddlemyer, A., and C. Smythe, eds. *Lady Gregory Fifty Years After.* Gerrards Cross, Bucks.: Colin Smythe, 1987.

Sekine, M., ed. *Irish Writers and the Theatre.* Gerrards Cross, Bucks.: Colin Smythe, 1986.

Shannon-Mangan, E. *James Clarence Mangan: A Biography.* Dublin: Irish Academic Press, 1995.

Sheehy, J. *The Rediscovery of Ireland's Past: The Celtic Revival, 1830–1930.* London: Thames and Hudson, 1980.

Sloan, B. *The Pioneers of Anglo-Irish Fiction, 1800–1850.* Gerrards Cross, Bucks.: Colin Smythe, 1986.

Small, I. *Oscar Wilde Revalued: An Essay on New Material and Methods of Research.* Greensboro, N.C.: ELT Press, University of North Carolina, 1993.

Thuente, M. H. "Violence in Pre-Famine Ireland: The Testimony of Irish Folklore and Fiction." *Irish University Review,* 15 (1985): 129–47.

Vance, N. "Celts, Carthaginians and Constitutions: Anglo-Irish Literary Relations, 1780–1820." *Irish Historical Studies,* 22 (1981): 216–38.

———. *Irish Literature: A Social History, Tradition, Identity and Difference.* Oxford: Basil Blackwell, 1990.

Warner, A. *William Allingham.* Lewisburg/London: Bucknell University Press, 1975.

———. *A Guide to Anglo-Irish Literature.* Dublin: Gill and Macmillan, 1981.

Watson, G. J. *Irish Identity and the Literary Revival: Synge, Yeats, Joyce and O'Casey.* London: Croom Helm, 1979.

Welch, R., ed. *Irish Writers and Religion.* Gerrards Cross, Bucks.: Colin Smythe, 1992.

Woodman, K. *Media Control in Ireland, 1923–1983.* Galway: Galway University Press, 1985.

Worth, K. *Sheridan and Goldsmith.* London: Macmillan, 1992.

13. Art, Architecture, and Music

Bowe, N. G. *The Life and Work of Harry Clarke.* Dublin: Irish Academic Press, 1990.

Boydell, B. *A Dublin Musical Calendar, 1700–1760.* Dublin: Irish Academic Press, 1988.

———. *Rotunda Music in Eighteenth-Century Ireland.* Dublin: Irish Academic Press, 1992.

Cone, P., ed. *Treasures of Early Irish Art, 1500 B.C. to 1500 A.D.* New York: A. A. Knopf, 1977.

Craig, M. *Dublin 1660–1860.* Dublin, 1969. Reprint, Dublin: Allen Figgis 1980.

———. *The Architecture of Ireland from the Earliest Times to 1880.* London: Batsford, 1982.

Danaher, K. *Ireland's Vernacular Architecture.* Cork: Mercier, 1975.

Elmes, R. M. *Catalogue of Irish Topographical Prints and Original Drawings.* Dublin: Malton Press for the National Library of Ireland, 1975.

Gillen, G., and H. White, eds. *Irish Musical Studies. Vol. 1, Musicology in Ireland.* Dublin: Irish Academic Press, 1990.

———. *Irish Musical Studies. Vol. 2, Music and the Church,* Dublin: Irish Academic Press, 1992.

———. *Irish Musical Studies. Vol. 3, Music and Irish Cultural History.* Dublin: Irish Academic Press, 1995.

Grindle, W. H. *Irish Cathedral Music: A History of Music at the Cathedrals of the Church of Ireland.* Belfast: Queen's University, Institute of Irish Studies, 1989.

Hamilton, C. *A Social History of Irish Traditional Music.* Dublin: Four Courts Press, 1995.

Henry, F. *Irish High Crosses.* Dublin: The Three Candles, 1964.

———. *Irish Art in the Early Christian Period to A.D. 800.* London: Methuen, 1965.

———. *Irish Art during the Viking Invasions, 800–1020 A.D.* London: Methuen, 1967.

———. *Irish Art during the Romanesque Period, 1020–1170.* London: Methuen, 1970.

———. *The Book of Kells.* London: Thames and Hudson, 1974.

———. *Studies in Early Christian and Medieval Irish Art.* 3 vols. London: Pindar, 1983–85.

Henry, F., and G. Marsh-Micheli. "A Century of Irish Illumination (1070–1170)." *Proceedings of the Royal Irish Academy,* 62C (1962): 101–64.

Henry, P. *An Irish Portrait: The Autobiography of Paul Henry.* London: Batsford, 1951.

Higgitt, J., ed. *Early Medieval Sculpture in Britain and Ireland.* Oxford: British Archaeological Reports 152, 1986.

Hunt, J. *Irish Medieval Figure Sculpture.* 2 vols. Dublin: Sotheby Publications, 1974.

Kelly, D. "The Heart of the Matter: Models for Irish High Crosses." *Journal of the Royal Society of Antiquaries of Ireland,* 121 (1991): 105–45.

Kennedy, S. B. *Frank McKelvey: A Painter in His Time.* Dublin: Irish Academic Press, 1993.

Kerrigan, P. M. *Castles and Fortifications in Ireland, 1485–1945.* Cork: Spellmount, 1995.

Leask, H. G. *Irish Castles and Castellated Houses.* Dundalk: Dundalgan, 1941.

———. *Irish Churches and Monastic Buildings.* 3 vols. Dundalk: Dundalgan, 1955–60.

McCullough, N., and V. Mulvin. *A Lost Tradition: The Nature of Architecture in Ireland.* Dublin: Gandon Editions, 1987.

McParland, E. "Francis Johnston, Architect, 1760–1829." *Quarterly Bulletin of the Irish Georgian Society.* 12 (1969): 61–139.

———. "A Bibliography of Irish Architectural History." *Irish Historical Studies.* 26 (1988): 161–212.

Megaw, R., and V. Megaw. *Celtic Art: From Its Beginnings to the Book of Kells.* London: Thames and Hudson, 1989.

O'Grady, J. *The Life and Works of Sarah Purser*. Dublin: Four Courts Press, 1995.

Ó Meadhra, U. *Early Christian, Viking and Romanesque Art: Motif-Pieces from Ireland*. Stockholm: Almqvist/Humanities Press, 1979.

O'Sullivan, M. "Approaches to Passage Tomb Art." *Journal of the Royal Society of Antiquaries of Ireland*, 116 (1986): 68–83.

Piggott, P. *The Life and Music of John Field*. London: Faber, 1973.

Pyle, H. *Jack B. Yeats: A Biography*. London: Routledge, 1970.

Pyle, J. B. *The Different Worlds of Jack B. Yeats: His Cartoons and Illustrations*. Dublin: Irish Academic Press, 1994.

———. *Jack B. Yeats: His Watercolours, Drawings, and Pastels*. Dublin: Irish Academic Press, 1991.

Rowan, A. *The Buildings of Ireland: North West Ulster: The Counties of Londonderry, Donegal, Fermanagh, and Tyrone*. Harmondsworth, England: Penguin, 1979.

Ryan, M., ed. *Treasures of Ireland: Irish Art, 3000 BC–1500 AD*. Dublin: Royal Irish Academy, 1983.

———. "The Formal Relationships of Insular Early Medieval Eucharistic Chalices." *Proceedings of the Royal Irish Academy*, 90C (1990): 281–356.

Shields, H. *Narrative Singing in Ireland*. Dublin: Irish Academic Press, 1993.

Stalley, R. A. "Mellifont Abbey: A Study of its Architectural History." *Proceedings of the Royal Irish Academy*, 80C (1980): 263–354.

Williams, J. *A Companion Guide to Architecture in Ireland, 1837–1921*. Dublin: Irish Academic Press, 1994.

14. Press and Publishing

Adams, J. R. R. *The Printed Word and the Common Man: Popular Culture in Ulster, 1700–1900*. Belfast: Queen's University, Institute of Irish Studies, 1987.

Cole, R. C. *Irish Booksellers and English Writers, 1740–1800*. London: Mansell, 1986.

Hayley, B., and E. McKay, eds. *300 years of Irish Periodicals*. Mullingar: Association of Irish Learned Journals, 1987.

Inglis, B. *The Freedom of the Press in Ireland, 1784–1841*. London: Greenwood, 1954.

Munter, R. L. *The History of Irish Newspapers, 1685–1760*. Cambridge: Cambridge University Press, 1967.

———. *A Dictionary of the Print Trade in Ireland, 1550–1775*. New York: Fordham University Press, 1988.

Oram, H. *The Newspaper Book: A History of Newspapers in Ireland, 1649–1983*. Dublin: MO Books, 1983.

Phillips, J. W. *Printing and Bookselling in Dublin, 1670–1800: A Bibliographical Enquiry*. Dublin: Irish Academic Press, 1995.

Pollard, M. *Dublin's Trade in Books, 1550–1800*. Oxford: Clarendon Press, 1989.

15. Agriculture, Land Ownership, and Rural Society

Aalen, F. H. A. "The Rehousing of Irish Rural Labourers under the Labourers (Ireland) Acts." *Journal of Historical Geography* (23) 1986: 287–306.

Arnold, L. J. *The Restoration Land Settlement in Co. Dublin, 1660–88.* Dublin: Irish Academic Press, 1993.

Bell, J., and M. Watson. *Irish Farming, Implements, and Techniques, 1750–1900.* Edinburgh: John Donald, 1986.

Bew, P. *Land and the National Question in Ireland, 1858–82.* Dublin: Humanities Press, 1978.

Black, R. D. C. *Economic Thought and the Irish Question, 1817–1870.* Cambridge: Cambridge University Press, 1960.

Bric, M. J. "The Tithe System in Eighteenth-Century Ireland." *Proceedings of the Royal Irish Academy,* 86C (1986): 271–88.

Butler, H. J., and H. E. Butler. *The Black Book of Edgeworthstown and Other Edgeworth Memories, 1585–1817.* London: Faber and Gwyer, 1927.

Clark, S. *Social Origins of the Irish Land War.* Princeton, N.J.: Princeton University Press, 1979.

Connell, K. H. "The Colonisation of Waste Land in Ireland, 1780–1845." *Economic History Review* 3 (1950–51): 44–71.

———. *Irish Peasant Society.* Oxford: Oxford University Press, 1968.

Crawford, W. H. "The Significance of Landed Estates in Ulster, 1600–1820." *Irish Economic and Social History,* 17 (1990): 44–61.

Crotty, R. D. *Irish Agricultural Production.* Cork: Cork University Press, 1966.

Curtis, L. P. Incumbered Wealth: Landed Indebtedness in Post-Famine Ireland. *American Historical Review* 85 (190): 332–68.

D'Arcy, F. A. *Horses, Lords, and Racing Men: The Turf Club, 1790–1990.* Kildare: Turf Club, 1991.

Donnelly, J. S. *The Land and People of Nineteenth-Century Cork: The Rural Economy and the Land Question.* London: Routledge and Kegan Paul, 1975.

Duffy, P. "Irish Landholding Structure and Population in the Mid-Nineteenth century." *Maynooth Review* 3 (1977): 3–27.

———. "The Territorial Organisation of Gaelic Landownership and Its Transformation in County Monaghan, 1591–1640." *Irish Geography,* 14 (1981): 1–26.

Fox, R. *The Tory Islanders: A People of the Celtic Fringe.* Cambridge: Cambridge University Press, 1978.

Genet, J., ed. *The Big House in Ireland: Reality or Representation?* Savage, Md./Dingle: Barnes and Noble/Brandon, 1991.

Gillespie, R. "Harvest Crises in Early Seventeenth-Century Ireland." *Irish Economic and Social History* 11 (1984): 5–18.

Graham, J. M. "South-west Donegal in the Seventeenth Century." *Irish Geography,* 6 (1970): 136–52.

Hannan, D. F. *Rural Exodus: A Study of the Forces Influencing the Large Scale Migration of Irish Youth*. London/Dublin: Geoffrey Chapman, 1970.

———. "Kinship, Neighbourhood, and Social Change in Irish Rural Communities." *Economic and Social Review* 3 (1972): 163–88.

———. *Displacement and Development: Class, Kinship, and Social Change in Irish Rural Communities*. Dublin: Economic and Social Research Institute, 1979.

Hooker, E. R. *Readjustments of Agricultural Tenure in Ireland*. Chapel Hill, N.C.: University of North Carolina Press, 1938.

Horner, A. A. "Sir Robert Kane's Land Classification Maps: A Mid-Nineteenth Century Cartographic Initiative." *Irish Geography* 27 (1994): 107–21.

Hughes, T. J. "Land Holding and Settlement in the Cooley Peninsula of Louth. *Irish Geography* 4 (1961): 149–74.

———. "Society and Settlement in Nineteenth-Century Ireland." *Irish Geography* 5 (1965): 79–96.

Jackson, A. *Colonel Edward Sanderson: Land and Loyalty in Victorian Ireland*. Oxford: Oxford University Press, 1995.

Jenkins, B. *Sir William Gregory of Coole: A Biography*. Gerrards Cross, Bucks.: Colin Smythe, 1986.

Kelly, J. "Harvests and Hardship: Famine and Scarcity in Ireland in the Late 1720s." *Studia Hibernica* 26 (1991–92): 65–106.

Kennedy, L. "Adoption of a Group Innovation in Irish Agriculture, 1890–1914: An Exercise in Applied History." *Oxford Agrarian Studies* 6 (1977): 57–70.

Lowe, W. J. "Landlord and Tenant on the Estate of Trinity College, Dublin, 1851–1903." *Hermathena* 120 (1976): 5–24.

Lucas, A. T. *Cattle in Ancient Ireland*. Kilkenny: Boethius, 1989.

MacCarthy, R. B. *The Trinity College Estates, 1800–1923: Corporate Management in an Age of Reform*. Dundalk: Dundalgan, 1992.

McCourt, D. "Traditions of Rundale in and around the Sperrin Mountains." *Ulster Journal of Archaeology* 16 (1953): 69–84.

———. "The Use of Oral Tradition in Irish Historical Geography." *Irish Geography* 6 (1972): 394–410.

Maguire, W. A. *The Downshire Estates in Ireland, 1801–1845: The Management of Irish Landed Estates in the Early Nineteenth Century*. Oxford: Clarendon, 1972.

Malins, E., and the Knight of Glin. *Los Demesnes: Irish Landscape Gardening, 1660–1845*. London: Barrie and Jenkins, 1977.

Nunan, D. "Price Trends for Agricultural Land in Ireland, 1901–1986." *Irish Journal of Agricultural Economics and Rural Sociology* 12 (1987): 51–78.

O'Connor, R., and C. Guiomard. "Agricultural Output in the Irish Free State Area before and after Independence." *Irish Economic and Social History* 12 (1985): 89–97.

O'Flanagan, P. "Rural Change South of the River Bride in Counties Cork and Waterford: The surveyors' evidence, 1716–1851." *Irish Geography* 15 (1982): 51–69.

O'Rourke, K., and B. Polak. "Property Transactions in Ireland, 1708–1988: An Introduction." *Irish Economic and Social History* 21 (1994): 58–71.

Proudfoot, L. J. "The Management of a Great Estate: Patronage, Income, and Expenditure on the Duke of Devonshire's Irish Property, c. 1816–1891." *Irish Economic and Social History* 13 (1986): 32–55.

Roebuck, P. "The Making of an Ulster Great Estate: The Chichesters, Barons of Belfast and Viscounts of Carrickfergus, 1599–1648." *Proceedings of the Royal Irish Academy* 79C (1979): 1–25.

Royle, S. A. "The Economy and Society of the Aran Islands, County Galway, in the Early Nineteenth Century." *Irish Geography* 16 (1983): 36–54.

Smyth, W. J. "Continuity and Change in the Territorial Organisation of Irish Rural Communities." *Maynooth Review,* 1, no. 1 (1975): 51–78 and 1, no. 2 (1975): 52–101.

Somerville-Large, P. *The Irish Country House: A Social History.* London: Sinclair-Stevenson, 1995.

Steele, E. D. *Irish Land and British Politics: Tenant Right and Nationality, 1865–1870.* Cambridge: Cambridge University Press, 1974.

Thomas, C., ed. *Rural Landscapes and Communities: Essays Presented to Desmond McCourt.* Dublin: Irish Academic Press, 1986.

Turner, M. "Output and Productivity in Irish Agriculture from the Famine to the Great War." *Irish Economic and Social History* 17 (1990): 62–78.

Vaughan, W. E. "Potatoes and Agricultural Output." *Irish Economic and Social History* 17 (1990): 79–92.

———. *Landlords and Tenants in Ireland, 1848–1904.* Dundalk: Economic and Social History Society of Ireland, 1984.

———. *Landlords and Tenants in Mid-Victorian Ireland.* Oxford: Oxford University Press, 1994.

16. Development

Attwood, E. A. "Agriculture and Economic Growth in Western Ireland." *Journal of the Statistical and Social Inquiry Society of Ireland* 20 (1961–62): 172–95.

Bolger, P. *The Irish Co-operative Movement: Its History and Development.* Dublin: Institute of Public Administration, 1977.

Crafts, N. F. R. "The Golden Age of Economic Growth in Postwar Europe: Why Did Northern Ireland Miss Out?" *Irish Economic and Social History* 22 (1995): 5–25.

Crotty, R. *Ireland in Crisis: A Study in Capitalist Colonial Under-development.* Dingle: Brandon, 1986.

Cullen, L. M. *An Economic History of Ireland since 1660.* London: Batsford, 1976.

———. *The Emergence of Modern Ireland, 1600–1900.* Dublin: Holmes and Meier, 1981.

Cullen, L. M., and T. C. Smout, eds. *Comparative Aspects of Scottish and Irish Economic and Social History, 1600–1900.* Edinburgh: John Donald, 1978.

Department of Agriculture and Technical Instruction. *Ireland Industrial and Agricultural.* Dublin/Cork/Belfast: Browne and Nolan, 1902.

Devine, T. M., and D. Dickson, eds. *Ireland and Scotland, 1600–1850: Parallels and Contrasts in Economic and Social Development.* Edinburgh: John Donald, 1983.

Girvin, B. *Between Two Worlds: Politics and Economy in Independent Ireland.* Dublin: Gill and Macmillan, 1988.

Goldthorpe, J. H., and C. T. Whelan, eds. *The Development of Industrial Society in Ireland.* Oxford: Oxford University Press, 1992.

Hardiman, N. *Pay, Politics, and Economic Performance in Ireland, 1970–1987.* Oxford: Clarendon, 1988.

Kennedy, K. A., T. Giblin, and D. McHugh. *The Economic Development of Ireland in the Twentieth Century.* London: Routledge, 1988.

Kennedy, L. "Studies in Irish Econometric History." *Irish Historical Studies* 23 (1983): 193–213.

Kennedy, L., and P. Ollerenshaw, eds. *An Economic History of Ulster, 1820–1940.* Manchester: Manchester University Press, 1985.

King, R., ed. *Ireland, Europe, and the Single Market.* Dublin: Geographical Society of Ireland, 1993.

Lee, J. J. *The Modernisation of Irish Society, 1848–1918.* Dublin: Gill and Macmillan, 1989.

Litton, F., ed. *Unequal Achievement: The Irish Experience, 1957–1982.* Dublin: Institute of Public Administration, 1982.

Lynch, P., and J. Vaizey. *Guinness's Brewery in the Irish Economy, 1759–1876.* Cambridge: Cambridge University Press, 1960.

McCracken, E. *The Irish Woods since Tudor Times: Their Distribution and Exploitation.* Newton Abbot: David and Charles, 1971.

Meenan, J. *The Irish Economy since 1922.* Liverpool: Liverpool University Press, 1970.

Mitchison, R., and P. Roebuck, eds. *Economy and Society in Scotland and Ireland 1500–1939,* Edinburgh: John Donald, 1988.

Neary, J. P., and C. Ó Gráda. "Protection, Economic War, and Structural Change: The 1930s in Ireland." *Irish Historical Studies* 27 (1991): 250–66.

O'Flanagan, P., P. Ferguson, and K. Whelan, eds. *Rural Ireland: Modernisation and Change, 1600–1900.* Cork: Cork University Press, 1987.

Ó Gráda, C. *Ireland: A New Economic History, 1780–1939.* Oxford: Oxford University Press, 1994.

Rottman, D. B., D. F. Hannan, N. Hardiman, and M. M. Wiley. *The Distribution of Income in the Republic of Ireland: A Study in Social Class and Family Cycle Inequalities.* Dublin: Economic and Social Research Institute, 1982.

Shiel, M. J. *The Quiet Revolution: The Electrification of Rural Ireland, 1946–1976.* Dublin: O'Brien Press, 1984.

Whelan, B. "Ireland and the Marshall Plan." *Irish Economic and Social History* 19 (1992): 49–70.

Whelan, C. T., ed. *Values and Social Change in Ireland*. Dublin: Gill and Macmillan, 1994.

Williamson, J. G. "Economic Convergence: Placing Post-Famine Ireland in Comparative Perspective." *Irish Economic and Social History* 21 (1994): 1–27.

17. Trade

Crawford, W. H. "The Evolution of the Linen Trade in Ulster before Industrialisation." *Irish Economic and Social History* 15 (1988): 32–53.

Doherty, C. "Exchange and Trade in Early Medieval Ireland." *Journal of the Royal Society of Antiquaries of Ireland* 110 (1980): 647–89.

Holm, P. "The Slave Trade of Dublin, Ninth to Twelfth Centuries." *Peritia* 5 (1986): 317–45.

Kelly, J. "The Irish Trade Dispute with Portugal, 1780–87." *Studia Hibernica* 25 (1989–90): 7–48.

Ollerenshaw, P. *Banking in Nineteenth Century Ireland: The Belfast Banks, 1825–1914*. Manchester: Manchester University Press, 1987.

O'Neill, T. *Merchants and Mariners in Medieval Ireland*. Dublin: Irish Academic Press, 1987.

Solar, P. M. "The Reconstruction of Irish External Trade Statistics for the Nineteenth Century." *Irish Economic and Social History* 12 (1985): 63–78.

———. "The Irish Butter Trade in the Nineteenth Century: New Estimates and Their Implications." *Studia Hibernica* 25 (1989–90): 134–61.

Truxes, T. M. *Irish-American Trade, 1660–1783*. Cambridge: Cambridge University Press, 1988.

18. Industry

Almqvist, E. L. "Pre-Famine Ireland and the Theory of European Proto-Industrialization: Evidence from the 1841 Census." *Journal Economic History* 39 (1979): 699–718.

Andrews, J. H. "Notes on the Historical Geography of the Irish Iron Industry." *Irish Geography* 3 (1956): 139–49.

Armstrong, D. L. "Social and Economic Conditions in the Belfast Linen Industry, 1850–1900." *Irish Historical Studies* 7 (1951): 235–69.

Barnard, T. C. "Sir William Petty as Kerry Ironmaster." *Proceedings of the Royal Irish Academy* 82C (1982): 1–32.

———. "An Anglo-Irish Industrial Enterprise: Iron Making at Enniscorthy, Co. Wexford, 1657–92." *Proceedings of the Royal Irish Academy* 85C (1985): 101–44.

Browne, R. F. "The Electricity Supply Board." *Journal of the Statistical and Social Inquiry Society of Ireland* 18 (1951–52): 564–84.

Crawford, W. H. "The Origins of the Linen Industry in North Armagh and the Lagan Valley." *Ulster Folklife* 17 (1971): 42–51.

———. *Domestic Industry in Ireland: Experience of the Linen Industry*. Dublin: Gill and Macmillan, 1972.

———. "A Handloom Weaving Community in County Down." *Ulster Folklife* 39 (1993): 1–14.

Dwyer, D. J., and L. J. Symons. "The Development and Location of the Textile Industries in the Irish Republic." *Irish Geography* 4 (1963): 415–31.

Geary, F., and W. Johnson. "Shipbuilding in Belfast, 1861–1986." *Irish Economic and Social History* 16 (1989): 42–64.

Gill, C. *The Rise of the Irish Linen Industry*. Oxford: Clarendon, 1925.

Gribbon, H. D. *The History of Water Power in Ulster*. Newton Abbot, David & Charles, 1969.

Hughes, N. J. *Irish Engineering, 1760–1960*. Dublin: Institute of Engineers of Ireland, 1982.

Jacobson, D. S. "The Motor Industry in Ireland." *Irish Economic and Social History* 12 (1985): 109–16.

Kinahan, G. H. "Irish Metal Mining." *Proceedings of the Royal Dublin Society* 5 (1886): 200–317.

Ludlow, C. G. "An Eighteenth Century Irish Saltworks As Described in the Castleward Papers." *Ulster Folklife* 38 (1992): 25–33.

McCutcheon, W. A. *The Industrial Archaeology of Northern Ireland*. Belfast: Fairleigh Dickinson, 1983.

O'Malley, E. "The Decline of Irish Industry in the Nineteenth Century." *Economic and Social Review* 14 (1981): 21–42.

Solar, P. M. "A Belgian View of the Ulster Linen Industry in the 1840s." *Ulster Folklife* 34 (1988): 16–25.

Takei, A. "The First Irish Linen Mills, 1800–1824." *Irish Economic and Social History* 21 (1994): 28–38.

Williams, R. A. *The Berehaven Copper Mines*. Sheffield: Northern Mine Research Society, 1991.

19. Labor

Bourke, J. *Husbandry to Housewifery: Women, Economic Change, and Housework in Ireland, 1890–1914*. Oxford: Clarendon Press, 1993.

Boyle, J. W. *The Irish Labour Movement in the Nineteenth Century*. Washington, D.C.: Catholic University of America, 1988.

Buckley, A. D. 'On the club': Friendly societies in Ireland." *Irish Economic and Social History* 14 (1987): 39–58.

Connolly, J. *Labour in Irish History*. Dublin, 1910. Reprint, Dublin: New Books, 1973.

Cradden, T. *Trade Unionism, Socialism, and Partition: The Labour Movement in Northern Ireland, 1939–53*. Belfast: December Publications, 1993.

Daly, M. E. "Social Structure of the Dublin Working Class, 1871–1911." *Irish Historical Studies* 23 (1982): 121–33.

Ellis, P. B. *History of the Irish Working Class*. London: Pluto, 1985.

Fitzpatrick, D. "The Disappearance of the Irish Agricultural Labourer, 1841–1912." *Irish Economic and Social History* 7 (1980): 66–92.

Hearn, M. *Below Stairs: Domestic Service Remembered in Dublin and Beyond, 1880–1922*. Dublin: Lilliput, 1993.

Jones, M. *These Obstreperous Lassies: A History of the Irish Women Workers Union*. Dublin: Gill and Macmillan, 1988.

Keogh, D. *The Rise of the Irish Working Class: The Dublin Trade Union Movement and Labour Leadership, 1890–1914*. Belfast: Appletree, 1982.

Larkin, E. *James Larkin: Irish Labour Leader*. London: Routledge and Kegan Paul, 1965.

Maguire, M. "The Organisation and Activism of Dublin's Protestant Working Class, 1883–1935." *Irish Historical Studies* 29 (1994): 65–87.

Morrissey, P. J. *Working Conditions in Ireland and Their Effect on Irish Emigration*. New York: P. J. Morrissey and Son, 1958.

O'Connor, E. *A Labour History of Ireland, 1824–1960*. Dublin: Macmillan, 1992.

Patterson, H. "Independent Orangeism and Class Conflict in Edwardian Belfast: An Interpretation." *Proceedings of the Royal Irish Academy* 80C (1980): 1–27.

———. *Class Conflict and Sectarianism: The Protestant Working Class and the British Labour Movement, 1868–1920*. Belfast: Blackstaff, 1980.

Walsh, B. M. *The Structure of Unemployment in Ireland, 1954–1972*. Dublin: Economic and Social Research Institute, 1974.

———. *The Unemployment Problem in Ireland*. Dublin: Kincora, 1978.

20. Transport and Communications

Andrews, J. H. "Road Planning in Ireland before the Railway Age." *Irish Geography* 5 (1964): 17–41.

Casserley, H. C. *Outline of Irish Railway History*. Newton Abbot: David and Charles, 1974.

Conroy, J. C. *A History of Railways in Ireland*. London: Longmans Green, 1928.

Currie, J. R. L. *Northern Counties Railway*. Newton Abbot: David and Charles, 1973.

Delany, V. T. H., and D. R. Delaney. *The Canals of the South of Ireland*. Newton Abbot: David and Charles, 1966.

Doyle, O., and S. Hirsch. *Railways in Ireland, 1834–1984*. Dublin: Signal Press, 1983.

Fayle, H. *The Narrow Gauge Railways of Ireland*. London: Greenlake Publications, 1946.

Herring, I. J. "Ulster Roads on the Eve of the Railway Age c. 1800–40." *Irish Historical Studies* 2 (1940–41): 160–88.

Lucas, A. T. "Toghers or Causeways: Some Evidence from Archaeological, Literary, Historical, and Place-name Sources." *Proceedings of the Royal Irish Academy* 85C (1985): 37–60.

McCaughan, M. "Irish Vernacular Boats and Their European Connections." *Ulster Folklife* 24 (1978): 1–22.

McCutcheon, W. A. *Railway History in Pictures: Ireland*. 2 vols. Newton Abbot: David and Charles, 1969–71.

O'Connell, M. J. *Charles Bianconi, 1786–1875*. London, 1878.

Share, B. *The Flight of the Iolar: The Aer Lingus experience, 1936–86*. Dublin: Gill and Macmillan, 1986.

21. Towns

Beckett, J. C., and R. E. Glasscock, eds. *Belfast: Origin and Growth of an Industrial City*. London: British Broadcasting Corporation, 1967.

Beckett, J. C., et al. *Belfast: The Making of the City, 1800–1914*. Belfast: Salem House, 1983.

Bielenberg, A. *Cork's Industrial Revolution, 1780–1880; Development or Decline?* Cork: Cork University Press, 1991.

Burke, N. T. "An Early Modern Dublin Suburb: The Estate of Francis Aungier, Earl of Longford." *Irish Geography* 6 (1972): 365–85.

Butel, P., and L. M. Cullen, eds. *Cities and Merchants: French and Irish Perspectives on Urban Development, 1500–1900*. Dublin: Trinity College, Department of Modern History, 1986.

Camblin, G. *The Town in Ulster*. Belfast: Mullan, 1951.

Clarke, H. B., ed. *Medieval Dublin*. 2 vols. Dublin: Irish Academic Press, 1990.

———. *Irish Cities*. Cork: Mercier Press, 1995.

Daly, M. E. *Dublin, the Deposed Capital: A Social and Economic History, 1860–1914*. Cork: Cork University Press, 1984.

Fagan, P. *The Second City: Portrait of Dublin, 1700–1760*. Dublin: Branar, 1986.

Hardiman, J. *The History of the Town and County of Galway*. Dublin, 1820. Reprint, Galway: Kenny, 1975.

Harkness, D., and M. O'Dowd, eds. *The Town in Ireland*. Belfast: Appletree, 1981.

Hepburn, A. C. "Work, Class, and Religion in Belfast, 1871–1911." *Irish Economic and Social History* 10 (1983): 33–50.

Jones, E. *A Social Geography of Belfast*. London/Oxford: Oxford University Press, 1960.

Lacy, B. *Siege City: The Story of Derry and Londonderry*. Belfast: Blackstaff, 1990.

McCullough, N. *Dublin: An Urban History*. Dublin: Anne Street Press, 1989.

McManus, M. "The Functions of Small Ulster Settlements in 1854, 1899, and 1916." *Ulster Folklife* 39 (1993): 50–72.

Maxwell, C. *Dublin under the Georges, 1714–1830.* London/Dublin: Harrap/Hodges Figgis, 1937. Revised ed., London: Faber, 1956.

Ó Cearbhaill, D. ed. *Galway: Town and Gown, 1484–1984.* Dublin: Gill and Macmillan, 1984.

O'Donnell, E. E. *The Annals of Dublin, Fair City.* Dublin: Wolfhound, 1987.

O'Sullivan, M. D. *Old Galway: The History of a Norman Colony in Ireland.* Cambridge: Cambridge University Press, 1942. Second ed., Galway: Kenny, 1983.

O'Sullivan, W. *The Economic History of Cork City from the Earliest Time to the Act of Union.* Dublin/Cork: Educational Company of Ireland/Cork University Press, 1937.

Pettit, S. F. *This City of Cork, 1700–1900.* Cork: Studio Publications, 1977.

Prunty, J. *Dublin Slums, 1800–1925: A Study in Urban Geography.* Dublin: Irish Academic Press, 1995.

Robinson, P. "Urbanisation in North-west Ulster, 1609–1670." *Irish Geography* 15 (1982): 35–50.

Simms, A. "Medieval Dublin: A Topographic Analysis." *Irish Geography* 12 (1979): 25–41.

Simms, A., and J. H. Andrews, eds. *Irish Country Towns.* Cork: Mercier, 1994.
———. *More Irish Country Towns.* Cork: Mercier, 1995.

Thomas, A. *The Walled Towns of Ireland.* 2 vols. Dublin: Irish Academic Press, 1992.

Wallace, P. *Viking and Medieval Dublin, 900–1315.* Dublin: University Press, 1980.

22. History: Pre-Norman

Bieler, L. *The Life and Legend of St. Patrick.* Dublin, 1949.

Binchy, D. A. "Patrick and His Biographers: Ancient and Modern." *Studia Hibernica* 2 (1962): 7–173.

Bowen, E. G. *Saints, Seaways, and Settlements in the Celtic Lands.* Cardiff: University of Wales Press, 1969.

Byrne, F. J. "Derrynaflan: The Historical Context." *Journal of the Royal Society of Antiquaries of Ireland* 110 (1980): 116–26.

de Paor, M., and L. de Paor. *Early Christian Ireland.* London: Thames and Hudson, 1978.

Harbison, P. *Pre-Christian Ireland.* London: Thames and Hudson, 1988.

Herbert, M., and P. O'Riain, eds. *Betha Adamnain: The Life of Adamnan.* London: Irish Texts Society, 1988.

Hughes, K. "The Cult of St. Finnian of Clonard from the Eighth to the Eleventh Century." *Irish Historical Studies* 9 (1954): 13–27.
———. *Early Christian Ireland: Introduction to the Sources.* London/Cambridge: Cambridge University Press, 1976.

Jackson, K. H. *The Oldest Irish Tradition: A Window on the Iron Age.* Cambridge: Cambridge University Press, 1964.

Laing, L., and J. Laing. *Celtic Britain and Ireland, AD 200–800: The Myth of the Dark Ages*. Dublin: Irish Academic Press, 1990.

Laing, L. "The Romanisation of Ireland in the Fifth Century." *Peritia* 4 (1985): 261–78.

O'Rahilly, T. F. *Early Irish History and Mythology*. Dublin: Institute for Advanced Studies, 1946; Reprint, 1976.

Ryan, J. "The Battle of Clontarf." *Journal of the Royal Society of Antiquaries of Ireland* 68 (1938): 1–50.

Smyth, A. P. *Scandinavian York and Dublin: The History and Archaeology of Two Related Viking Kingdoms*. 2 vols. Dublin: Irish Academic Press, 1975–79.

———. *Celtic Leinster*. Dublin: Irish Academic Press, 1982.

23. History: Medieval

Bieler, L. *Ireland, Harbinger of the Middle Ages*. Oxford: Oxford University Press, 1963.

Carney, J. *Studies in Irish Literature and History*. Dublin: Institute for Advanced Studies, 1955; Revised ed., 1979.

Cosgrove, A. *Late Medieval Ireland, 1370–1541*. Dublin: Helicon, 1981.

———, ed. *Medieval Ireland, 1169–1534*. Oxford: Clarendon, 1993.

Flanagan, M. T. *Irish Society, Anglo-Norman Settlers, Angevin Kingship: Interactions in Ireland in the Late Twelfth Century*. Oxford: Clarendon, 1989.

Frame, R. "Power and Society in the Lordship of Ireland, 1272–1372." *Past and Present* 76 (1977): 3–33.

———. *Colonial Ireland, 1169–1369*. Dublin: Helicon, 1981.

Gwynn, A., and R. N. Hadcock. *Medieval Religious Houses: Ireland*. London: Harlow, Longmans, 1970.

Lydon, J. F. *The Lordship of Ireland in the Middle Ages*. Dublin: Gill and Macmillan, 1972.

———. *Ireland in the Later Middle Ages*. Dublin: Gill and Macmillan, 1983.

———, ed. *The English in Medieval Ireland*. Dublin: Royal Irish Academy, 1984.

———. "Ireland and the English Crown, 1171–1541." *Irish Historical Studies* 29 (1995): 281–94.

MacNiocaill, G. *Na Buirgéisí*. 2 vols. Dublin: Clo Morainn, 1964.

MacNiocaill, G., and P. F. Wallace, eds. *Keimelia: Studies in Medieval Archaeology and History in Memory of Tom Delaney*. Galway: Galway University Press, 1988.

Nicholls, K. W. *Gaelic and Gaelicised Ireland in the Middle Ages*. Dublin: Gill and Macmillan, 1972.

Norman, E. R., and J. K. S. St. Joseph. *The Early Development of Irish Society: The Evidence of Aerial Photography*. Cambridge: Cambridge University Press, 1967.

Ó Corrain, D. *Ireland before the Normans*. Dublin: Gill and Macmillan, 1972.

————, ed. *Irish Antiquity: Essays and Studies Presented to Professor M. J. O'Kelly.* Cork: Tower Books, 1981.

O'Riordain, M. *The Gaelic Mind and the Collapse of the Gaelic World.* Cork: Cork University Press, 1991.

Orpen, G. H. *Ireland under the Normans, 1169–1333.* 4 vols. Oxford: Oxford University Press, 1911–20. Reprint, Oxford: Oxford Reprints, 1968.

Otway-Ruthven, A. J. "Anglo-Irish Shire Government in the Thirteenth Century." *Irish Historical Studies* 5 (1946): 1–28.

————. *A History of Medieval Ireland.* London/New York: Ernest Benn/Barnes and Noble, 1968. Second ed., New York: St. Martin's Press, 1979.

Richter, M. "The Interpretation of Medieval Irish History." *Irish Historical Studies* 24 (1985): 289–98.

————. "The European Dimension of Irish History in the Eleventh and Twelfth Centuries." *Peritia* 4 (1985): 328–45.

Simms, K. *From Kings to Warlords.* Woodbridge, Suffolk: Boydell, 1987.

Stalley, R. A. *The Cistercian Monasteries of Ireland.* New Haven/London: Yale University Press, 1987.

Whitelock, D., R. McKitterick, and D. Dumville, eds. *Ireland in Early Medieval Europe: Studies in Memory of Kathleen Hughes.* Cambridge: Cambridge University Press, 1982.

24. History: The Tudor-Stuart Plantations

Andrews, K. R., N. P. Canny, and P. E. H. Hair, eds. *The Westward Enterprise: English Colonisation in Ireland, the Atlantic, and America, 1480–1650.* Liverpool: Liverpool University Press, 1978.

Appleby, J. C. "Settlers and Pirates in Early Seventeenth-Century Ireland: A Profile of Sir William Hull." *Studia Hibernica* 25 (1989–90): 76–104.

Berleth, R. *The Twilight Lords: The Epic Struggle of the Last Feudal Lords of Ireland against the England of Elizabeth I.* London: Allen Lane, 1979.

Bradshaw, B., A. Hadfield, and W. Maley, eds. *Representing Ireland: Literature and the Origins of Conflict, 1534–1660.* Cambridge: Cambridge University Press, 1993.

Brady, C. "Faction and the Origins of the Desmond Rebellion of 1579." *Irish Historical Studies* 22 (1981): 289–312.

Brady, C., and R. Gillespie, eds. *Natives and Newcomers: Essays on the Making of Irish Colonial Society, 1534–1641.* Dublin: Irish Academic Press, 1986.

Canny, N. "Hugh O'Neill, Earl of Tyrone, and the Changing Face of Gaelic Ulster." *Studia Hibernica* 10 (1970): 7–35.

————. "The Flight of the Earls, 1607." *Irish Historical Studies* 16 (1972): 380–99.

————. *The Elizabethan Conquest of Ireland: A Pattern Established 1565–76.* Hassocks: Harvester, 1976.

————. *The Upstart Earl: A Study of the Social and Mental World of Richard*

Boyle, First Earl of Cork, 1566–1643. Cambridge: Cambridge University Press, 1982.

————. *From Reformation to Restoration: Ireland 1534–1660*. Dublin: Helicon, 1987.

Clarke, A. *The Old English in Ireland, 1625–42*. London: MacGibbon and Kee, 1966.

Coughlan, P., ed. *Spenser and Ireland, An Interdisciplinary Perspective*. Cork: Cork University Press, 1989.

Curl, J. S. *The Londonderry Plantation, 1609–1914*. Chichester: Phillimore, 1986.

Ellis, S. G. *Tudor Ireland: Crown, Community and Conflict of Cultures, 1470–1603*. London: Longmans, 1985.

Emery, F. V. "Irish Geography in the Seventeenth Century." *Irish Geography* 3 (1958): 263–76.

Fitzpatrick, B. *Seventeenth Century Ireland: The War of Religions*. Dublin: Gill and Macmillan, 1988.

Gillespie, R. *Colonial Ulster: The Settlement of East Ulster, 1600–1641*. Cork: Cork University Press, 1985.

Hunter, R. J. "Towns in the Ulster Plantation." *Studia Hibernica* 11 (1971): 40–78.

Lindley, K. J. "The Impact of the 1641 Rebellion upon England and Wales, 1641–5." *Irish Historical Studies* 18 (1972): 143–76.

Loeber, R. *The Geography and Practice of English Colonisation in Ireland from 1534 to 1609*. Athlone/Dublin: Group for the Study of Irish Historic Settlement, 1991.

MacCarthy-Morrogh, M. *The Munster Plantation: English Migration to Southern Ireland, 1583–1641*. Oxford: Clarendon, 1986.

MacCuarta, B., ed. *Ulster 1641: Aspects of the Rising*. Belfast: Queen's University Institute of Irish Studies, 1993.

McCurtain, M. *Tudor and Stuart Ireland*. Dublin: Gill and Macmillan, 1972.

McKenny, K. *For King or Ulster: The Landed Interests, Political Ideologies and Military Campaigns of the British Settler Armies of North West Ulster, 1620–85*. Dublin: Irish Academic Press, 1995.

Moody, T. W. *The Londonderry Plantation, 1609–41*. Belfast: Mullan, 1939.

Morgan, H. "The End of Gaelic Ulster: A Thematic Interpretation of Events between 1534 and 1610." *Irish Historical Studies* 26 (1988): 8–32.

————. *Tyrone's Rebellion: The Outbreak of the Nine Years War in Tudor Ireland*. Dublin: Gill and Macmillan, 1993.

Ohlmeyer, J. H. *Civil War and Restoration in the Three Stuart Kingdoms: The Career of Randal MacDonnell, Marquis of Antrim, 1609–1683*. Cambridge: Cambridge University Press, 1993.

————. ed. *Ireland from Independence to Occupation 1641–1660*. Cambridge: Cambridge University Press, 1995.

Pawlisch, H. *Sir John Davies and the Conquest of Ireland*. Cambridge: Cambridge University Press, 1985.

Perceval-Maxwell, M. *The Scottish Migration to Ulster in the Reign of James I.* London: Routledge and Kegan Paul, 1973.

————. *The Outbreak of the Irish Rebellion of 1641.* Dublin: Gill and Macmillan, 1994.

Quinn, D. B. "The Munster Plantation: Problems and Opportunities." *Cork Historical and Archaeological Society Journal* 71 (1966): 19–40.

————. *The Elizabethans and the Irish.* Ithaca, N.Y.: Cornell University Press, 1966.

Robinson, P. "British Settlement in County Tyrone." *Irish Economic and Social History* 5 (1978): 5–26.

————. *The Plantation of Ulster: British Settlement in an Irish Landscape, 1600–1700.* Dublin/New York: Gill and Macmillan/St. Martin's Press, 1984. Reprint, Belfast: Ulster Historical Foundation, 1994.

Sheehan, A. J. "The Population of the Plantation of Munster: Quinn Reconsidered." *Cork Historical Society Journal* 87 (1982): 107–17.

Simington, R. C., ed. *The Civil Survey, 1654–56.* 10 vols. Dublin: Irish Manuscripts Commission, 1931–61.

Simms, J. G. "The Civil Survey, 1654–6." *Irish Historical Studies* 9 (1955): 253–63.

Smyth, W. J. "The Western Isle of Ireland and the Eastern Seaboard of America: England's First Frontiers." *Irish Geography* 11 (1978): 1–22.

Stevenson, D. *Scottish Covenanters and Irish Confederates.* Belfast: Ulster Historical Foundation, 1981.

25. History: The Great Famine

Crawford, E. M., ed. *Famine, the Irish Experience, 900–1900: Subsistence Crises and Famines in Ireland.* Edinburgh: John Donald, 1989.

Daly, M. *The Famine in Ireland,* Dundalk: Dundalgan, 1986.

Edwards, R. D., and T. D. Williams, eds. *The Great Famine: Studies in Irish History, 1845–52.* Dublin: Browne and Nolan, 1956. New ed., Dublin: Lilliput, 1994.

Gray, P. *Famine, Land and Politics: British government and Irish society, 1843–50.* Dublin: Irish Academic Press, 1995.

Hill, J., and C. O Gráda, eds. *Austin Bourke, "The Visitation of God"? The Potato and the Great Irish Famine.* Dublin: Lilliput, 1993.

Miller, D. W. "Irish Catholicism and the Great Famine." *Journal of Social History* 9 (1975): 81–94.

Mokyr, J. *Why Ireland Starved: A Quantitative and Analytical History of the Irish Economy, 1800–1850.* London: Allen Unwin, 1982.

Morash, C., and R. Hayes, eds. *"Fearful Realities": New Perspectives on the Famine.* Dublin: Irish Academic Press, 1995.

Ó Gráda, C. *The Great Irish Famine.* London: Macmillan, 1989.

————. *Ireland before and after the Famine: Explorations in Economic History, 1800–1930.* Manchester: Manchester University Press, 1988; revised ed., 1993.

Póirtéir, C., ed. *The Great Irish Famine.* Cork: Mercier, 1995.
Woodham-Smith, C. *The Great Hunger: Ireland 1845–49.* London: Hamish Hamilton, 1962. New ed., London: Dutton, 1980.

26. History: Post-Famine

Bew, P. *Conflict and Conciliation in Ireland, 1890–1910: Parnellites and Radical Agrarians.* Oxford: Clarendon, 1987.
———. *Charles Stewart Parnell.* Dublin: Gill and Macmillan, 1991.
Boyce, D. G. *The Irish Question and British Politics, 1868–1986.* Basingstoke: Macmillan Education, 1988.
———, ed. *The Revolution in Ireland, 1879–1923.* Basingstoke/Dublin: Macmillan Education/Gill and Macmillan, 1988.
Boyce, D. G., and A. O'Day, eds. *Parnell in Perspective.* London: Routledge, 1991.
Callanan, F. *The Parnell Split, 1890–91.* Cork: Cork University Press, 1992.
Comerford, R. V. "Patriotism as Pastime: The Appeal of Fenianism in the Mid-1860s." *Irish Historical Studies* 22 (1981): 239–50.
———. *The Fenians in Context: Irish Politics and Society.* Dublin: Wolfhound, 1985.
Kee, R. *The Laurel and the Ivy: The Story of Charles Stewart Parnell and Irish Nationalism.* London: Hamish Hamilton, 1993.
Kissane, N. *Parnell: A Documentary History.* Dublin: National Library of Ireland, 1991.
Lyons, F. S. L. *The Irish Parliamentary Party, 1890–1910.* London, 1951. New ed., London: Greenwood, 1976.
———. *The Fall of Parnell, 1890–91.* London: Routledge and Kegan Paul, 1960.
———. *John Dillon.* London: Routledge and Kegan Paul, 1968.
———. *Ireland since the Famine.* London: Fontana, 1973.
———. *Charles Stewart Parnell.* London: Collins, 1977. New ed., London: Fontana, 1991.
Mansergh, N. *The Irish Question, 1840–1921.* London: Allen and Unwin, 1975.
Martin, F. X. *The Irish Volunteers.* Dublin: Duffy, 1963.
Moody, T. W. *Davitt and Irish Revolution, 1846–1882.* Oxford: Oxford University Press, 1981.
———, ed. *The Fenian Movement.* Dublin: Mercier Press, 1968.
Muenger, E. A. *The British Military Dilemma in Ireland: Occupation Politics, 1886–1914.* Dublin: Gill and Macmillan, 1991.
O'Brien, C. C. *Parnell and His Party, 1880–90.* Oxford: Clarendon Press, 1964.
Takagami, S. "The Fenian Rising in Dublin, March 1867." *Irish Historical Studies* 29 (1995): 340–62.
Thornley, D. *Isaac Butt and Home Rule.* London, 1964. Reprint, London: Greenwood Press, 1976.

Travers, P. *Settlements and Divisions: Ireland, 1870–1922*. Dublin: Helicon, 1989.

Valiulis, M. G. *Portrait of a Revolutionary: General Richard Mulcahy and the Founding of the Irish Free State*. Dublin: Irish Academic Press, 1992.

Walker, B. M. "The Irish Electorate, 1868–1915." *Irish Historical Studies* 18 (1973): 359–406.

———. *Ulster Politics: The Formative Years, 1868–86*. Belfast: Ulster Historical Foundation and Queen's University, Institute of Irish Studies, 1989.

Warwick-Haller, S. *William O'Brien and the Irish Land War*. Dublin: Irish Academic Press, 1990.

West, T. *Horace Plunkett: Co-operation and Politics*. Gerrards Cross, Bucks.: Colin Smythe, 1987.

Whyte, J. H. "The Influence of the Catholic Clergy on Elections in Nineteenth-century Ireland." *English Historical Review* 85, 1960, 239–259.

27. History: Twentieth Century

Andrews, J. H. "The 'Morning Post' Line." *Irish Geography* 4 (1960): 99–106.

Bell, J. B. *The Gun in Politics: An Analysis of Irish Political Conflict, 1916–1986*. London/New Brunswick, N.J.: Transaction Books, 1991.

———. *The Irish Troubles: A Generation of Violence, 1967–1992*. Dublin: Gill and Macmillan, 1993.

Blake, J. W. *Northern Ireland in the Second World War*. Belfast: HMSO, 1956.

Bowman, J. *De Valera and the Ulster Question, 1917–1973*. Oxford: Oxford University Press, 1982.

Breen, R., D. F. Hannan, D. B. Rottman, and C. T. Whelan. *Understanding Contemporary Ireland: State, Class, and Development in the Republic of Ireland*. Basingstoke: Gill and Macmillan, 1990.

Cahill, L. *Forgotten Revolution: Limerick Soviet 1919: A Threat to British Power in Ireland*. Dublin: O'Brien, 1990.

Carroll, F. M. "The American Committee for Relief in Ireland, 1920–22." *Irish Historical Studies* 23 (1982): 30–49.

Cathcart, R. *The Most Contrary Region: The B.B.C. in Northern Ireland, 1924–1984*. Belfast: Blackstaff, 1984.

Coogan, T. P. *Michael Collins: A Biography*. London: Hutchinson, 1991.

Curran, J. M. *The Birth of the Irish Free State, 1921–1923*. Huntsville: University of Alabama Press, 1980.

Fitzpatrick, D. *Politics and Irish Life, 1913–21: Provincial Experience of War and Revolution*. Dublin: Gill and Macmillan, 1977. New ed., Aldershot: Gregg Revivals, 1993.

Forester, M. *Michael Collins: The Lost Leader*. London: Sidgwick and Jackson, 1971. New ed., Dublin: Gill and Macmillan, 1989.

Gwynn, S. *John Redmond's Last Years*. London: Arnold, 1919.

Hawkings, F. M. A. "Defence and the Role of Erskine Childers in the Treaty Negotiations of 1921." *Irish Historical Studies* 22 (1981): 251–70.

Hopkinson, M. "Biography of the Revolutionary Period: Michael Collins and Kevin Barry." *Irish Historical Studies* 28 (1993): 310–16.

———. *Green against Green: A History of the Irish Civil War.* Dublin: Gill and Macmillan, 1988.

———. "President Woodrow Wilson and the Irish Question." *Studia Hibernica* 27 (1993): 89–111.

Hutchinson, J. *The Dynamics of Cultural Nationalism: The Gaelic Revival and the Creation of the Irish Nation State.* London: Allen and Unwin, 1987.

Johnson, D. S. "Northern Ireland as a Problem in the Economic War, 1932–38." *Irish Historical Studies* 22 (1980): 144–61.

Kennedy, M. J. *Ireland and the League of Nations.* Dublin: Irish Academic Press, 1995.

Keogh, D. *Ireland and Europe, 1919–1948.* Dublin: Gill and Macmillan, 1988.

Lawlor, S. M. "Ireland from Truce to Treaty: War or Peace? July to October 1921." *Irish Historical Studies* 22 (1980): 49–64.

Lyons, F. S. L. *Culture and Anarchy in Ireland, 1890–1939.* Oxford: Oxford University Press, 1979.

McEvoy, F. J. "Canada, Ireland, and the Commonwealth: The Declaration of the Irish Republic, 1948–49." *Irish Historical Studies* 24 (1985): 506–27.

McMahon, D. " 'A transient apparition': British Policy Towards the de Valera Government, 1932–35." *Irish Historical Studies* 22 (1981): 331–61.

Mansergh, N. *The Unresolved Question: The Anglo-Irish Settlement and Its Undoing, 1912–72.* London: Yale University Press, 1991.

Murphy, B. P. *Patrick Pearse and the Lost Republican Ideal.* Dublin: James Duffy, 1991.

———. *John Chartres: Mystery Man of the Treaty.* Dublin: Irish Academic Press, 1995.

O'Connor, F. *The Big Fellow.* London, 1937. Reprint, Swords, Co. Dublin: Poolbeg, 1979.

Rosenberg, J. L. "The 1914 Mission of Frank Aiken to the United States: An American Perspective." *Irish Historical Studies* 22 (1980): 162–77.

Skelly, J. M. *National Interests and the International Order: Irish Diplomacy at the United Nations General Assembly.* Dublin: Irish Academic Press, 1995.

28. Government

Barrington, T. J. *The Irish Administrative System.* Dublin: Institute of Public Administration, 1980.

Birrell, D., and A. Murie. *Policy and Government in Northern Ireland: Lessons of Devolution.* Dublin: Barnes and Noble, 1980.

Bradshaw, B. *The Irish Constitutional Revolution of the Sixteenth Century.* Cambridge: Cambridge University Press, 1979.

Burns, R. E. *Irish Parliamentary Politics in the Eighteenth Century.* 2 vols. Washington, D.C.: Catholic University of America Press, 1989–90.

Chubb, B. *The Constitution and Constitutional Change in Ireland.* Dublin: Institute of Public Administration, 1978.

———. *The Government and Politics of Ireland.* London: Longmans/Stanford University Press, 1982.

Crawford, J. G. *Anglicizing the Government of Ireland: The Irish Privy Council and the Expansion of Tudor Rule, 1556–1578.* Dublin: Irish Academic Press, 1993.

Crossman, V. *Local Government in Nineteenth Century Ireland.* Belfast: Queen's University, Institute of Irish Studies, 1994.

Doolan, B. *Constitutional Law and Constitutional Rights in Ireland.* Dublin: Gill and Macmillan, 1988.

Duggan, J. P. *A History of the Irish Army.* Dublin: Gill and Macmillan, 1991.

Ellis, S. G. "The Irish Customs Administration under the Early Tudors," *Irish Historical Studies* 22 (1981): 271–77.

———. *Reform and Revival: English Government in Ireland, 1470–1534.* Woodbridge, Suffolk: Boydell, 1986.

Farrell, B. ed. *The Creation of the Dáil.* Dublin: Gill and Macmillan, 1994.

Flanagan, K. "The Chief Secretary's Office, 1853–1914: A Bureaucratic Enigma." *Irish Historical Studies* 24 (1984): 197–225.

Hand, G. J. *Report of the Boundary Commission, 1925.* Shannon: Irish University Press, 1969.

Johnston, E. M. *Great Britain and Ireland, 1760–1800: A Study in Political Administration.* Edinburgh, 1963. Reprint, London: Greenwood, 1978.

Kelly, J. M. *The Irish Constitution.* Dublin: Jurist Publishing, 1984.

Kendle, J. *Ireland and the Federal Solution: The Debate over the United Kingdom Constitution, 1870–1921.* Montreal: McGill-Queen's University Press, 1989.

Kotsonouris, M. *Retreat from Revolution: The Dáil Courts, 1920–24.* Dublin: Irish Academic Press, 1994.

Lowe, W. J., and E. L. Malcolm. "The Documentation of the Royal Irish Constabulary, 1836–1922." *Irish Economic and Social History* 19 (1992): 29–48.

McCartney, D. *The Dawning of Democracy: Ireland, 1800–1870.* Dublin: Helicon, 1987.

McCormack, W. J., ed. *The Debate on the Union between Great Britain and Ireland, 1797–1800.* Dublin: Irish Academic Press, 1995.

McCracken, J. L. *Representative Government in Ireland: A Study of Dail Eireann, 1914–48.* London, 1958. Reprint, London: Greenwood, 1976.

McDowell, R. B. *The Irish Administration, 1801–1914.* London, 1964. New ed., London: Greenwood, 1977.

Micks, W. L. *An Account of the Constitution, Administration, and Dissolution of the Congested Districts Board for Ireland from 1891 to 1923.* Dublin: Eason, 1925.

Mitchell, A., and P. O'Snodaigh, eds. *Irish Political Documents, 1869–1916.* Dublin: Irish Academic Press, 1989.

Mulloy, S., ed. *Franco-Irish Correspondence, December 1688–February 1692.* 3 vols. Dublin: Irish Manuscripts Commission, 1983–84.

Nowlan, K. B. *The Politics of Repeal: A Study in the Relations between Great Britain and Ireland, 1841–1850.* London, 1965. Reprint, London: Greenwood, 1976.

O'Brien, G. "The Establishment of Poor-Law Unions in Ireland, 1838–43." *Irish Historical Studies* 23 (1982): 97–120.

———. "Workhouse Management in Pre-Famine Ireland." *Proceedings of the Royal Irish Academy* 86C (1986): 113–34.

Ó Dúill, G. "Founding the Office: Archival Reform in the Nineteenth Century." *Administration* 25 (1977): 561–80.

———. "Sir Samuel Ferguson, Administrator and Archivist." *Irish University Review* 16 (1986): 117–40.

O'Halpin, E. *The Decline of the Union: British Government in Ireland, 1892–1920.* Dublin: Gill and Macmillan, 1987.

Palmer, S. H. *Police and Protest in England and Ireland, 1780–1850.* Cambridge: Cambridge University Press, 1988.

Quekett, A. S. *The Constitution of Northern Ireland.* 3 parts. Belfast: HMSO, 1928–46.

Roche, D. *Local Government in Ireland.* Dublin: Institute of Public Administration, 1982.

Sainty, J. C. "The Secretariat of the Chief Governors of Ireland, 1690–1800." *Proceedings of the Royal Irish Academy* 77C (1977): 1–33.

Sexton, B. *Ireland and the Crown, 1922–1936: The Governor-Generalship of the Irish Free State.* Dublin: Irish Academic Press, 1989.

Smyth, J. M. *The Houses of the Oireachtas.* Dublin: Institute of Public Administration, 1979.

Thompson, W. J. "The Development of the Irish Census." *Journal of the Statistical and Social Inquiry Society of Ireland,* 1910–11, 474–88.

Townshend, C. *Political Violence in Ireland: Government and Resistance since 1848.* Oxford: Oxford University Press, 1983.

Wallace, M. *British Government in Northern Ireland from Devolution to Direct Rule.* Newton Abbot: David and Charles, 1982.

Ward, A. J. *The Irish Constitutional Tradition: Responsible Government and Modern Ireland, 1782–1992.* Dublin: Irish Academic Press, 1995.

Wilkinson, D. "The Fitzwilliam Episode, 1795: A Reinterpretation of the Role of the Duke of Portland." *Irish Historical Studies* 29 (1995): 315–39.

29. Law

Ball, J. E. *The Judges in Ireland, 1221–1921.* 2 vols. Dublin: Round Hall Press, 1993.

Binchy, D. A., ed. *Corpus Iuris Hibernici.* 6 vols. Dublin: Institute for Advanced Studies, 1978.

Burke, H. *The People and the Poor Law in Nineteenth Century Ireland*. Dublin: Women's Education Bureau, 1987.

Casey, J. P. *The Office of the Attorney General in Ireland*. Dublin: Institute of Public Administration, 1980.

Doolan, B. *Principles of Irish Law*. Dublin: Gill and Macmillan, 1986.

Ellis, E., and P. B. Eustace, eds. *Registry of Deeds Dublin: Abstract of Wills. Vol. 3, 1785–1832*. Dublin: Irish Manuscripts Commission, 1984.

Henry, B. *Dublin Hanged: Crime, Law Enforcement, and Punishment in Late 18th-century Dublin*. Dublin: Irish Academic Press, 1994.

Hogan, D. H., and W. N. Osborough. *Brehons, Serjeants, and Attorneys: Studies in the History of the Irish Legal Profession*. Dublin: Irish Academic Press, 1990.

Keane, E., P. B. Phair, and T. U. Sadleir, eds. *King's Inns Admission Papers, 1607–1867*. Dublin: Irish Manuscripts Commission, 1982.

Kelly, F. *A Guide to Early Irish Law*. Dublin: Institute for Advanced Studies, 1988.

Kenny, C. *King's Inns and the Kingdom of Ireland: The Irish 'Inn of Court' 1541–1800*. Dublin: Irish Academic Press, 1992.

Nicholls, G. *A History of the Irish Poor Law*. London, 1856. New ed., London: Frank Cass, 1968.

O'Brien, G. "The New Poor Law in Pre-Famine Ireland." *Irish Economic and Social History* 12 (1985): 33–49.

Ó Corrain, D., L. Breatnach, and A. Breen. "The Laws of the Irish," *Peritia* 3 (1984): 382–438.

O'Flaherty, E. "Ecclesiastical Politics and the Dismantling of the Penal Laws in Ireland, 1774–82." *Irish Historical Studies* 26 (1988): 33–50.

Osborough, W. N., ed. *Explorations in Law and History*. Dublin: Irish Academic Press, 1995.

30. Politics

Allen, K. *The Politics of James Connolly*. London: Pluto, 1990.

Anderson, W. K. *James Connolly and the Irish Left*. Dublin: Irish Academic Press, 1994.

Barton, B. *Brookeborough: The Making of a Prime Minister*. Belfast: Queen's University, Institute of Irish Studies, 1988.

Bew, P., and H. Patterson. *Seán Lemass and the Making of Modern Ireland, 1945–66*. Dublin: Gill and Macmillan, 1982.

Bew, P., E. Hazelkorn, and H. Patterson. *The Dynamics of Irish Politics*. London: Lawrence and Wishart, 1989.

Bolton, G. C. *The Passing of the Irish Act of Union: A Study in Parliamentary Politics*. Oxford/London: Oxford University Press, 1966.

Boyce, D. G. *Nineteenth-Century Ireland: The Search for Stability*. Dublin: Gill and Macmillan, 1990.

————. *Nationalism in Ireland.* London: Routledge, 1995.

Boyce, D. G., R. Eccleshall, and V. Geoghegan, eds. *Political Thought in Ireland since the Seventeenth Century.* London: Routledge, 1993.

Boylan, T. A., and T. P. Foley. *Political Economy and Colonial Ireland: The Propagation and Ideological Function of Economic Discourse in the Nineteenth Century.* London: Routledge, 1992.

Buckley, D. N. *James Fintan Lalor: Radical.* Cork: Cork University Press, 1990.

Busteed, M. A. *Voting Behaviour in the Republic of Ireland: A Geographical Perspective.* Oxford: Clarendon Press, 1990.

Carty, R. K. *Party and Parish Pump: Electoral Politics in Ireland.* Waterloo, Ontario: Wilfrid Laurier University Press, 1981.

Casway, J. I. *Owen Roe O'Neill and the Struggle for Catholic Ireland.* Philadelphia: University of Pennsylvania Press, 1984.

Clark, S., and J. S. Donnelly, eds. *Irish Peasants: Violence and Political Unrest, 1780–1914.* Manchester: Manchester University Press, 1983.

Coakley, J., and M. Gallagher, eds. *Politics in the Republic of Ireland.* Dublin: Folens Publishers, 1993.

Coldrey, B. M. *Faith and Fatherland: The Christian Brothers and the Development of Irish Nationalism, 1838–1921.* Dublin: Gill and Macmillan, 1988.

Collins, N. ed. *Political Issues in Ireland Today.* Manchester: Manchester University Press, 1994.

Collins, N., and F. McCann. *Irish Politics Today.* Manchester: Manchester University Press, 1991.

Corish, P. J., ed. *Radicals, Rebels, and Establishments.* Belfast: Appletree, 1985.

Coyle, C., and R. Sinnott. "Regional Élites, Regional 'Powerlessness,' and European Regional Policy in Ireland." *Regional Politics and Policy* 2 (1992): 71–108.

Curtin, N. J. "The Transformation of the Society of United Irishmen into a Mass-Based Revolutionary Organisation, 1794–76." *Irish Historical Studies* 24 (1985): 463–92.

————. *The United Irishmen: Popular Politics in Ulster and Dublin, 1791–1798.* Oxford: Clarendon, 1994.

Dangerfield, G. "James Joyce, James Connolly, and Irish Nationalism." *Irish University Review* 16 (1986): 5–21.

Davis, R. *The Young Ireland Movement.* Dublin: Gill and Macmillan, 1987.

Dickson, D., D. Keogh, and K. Whelan. *The United Irishmen, Republicism, Radicalism, and Rebellion.* Dublin: Lilliput, 1993.

Dunleavy, J. E., and G. W. Dunleavy. *Douglas Hyde: A Maker of Modern Ireland.* Berkeley/Oxford: University of California Press, 1991.

Dunne, T. "La Trahison Des Clercs: British Intellectuals and the First Home-Rule Crisis." *Irish Historical Studies* 23 (1982): 134–73.

Dwyer, T. R. *Charlie: The Political Biography of Charles J. Haughey.* Dublin: Gill and Macmillan, 1987.

Edwards, R. D. *Patrick Pearse: The Triumph of Failure*. London: Faber and Faber, 1980.

Elliott, M. "The Origins and Transformation of Early Irish Republicanism." *International Review of Social History* 23 (1978): 405–28.

————. *Partners in Revolution: The United Irishmen and France*. New Haven/London: Yale University Press, 1982.

————. *Wolfe Tone, Prophet of Irish Independence*. New Haven/London: Yale University Press, 1989.

Farrell, B. *Seán Lemass*. Dublin: Gill and Macmillan, 1983.

Farrell, D. M. "Age, Education, and Occupational Backgrounds of TDs and 'Routes' to the Dáil: The Effects of Localism in the 1980s." *Administration* 32 (1984): 323–41.

FitzGerald, G. *All in a Life: An Autobiography*. Dublin: Gill and Macmillan, 1991.

Gailey, A. *Ireland and the Death of Kindness: The Experience of Constructive Unionism, 1890–1905*. Cork: Cork University Press, 1987.

Gallagher, M. *Electoral Support for Irish Political Parties, 1927–1973*. London: Sage Publications, 1976.

————. *The Irish Labour Party in Transition, 1957–82*. Manchester: Manchester University Press, 1982.

————. *Political Parties in the Republic of Ireland*. Dublin: Gill and Macmillan, 1985.

Gallagher, M., and R. Sinnott. *How Ireland Voted: The Irish General Election, 1989*. Galway: Centre for the Study of Irish Elections, 1990.

Garvin, T. "Political Cleavages, Party Politics, and Urbanisation in Ireland: The Case of the Periphery-Dominated Centre." *European Journal of Political Research* 2 (1974): 307–27.

————. *The Evolution of Irish Nationalist Politics*. Dublin: Gill and Macmillan, 1981.

————. *Nationalist Revolutionaries in Ireland, 1858–1928*. Oxford: Clarendon, 1987.

Girvin, B., and R. Sturm, eds. *Politics and Society in Contemporary Ireland*. Aldershot: Gower, 1986.

Gough, H., and D. Dickson, eds. *Ireland and the French Revolution*. Dublin: Irish Academic Press, 1990.

Greaves, C. D. *Life and Times of James Connolly*. London: Lawrence and Wishart, 1972.

Grogan, G. F. *The Noblest Agitator: Daniel O'Connell and the German Catholic Movement, 1830–1850*. Dublin: Veritas, 1991.

Hepburn, A. C. *The Conflict of Nationality in Modern Ireland*. London: Edward Arnold/St. Martin's Press, 1980.

Hoppen, K. T. *Elections, Politics, and Society in Ireland, 1832–1885*. Oxford: Clarendon, 1984.

Hughes, E., ed. *Culture and Politics in Northern Ireland, 1960–90*. Milton Keynes, Bucks.: Open University Press, 1991.

Hussey, G. *At the Cutting Edge: Cabinet Diaries, 1982–87*. Dublin: Gill and Macmillan, 1990.

Hyde, H. M. *Carson: The Life of Sir Edward Carson, Lord Carson of Duncairn*. London: Heinemann, 1953. Reprint, London: Constable, 1987.

Jalland, P. *The Liberals and Ireland: The Ulster Question in British Politics to 1914*. Brighton: Harvester, 1980.

Jenkins, R. *Gladstone*. London: St. Martin's Press, 1995.

Kearney, R. ed. *The Irish Mind: Exploring Intellectual Traditions*. Dublin: Wolfhound, 1985.

Kelly, J. "The Origins of the Act of Union: An Examination of Unionist Opinion in Britain and Ireland, 1650–1800." *Irish Historical Studies* 25 (1987): 263–63.

———. *Prelude to Union: Anglo-Irish Politics in the 1780s*. Cork: Cork University Press, 1992.

Laffan, M. "The Unification of Sinn Féin in 1917." *Irish Historical Studies* 17 (1971): 353–79.

Laver, M. "Ireland: Politics with Some Social Bases." *Economic and Social Review* 17 (1986): 107–31; 193–213.

Laver, M., P. Mair, and R. Sinnott, eds. *How Ireland Voted: The Irish General Election, 1987*. Dublin: Poolbeg, 1987.

Lee, J. J. *Ireland, 1912–1985: Politics and Society*. Cambridge: Cambridge University Press, 1989.

Longford, Earl of, and T. P. O'Neill. *Eamon de Valera*. Dublin/London: Gill and Macmillan/Hutchinson, 1970. New ed., London: Arrow Books, 1974.

Longford, E. *Wellington*. 2 vols. London: Weidenfeld and Nicholson, 1969–72.

Loughlin, J. *Gladstone, Home Rule, and the Ulster Question, 1882–93*. Dublin/Atlantic Highlands, N.J.: Gill and Macmillan/Humanities Press International, 1986.

McAllister, I. *The Northern Ireland Social Democratic and Labour Party: Political Opposition in a Divided Society*. London: Macmillan, 1977.

McCartney, D. *The Dawning of Democracy: Ireland, 1800–1870*. Dublin: Helicon, 1987.

MacDonagh, O. *The Hereditary Bondsman: Daniel O'Connell, 1775–1829*. London: Weidenfeld and Nicholson, 1988.

———. *The Emancipist: Daniel O'Connell, 1830–47*. London: Weidenfeld and Nicolson, 1989.

McDowell, R. B. *Irish Public Opinion, 1750–1800*. London: Faber and Faber, 1944.

McDowell, R. B., et al., eds. *The Writings and Speeches of Edmund Burke*. 2 vols. Oxford: Clarendon, 1992.

MacIntyre, A. *The Liberator: Daniel O'Connell and the Irish Party*. London: Hamish Hamilton, 1965.

Maguire, W. A., ed. *Kings in Conflict: Revolutionary War in Ireland and Its Aftermath, 1689–1750*. Belfast: Blackstaff, 1990.

Mair, P. *The Changing Irish Party System: Organisation, Ideology, and Electoral Competition*. London: Pinter, 1987.

Mandle, W. F. *The Gaelic Athletic Association and Irish Nationalist Politics, 1844–1924.* London: Christopher Helm, 1987.

Manning, M. *The Blueshirts.* Dublin: Gill and Macmillan, 1987.

O'Brien, C. C. *The Great Melody: A Thematic Biography and Commented Anthology of Edmund Burke.* London: Sinclair-Stevenson, 1992.

———. *Ancestral Voices: Religion and Nationalism in Ireland.* Dublin: Poolbeg, 1994.

O'Brien, G. *Anglo-Irish Politics in the Age of Grattan and Pitt.* Dublin: Irish Academic Press, 1988.

———. *The Politics of Conciliation: The Pursuit of Catholic Emancipation in Ireland, England, and Scotland, 1660–1829.* Dublin: Irish Academic Press, 1995.

Ó Cathaoir, B. *John Blake Dillon: Young Irelander.* Dublin: Irish Academic Press, 1990.

O'Connell, M. R., ed. *Daniel O'Connell: Political Pioneer.* Dublin: Institute of Public Administration, 1991.

O'Day, A., ed. *Reactions to Irish Nationalism, 1865–1914.* Dublin: Gill and Macmillan, 1987.

O'Ferrall, F. *Catholic Emancipation, Daniel O'Connell, and the Birth of Irish Democracy, 1820–30.* Dublin: Gill and Macmillan, 1985.

O'Leary, C. *Irish Elections, 1918–1977: Parties, Voters, and Proportional Representation.* Dublin: Gill and Macmillan, 1979.

Orridge, A. "The Blueshirts and the 'Economic War': A Study of Ireland in the Context of Dependency Theory." *Political Studies* 31 (1983): 351–69.

O'Sullivan, E. "The 1990 Presidential Election in the Republic of Ireland." *Irish Political Studies* 6 (1991): 85–948.

Pakenham, T. *The Year of Liberty: The Irish Rebellion of 1798.* London: Orion, 1992.

Reid, C. *Edmund Burke and the Practice of Political Writing.* New York/Dublin: St. Martin's Press, 1985.

Rumpf, E., and A. C. Hepburn. *Nationalism and Socialism in Twentieth-Century Ireland.* Liverpool: Liverpool University Press, 1977.

Senior, H. *Orangeism in Ireland and Britain, 1795–1836.* London: Routledge and Kegan Paul, 1966.

Shannon, C. B. *Arthur J. Balfour and Ireland, 1874–1922.* London/Washington, D.C.: Catholic University of America Press, 1988.

Sinnott, R. "The North: Party Images and Party Approaches in the Republic." *Irish Political Studies* 1 (1986): 15–31.

———. *Irish Voters Decide: Voting Behaviour in Elections and Referendums since 1918.* Manchester: Manchester University Press, 1995.

Smyth, J. *The Men of No Property: Irish Radicals and Popular Politics in the Late Eighteenth Century.* Dublin/Basingstoke: Macmillan, 1992.

Stewart, A. T. Q. *The Narrow Ground: Aspects of Ulster, 1609–1969.* London: Faber, 1977.

———. *Edward Carson.* Dublin: Gill and Macmillan, 1981.

Ward, A. J. *The Easter Rising: Revolution and Irish Nationalism*. Wheeling, Ill.: Harlan Davidson, 1980.

Ward, M. *Maud Gonne: Ireland's Joan of Arc*. London: Pandora, 1990.

Wauchope, P. *Patrick Sarsfield and the Williamite War*. Dublin: Irish Academic Press, 1992.

White, T. de Vere. *Kevin O'Higgins*. London: Methuen, 1948. New ed., Dublin: Anvil, 1986.

Whyte, J. *Interpreting Northern Ireland*. Oxford: Clarendon, 1991.

31. Geography

Aalen, F. H. A. *Man and the Landscape in Ireland*. New York/London: Academic Press, 1978.

Brunt, B. *The Republic of Ireland*. London: Paul Chapman, 1988.

Carter, R. W. G., and A. J. Parker, eds. *Ireland: A Contemporary Geographical Perspective*. London: Routledge, 1989.

Fitzpatrick, D. "The Geography of Irish Nationalism." *Past and Present* 81 (1978): 113–44.

Freeman, T. W. *Pre-Famine Ireland: A Study in Historical Geography*. Manchester: Manchester University Press, 1957.

———. *Ireland: A General and Regional Geography*. London: Methuen, 1950. There are numerous revised editions to 1969.

Gillmor, D. A. *Economic Activities in the Republic of Ireland: A Geographical Perspective*. Dublin: Gill and Macmillan, 1985.

Graham, B. J., and L. J. Proudfoot, eds. *An Historical Geography of Ireland*. London: Academic Press, 1993.

Mendyk, S. "Gerard Boate and *Irelands Naturall History*." *Journal of the Royal Society of Antiquaries of Ireland* 115 (1985): 5–12.

Mitchell, G. F. *The Irish Landscape*. London: Collins, 1976.

Orme, A. R. *The World's Landscapes: Ireland*. London: Longmans, 1970.

Praeger, R. L. *The Way That I Went: An Irishman in Ireland*. Dublin/London: Hodges, Figgis/Methuen, 1937.

Smyth, W. J., and K. Whelan, eds. *Common Ground: Essays on the Historical Geography of Ireland Presented to T. Jones Hughes*. Cork: Cork University Press, 1988.

Stephens, N., and R. E. Glasscock, eds. *Irish Geographical Studies in Honour of E. Estyn Evans*. Belfast: Queen's University, Department of Geography, 1970.

32. Regional Studies

Aalen, F. H. A., and K. Whelan, eds. *Dublin City and County: From Prehistory to Present: Studies in Honour of J. H. Andrews*. Dublin: Geography Publications, 1992.

Bardon, J. *A History of Ulster*. Belfast: Blackstaff, 1992.

Boal, F. W., and J. N. H. Douglas, eds. *Integration and Division: geographical perspectives on the Northern Ireland problem.* Belfast: Academic Press, 1982.

Evans, E. E., ed. *Belfast in its regional setting.* Belfast: British Association for the Advancement of Science, 1952.

———. *Mourne Country.* Dundalk: Dundalgan Press, 1978.

Freeman, T. W. "The Congested Districts of Western Ireland." *Geographical Review* 33 (1943): 1–14.

Gillespie, R., and G. Moran, eds. *A Various Country: Essays in Mayo History, 1500–1900.* Westport: Foilseachain Naisiunta Teoranta, 1987.

Gillespie, R., and H. O'Sullivan, eds. *The Borderlands: Essays on the History of the Ulster-Leinster Border.* Belfast: Queen's University, Institute of Irish Studies, 1989.

Gillespie, R., ed. *Cavan: An Irish County History.* Dublin: Irish Academic Press, 1995.

Green, E. R. R. *The Lagan Valley, 1800–50: A Local History of the Industrial Revolution.* London: Faber and Faber, 1949.

Hannigan, K., and W. Nolan, eds. *Wicklow: History and Society: Interdisciplinary Essays on the History of an Irish County.* Dublin: Geography Publications, 1994.

Heslinga, M. W. *The Irish Border as a Cultural Divide.* Assen, 1962. Reprint, Atlantic Highlands, N.J.: Humanities, 1980.

Horner, A. A., and A. J. Parker, eds. *Geographical Perspectives on the Dublin Region.* Dublin: Geographical Society of Ireland, 1987.

Kearns, K. C. "The Resuscitation of the Irish Gaeltacht." *Geographical Review* 64 (1974): 82–110.

MacAodha, B. S. *Galway Gaeltacht Survey.* Galway: University College, Social Science Research Centre, 1969.

Murtagh, H. ed. *Irish Midland Studies: Essays in Commemoration of N. W. English.* Athlone: Old Athlone Society, 1980.

Nolan, W., and T. G. McGrath, eds. *Tipperary: History and Society: Interdisciplinary Essays on the History of an Irish County.* Dublin: Geography Publications, 1985.

Nolan, W., L. Ronayne, and M. Dunlevy, eds. *Donegal: History and Society: Interdisciplinary Essays on the History of an Irish County.* Dublin: Geography Publications, 1995.

Nolan, W., and K. Whelan, eds. *Kilkenny: History and Society: Interdisciplinary Essays on the History of an Irish County.* Dublin: Geography Publications, 1990.

Nolan, W., and T. P. Power, eds. *Waterford: History and Society: Interdisciplinary Essays on the History of an Irish County.* Dublin: Geography Publications, 1992.

O'Brien, I. *O'Brien of Thomond: The O'Briens in History, 1500–1865.* Chichester: Phillimore, 1986.

O'Flanagan, P., and C. G. Buttimer, eds. *Cork: History and Society: Interdisciplinary Essays on the History of an Irish County*. Dublin: Geography Publications, 1993.

Whelan, K. ed. *Wexford: History and Society: Interdisciplinary Essays on the History of an Irish County*. Dublin: Geography Publications, 1987.

33. Education

Akenson, D. H. *The Irish Education Experiment: The National System of Education in the Nineteenth Century*. London: Routledge and Kegan Paul, 1970.

———. *A Mirror to Kathleen's Face: Education in Independent Ireland, 1922–60*. Montreal: McGill-Queen's University Press, 1975.

Coolahan, J. *Irish Education: Its History and Structure*. Dublin: Institute of Public Administration, 1981.

Costello, P. *Clongowes Wood: A History of Clongowes Wood College, 1814–1989*. Dublin: Gill and Macmillan, 1989.

Daly, M., and D. Dickson, eds. *The Origins of Popular Literacy in Ireland: Language and Educational Development, 1700–1920*. Dublin: Trinity College, Department of Modern History, and University College, Department of Modern Irish History, 1990.

Dowling, P. J. *The Hedge Schools of Ireland*. London: Longmans Green, 1935. Reprint, Cork: Mercier, 1968.

Hyland, A., and K. Milne, eds. *Irish Educational Documents*. Vols. 1–3. Dublin: Church of Ireland College of Education, 1987–95.

Luce, J. V. *Trinity College Dublin: The First 400 Years*. Dublin: Trinity College Press, 1992.

McCarthy, M. *All Graduates and Gentlemen: Marsh's Library*. Dublin: O'Brien, 1980.

McDowell, R. B., and D. A. Webb. *Trinity College, Dublin, 1592–1952: An Academic Study*. Cambridge: Cambridge University Press, 1982.

Mahaffy, J. P. *An Epoch in Irish History: Trinity College, Dublin, 1591–1640*. London/Chicago: T. Fisher Unwin/University of Chicago Press, 1903.

Maxwell, C. E. *A History of Trinity College, Dublin, 1591–1892*. Dublin: University Press, 1946.

Moody, T. W., and J. C. Beckett. *Queen's, Belfast, 1845–1949: The History of a University*. 2 vols. London: Faber, 1959.

Ó Buachalla, S. *Education Policy in Twentieth Century Ireland*. Dublin: Wolfhound, 1988.

Ó Cuiv, B. *Seven Centuries of Irish Learning, 1000–1700*. Dublin: Stationery Office, 1961.

Ó Raifeartaigh, T. "Mixed Education and the Synod of Ulster, 1831–40." *Irish Historical Studies* 9 (1955): 281–99.

Parkes, S. M. *Kildare Place: The History of the Church of Ireland Training College, 1811–1969*. Dublin: Church of Ireland College of Education, 1984.

Stevenson, J. "The Beginnings of Literacy in Ireland." *Proceedings of the Royal Irish Academy* 89C, (1989): 127–65.

Tynan, M. *Catholic Instruction in Ireland, 1720–1950*. Dublin: Four Courts Press, 1985.

34. Religion

Abbott, V. *An Irishman's Revolution: The Abbé Edgeworth and Louis XVI*. Newbridge, Co. Kildare: Kavanagh, 1989.

Akenson, D. H. *The Church of Ireland: Ecclesiastical Reform and Revolution, 1800–1885*. New Haven/London: Yale University Press, 1971.

————. *Small Differences: Irish Catholics and Irish Protestants, 1815–1922*. Kingston/Montreal: McGill-Queen's University Press, 1991.

Bartlett, T. *The Fall and Rise of the Irish Nation: The Catholic Question, 1690–1830*. Dublin: Gill and Macmillan, 1992.

Beckett, J. C. *Protestant Dissent in Ireland, 1687–1780*. London, 1948. Reprint, Connecticut: Hyperion, 1980.

Bethell, D. L. T. "The Originality of the Early Irish Church." *Journal of the Royal Society of Antiquaries of Ireland* 111 (1981): 36–49.

Bowen, D. *The Protestant Crusade in Ireland, 1800–1870: A Study of Protestant-Catholic Relations between the Act of Union and Disestablishment*. Dublin: McGill-Queen's University Press, 1978.

————. *Paul Cardinal Cullen and the Shaping of Modern Irish Catholicism*. Dublin: Gill and Macmillan, 1983.

Bradshaw, B. *The Dissolution of the Religious Orders in Ireland under Henry VIII*. Cambridge: Cambridge University Press, 1974.

Brockliss, L. W. B., and P. Ferte. "Irish Clerics in France in the Seventeenth and Eighteenth Centuries: A Statistical Study." *Proceedings of the Royal Irish Academy* 87C (1987): 527–72.

Brooke, P. *Ulster Presbyterianism*. Dublin: Gill and Macmillan, 1987.

Caldicott, C. E. J., H. Gough, and J. P. Pittion, eds. *The Huguenots and Ireland: Anatomy of an Emigration*. Dun Laoghaire: Glendale, 1987.

Campbell, F. *The Dissenting Voice: Protestant Democracy in Ulster from Plantation to Partition*. Belfast: Blackstaff, 1991.

Clear, C. *Nuns in Nineteenth-Century Ireland*. Dublin: Gill and Macmillan, 1987.

Cole, R. L. *One Methodist Church, 1860–1960*. Belfast: Irish Methodist Publishing Co., 1960. vol. 4 of C. H. Crookshank, *A History of Methodists in Ireland*.

Comerford, R. V., M. Cullen, J. R. Hill, and C. Lennon, eds. *Religion, Conflict, and Coexistence in Ireland*. Dublin: Gill and Macmillan, 1990.

Connolly, S. J. *Priests and People in pre-Famine Ireland, 1780–1845*. Dublin: St. Martin's Press, 1982.

————. *Religion and Society in Nineteenth-Century Ireland*. Dundalk: Dundalgan, 1985.

———. *Religion, Law, and Power: The Making of Protestant Ireland, 1660–1760.* Oxford: Clarendon, 1992.

Corish, P. J., ed. *A History of Irish Catholicism.* 6 vols. Dublin: Gill and Macmillan, 1967–72.

———. *The Catholic Community in the Seventeenth and Eighteenth Centuries.* Dublin: Helicon, 1981.

———. *The Irish Catholic Experience: A Historical Survey.* Dublin: Gill and Macmillan, 1985.

Fagan, P. *Dublin's Turbulent Priest: Cornelius Nary (1658–1738).* Dublin: Royal Irish Academy, 1991.

———. *An Irish Bishop in Penal Times: The Chequered Career of Sylvester Lloyd, O.F.M., 1680–1747.* Dublin: Four Courts Press, 1993.

Faughnan, S. "The Jesuits and the Drafting of the Irish Constitution of 1937." *Irish Historical Studies* 26 (1988): 79–102.

Fenning, H. *The Irish Dominican Province, 1698–1797.* Dublin: Dominican Publications, 1990.

Flynn, T. S. *The Irish Dominicans, 1536–1641.* Dublin: Four Courts Press, 1993.

Ford, G. A. *The Protestant Reformation in Ireland, 1590–1641.* Frankfurt-am-Main: Lang, 1985.

Freeman, T. W. "John Wesley in Ireland." *Irish Geography* 8 (1975): 86–96.

Gaustad, E. S. *George Berkeley in America.* New Haven/London: Yale University Press, 1979.

Gwynn, A. "The origins of the See of Dublin." *Irish Ecclesiastical Record* 57 (1941): 40–55; 97–112.

———. "St. Malachy of Armagh." *Irish Ecclesiastical Record* 70 (1948): 961–78; 71, (1949): 134–48; 317–331.

Harris, M. *The Catholic Church and the Foundation of the Northern Irish State.* Cork: Cork University Press, 1993.

Hempton, D. N. "The Methodist Crusade in Ireland, 1795–1845." *Irish Historical Studies* 22 (1980): 33–48.

Hempton, D., and M. Hill. *Evangelical Protestantism in Ulster Society, 1740–1890.* London: Routledge, 1992.

Hendricks, C. "The Moravian connection: Gracehill and Salem." *Ulster Folklife* 36 (1990): 55–65.

Hickey, J. *Religion and the Northern Ireland Problem.* Dublin: Barnes and Noble, 1984.

Hogan, E. M. *The Irish Missionary Movement: A Historical Survey, 1830–1980.* Dublin: Gill and Macmillan, 1991.

Hughes, K. "The Changing Theory and Practice of Irish Pilgrimage." *Journal of Ecclesiastical History* 11 (1960): 143–51.

———. *The Church in Early Irish Society.* London: Methuen, 1980.

Hurley, M., ed. *Irish Anglicanism, 1869–1969.* Dublin: Allen Figgis, 1970.

Inglis, T. *Moral Monopoly: The Catholic Church in Modern Irish Society.* Dublin: Gill and Macmillan, 1987.

Jeffrey, F. *Irish Methodism: An Historical Account of its Traditions, Theology, and Influence.* Belfast: Irish Methodist Publishing Co., 1964.

Keenan, D. *The Catholic Church in Nineteenth-Century Ireland: A Sociological Study.* Dublin: Gill and Macmillan, 1983.

Keogh, D. *"The French Disease": The Catholic Church and Radicalism in Ireland, 1790–1800.* Dublin: Four Courts Press, 1993.

————. *Ireland and the Vatican: The Politics and Diplomacy of Church-State Relations.* Cork: Cork University Press, 1995.

Kilroy, P. *Protestant Dissent and Controversy in Ireland, 1660–1714.* Cork: Cork University Press, 1994.

Knox, R. B. *James Ussher, Archbishop of Armagh.* Cardiff: University of Wales Press, 1967.

Larkin, E. *The Roman Catholic Church and the Creation of the Modern Irish State, 1878–1886.* Philadelphia/Dublin: American Philosophical Society/Gill and Macmillan, 1975.

————. *The Roman Catholic Church and the Plan of Campaign, 1886–1888.* Cork: Cork University Press, 1978.

————. *The Roman Catholic Church and the Fall of Parnell, 1888–1891.* Liverpool: Liverpool University Press, 1979.

————. *The Making of the Roman Catholic Church in Ireland, 1850–1860.* Chapel Hill, N.C.: University of North Carolina Press, 1980.

————. *The Consolidation of the Roman Catholic Church in Ireland, 1860–1870.* Chapel Hill, N.C.: Gill and Macmillan, 1987.

Luce, A. A. *The Life of George Berkeley, Bishop of Cloyne.* London, 1949. Reprint, Westport, Conn./London: Greenwood, 1968.

Luce, A. A., and T. E. Jessop. *The Works of George Berkeley.* 9 vols. London: Nelson, 1948–57.

McDowell, R. B. *The Church of Ireland, 1869–1969.* London: Routledge and Kegan Paul, 1975.

McElroy, G. *The Catholic Church and the Northern Ireland Crisis, 1968–86.* Dublin: Gill and Macmillan, 1991.

McMinn, J. "Presbyterianism and Politics in Ulster, 1871–1906." *Studia Hibernica* 21 (1981): 127–46.

————. *Jonathan's Travels: Swift and Ireland.* Belfast: Appletree, 1994.

McMinn, J. R. B., ed. *Against the Tide: A Calendar of the Papers of the Rev. J. B. Armour, Irish Presbyterian Minister and Home Ruler.* Belfast: PRONI, 1985.

McNally, P. " 'Irish and English Interests': National Conflict within the Church of Ireland Episcopate in the Reign of George I." *Irish Historical Studies* 29 (1995): 295–314.

Macaulay, A. *Patrick Dorrian: Bishop of Down and Connor.* Dublin: Irish Academic Press, 1987.

————. *William Crolly: Archbishop of Armagh, 1835–1849.* Dublin: Four Courts Press, 1994.

Ní Chatháin, P. "The Liturgical Background of the Derrynaflan Altar Service." *Journal of the Royal Society of Antiquaries of Ireland* 110 (1980): 127–48.

Norman, E. R. *The Catholic Church and Ireland in the Age of Rebellion.* Ithaca, N.Y./London: Cornell University Press, 1965.

O'Flaherty, E. "Clerical Indiscipline and Ecclesiastical Authority in Ireland, 1690–1750." *Studia Hibernica* 26 (1991–92): 7–30.

Phillips, W. A. *History of the Church of Ireland from the Earliest Times to the Present Day.* 3 vols. Oxford, 1933–34. Reprint, Oxford: Octagon, 1972.

Power, T. P., and K. Whelan, eds. *Endurance and Emergence: Catholics in Ireland in the Eighteenth Century.* Dublin: Irish Academic Press, 1990.

Ryan, J. *Irish Monasticism, its origins and early development.* London: Longmans Green, 1931.

Seymour, St.J, D. *The Puritans in Ireland, 1647–1661.* Oxford: Clarendon, 1912; reprint, 1969.

Sheils, W. J., and D. Woods, eds. *The Churches, Ireland, and the Irish.* Oxford: Blackwell, 1989.

Simms, K. "The Origins of the Diocese of Clogher." *Clogher Record* 10 (1980): 180–98.

Watt, J. *The Church in Medieval Ireland.* Dublin: Gill and Macmillan, 1972.

35. Population

Barkley, J. "Marriage and the Presbyterian Tradition." *Ulster Folklife* 39 (1993): 29–40.

Brothwell, D. "Variation in Early Irish Populations: A Brief Survey of the Evidence." *Ulster Journal of Archaeology* 48 (1985): 5–9.

Butlin, R. A. "The Population of Dublin in the Late Seventeenth Century." *Irish Geography* 5 (1965): 51–66.

Cawley, M. E. "Town Population Change, 1971–1986: Patterns and Distributional Effects." *Irish Geography* 24 (1991): 106–16.

Compton, P. A. "Religious Affiliation and Demographic Variability in Northern Ireland." *Transactions of the Institute of British Geographers* n.s. 1 (1976): 433–52.

———. "Fertility Differentials and Their Impact on Population Distribution and Composition in Northern Ireland." *Environment and Planning* (10) 1978: 1397–1411.

———, ed. *The Contemporary Population of Northern Ireland and Population-Related Issues.* Belfast: Queen's University, Institute of Irish Studies, 1981.

Connell, K. H. "The Population of Ireland in the Eighteenth Century." *Economic History Review* 16 (1946): 111–24.

———. Land and Population in Ireland, 1780–1845. *Economic History Review,* 2 (1950): 278–90.

———. *The Population of Ireland, 1750–1845.* Oxford: Clarendon, 1950. Reprint, London: Greenwood, 1976.

Cosgrove, A., ed. *Marriage in Ireland*. Dublin: College Press, 1985.

Cousens, S. H. "Regional Variations in Population Changes in Ireland, 1881–1891." *Transactions of the Institute of British Geographers* 33 (1963): 145–62.

Coward, J. "Regional Variations in Family Size in the Republic of Ireland." *Journal of Biosocial Science* 12 (1980): 1–14.

————. "Recent Characteristics of Roman Catholic Fertility in Northern and Southern Ireland." *Population Studies* 34 (1980): 31–44.

————. "Fertility Changes in the Republic of Ireland during the 1970s." *Area* 14 (1982): 109–17.

Cullen, L. M. "Population Trends in Seventeenth-Century Ireland." *Economic and Social Review* 6 (1975): 149–65.

de Paor, L. *The Peoples of Ireland from Prehistory to Modern Times*. London: Hutchinson, 1986.

Dickson, D., C. Ó Gráda, and S. Daultrey. "Hearth Tax, Household Size, and Irish Population Change, 1672–1821." *Proceedings of the Royal Irish Academy* 82C (1982): 125–82.

Garvey, D. "The History of Migration Flows in the Republic of Ireland." *Population Trends* 39 (1985): 22–30.

Geary, R. C., and J. G. Hughes. *Internal Migration in Ireland*. Dublin: Economic and Social Research Institute, 1970.

Goldstrom, J. M., and L. A. Clarkson, eds. *Irish Population, Economy, and Society: Essays in Honour of the Late K. H. Connell*. Oxford: Oxford University Press, 1981.

Hughes, J. G., and B. M. Walsh. *Internal Migration Flows in Ireland and Their Determinants*. Dublin: Economic and Social Research Institute, 1980.

Kelly, J. "Infanticide in Eighteenth Century Ireland." *Irish Economic and Social History* 19 (1992): 5–26.

Kennedy, R. E. *The Irish: Emigration, Marriage and Fertility*. Berkeley: University of California Press, 1973.

Larcom, T. A. "Observations on the Census of the Population of Ireland in 1841." *Journal Statistical Society of London* 6 (1843): 323–51.

McCarthy, M. D. "The 1961 Census of Population." *Journal of the Statistical and Social Inquiry Society of Ireland* 20 (1961): 73–93.

Macourt, M. P. A. "The Religious Inquiry in the Irish Census of 1861." *Irish Historical Studies* 21 (1979): 168–87.

Nicholas, S., and P. R., Shergold. "Irish Intercounty Mobility before 1840." *Irish Economic and Social History* 17 (1990): 22–43.

Ó Gráda, C. "Did Ulster Catholics Always Have Larger Families?" *Irish Economic and Social History* 12 (1985): 79–88.

Oldham, C. H. "The Reform of the Irish Census." *Journal of the Statistical and Social Inquiry Society of Ireland* 1925–26, pp. 197–.

Robins, J. *The Lost Children: A Study of Charity Children in Ireland, 1700–1900*. Dublin: Institute of Public Administration, 1980.

Verriere, J. *La population de l'Irlande*. Paris: Mouton, 1979.

Walsh, B. M. *Religion and Demographic Behaviour in Ireland*. Dublin: Economic and Social Research Institute 1970.

―――. "Ireland's Demographic Transformation, 1958–1970." *Economic and Social Review* 3 (1972): 251–75.

―――. "Trends in the Religious Composition of the Republic of Ireland, 1946–71." *Economic and Social Review* 6 (1975): 543–56.

Walsh, J. A. "Immigration to the Republic of Ireland, 1946–71." *Irish Geography* 12 (1979): 104–10.

36. Emigration

Akenson, D. H. *Half the World from Home: Perspectives on the Irish in New Zealand, 1860–1950*. Wellington: Victoria University Press, 1990.

―――. *The Irish Diaspora: A Primer*. Toronto/Belfast: P. D. Meany/Queen's University Institute of Irish Studies, 1993.

Canny, N. "Migration and Opportunity: Britain, Ireland, and the New World." *Irish Economic and Social History* 12 (1985): 7–32.

Cousens, S. H. "The Regional Pattern of Emigration during the Great Irish Famine." *Transactions of the Institute of British Geographers* 28 (1960): 119–34.

―――. "Emigration and Demographic Change in Ireland, 1851–1861." *Economic History Review* 14 (1961): 275–88.

Davis, G. *The Irish in Britain, 1815–1914*. Dublin: Gill and Macmillan, 1991.

Devine, T. M. *Irish Immigrants and Scottish Society in the Nineteenth and Twentieth Centuries*. Edinburgh: John Donald, 1991.

Dickson, R. J. *Ulster Emigration to Colonial America, 1718–1775*. Belfast, 1966. Reprint, Belfast: Ulster Historical Foundation, 1976.

Doyle, D. N. "The Irish in Australia and the United States: Some Comparisons, 1800–1939." *Irish Economic and Social History* 16 (1989): 73–94.

Elliott, B. S. *Irish Migrants in the Canadas: A New Approach*. Belfast: McGill-Queen's University Press, 1988.

Fielding, S. *Class and Ethnicity: Irish Catholics in England, 1880–1939*. Milton Keynes, Bucks.: Open University Press, 1993.

Fitzpatrick, D. "Irish Emigration in the Later Nineteenth Century." *Irish Historical Studies* 22 (1980): 126–43.

―――. *Irish Emigration, 1801–1921*. Dublin: Economic and Social History Society of Ireland, 1984.

Handley, J. E. *The Irish in Scotland, 1798–1845*. Cork: Cork University Press, 1943.

Houston, C. J., and W. J. Smyth. *The Sash Canada Wore: A Historical Geography of the Orange Order in Canada*. Toronto: University of Toronto Press, 1980.

―――. *Irish Emigration and Canadian Settlement*. Toronto/Belfast: University of Toronto Press/Ulster Historical Foundation, 1990.

Hughes, A. J. "An Account of a Sea-Voyage from Derry to America, 1818." *Ulster Folklife* 35 (1989): 18–41.

Jackson, J. A. *The Irish in Britain*. London: Routledge and Kegan Paul, 1963.

Johnson, J. H. "Harvest Migration from Nineteenth Century Ireland." *Transactions of the Institute of British Geographers* 41 (1967): 97–112.

Kelly, J. "The Resumption of Emigration from Ireland after the American War of Independence: 1783–1787." *Studia Hibernica* 24 (1984–88): 61–88.

Kerr, B. M. "Irish Seasonal Migration to Great Britain, 1800–38." *Irish Historical Studies* 3 (1942–43): 365–80.

King, R., ed. *Contemporary Irish Migration*. Dublin: Geographical Society of Ireland, 1991.

Lawton, R. "Irish Migration to England and Wales in the Mid-Nineteenth Century." *Irish Geography* 4 (1959): 35–54.

Lees, L. H. *Exiles of Erin: Irish Migrants in Victorian London*. Manchester: Manchester University Press, 1979.

Lowe, W. J. *The Irish in Mid-Victorian Lancashire: The Shaping of a Working Class Community*. New York: Peter Lang, 1989.

McCracken, D. P. "Irish Settlement and Identity in South Africa before 1910." *Irish Historical Studies* 28 (1992): 134–49.

MacDonagh, O. "The Regulation of the Emigrant Traffic from the United Kingdom, 1842–55." *Irish Historical Studies* 9 (1955): 162–89.

———. "The Irish Famine Emigration to the United States." *Perspectives in American History* 10 (1976): 357–446.

Mannion, J. J. *Irish Settlements in Eastern Canada*. Toronto: University of Toronto Press, 1974.

———. "Migration and Upward Mobility: The Meagher Family in Ireland and Newfoundland, 1780–1830." *Irish Economic and Social History* 15 (1988): 54–70.

Miller, K. A., et al. "Emigrants and Exiles: Irish Cultures and Irish Emigration to North America, 1790–1922." *Irish Historical Studies* 22 (1980): 97–125.

———. *Emigrants and Exiles: Ireland and the Irish Exodus to North America*. Oxford: Oxford University Press, 1985.

Mokyr, J., and C. Ó Gráda. "Emigration and Poverty in Pre-Famine Ireland." *Explorations in Economic History* 19 (1982): 360–84.

Neal, F. "Lancashire, the Famine Irish, and the Poor Laws: A Study in Crisis Management." *Irish Economic and Social History* 22 (1995): 26–48.

O'Brien, J., and P. Travers, eds. *The Irish Emigrant Experience in Australia*. Dublin: Poolbeg, 1991.

O'Dowd, A. *Spalpeens and Tattie Hokers: History and Folklore of the Irish Migratory Agricultural Worker in Ireland and Britain*. Dublin: Irish Academic Press, 1991.

O'Farrell, P. *Letters from Irish Australia, 1825–1929*. Sydney/Belfast: New South Wales University Press/Ulster Historical Foundation, 1984.

———. *The Irish in Australia*. Sydney/Belfast: New South Wales University Press/Ulster Historical Foundation, 1986.

Ó Gráda, C. "Seasonal Migration and Post-Famine Adjustment in the West of Ireland." *Studia Hibernica* 13 (1973): 48–76.

Reece, B. ed. *Exiles from Erin: Convict Lives in Ireland and Australia.* Dublin: Gill and Macmillan, 1991.

———. *Irish Convict Lives.* Sydney: Crossing Press, 1993.

Richards, E. "Irish Life and Progress in Colonial South Australia." *Irish Historical Studies* 27 (1991): 216–36.

Swift, R., and S. Gilley, eds. *The Irish in the Victorian City.* London: Croom Helm, 1985.

———. *The Irish in Britain, 1815–1939.* London: Pinter, 1989.

Wyman, M. *Round-trip to America: The Immigrants' Return to Europe, 1880–1930.* Ithaca, N.Y.: Cornell University Press, 1993.

37. Health and Medicine

Barrington, R. *Health, Medicine, and Politics in Ireland, 1900–1970.* Dublin: Institute of Public Administration, 1987.

Connolly, S. J. "The 'Blessed Turf': Cholera and Popular Panic in Ireland, June 1832." *Irish Historical Studies* 23 (1983): 214–32.

Froggatt, P. "Sir William Wilde, 1815–1876, a Centenary Appreciation: Wilde's Place in Medicine." *Proceedings of the Royal Irish Academy* 78C (1977): 261–78.

Griffin, B. " 'Mad Dogs and Irishmen': Dogs and Rabies in the Eighteenth and Nineteenth Centuries." *Ulster Folklife* 40 (1994): 1–15.

Kirkpatrick, T. P. C. *The History of Doctor Steeven's Hospital, Dublin, 1720–1920.* Dublin, 1924.

Lyons, J. B. *Surgeon-Major Parke's African Journey, 1887–89.* Dublin: Lilliput, 1994.

———. *Brief Lives of Irish Doctors, 1600–1965.* Dublin: Blackwater, 1978.

Malcolm, E. *Swift's Hospital: A History of St. Patrick's Hospital, Dublin, 1746–1989.* Dublin: Gill and Macmillan, 1989.

Nic Suibhe, F. " 'On the Straw' and Other Aspects of Pregnancy and Childbirth from the Oral Tradition of Women in Ulster." *Ulster Folklife* 38 (1992): 12–24.

O'Brien, E., and A. Crookshank. *A Portrait of Irish Medicine.* Swords, Co. Dublin: Ward River, 1984.

38. Science

Andrews, J. H. *A Paper Landscape: The Ordnance Survey in Nineteenth-Century Ireland.* Oxford: Oxford University Press, 1975.

———. "Science and Cartography in the Ireland of William and Samuel Molyneux." *Proceedings of the Royal Irish Academy* 80C (1980): 231–50.

———. *Plantation Acres: An Historical Study of the Irish Land Surveyor and His Maps.* Belfast: Ulster Historical Foundation, 1985.

Berry, H. F. *A History of the Royal Dublin Society*. London: Longmans, 1915.

Clarke, D. *The Ingenious Mr. Edgeworth*. London: Oldbourne, 1965.

Clarke, M. *The Book of Maps of the Dublin City Surveyors, 1695–1827*. Dublin: Dublin Corporation, 1983.

Davies, G. L. H., and R. C. Mollan, eds. *Richard Griffith, 1784–1878*. Dublin: Royal Dublin Society, 1980.

Davies, G. L. H. *Sheets of Many Colours: The Mapping of Ireland's Rocks, 1750–1890*. Dublin: Royal Dublin Society, 1983.

Doherty, F. "An Eighteenth-Century Intellectual Friendship: Letters of Richard Lovell Edgeworth and the Wedgwoods." *Proceedings of the Royal Irish Academy* 86C (1986): 231–69.

Dreyer, J. L. E. *An Historical Account of the Armagh Observatory*. Armagh, 1883.

Friendly, A. *Beaufort of the Admiralty: The Life of Sir Francis Beaufort, 1774–1857*. London: Hutchinson, 1977.

Jarrell, R. A. "The Department of Science and Art and Control of Irish Science, 1853–1905." *Irish Historical Studies* 23 (1983): 330–47.

Meenan, J., and D. Clarke, eds. *RDS: The Royal Dublin Society, 1731–1981*. Dublin: Gill and Macmillan, 1981.

Mollan, R. C., W. Davis, and B. Finucane, eds. *Some People and Places in Irish Science and Technology*. Dublin: Royal Irish Academy, 1985.

——————. *More People and Places in Irish Science and Technology*. Dublin: Royal Irish Academy, 1990.

More, L. T. *The Life and Works of the Honourable Robert Boyle*. Oxford: Oxford University Press, 1944.

Ó Raifeartaigh, T., ed. *The Royal Irish Academy: A Bicentennial History, 1785–1985*. Dublin: Royal Irish Academy, 1985.

Partington, J. R., and T. S. Wheeler. *The Life and Works of William Higgins, Chemist (1763–1825)*. London: Pergamon, 1960.

Scaife, B. K. P. "James MacCullagh, M.R.I.A., F.R.S., 1809–47." *Proceedings of the Royal Irish Academy* 90C (1990): 68–106.

Simms, J. G. *William Molyneux of Dublin, 1656–1694*. Dublin: Irish Academic Press, 1982.

White, T. de Vere. *The Story of the Royal Dublin Society*. Tralee: The Kerryman, 1955.

39. Traditional Culture and Folklore

Arensberg, C. M. *The Irish Countryman: An Anthropological Study*. London, 1937. Reprint, London: Doubleday, 1968.

Arensberg, C. M., and S. T. Kimball. *Family and Community in Ireland*. Cambridge, Mass.: Harvard University Press, 1940, 1968.

Boyne, P. *John O'Donovan (1806–61): A Biography*. Kilkenny: Boethius, 1987.

Casey, D. J., and R. E. Rhodes, eds. *Views of the Irish Peasantry, 1800–1916*. Hamden, Conn.: Archon Books, 1977.

Danaher, K. *Irish Country People*. Cork: Mercier, 1966.

————. *The Hearth, the Stool and All! Irish Rural Households*. Cork: Mercier, 1986.

————. *The Year in Ireland: Irish Calendar Customs*. Cork: Mercier, 1994.

Downey, G., and G. Stockman. "From Rathlin and the Antrim Glens: Gaelic Folktales in Translation." *Ulster Folklife* 37 (1991): 71–96.

Evans, E. E. *Irish Folk Ways*. London, 1957. Reprint, London: Routledge and Kegan Paul, 1966.

————. *Irish Heritage: The Landscape, the People and Their Work*. Dundalk: Dundalgan, 1967.

————. *The Personality of Ireland*. Cambridge: Cambridge University Press, 1973.

Gailey, R. A. "The Housing of the Rural Poor in Nineteenth-Century Ulster. *Ulster Folklife* 22 (1976): 34–58.

————, ed. *Gold under the Furze: Studies in Folk Tradition Presented to Caoimhín Ó'Danachair*. Dublin: Glendale, 1982.

————. *Rural Houses of the North of Ireland*. Edinburgh: John Donald, 1984.

————. "Creating Ulster's Folk Museum." *Ulster Folklife* 32 (1986): 54–77.

————. " '. . . such as pass by us daily . . .': The Study of Folklife: The Estyn Evans Lecture, March 1989. *Ulster Folklife* 36 (1990): 4–22.

Glassie, H. ed. *Irish Folk Tales*. Harmondsworth, England: Penguin, 1985.

Harvey, B. "Changing Fortunes on the Aran Islands in the 1890s." *Irish Historical Studies* 27 (1991): 237–49.

Hughes, A. J., and R. J. Hannan, eds. *Place-names in Northern Ireland. Vol. 2, County Down II: The Ards*. Belfast: Queen's University, Institute of Irish Studies, 1992.

Joyce, P. W. *The Origin and History of Irish Names of Places*. 3 vols. London: Longmans Green, 1910–13. Facsimile ed., Wakefield: EP Publishing, 1973–76.

Kinmonth, C. *Irish Country Furniture*. New Haven/London: Yale University Press, 1993.

Lucas, A. T. "The Social Role of Relics and Reliquaries in Ancient Ireland." *Journal of the Royal Society of Antiquaries of Ireland* 116 (1986): 5–37.

Lysaght, P. *The Banshee: The Irish Supernatural Death-Messenger*. Dublin: Glendale, 1986.

————. " 'When I Makes Tea, I Makes Tea. . .': Innovation in Food: The Case of Tea in Ireland." *Ulster Folklife* 33 (1987): 44–71.

Mahon, B. *Land of Milk and Honey: The Story of Traditional Irish Food and Drink*. Dublin: Poolbeg, 1991.

Mogey, J. M. *Rural Life in Northern Ireland*. Oxford: Oxford University Press, 1947.

Nelson, E. C. *Shamrock: Botany and History of an Irish Myth*. Aberystwyth/Kilkenny: Boethius, 1991.

Ó Coileain, S. "The Irish Lament: An Oral Genre." *Studia Hibernica* 24 (1984–88): 97–117.

Ó Danachair, C. "Some Distribution Patterns in Irish Folklife." *Béaloideas* 25 (1957–59): 108–25.

————. *Folk and Farm: Essays in Honour of A. T. Lucas.* Dublin: Royal Society of Antiquaries of Ireland, 1976.

Robinson, P. "Vernacular Housing in Ulster in the Seventeenth Century." *Ulster Folklife* 25 (1979): 1–28.

————. "From Thatch to Slate: Innovation in Roof Covering Materials of Traditional Houses in Ulster." *Ulster Folklife* 31 (1985): 21–35.

————. "The Use of the Term 'Clachan' in Ulster." *Ulster Folklife* 37 (1991): 30–35.

Smyth, D. *A Guide to Irish Mythology.* Dublin: Irish Academic Press, 1988.

Toner, G., and M. B. O'Mainnin, eds. *Place-names in Northern Ireland. Vol 1, County Down I: Newry and South-West Down.* Belfast: Queen's University, Institute of Irish Studies, 1992.

40. Women in Irish Society

Fitzpatrick, D. "Women, Gender and the Writing of Irish History." *Irish Historical Studies* 27 (1991): 267–73.

Holmes, J., and D. Urquhart, eds. *Coming into the Light: The Work, Politics, and Religion of Women in Ulster, 1840–1940.* Belfast: Queen's University, Institute of Irish Studies, 1994.

Luddy, M. *Women and Philanthropy in Nineteenth-Century Ireland.* Cambridge: Cambridge University Press.

McCurtain, M., M. O'Dowd, and M. Luddy. "An Agenda for Women's History in Ireland, 1500–1900." *Irish Historical Studies* 28 (1992): 1–37.

McCurtain, M., and M. O'Dowd, eds. *Women in Early Modern Ireland.* Dublin/Edinburgh: Wolfhound/Edinburgh University Press, 1991.

McLoughlin, D. *Shovelling Out Paupers: Female Emigration from Irish Workhouses, 1840–70.* Dublin: Irish Academic Press, 1995.

Murphy, C. *The Women's Suffrage Movement and Irish Society in the Early Twentieth Century.* New York/London: Harvester Wheatsheaf, 1989.

Sawyer, R. *We Are but Women: Women in Ireland's History.* London: Routledge, 1993.

41. Economic, Political and Social Protest Movements

Beames, M. R. "The Ribbon Societies: Lower-class Nationalism in Pre-Famine Ireland." *Past and Present* 97 (1982): 157–71.

————. *Peasants and Power: The Whiteboy Movements and Their Control in Pre-Famine Ireland.* New York: St. Martin's Press, 1983.

Broeker, G. *Rural Disorder and Police Reform in Ireland, 1812–1836.* London: Routledge and Kegan Paul, 1970.

Donnelly, J. S. "Irish Agrarian Rebellion: The Whiteboys of 1769–76." *Proceedings of the Royal Irish Academy* 83C (1983): 293–331.

————. *Irish Agrarian Rebellion, 1760–1800*. Dublin: Irish Academic Press, 1995.

Garvin, T. "Defenders, Ribbonmen, and others: Underground Political Networks in Pre-Famine Ireland." *Past and Present* 96 (1982): 133–55.

Graham, B. J., and S. Hood. "Town Tenant Protest in Late Nineteenth- and Early Twentieth-Century Ireland." *Irish Economic and Social History* 21 (1994): 39–57.

Kerrigan, C. *Father Matthew and the Irish Temperance Movement, 1838–1849*. Cork: Cork University Press, 1992.

Malcolm, E. "The Catholic Church and the Irish Temperance Movement, 1838–1901." *Irish Historical Studies* 23 (1982): 1–16.

————. *"Ireland Sober, Ireland Free": Drink and Temperance in Nineteenth-Century Ireland*. Dublin: Gill and Macmillan, 1986.

Murray, A. C. "Agrarian Violence and Nationalism in Nineteenth Century Ireland: The Myth of Ribbonism." *Irish Economic and Social History* 13 (1986): 56–73.

Philpin, C. H. E. *Nationalism and Popular Protest in Ireland*. Cambridge: Cambridge University Press, 1987.

Pollard, H. B. C. *The Secret Societies of Ireland: Their Rise and Progress*. London: Allen, 1922.

Williams, T. D., ed. *Secret Societies in Ireland*. Dublin: Gill and Macmillan, 1973.

About the Authors

Colin Thomas was born in Wales and graduated in geography and anthropology at the University College of Wales, Aberystwyth, where he received a Ph.D. in 1965. In addition to numerous publications on Wales, Ireland, Eastern Europe, and the former Soviet Union, he edited *Rural Landscapes and Communities: Essays Presented to Desmond McCourt* (Dublin: Irish Academic Press, 1986) and contributed sections on Northern Ireland to the BBC's *Domesday Britain* (London, 1986) interactive video disc. He is a member of the International Union for the Scientific Study of Population and has served on the Royal Irish Academy's National Committee for Geography since 1984. Having held several university posts elsewhere in Britain, since 1970 he has taught at the University of Ulster at Coleraine. He is currently editing several volumes of the registers of St. Columb's Cathedral, Londonderry.

Avril Thomas was born in Dublin, where she was educated at Alexandra College and Trinity College, graduating in natural science. Subsequently she taught at the University of Leicester and at Trinity College, Dublin. In 1990 she was awarded a D.Phil. from the University of Ulster for a thesis on "The Walled Towns of Ireland." It was published by Irish Academic Press, Dublin, in two volumes in 1992. She contributed to the 1995 Thomas Davis Lecture series on Radio Telefis Eireann, published as *Irish Cities* (Mercier Press, Cork), and is at present preparing the fascicle on Londonderry in the *Irish Historic Towns Atlas* series published by the Royal Irish Academy.